Cc

Roll the Bones

The History of Gambling

David G. Schwartz

WINCHESTER

WINCHESTER BOOKS

Las Vegas, Nevada

Roll the Bones: The History of Gambling
Casino Edition

A portion of chapter 13, "The Burger King Revolution," previously published in *Gaming Law Review and Economics* 14, no. 4 (2010).

First edition © 2006 David G. Schwartz, published by Gotham Books, a division of Penguin Group (USA) Inc.

Photo credits are listed on pages 414-416 and constitute an extension of this copyright page.

Library of Congress Cataloging-in-Publication Data
Schwartz, David G., 1973-
Roll the Bones: The History of Gambling Casino Edition/ David G. Schwartz
p.   cm.
Includes bibliographical references
ISBN 978-1-939546-00-5 (paperback)
1. Gambling—History I. Title
HV6710.S382 2013

Cover design by Charles S. Monster, 15-North

Set in Adobe Caslon Pro

For Eric H. Monkkonen (1942–2005),
my dissertation advisor, mentor, and friend.

Contents

Acknowledgements   vii

Author's Note   ix

Prologue: The Rainmaker Reborn   xi
Casino gambling's power to recreate

1: The Ridotto Revolution   1
Mercantile gamblers create the casino

2: Seeking the Cure   22
Europe wins and loses at spas

3: A Sunny Place for Shady People   57
Gambling on the French Riviera

4: Baiting John Bull   90
The British bet big

5: Star-Spangled Gamblers   110
The birth of American gambling

6: Wild Cards   128
Seeking fortunes in the West

7: Fools of Fortune   154
American gambling becomes urban

8: Wise Guys and One-Armed Bandits   181
Big city gambling in the gangster age

9: Hard to Resist   197
Nevada becomes America's gambling oasis

10: A Place in the Sun   218
The Las Vegas Strip is born

11: The Sky's the Limit   243
Las Vegas reaches for the stars

12: America's Playground…Again   262
Atlantic City becomes the casino capital of the East

13: The Burger King Revolution   282
Las Vegas bounces back for the first time

14: Runaway American Dream   303
Casino gambling in the public interest

15: A Clockwork Volcano   320
Las Vegas strikes back

16: All In   337
Casino gambling's global spread

17: Reinventing the Wheel   368
Las Vegas hangs on as gambling goes digital

Epilogue: Still Betting   385
A hard seven

Notes   388

Illustrations   414

Index   417

Acknowledgements

It goes without saying that a book is never an entirely solo effort, and I've had a plenty of help getting here.

The book you're reading now happened in two stages: the original edition started with a call from Gotham's Brendan Cahill, who persuaded me that a comprehensive history of world gambling could be written, and that I could do it. He did a great job of convincing me to attempt the book, and of shepherding me through the editorial process. He and Patrick Mulligan provided excellent suggestions for revisions, additions, and other changes.

At the University of Nevada Las Vegas, where I'm the Director of the Center for Gaming Research in Lied Library, I got help from everyone then in Special Collections, including Peter Michel, Su Kim Chung, Toby Murray, Kathy War, Jonnie Kennedy, Joyce Moore, Michael Frazier, and Dana Miller, and the staff of Document Delivery, who answered my interlibrary loan requests with incredible speed. Thanks also go to Dean of Libraries Patricia Iannuzzi. At the Nevada State Museum and Historical Society, David Millman generously helped me find the only extant picture of Nick the Greek Dandolos that I've ever seen.

I also had help at the University of Nevada Reno from Bill Eadington and Judy Cornelius at the Institute for the Study of Gambling and Commercial Gaming, and visiting professor Ricardo Siu. Dr. Eadington's offer of a guest lecture in his class let me try out some of the material from the first few chapters on a captive audience, and his friendship and encouragement over the years is much appreciated. The staff of UNR Special Collections, particularly Jacquelyn Sundstrand, was very accommodating, particularly in facilitating my access to the papers of Russell T. Barnhart.

A host of academic experts from around the world contributed their thoughts and, sometimes, bibliographies, including Larry

Gragg at the Missouri University of Science and Technology; Annie Chan, Jason Gao, Davis Fong, and Carmen Cheng at the University of Macau,;Raymond Chan and Claudia Mendes Khan at the Macau Tourism and Career Center, Kai Cheong Fok at the Macau Millennium College, Il-Yong Yang at Cheju Tourism College, Mark Balestra and Sue Schneider at the River City Group, and Stephen M. Stigler at the University of Chicago.

In the gaming industry, several people granted me access to current operations and helped me track down information about the past, including Nick Spencer at the Hong Kong Jockey Club; George Tanasijevich and Lisa Cheong at Venetian/Sands Macau; Grant Bowie at Wynn Macau; Rich Westfall at Isle of Capri; Bruce Mac Donald at Foxwoods; Denise Randazzo, Roger Thomas, Steve Wynn and Elaine Wynn at Wynn Resorts; Tex Whitson (a font of information about Binion's, poker, and the World Series of Poker); Crandell Addington; Debbie Munch of Caesars Entertainment; Yvette Monet and Alan Feldman of MGM Resorts International; and Mando Rueda.

For the current edition, I've had a lot more help from a whole new set of friends and colleagues. UNLV Special Collections has had some additions including Claytee White, Barbara Tabach, Tom Sommer, and Kelli Luchs, whose photo assistance was invaluable. At Santo Gaming, Steve Rosen and Tony Santo have been great friends with a depth of knowledge about the industry that is hard to surpass. Roger Gros at *Global Gaming Business* has also been a true friend; the series of Atlantic City history articles that I wrote for *Casino Connection* gave me a much better insight into many casinos that I've condensed into the new Atlantic City chapter here.

For the past two years, I've also had the pleasure of writing about gaming and hospitality for *Vegas Seven* magazine. Working with everyone there, particularly Phil Hagen, Greg Blake Miller, and Paul Szydelko, has been great for me, and has helped to shape the "recent history" chapters of this book.

And I've had a ball talking Vegas with a whole bunch of passionate, interesting people who I'd never have met if it weren't for the Internet. Called the Vegas Internet Mafia, the list starts with Hunter Hillegas and Chuck Monster, who I'm privileged to join on the Vegas Gang Podcast, and Tim and Michelle Dressen at Five Hundy by Midnight, and includes all of the VegasTrippers and everyone in the Five Hundy community. There are also a ton of people who I interact with every day on Twitter (@unlvgaming), who always give me new insights and idea. Thanks.

My wife Suni has been a source of strength and clarity as I got this edition over the finish line, a process that wasn't always easy. And our two children are an inspiration and a joy every day.

For specific production-related gratitude: thanks go to Mike Gavin and Thomas Speak for unlocking the mysteries of InDesign for me, to Svetvlana Miller for her excellent copy-editing (and Greg Miller for his contributions there as well), and to Meg Daniel for her index. Chuck Monster designed the outstanding cover. And my "beta testers" Mike Adey, Steve Grantz, Katherine Jackson, Steve King, Barry Kuan, and Derek Miller caught plenty of mistakes that evaded me, for which I am grateful.

A heartfelt thanks goes to my agent, Susan Ginsburg of Writers House, who was able to get the rights to this book back to me, letting me take the big leap and get a new edition out. Throughout, she has given me sage advice and strong encouragement and put me in a position to be a better writer.

I'd like to offer a thank you to all of the enthusiasts, scholars, and gamblers who left behind the collections of stories, legends, and facts that I pored over while putting this book together.

Finally, thanks to you, the reader, for having the trust that I'm going to deliver on my promise to tell you a little about the history of gambling. I hope you have as much fun reading this as I did researching and writing it.

Author's Note on the Casino Edition

What's new and different

Roll the Bones: The History of Gambling was first published in 2006 and mostly completed (on the author's end, at least) by the summer of 2005. If you're at all familiar with the casino business, you'll know that there have been, to put it mildly, many changes since then. That's the primary reason that I've put together a new edition of the book, which focuses more strongly on elements that most readers found of interest and incorporates recent history into the story.

For American readers, the most obvious is the recession, which forced many changes in the gaming landscape, not the least of which was the sudden discovery that, perhaps, gambling was not as recession-proof as had earlier been assumed. The other change globally is the surging popularity of casino gaming in Asia, particularly Macau and Singapore.

The current edition incorporates those changes. Since this book is mostly concerned with gambling's past, recent developments haven't forced alterations in much of the text, though they have made it clear that, in some cases, more perspective was needed. For example, I have expanded the material on Atlantic City, New Jersey into a complete chapter, and not just because I'm feeling nostalgic for my hometown: I think that its current decline is both of historical importance and balances the earlier, more exuberant narrative, which needed more fleshing out.

I also updated material on newer domestic markets like Pennsylvania and, naturally, added material to bring Macau more or less up-to-date and to account for the rise of Singapore.

Las Vegas also gets more attention this time around. I've split the chapter on the rise of the Las Vegas Strip from roughly 1941 to 1970 into two, "A Place in the Sun" and "The Sky's the Limit."

this gave me room to tackle a much more extended discussion of the role of the mob in building up the Las Vegas gaming industry. Like so much else, this is because of reader feedback. I noticed when I gave talks about gambling history, the first question I'd invariably get would be about the mob. It didn't take long for me to figure out that the mob should be in the main part of the talk, and I've incorporated much of my research into that chapter. It's impossible to really tell the story of the development of casinos in Las Vegas without discussing the impact of organized crime in some way, and I hope that readers get something out of the additional perspective I've added here.

The really big news in Las Vegas since the first edition rolled off the presses has been the recession. It's also been driving a good portion of my work. A short while ago, based on recession-inspired research, I wrote an article for *Gaming Law Review and Economics* in 2010 that considered the impact of the early 1980s recession on Las Vegas, and how it bounced back. Essentially, I wanted to learn how Las Vegas responded to its first major economic challenge. The results were surprising, and forced me to reconsider much of what I thought I knew about the period. I've incorporated much of that material, and a new section on how the mob was forced out of Nevada gaming in roughly the same period into a new chapter, "The Burger King Revolution." That chapter begins with a section describing the decline of the mob in Las Vegas casinos, a bookend to the earlier new material in "A Place in the Sun."

The Las Vegas Strip gets a more comprehensive treatment in "A Clockwork Volcano," with added material on the impact of The Mirage, and several other innovative operators.

The final addition is an entirely new chapter, "Reinventing the Wheel," which pulls in earlier material about the rise of online gaming in the 2000s and updates it, then discusses the setbacks the Las Vegas casino business suffered in that decade, as well as its efforts to respond.

If you have the original edition, you might notice this one is a little lighter. In the copious feedback and criticism I've received on the original, I've found that the vast majority of readers preferred the sections focusing on casino gaming to those chronicling other forms of gambling. For that reason, I've chosen, for this "casino" edition, to eliminate several early chapters and sections focusing on lotteries, horse racing, and other forms of gambling. This edition starts with a brief background into the nature of gambling before jumping in to the story of the first legal European casino, Venice's Ridotto.

The result is, I hope, a book that's more enjoyable for the reader, which can give a better perspective on recent and future events. I realize that, like anything else, making additions and deletions to the book is a gamble, but if there's one thing that my studies in gambling have taught me, it's never to be afraid to toss the dice.

David G. Schwartz
Las Vegas, Nevada, December 2012

Prologue
The Rainmaker Reborn

Casino Gambling's Power to Recreate

June 5, 1637. The Puritans are on the march, and for the Pequot of the Connecticut River Valley, the world is ending.

Pequot translates as "destroyer" in the Algonquian language, and the name underscores that nation's fearsome reputation. Centuries ago, the Pequot and Mohegan had migrated together into Connecticut from the Hudson River Valley, then split into two warring tribes. When not warring with the Mohegan and Narragansett, the Pequot collect tribute from surrounding villages whose residents cringe with fear at the mention of the Pequot and their fierce sachem Sassacus. But as the "Great Migration" of Puritans overspills its original plantings at Massachusetts Bay, the encroaching English colonists begin to threaten Pequot dominance of the area. A showdown is inevitable.

An escalating series of kidnappings, raids, and assaults soon leads to open warfare between the Pequot and English. Years earlier, the newcomers had celebrated the first Thanksgiving by feasting on wild turkey and venison with their new Indian neighbors. Now, old friendships are forgotten in the name of expansion, and English guns are matched against the legendary ferocity of the Pequot.

Initially, the Pequot faired well. But by May 1637, English forces led by Captain John Mason allied with the Mohegan and Narragansett, who had earlier rebuffed a Pequot overture to join a pan-Indian alliance and drive the invaders into the sea. Together, they launched damaging counterattacks and began to turn the tide.

On that fateful June day, Mason leads 150 Englishmen and 60 Mohegan warriors under the command of the sachem Uncas against the fortified Pequot village at Mystic. After firing their muskets on the palisades, the English burst through the wall into the village itself. Crying, "We must burn them!" Mason touches a firebrand to a wigwam, then leads a retreat from the village. The English and their Indian allies form a ring around the palisades, watching as flames swiftly overrun the fort "to the extream Amazement of the Enemy, and the great Rejoycing of ourselves," according to Mason. The blaze spreads rapidly that hot and dry morning; the entire village is soon afire. The English indiscriminately shoot at Pequot fleeing the conflagration and cut down with swords those who escape the burning palisades. As many as 700 Pequot men, women, and children perish in the attack.

In less than an hour, Mason has obliterated a major Pequot village and snapped the will of the Pequot fighters. Over the next few months, the colonists and their Indian allies track down, capture, and kill the remaining Pequot. Captives are dispersed as slaves among surrounding tribes, in English households, and as far south as the Caribbean. The Mohegan kill the terrible Sassacus in August, sending his head to the English at Hartford as a gesture of friendship. The Pequot power is broken.

In the peace settlement of September 21, 1638, the English and their Indian allies agree that the Pequot must never threaten revenge. The victors prohibit any survivors from speaking the Pequot language or even identifying themselves as Pequot. The river that bears their name is renamed the Thames, and their eponymous central village is re-christened New London. The Connecticut countryside, which once reverberated with the sounds of Pequot warriors demanding tribute, fears them no more.

February 6, 2004. A nation has risen from the ashes.

Popular comedian Chris Rock entertains a crowd paying as much as $110 per ticket at the Fox Theater, a venue that legendary crooner Frank Sinatra opened in 1993. On this night, Rock was simply one attraction at Foxwoods Resort Casino, a collection of six casinos with 350 table games and 6,400 slot machines, the world's largest bingo hall, over 1,400 rooms and suites, twenty-four restaurants (including the aptly-named Rainmaker Café), a convention center, a 4,000-seat arena, and a championship golf course, all rising incongruously out of the once-quiet woods near Ledyard, Connecticut.

While the god-fearing Puritans would be aghast at the notion that a 4.7 million square-foot complex dedicated to pleasure and indulgence had been erected in their former dominion, they would be shocked to learn that the Mashantucket Pequot, a resurgent remnant of the tribe they had attempted to wipe from history, owned it. Nearly four centuries after their supposed eradication, the descendants of Sassacus no longer send war parties to neighboring villages to collect tribute; instead, 40,000 visitors come to Foxwoods each day with the primary purpose of losing their money in the name of a good time, leaving somewhere in the neighborhood of $67 million in monthly slot losses as tribute. Of this, a cut of about $16.5 million is forwarded to the state of Connecticut for the privilege of operating the casino.

The Pequot had an improbable journey back from obscurity. Granted two reservations in 1683, the tribe's membership declined precipitously over the next three centuries; by 1910, only three families lived on the Ledyard reservation, which had been reduced to less than 200 acres. But in 1983, tribal chairman Skip Hayward, assisted by Indian rights attorney Tom Tureen, won the tribe federal recognition over the initial veto of President Ronald Reagan. The sovereign tribe started offering high-stakes bingo in a hastily-constructed hall in 1986. This humble beginning would ultimately yield (for a time) the world's most profitable casino. In 1992, after striking a compact with the state of Connecticut, the tribe added table games, and in the next following year, slot machines started accepting coins. Since then, the casino has expanded regularly, clogging Route 2 with traffic that was unimaginable a scant decade earlier. Although most visitors hail from New York and New England, travelers from as far as Abu Dhabi, Taiwan, and Singapore arrive weekly for flings at fate. Foxwoods is a truly cosmopolitan island in the New England woods—even the money to build Foxwoods came from Malaysian multi-billionaire Lim Goh Tong, owner of that country's monopoly casino, Genting Highlands.

As purveyors of casino entertainment and collectors of tribute, the Pequot are not alone. About ten miles away, their erstwhile mortal enemies the Mohegan operate their own gargantuan gambling/ entertainment complex in Uncasville, named for the sachem who sent the head of Sassacus to the English. In a 1994 agreement, the tribes guaranteed the state of Connecticut an annual payment of $80 million or 25 percent of their slot revenue, whichever was greater (invariably, it is the percentage). This pact has lifted the Indian tribes out of poverty, luring millions of supplicants to chance within the palisades of the Pequot and Mohegan, and garnering nearly $2 billion in tax revenue for the state since its signing. It has brought these Connecticut Indians money and influence. For decades, "friends of the Indian" had labored to bring Indians into the mainstream of American economic life with little result. Where they failed, gambling has succeeded, reversing the course of 400 years of Anglo-Indian relations.

The story of Connecticut's casinos is remarkable, but hardly unusual. Many Americans think that "serious gambling" is confined to the well-known casino destinations of Las Vegas and Atlantic City, but it is actually nearly everywhere. With a growing assortment of casinos, racetracks, bingo halls, and lottery tickets available at convenience stores in nearly every state, Americans are never far from a chance to take a chance. Gambling is more than a pastime—it is big business. In 2011, American casinos won more than $60 billion.

Las Vegas is the first city many Americans think of when they hear the word "casino," but the desert metropolis lost its bragging rights as the world's casino capital in 2007, when Macau, a Special Administrative Region in China, roared past it. In 2011, Macau casinos brought in over three times as much revenue as all of the casinos of Nevada combined, and nearly as much as all commercial (non-tribal) casinos in the United States. The ascent of Macau—followed by the just-as-meteoric rise of Singapore—highlights the growing dominance of the Asian casino industry and the increasingly global nature of the casino business.

What many people don't know, however, is that casinos have a decidedly global past, as gambling is an ancient and widespread pastime. Gambling and gamblers have left footprints throughout history in curious, sometimes-surprising ways. Games of chance have evolved over many centuries, changing along with civilization. As new technologies—from block printing to the Internet—have become available, people have used them to gamble. Early mathematics and statistical sciences developed in part to explain the vagaries of chance. Card games flourished in the neighborhood of Shakespeare's Globe Theater and in the imperial courts of China. European colonial ventures, including the Virginia Company, funded themselves through lotteries, and the British Stamp Tax, which included levies on playing cards, helped spur the colonials into rebellion against the Crown. The consolidation of German principalities into Prussia forced the closure of German casinos and led to the rise of Monte Carlo as the grand casino of Europe. Nevada's modern casino industry was born in the gloom of the Great Depression, and the late-20th century post-industrial slump helped spur the wave of casino expansion than began in Atlantic City, New Jersey and still continues. The presence of American casino operators in China reflects the changing global economy, as does the fact that these companies are becoming more Chinese than American.

Gambling is ancient; casinos are of a more recent vintage, but their story is still long and not without lessons for today. The appeal of casinos explains their power to raise up the weak and, more often, bring low the mighty. For plenty of examples of both, just keep on reading.

Roll the Bones

The History of Gambling

Casino Edition

1

The Ridotto Revolution

Mercantile gamblers create the casino

In Our Bones

Where did gambling come from? Storytellers once said that a cunning god or hero first taught people to gamble. Whether it was the coyote or spider trying to trick his fellows or a siege-bound king hoping to rally his troops, the invention of gambling was a single dramatic moment to be cherished or cursed.

Modern historians can't give their audiences such easy explanations of gambling's origin. Their gambling tale starts with an anonymous Paleolithic rounder who rolled a few bones and took action on which sides would come up. But this is not unusual. No one can say exactly who invented prayer, music, farming, medicine, or money. The same must be said for gambling: it is simply older than history.

The gambling impulse even predates humanity: a variety of animals from bees to primates have been observed to embrace risk for a chance at a reward. A 2005 Duke University study found that macaque monkeys preferred to follow a "riskier" target, which gave them varying amounts of juice, over a "safe" one, which always gave the same. They just like gambling. Intriguingly, the monkeys preferred the riskier target even when it gave them consistently less juice than the safe one, and continued to choose the riskier target in the face of diminishing returns when a single large one was still in memory. Chasing the jackpot is nothing new.

Whatever the secret gambling lives of our primate ancestors, humans have long been apt gamblers. The hunter-gatherer lifestyle of early cultures was, like mining or fishing today, predicated on risk: on any given day, one might either find lunch or become lunch. The unknown was omnipresent yet still mysterious, something approached with mingled hope, fear, and superstition. As they discovered new technologies, proto-humans gained more control over their environment, but they still retained a fascination with chance. When the ancestors of modern humans began using tools more than half a million years ago, they also had the potential to modify stone, wood, and bone that could be used to test the unknown. These were the first gambling tools.

But these early "gamblers" weren't simply playing for amusement: early ventures into chance were usually more religious than recreational. Divination is the practice of using supernatural or intuitive means to tell the future or reveal information hidden to reason. Creative diviners have invented dozens of randomizing mechanisms. Some are downright messy: haruspicy, a favorite of the ancient Greeks and Etruscans, involves reading the entrails—particularly the liver—of ritually slaughtered beast. Others are more fragrant: karydaomancers tell the future using coconut shells. Oomancers interpret the patterns made by broken eggs; their clients can presumably enjoy a glimpse into the future along with a tasty omelet. Copromancers and uromancers look for signs in feces and urine, respectively; phyllorhodomancy uses rose petals to divine. And, of course, there are the better-known forms of fortune telling, involving tea leaves, palmistry, astrology, and tarot card reading—a modern form of divination that was, ironically, once a gambling game.

Divination by sortilege (interpreting patterns in thrown objects) allows for many shades of meaning. Early humans threw and read virtually anything for portents, including plants, sticks, stones, and bones. Cleromancy, the casting of lots, would gradually evolve from sacred ritual to profane amusement—dice. Lots could be made from anything, but small bones became the preferred medium. The astragalus (plural, astragali), also called the huckle-bone, is immediately above the talus, or heel bone. The astragalus of many animals—particularly domesticated sheep and goats—can be thrown to produce a more or less random result, though modern day craps players bear little resemblance to Sumerian priests "rolling the bones" for hopeful supplicants.

The precursors of modern dice were sheep huckle-bones or astragali, known to the Romans as tali. At some point, people conflated huckle-bone with knuckle-bone, and began referring to astragali as knucklebones, though they are not, strictly speaking, skeletal remains of knuckles.

The astragalus had four unsymmetrical large sides—concave, convex, broad, and narrow (it was impossible for the bone to come to rest on either of its two rounded ends). Each side stood for a distinct outcome. From using astragali to forecast future events, it was a simple step to simply put stakes on the outcome of a throw. The line between divination and gambling is blurred. One hunter, for example, might say to another, "if the bones land short side up, we will search for game to the south; if not, we look north," thus using the astragali to plumb the future. But after the hunt, the hunters might cast bones to determine who went home with the most desirable cuts. If ascribing the roll of the bones to the will of a divine presence, that would be divination; if the hunters simply rolled and hoped for the best, they were gambling.

Several early archaeological sites throughout Europe, the Mediterranean, and the Near East include astragali and collections of small, differently colored stones—possibly counters. This could be the earliest known craps game, complete with primitive dice and ancient chips. The relative ubiquity of ancient astragali suggests that they must have had some everyday function—they are simply too common to have been used only by a small priestly caste. Unless people did not make day-to-day decisions without rolling the bones, the best explanation for their ubiquity is that astragali were used for entertainment as well.

Anthropologists have identified Mesopotamia, the land between the Tigris and Euphrates rivers in present-day Iraq, as the place where modern urban society originated when, 7,000 years ago, Mesopotamians began building the first cities. Archaeologists have discovered astragali in all periods of Mesopotamian history. The Mesopotamians used astragali to gamble, and gave the convex narrow side a value of one, the convex broad side three, the concave broad side four, and the concave narrow side six: this would become the accepted standard throughout the Middle East and Mediterranean.

When Mesopotamian fortunetellers filed down their knucklebones and marked them with insignia, modern dice were born. It is easy to imagine the evolution from astragali to dice: the four-sided astragali simply were at first filed down into cubes, most likely to make them roll more randomly. Because of variations in bone density and structure, though, these cubical astragali would have inevitably rolled unevenly; it was a logical step to carve more honest dice out of ivory, wood, and other materials. The earliest six-sided dice yet discovered, dating from about 3000 B.C., were unearthed in what is today Northern Iraq.

Eastern Origins

Farther east, the cultures of eastern Asia place as high a premium on gambling as any in the world. While the frequency of gambling activity in many parts of the world, including Europe and North America, was high in ancient times, East Asia had perhaps the greatest intensity of gambling, with higher stakes played for more regularly. From playing cards to keno, Asian cultures have made several important contributions to today's global culture of gambling.

China has a long gambling tradition. The ancient Chinese held random events in high regard; as early as the Shang period (beginning circa 1700 B.C.), they consulted oracles for guidance in making major decisions. Instead of eviscerating farm animals like the Etruscans, these diviners engraved turtle shells or animal bones with written characters, applied heated bronze pins to the opposite sides, then compared the pattern of the cracks to the characters. These oracles, or shih, eventually became the respected scholar gentry of China, proof that, as much as many societies have damned gambling, those who can harness and interpret random events, be it cracked bones or rolled ones, can frequently gain power and respect.

By the Chou period (circa the first millennium B.C.), Chinese culture and cities were flourishing, and gambling was entrenched as a common pastime. In addition to shops selling jewels, clothing, and food, most Chinese cities had gambling houses on their commercial streets. Betting on fighting animals, from quails and thrushes to fish and even crickets (otherwise placid crickets would have their heads tickled with a feather until they charged each other), was quite widespread. Interestingly, even in the age of mechanical and digital gambling, this ancient tradition persists. In the summer of 2004, Hong Kong police arrested 115 people after breaking up an insect-fighting ring in Kowloon, seizing nearly 200 crickets, some of them worth as much as $20,000. Subsequent raids proved that the sport would not die easily.

The Chinese played a version of the lotto game as early as the tenth century A.D., about five centuries before it appeared in Europe. In the Game of Thirty-Six Animals or Hua-Hoey Lottery, one of 36 cards illustrated with different animals was selected at random. Betting schemes on this game varied, but it survived into the 19th century and emigrants from the Celestial Empire brought it with them to Europe and the Americas (it is similar to the Brazilian *jogo du bichos*, which remains popular today).

In the fourth century B.C., players bet on the board game *po*, which mingled skill and chance, as well as other diversions. The Chinese soon found new, more robust ways to gamble. By 200 B.C., betting on cock fights, horse and dog races, and other sports was common in China. The *Han Shu*, a classic Chinese history dating from 115 B.C., laments that young, wealthy government officials were throwing the common people into confusion through an overindulgence in games of chance.

But few heeded the scribe's warnings. Over the following centuries, Chinese gamblers continued to play heartily and even found new ways to gamble. They adopted Western-style dice around the seventh century A.D. and by 900 had turned them into dominoes, which they called *kwat pai*, or "bone tablets." A set of Chinese dominoes consisted of 21 numbers, of which 11 appeared twice, giving a total of 32 tiles. These tiles were made of ivory, in which case their pips were red and black, or ebony, in which case the pips were red and white. As with the modern game of pai gow, players attempted to pair tiles according to their values. Domino games had descriptive titles: English translations such as "to dispute for tens" and "turning heavens and nines," barely suggest their poetry. The Chinese also devised mahjong tiles, fantan (a game played with circular disks), and the forerunners of lotteries, bingo, and keno. Gamblers would owe their greatest debt, though, to a comparatively late Chinese invention: playing cards.

Gambling cultures in the rest of Asia varied widely. Koreans gambled on a number of board games as well as rather obscure events such as oxen fights, kite battles, and the fall of a rake. They also adopted most of the games invented by the Chinese: Korean dominoes are known as *ho hpai*, or "foreign tablets," suggesting their Chinese origin. Until relatively recent historic times, the Japanese had far less gambling than either Koreans or the Chinese. To the north of China, the Mongols were reputed to shun gambling for physical exercise. Further to the west, the Turks adopted dice around A.D. 600, which facilitated the spread of dice gambling across Central Asia. Not to be left out, the Kazakhs also embraced gambling by casting lots, wagering on races, and betting on an indigenous rodeo-style event known as "goat wrestling." The latter was particularly inventive, as riders tried to hoist a decapitated goat onto their horse without falling off, while others tried to recapture it. If nothing else, this proves the incredible creativity of those intent on a good game of chance.

The Invention of Mercantile Gambling

Casinos, places where the general public is free to bet against a fixed bank, are institutions built on mercantile gambling, or gambling run by professionals for profit. Mercantile gambling, also known as commercial gambling, is contrasted with social gambling, where the players bet against each other, not a fixed bank or house. Playing a slot machine in a casino is a prime example of mercantile gambling; a Tuesday night poker game in your friend's basement is the quintessential social gamble.

Lotteries were only the tip of the gambling iceberg in 16th-century Italy. Even before mathematicians had elaborated a systematic consideration of chance, wily gamblers in the Italian city of Venice were beginning to apply theories of probability in practical ways that would revolutionize the world of gambling. Just as the lottery offered citizens a chance to get rich while underwriting charities or government programs, mercantile gambling let people play against an impersonal house for the price of the house edge.

In many ways, the invention of mercantile gambling mirrored the development of modern banking. The development of these "bank games" had as much importance for gambling as the rise of banks themselves did for finance. Banknotes had circulated in China as early as the seventh century A.D., but did not become a regular feature of European life until the 18th century—around the same time that mercantile gambling became widespread. As investors were experimenting with joint stock companies and speculative ventures, gamblers began, increasingly, to view gambling as a business transaction rather than a friendly game between equals.

Social gambling made sense for people who gambled only in order to relieve tedium or to enjoy special occasions. This is why ancient societies from China to Rome permitted gambling during year-end holidays, and why writers from Spanish king Alphonso X to Girolamo Cardano condoned recreational social gambling as a fitting diversion, if indulged infrequently and according to prescribed rules. But there were always those who saw gambling not as a rare entertainment, but as a shortcut to wealth and leisure. Those who wished to extend their gambling from occasional recreation to habitual pursuit needed to possess both an unlimited income independent of unreliable gambling winnings and more free time than responsibilities. The only way to "earn" a living from gambling was to either hope for incredibly good luck, accept stretches of poverty as the price of the game, or to regularly cheat without scruple or detection.

The invention of mercantile gambling provided a way to legitimately make a living from gambling by running houses where gambling was permitted. It also freed players from the bonds of sociability—they could now gamble against professionals whenever they wished. At the same time, the games themselves changed, becoming far more direct as rules were simplified and game durations shortened.

Social gamblers might want to while away the hours over sprawling games of trappola with their friends, but those looking for action in gambling houses wanted a quick fix: the turn of the card at bassett or faro, the spin of the roulette wheel, or a single throw of the dice.

With the introduction of bank games and the proliferation of professional gambling houses, a gambling mania swept over much of Europe. It hit different countries at slightly different times, but it is safe to say from 1650 to 1850 gambling's place in European society was far more prominent than before or since. There had always been gambling, but in these years it was universally common on a level never before seen. With the rise of mercantile capitalism, money circulated more freely and accumulations of wealth became greater than before. During the same years that governments sponsored lotteries, all social classes gambled more. The emergence of mercantile gambling provided the catalyst for the increasing interest of governments in gambling.

One of the earliest bank games was the German lansquenet, which derived its name from the Landsknechte, roving German mercenary knights of the 16th century who apparently had a nose for favorable house odds. Lansquenet was relatively straightforward: the banker matched stakes with a player or players, then dealt one card to the right and one to the left. If they were of the same suit, the bank won automatically. If not, the dealer continued laying out cards in the middle until a match appeared: if it matched the left, the bank swept the players' stakes, and if it matched the right, the players took the banks. The lansquenet bank wasn't held by a fixed house, but could rotate from player to player. In coming years, bank games would develop much greater sophistication, nowhere with as much passion as in northern Italy.

The First Casino

Post-renaissance Italy (it was not then a nation, but a collection of several principalities and city-states) was notorious for its gamblers. Gambling flourished in taverns and private houses throughout the peninsula.

Italians were passionate about gambling, but they above all others turned it into a business. Northern Italy—Europe's most economically, socially, and culturally advanced region—was the cradle of mercantile gambling. Venice had long been a gambling mecca: in the late 14th century, it was one of the first centers of playing cards, and though the lottery wasn't invented there, it gained widespread acceptance there in the 16th century. Especially during the Carnival season, women and men of all Venetian social classes gambled. Less affluent Venetians enjoyed card and dice games in public places, such as street corners, bridges, grand squares, and wine shops. Though these games were occasionally disrupted by the police and convicted gamblers could face fines and imprisonment, they usually ran more or less openly. Members of the nobility offered a more refined setting for their gambling: at private parties, they presented their guests with games of chance and, as most were politically well connected, these games were rarely stopped by police.

Municipal edicts banning gambling did nothing to stop its dramatic transformation in the 16th century. By 1567, legislation specified a new danger: the *ridotti* of nobles, places where gambling took place. The word *ridotto* is likely derived from *ridurre*, to reduce or close, or to make private. Generally, a *ridotto* could be anything closed—a top-secret meeting of government officials, or a private suite of rooms in a larger domicile. But the word soon came to suggest a semi-private place for gambling, dancing, eating, and gossip. These notorious houses remained the haunts of the aristocracy. For the rest, inns and other public places continued to serve as convenient gathering places.

By the turn of the 17th century, anti-gambling laws reflected a change in the status of *ridotti*. They were no longer merely places where nobles permitted gambling and drinking: they had become places where nobles, by taking a portion of the money staked, profited directly from gambling. The nobles apparently had specialized dealers, for the Executors against Blasphemy (Escutori contro la bestemmia) prosecuted both nobles who owned *ridotti* and their employees who actually ran the games.

Chief among the games of the *ridotti* was *bassetto* or basset, a Venetian game that was invented in the late 16th century. The game of basset, notably, was a banking game without even the pretense of equality between the dealer/banker and the bettor. In addition to its main bet, where the player tried to guess whether a card would be dealt to the player or dealer pile, basset also featured a series of long-shots that, though they paid off handsomely, were extremely unlikely. If a player bet his money on the king, for example, and had the first king in the deck placed in the player's pile, he could either collect three-to-one on his money or let his bet ride and hope to get the king when it was dealt again, in which case he would win seven times his original bet. If he won a second time, this bet, and the third, could also be kept alive: if he triumphed each time, he could collect up to 30 times his initial bet. This was known as the *paroli* (the origin of the English word "parlay"). Though the laws of probability declared such an eventuality highly unlikely, the willingness of bettors to press on in hopes of a larger payout made basset an extremely profitable game—for the banker.

Ridotti flourished, and, frustrated at the inability of the Venetian Inquisition to eliminate the gambling dens, the Great Council embarked on a novel plan—the legalization of gambling, at least during Carnival, within a single specified free zone. In 1638, the Great Council opened the Ridotto in the San Moise Palace, a four-story building owned by Marco Dandolo. This was the first legal, state-sanctioned public gambling house in European history—from this notable edifice that today's casino industry can rightfully claim descent. The opening of the Ridotto represented a historic union between mercantile gamblers, who ran games for profit, and government, who sought to legitimize the gamblers for purposes of public order and revenue enhancement.

Upon entering the Ridotto, one could visit two small rooms, one selling stimulating refreshments (coffee, tea, and chocolates), and the other which dispensed cheese, wine, fruit, and sausage. Past this initial vestibule one entered the Long Hall, a two-story room whose ceiling was painted with Gerolamo Colonna's The Triumph of Virtue, perhaps a warning against cheaters. Along the sides of the Long Hall, one found basset tables at which members of an impoverished clan of noblemen known as the *barnabotti* or Barnabots dealt cards and took wagers. The Barnabots, despite having limited financial means, were prohibited as nobles from regular employment, living at the public expense in the parish of St. Barnabas. Granting them the Ridotto monopoly was a step toward minimizing the public cost of maintaining them—an early example of public-interest gambling. According to Venetian law, the Barnabots who dealt games had to wear black robes and shoulder-length wigs. As these poor nobles at first lacked the money to bank games themselves, wealthier nobles or merchants sometimes put the Barnabots on salary, bankrolling their games in exchange for the lion's share of the profits.

Off the Long Hall, about six smaller rooms offered even more tables for basset, *biribisso* (the leather-sack version of roulette that the French called *biribi*), and a now-obscure Italian card game known as *panfil*. The windowless Long Hall was lit by six-armed chandeliers that hung from the ceiling and a municipally-specified two candles on each table. All gamblers, except for members of the nobility, had to wear masks while gambling, something that clearly ties the legality of the Ridotto to the permissive spirit that reigned at Carnival. The Ridotto began admitting customers between eight or ten in the morning, depending on the season, and stayed open until well past midnight; its votaries often emerged only in the morning, blinking in the sudden sunlight as the rest of Venice began its work day.

Though anyone wearing proper attire (a three-cornered hat, cape, and mask for men) could enter the Ridotto, the high minimum stakes served to restrict its play to the wealthy. Men and women (especially noblemen) were expected to gamble with a phlegmatic detachment that forbade both bettors and bankers from expressing even the slightest dismay at an astounding loss or the tiniest excitement over a victory. The Ridotto was nevertheless an exciting mishmash of Venetian society, with nobles, prostitutes, pimps, usurers, police informants, and degenerate gamblers mixing with curious visitors. The anonymity of the masked Carnival atmosphere no doubt lowered inhibitions. Those seeking adventure outside the bonds of marriage were seldom disappointed at the Ridotto. Its "Chamber of Sighs" was a famously darkened room upon whose couches unlucky gamblers could moan with despair, and lovers with passion.

The profit generated by the Ridotto for the Barnabots and the Venetian government only grew over the years. At the insistence of the city authorities, the Ridotto was enlarged in 1768 using money confiscated from convents, outraging the "social conservatives" of the era. A second legal ridotto opened at the San Cassian Theater, though the Ridotto at San Moise remained the focal point of the city's gambling. The Ridotto changed its games to keep up with the times. About midway through the 18th century, basset began to lose popularity at the expense of faro, a game that would remain popular in Europe and the United States for the next century and a half.

Faro was first known as pharaoh or pharaon, after a French deck of cards which boasted a picture of the Egyptian ruler. Contrary to later legend, it was not born in ancient Egypt, but was rather an adaptation of basset. Working on the same general principal as basset—that players bet on a card or cards that might be in the winning pile—faro had the advantage of a common layout upon which all players could bet. (In basset, a player had to produce from her own deck the card that she wished to bet on; in faro, each card was already represented on the gaming table, and she only had to place her stakes in the appropriate space.) There were other changes, as well. If the cards on a single turn formed a pair, the dealer kept half the money bet. Faro players also could bet with the bank, or losing pile, and could bet on multiple cards. A final innovation allowed players to "call the turn" and predict the correct order of the three penultimate cards to be drawn (the last card, the "hock," was an automatic discard).

Sin City on the Adriatic

Whether playing basset, faro, or other games, a parade of the rich and notorious saw the inside of the Ridotto during its golden years. Even those without a propensity for wagering visited the Ridotto at least once if they had the means. The enlightened philosopher Jean-Jacques Rousseau, perhaps looking for noble savages in an urban setting, gambled only once in his life, when he visited the Ridotto in 1744. But others found themselves trapped by fortune's temptations. Lorenzo Da Ponte, a poet best remembered as the librettist of three Mozart operas (The Marriage of Figaro, Cosi fan tutte, and Don Giovanni), nearly came to ruin in the Ridotto; the victim of an obsessive love for a female of the Barnabot clan, he gambled himself into desperation. After witnessing his own priest steal and sell his cloak for gambling money, Da Ponte vowed "no more gambling, no more women, no more Venice," and embarked on a long and varied career which brought him to the United States where he would ultimately die in poverty.

The infamous Giacomo Casanova frequented the Ridotto during his days in Venice. A notorious gambler, he was loath to part with money earned by other means, but freely lavished his gambling winnings on himself, extravagant gifts to women, and enormous gratuities to servants. Casanova himself said that his gambling was a great mistake, as he lacked the discipline to stop playing when luck was against him, though only felt at ease spending gambling money, because he felt that it had "cost him nothing." He crossed paths with Lorenzo Da Ponte at the Ridotto and may have collaborated with him on Don Giovanni.

Da Ponte and Casanova were not the only ones who found the Ridotto irresistible. The combination of the Venetian mania for gambling with the house advantage of the Ridotto, led to a sad phenomenon: nobles playing themselves into bankruptcy. Fortunes accumulated over generations were lost at the Ridotto, and furniture, artwork, and even palaces were pledged to money-lenders in order to secure funds for more gambling.

Perhaps alarmed by the growing impoverishment of its aristocratic families, the Great Council of Venice eventually took action. A reform-minded Barnabot named Giorgio Pisani urged his colleagues that, "to preserve the piety, sound discipline, and moderate behavior" of Venetian society, they had to close the Ridotto and end the experiment in legal public gambling. On November 27, 1774, by a vote of 720 to 21, the Council passed the measure, though, according to Casanova, its members had not intended that to be the case: each felt that since there would naturally be a majority of votes opposed to the bill, he could support it and thus claim the moral high ground. When the vote was announced, according to Casanova, the Solons blankly looked at each other, stupefied at the calamity they had just authored.

After 136 years, the Ridotto was silent. The wife of a French gambler penned an epitaph for the Ridotto when she declared that, with its closure, Venice had been gripped by a morbid depression: "usurers look as sour as lemons, shop-keepers can't sell a thing, mask-makers are starving, and the Barnabot noblemen, accustomed to dealing cards ten hours a day, find their hands are withering away. Clearly, no state can keep going without the aid of vice."

Yet the closure of the Ridotto did not mean the end of Venetian gambling, but only a new beginning. From its former center at San Moise, gambling spread to over a hundred illicit *ridotti* and *casini*. Originally, a *casino* was a small house used as a gathering place by a group of people: a club-house. The first references to casini appear in the early 17th century, and *casini* soon became centers for gambling and gossip. The closure of the public Ridotto increased the number of these little houses: by the end of the century, there were 136 operating in Venice.

Though it was hailed as one of the most sophisticated cities of 18th century Europe, Venice's days of glory did not long outlive its public Ridotto. The city's occupation by Napoleon in 1797 and its absorption into the Austrian Empire soon afterwards marked the beginning of a long decline. As the city suffered, its gambling culture waned as well, as other European principalities legalized gambling houses or, as they became known, casinos. When the government of Italy again authorized Venetian casinos in the 20th century, these could not bring back the wayward dissolution of the Ridotto during Carnival season, but the continuation of Venetian gambling and the universal name used to describe gambling houses featuring bank games—the casino—serve as lasting reminders of the impressive Venetian contribution to gambling history.

Modern Games Appear

Though the casino was born in Venice, most of today's popular casino games, including roulette, baccarat, and blackjack originated in France, a testament to the Gallic manifestation of the 1650-1850 European gambling craze. In these years, gambling received the sanction of the French monarch and, for a while, became the *sine qua non* of courtly life at Versailles. From there, it became a national obsession.

The French turned to gambling with wild abandon in the 17th century, but had already been playing for years, though at much lower levels. For centuries, gambling had been chiefly a pastime of nobles and soldiers, particularly during the Hundred Years War (1337-1453), with dicing originally the game of choice, though playing cards proliferated in the latter part of the war. During the reign of Charles VI (r. 1380-1422; sometimes known as Charles the Mad), the Hotel de Nesle attracted many nobles (it was barred to all others) who wished to gamble. A poet of the time lamented: "How many very eminent gentlemen have there lost their arms and horses, their money and lordship—a horrible folly."

Towards the end of the 16th century, though, gambling became more prevalent, as did those wishing to take advantage of the unwary. Upon hearing that King Henry III (r. 1574-1589) had opened gaming rooms in the Louvre, a band of Italian gamblers gained admission and took the king for 30,000 crowns, a tremendous sum. Yet perhaps because of the religious wars that engulfed France during his reign, gambling did not enjoy anything near the level of popularity it would find in that of his successor, Henry IV. Known as "good king Henry" to this day, Henry loved gambling. More greedy than skillful, Henry became extremely displeased when he lost. As a result, smart courtiers and nobles tripped over themselves to lose to him.

During Henry IV's reign, *Academies de Jeux*, or gaming academies, first appeared. These were not institutions of higher learning, but gaming houses which admitted all comers, from peasants to dukes, provided they could secure funds to play. These academies seem to have been in a grey area: though tolerated by city magistrates for a financial consideration (nearly 50 flourished in Paris alone), they do not seem to have had royal sanction. Nor is it clear if, as in the Ridotto, bank games predominated, or whether these academies were merely places for intense social gambling. Their first heyday was brief. With the ascension of Louis XIII to the French throne in 1610, existing laws against gambling were strengthened and the academies were closed. Still, clandestine private gambling amongst the nobility continued.

The accession of the young King Louis XIV to the kingship under the tutelage of Cardinal Mazarin is best remembered as the high point of French monarchical absolutism, though that time also saw the most dramatic expansion of gambling throughout France. Some claimed that Mazarin introduced gambling to the French nobility at

Versailles in 1648. In fact, French monarchs had long been familiar with gambling. At first, according to one chronicler, Mazarin encouraged only games with playing cards which might or might not have occasioned gambling. Before long, though, thanks to Mazarin's skill at play, games of chance soon predominated and, to the woe of one commentator, brought ruin to noble families. Even worse, it stultified the nobility: before the vogue for gambling, men and women had worked at improving the art of conversation by reading, but afterwards books were neglected, as were athletic pursuits and other games of skill, until men became "weaker and more sickly, more ignorant, less polished, and more dissipated." Women lost their previous mystique by spending all night out gambling with the boys and were "very ductile and complying" to those from whom they borrowed money.

Given royal imprimatur, gambling became *de rigeur* for members of gentle society. Respectable hosts thought nothing of mitigating their entertainment expenses by "entertaining" guests with bank games like faro, *biribi*, and *hoca*, another roulette ancestor. Curmudgeons complained that, before inviting a guest to dinner, the partygiver inquired as to whether he gambled.

According to one account, during these years card-playing spread from the army to the court, from the court to the city, and from the city to the country towns. Gambling became a French obsession during this time: everyone, it seemed, lived only to hope for the next big win, and gambling became a favorite topic in the period's fiction and drama. Mazarin's enemies charged that he had familiarized the court with gambling as part of a cynical plot to keep the young Sun King under his thrall and to bankrupt his enemies, but it seems obvious that gambling was avidly pursued throughout the nation. After Mazarin's death in 1661, gambling continued to increase in scale, and at the passing of Louis XIV himself in 1715, its primacy in France was undisputed. One early historian wrote that, at that time, three-quarters of the nation thought of nothing but cards and dice.

The official French approach to gambling was anything but enlightened. From 1643 to 1777, thirty-two official decrees announced that gambling was a crime to be sternly punished. Yet gambling only grew. The regency of Louis XV saw the royal finances and national wealth entrusted to a gambler, the notorious John Law, and licensed gambling houses known as *maisons de jeux* became fixtures of the Paris cityscape. They commonly glided by official prohibitions by maintaining a pretense of offering only card games requiring skill, collectively known as *jeux de commerce*. Games of pure chance, or *jeux de hazard*, also flourished in the *maisons de jeux*. Popular games included basset/faro, *biribi*, and lansquenet—all of them bank games, indicating that mercantile gamblers ran the houses. Gamblers also plied their trade without even superficial fear of the police at two seasonal fairs and within foreign embassies. In addition, hundreds of ostensibly illegal gambling rooms were widely known, proclaiming their existence by telltale lights at their entrance. For a kingdom that added new laws against gambling nearly every year, France had a great deal of it, both legal and illegal.

The French embraced the games played in Italy. *Hoca* enjoyed a great popularity, as did basset, faro, and the ultimate mercantile game, the lottery. Particularly among the upper classes, social gambling continued alongside the new mercantile games.

Wealthy Parisians soon found even more places to play. New gambling houses, called *enfers*, or hells, opened in Paris and its environs. Their sinister name revealed the intensity of gambling that took place there. One chronicler described how in the salon of one of these hells a nobleman offered his sword as his stake, a contravention of custom that appalled both the nobility and the bankers in attendance. Others retreated to spas under the pretense of seeking healthy respite at the healing springs, while they actually wanted to congregate with gamesters. Even those who could not afford bread gambled constantly, while merchants and craftsmen heaped gold upon the tables and one farmer even gambled away his harvest.

In the 1770s, government officials made two attempts to alleviate the problems of rampant unchecked gambling and divert some of its profits towards the public good. The first was the 1776 cooption of Casanova's lottery by the king, and the second was a scheme developed a year earlier by the Parisian lieutenant of police Antoine de Sartines to license and tax gambling establishments. He permitted twelve legal gaming houses, forwarding the resulting tax to hospitals, and required them to permit women to gamble two days a week. A reported rise in crime and financial misfortunes led to their supposed suppression three years later, but the contradictory French approach continued, as both licensed and unlicensed establishments continued to operate unabated.

French Casinos in the Revolutionary Era

As the social and economic conditions in France worsened and political tensions began to mount in the late 1780s, gambling's intensity continued to increase. One might have expected the shock of the sudden regime change in 1787 combined with the vicissitudes of war, internal and external, following the Revolution might have caused a sudden, sharp decline in gambling. But gambling continued, seemingly immune from any interruption, save the temporary hiatus of the lottery from 1793 to 1797. Perhaps the French Revolution most strongly changed gambling in Britain, where escaping émigrés brought the contagion of gambling fever with them, at least in the opinion of British moralists.

The path of revolutionary gambling is best seen at the Palais Royale, a four-story behemoth north of the Louvre. This palace was originally the hereditary home of the Orleans family. When Louis Phillipe Joseph I inherited it in 1785, his sumptuous lifestyle and wild betting threatened to bankrupt him. Rather than limit his spending, the liberal Phillipe Egalitie (as he was known) turned it into a commercial center. He converted the upper floors into apartments for rent, and installed 180 shops on the ground floor. The duke rented out basement and second-floor space for restaurants, cafes, and social clubs, which began offering games of chance. Soon over 100 gambling rooms were found there.

In the years before the Revolution, the Palais was the scene of ardent gambling. Marie-Antoinette stayed until dawn for weeks, losing spectacularly at faro. Other nobles disgraced themselves by losing unimaginable sums there as well. The liberal Phillipe also opened the Palais to the middle classes, giving them an elegant place to gamble. After the 1793 guillotining of the French monarchy (including the unfortunate Phillipe), gambling only escalated within the Palais Royale. The Directorate successfully reduced the number of gambling operations to five. Though the new government did not officially sanction these five rooms, they declined to close them, thus allowing gambling-mad Parisians an important safety valve.

Apocryphally, the French Revolution led to a singular change within the rules of cards: aces, not kings, became the highest-ranked card. But, as can be seen by looking at the rules of the much earlier game brelan, this was already a feature of at least some French games. Perhaps it is more fitting to say that games like brelan, where a single ace could sweep aside three kings, represented the building social turmoil. The Revolution's chief impact was to briefly change the composition of the French deck. With the ascension of the Republic in the 1790s, gambling with pictures of kings, queens, and their retainers became decidedly passé, and the customary court cards were replaced with representation of abstract republican virtues like Liberty or patriarchs of the new order like Voltaire. Even this change was temporary, as gamblers proved yet again to stubbornly resist innovation in the art of the playing card, and royalty soon returned.

During the years following the Revolution a new game appeared at the Palais Royale: roulette, which combined the numbers of *hoca/biribi* with an English wheel used in at least three games: roly poly or rowlet, ace of hearts, and EO (even and odd). The English had begun playing roly poly in 1720, when they spun a small ball around a horizontal wheel with several slots, including two that gave the banker an automatic victory. Around the same time, Ace of Hearts featured a faro-like layout and cards painted on the wheel. When the British Parliament outlawed roly poly and Ace of Hearts in 1739, one enterprising gamester circumvented the law by creating EO, a wheel with 40 slots: nineteen each marked odd or even, and two which denoted an instant bank win.

When the French first began playing roly poly or roulette, they played the un-numbered English original. Besides changing the wheel's colors to red and black from white and black, the French made no changes until, in 1796, someone fused the numbered balls and layout of the smaller, street version of *biribi* (which had 36 numbers to the indoor version's 70) with the wheel of roulette. The Palais Royale game of 1796 offered all of the features of today's game: straight-up betting, red/black and even/odd betting, column betting, and other splits and combinations. Like American roulette, it had both zero and double zero, marked in green, which were neither red, black, even, nor odd (though zero is actually an even number). Even at times of revolutionary crisis, the French remained inventive gamblers, and not even the chaos of revolution and war could stop the wheels from spinning.

Nor did the rise of Napoleon Bonaparte halt gambling. Salons, legal or not, continued, and French men and women remained drawn to them. In 1806 Napoleon created the first unambiguously legal gambling houses in France. In that year he finally legalized the five surviving gambling rooms of the Palais Royale, six more in the vicinity of that palace, and those at health resorts like Spa and Aix-les-Bains. After Napoleon's defeat at Waterloo in 1815, ironically, the Palais Royale enjoyed its most profitable year yet, as triumphant Englishmen, Prussians, Austrians, and Russians converged on Paris and celebrated by gambling at the Palais.

The emperor himself was a noted gambler, preferring the relatively new game of Vignt-et-un, better known to English speakers as "twenty-one" or blackjack. Twenty-one's roots are obscure, but it first appeared in France in the middle of the 18th century, probably developing from the earlier game of thirty-one, which had been played as early as 1464. The rules of thirty-one are unknown, but it is likely that drawing cards to its eponymous number was only one phase of the game, as it was with the games of cribbage and noddy. Twenty-one emerged as its own game when the rules were altered to permit the ace to represent one or eleven and play was shortened by drawing only to twenty-one. The game did not have the same popular appeal as faro, though it was a favorite of Louis XV's mistress Madame Du Barry, and in truth it would not be until the popularization of card counting in the 1960s that the game truly came into its own. This game, perhaps, comforted Napoleon during his years of exile, and it is interesting to speculate as to whether the great general developed any counting system of his own or meekly surrendered to fortune.

French gambling continued after the 1814 Bourbon Restoration. An 1818 Paris survey reported a total of twenty tables operating throughout nine legal houses. Nearly half of the tables were dedicated to roulette, with seven for *trente-et-un*, possibly the extended version of blackjack, which apparently survived alongside its quicker version. Other games played included the American craps, its ancestor hazard, and biribi. These licensed games operated until December 31, 1837 when the Chamber of Deputies "permanently" banned all games of chance, an act whose greatest consequence was the eventual development of Monte Carlo as a gambling haven. Even when banning gambling, the French could not help but encourage it.

2

Seeking the Cure

Europe wins and loses at spas

Across Europe, the turmoil of the French Revolution marked the end of the Ancien Regime. Gambling faced similar tumult. The French prohibition of gambling in 1837 augured a century of contraction for casino-style gambling across the continent. As other industrializing nations of Western Europe became more sensitive to the financial disorder unleashed by unlimited gambling, they also moved to suppress it. But gambling survived, and even prospered, in the unlikeliest of places—health resorts.

Initially, most of those who sojourned to the spas were legitimately ill. The therapeutic waters were plausibly the best recuperative option given the state of medicine at the time. But as time went on, spending time at a spa became de rigeur for those with sufficient wealth to do so. After they became the continent's au courant resorts, virtually anyone of social standing summered at one of them. The bored, healthy vacationers eagerly took up gambling to pass the time. Once home to those seeking the cure for various physical afflictions, the spas—and the wild gambling that took place within them—became notorious as the cure for nothing more serious than excess wealth.

The Spa at Spa

The first spa town to gain acclaim as both a health resort and an aristocratic gathering place was also the oldest. The town of Spa has since given its name generically to any place where healthy waters are the attraction, from posh enclaves like Canyon Ranch to apartment community Jacuzzis. Spa is nestled in a green valley in the hills of the Ardennes in Liege, today a province in eastern Belgium and can rightly claim an ancient lineage: Pliny the Elder praised its bubbling waters as curative of fevers and infections in the first century AD.

Spa's modern vogue dates to the 16th century. In 1559, Dr. Gilbert Lymborch wrote *Of the Acidulous Fountains of the Ardennes Forest and principally those found at Spa*. Despite its cumbersome title, this volume was quite the page-turner—translated into several languages, it was widely read throughout Europe. The book gave Europeans a plausible medical excuse for convalescing in Spa. Attracting visitors from throughout Europe (particularly Britons) due to the religious tolerance of the ruling prince-bishop, the principality of Liege became a haven for both Protestants and Catholics during the religious strife that marked the era.

By the beginning of the 18th century, Spa was well established as a health resort, thanks to the ingenuity and perseverance of the town's promoters, who even turned the decrepitude of the infamously muddy streets to their advantage. Cottage industries sprang up to make and sell oversized shoes and handmade walking sticks that allowed visitors to navigate the rubble-strewn thoroughfares. The town fathers probably kept the streets in deliberate disrepair to foster this industry. Typically, visitors awoke between five and seven in the morning, donned their shoes, grabbed their walking sticks, and trundled off to one of the three springs. Spa artisans eagerly sold them small watch-sized dials numbered one through twenty. As the visitor drank a glass of spring water, she rotated the dial to mark it, thus keeping track of her water consumption. Few water-takers were without another local item, a small box filled with orange peels, peppermint, or other spices to flavor the famous waters.

The healthy waters were the chief attraction, but a host of other amusements were easy to find. Strolling musicians serenaded visitors. Acrobats, jugglers, and tightrope walkers dazzled their audiences, as did ventriloquists and sleight-of-hand operators. Other attractions seem to be taken directly from a sideshow: armless, legless, and kneeless specimens of humanity performed various acts for the curious. Dwarves, strongmen, and prodigies rounded out the display.

The scene would not have been complete without gambling, and professional gamblers perched near the springs, offering mercantile games like faro, hazard, and biribi. Operating outdoors when the weather permitted, and moving indoors to private houses when it didn't, gamblers earned incredible profits during the fashionable summer season, when throngs of well-off health-seekers lounged near the springs. But others profited as well. It was reported that opportunists prowled the gambling grounds, some using wax-tipped canes to pick up dropped coins, while others trained dogs to leap forward and snatch up any loose change.

To provide visitors with more elegant—and presumably more private—gambling facilities, the reigning prince-bishop, Cardinal Jean-Theodore of Bavaria announced in 1762 plans for a two-story casino named the Redoute, the French translation of Ridotto. Lacking perhaps in originality, the Cardinal was certainly far-sighted: he planned for the Redoute to host balls, concerts, and plays, as well as have elegant gambling rooms. A temporary structure opened in 1765, and four years later the permanent Redoute debuted. It was widely acclaimed as a hall fit for kings. With two gambling rooms, a reading room, and a ballroom, the Redoute offered its guests suitably lavish facilities for aristocratic entertainment.

Others began diversifying Spa's gambling. In 1773, the Duke of Lauzun and Count Branicki began running horseracing on a track located between Spa and Verviers. They modeled the races on those being conducted at Newmarket, the home of the British Jockey Club. This racing enterprise, the first such one on the Continent, was successful.

Another facility competed more directly with the Redoute. In 1770, the Vaux Hall opened on a rise which commanded a superior view of Spa and its surroundings. With an elegant ballroom and two gaming salons, the Vaux Hall (named after the Thames gardens in an apparent attempt to appeal to British visitors) rivaled the Redoute in its splendor. Predictably, the proprietors of the Redoute, chagrined by the loss of their monopoly, demanded satisfaction from the reigning prince-bishop, Count Francois de Velbruck. The count responded with an edict that combined the wisdom of Solomon with naked self-interest. He commanded that the two feuding companies unite and share the profits from the two casinos equally, minus a thirty percent cut to be annually delivered to the prince-bishop. The casino managers combined their operations and, with heavy hearts, sent their annual tribute to Velbruck.

A group of British visitors opened the English Club in 1765. Although it was not open to the general public, the owners of the Redoute and Vauxhall resented its siphoning of gambling money away from them, and they continually petitioned the prince-bishop to suppress it. Despite the protests, the English Club persisted for about twenty years. This Club emulated the gentlemen's clubs of London's West End which were then beginning to flourish.

On August 13, 1785, a catastrophic fire destroyed an entire wing of the Redoute. This was, however, only the beginning of the disaster. Fanned by the winds, burning playing cards were blown to the southeast, where they set fire to as many as fifty thatch-roofed houses, killing three people and causing widespread destruction. Though this might have seemed to the pious to be a signal of divine disapproval of gambling, the Redoute soon continued as before, with the burnt section promptly rebuilt.

The Spa casinos were renowned for their haughty croupiers and for the swarms of adventurers they attracted. One critic wrote in 1784 that the croupiers grandiosely styled themselves "captain," "gendarme," or "hussar," while they rudely dealt games with a vulgarity unbecoming such ostensibly noble gentlemen. On the opposite side of the tables, cheaters often attempted to introduce loaded dice or marked cards, though they were usually discovered before much damage could be done. In 1779, a scandal rocked the Redoute when it was discovered that one of its trusted employees had been introducing marked cards into play, allowing a confederate to make off with tremendous sums. The anger of the Redoute's managers was apparently mitigated by the fact that the offending official was a close relative of one of the casino's directors. The casino did not press charges or even fire him, but merely reprimanded the cheater and removed him from his position of responsibility.

By 1789, faro, hazard, and biribi had largely been replaced by roulette and *trente-et-quarante* . The latter, also known as *rouge et noir,* was played in France as early as 1650 but first became popular at Spa around 1780. This game, whose name means "thirty and forty," is

The game of *trente-et-quarante* as it was played in the nineteenth century. It was, for much of the period, the second-most popular game in Europe, trailing only roulette.

rather simple, with only four possible bets, and it holds a razor-thin house advantage, making it one of the least-unbalanced mercantile games ever offered. Even during its heyday it was rarely found outside of France, and it never developed any traction in American casinos, legal or illegal.

To play, the player places a bet on rouge, noir, *coleur*, or *inverse*. The croupier then lays out two rows of cards marked red and black, dealing a standard fifty-two card deck from a six-deck shoe. Court cards count for ten, and all other cards hold their face value. When both rows total more than thirty, the game is over. The dealer then pays those who bet on the row that is closer to thirty. If the rows are tied, the money is returned to players, unless both rows equal thirty-one, in which case the house takes half of the wager, although players can buy insurance against this outcome. The "coleur" bet pays if the first card of the winning row matches that row's color (for example, a diamond or heart in "rouge"), while "inverse" is a bet for the opposite.

Most of the game's bets, then, are simple either/or propositions. The house's only advantage comes with the half-loss on tied thirty-ones. Roulette, which evolved at about the same time as *trente-et-quarante*, offered similarly clear-cut wagers, but the addition of one or two zeroes gave the house a stronger edge. Quicker than hazard and faro, both games gave players rapid decisions, and neither required a whit of skill: minus an unbalanced wheel, marked cards, or a crooked dealer, there was no way to use logic or reasoning to place a wager.

Though it was politically and administratively distinct from France as part of the Principality of Liege, Spa was no more immune from the turmoil of the French Revolution than the neighborhoods of Paris. In Spa, the revolutionary ferment centered on a casino. In 1784, a Liege businessman named Noel Levoz flouted the prince-bishop's imposition of a gaming monopoly and began building his own fashionable gambling salon. He hoped to force the managers of the existing casinos to buy him out. They refused, and asked the current prince-bishop, Prince Constantine de Hoensbroek, to close Levoz's large, richly-appointed gambling room.

In anticipation of a move by the prince-bishop to force him out, Levoz began stockpiling weapons and ammunition in his salon in 1787. Hoensbroek then dispatched troops who, following his orders, seized the arms and occupied the casino's environs. This episode might have been written off as nothing more than a sovereign exercising his rights to enforce a monopoly, but two years later, in the summer of 1789, revolution was in the air. Hoensbroek's high-handed action against Levoz had stirred up liberal resentment against him, and on August 18, 1789, the progressive citizens of Liege finally took action. As peasants from surrounding towns stormed Spa, causing aristocratic guests to flee, rebel burghers and artisans in Liege declared a revolutionary republic. The prince-bishop abdicated before taking flight in terror.

This excitement hardly boded well for the hospitality industry of Spa. But after the Holy Roman Emperor, Joseph II of Austria, occupied the principality, refugees from France began to pour into Spa, providing a boon for the local economy. The expatriate "aristos," many of whom had escaped with fortunes in gold coins, awaited the day that they could return to France. But on September 18, 1794, the Austrian army suffered a decisive defeat at the battle of Sprimont, and the armies of the old regime abandoned Liege to the onrushing revolutionary armies. The émigrés immediately began to flee, desperate to escape the guillotine that surely awaited them should they fall into the republican hands. Some nobles, unable to carry their gold-laden trunks, hid them in the surrounding forests, inspiring legends of hidden fortunes.

Liege was officially annexed to France the next year, and it never recovered from the disaster of the revolution. Those with the means left in search of better prospects, and with the tourist trade effectively ended, those left behind begged and foraged for food amid empty inns and vacant streets. Many starved to death. In 1802, the Treaty of Amiens gave momentary respite to the fighting that had disrupted Spa's trade, and visitors returned in small numbers. But when the fighting resumed again, even that trickle ceased. A catastrophic fire in 1807 destroyed nearly the entire town. Though most of the attractions, including the Redoute, were rebuilt, the town was doomed to obscurity. Even after the inauguration of peace with the Congress of Vienna in 1815, Spa held few attractions; though a few visitors came and gambled perfunctorily, they became fewer and fewer in number.

For the next several decades, Spa's gambling unmistakably declined. The Redoute now seemed dominated by mutual suspicion, as both croupiers and players now made no pretense at maintaining a constant vigil against cheating. A travel guide of the period declared that "the ball spins more slowly at roulette—the cards are dealt more gingerly at *trente-et-quarante* here than elsewhere. Nothing must be done quickly, lest somebody on one side or other should try to do [wrong to] somebody else." While the promenades and ball rooms remained pleasant enough, visitors to the gaming tables were warned to guard against the hustlers and opportunists who congregated there.

As railroads took travelers to other destinations quickly and cheaply, they bypassed Spa, and the town did not get a direct line until 1854. In the interim, a host of more fashionable mineral springs, particularly in today's Germany, had usurped Spa's place as the gathering point of polite and adventurous European society. Located along the banks of the Rhine River or in the hills of the Black Forest, these spas were eminently suited to the spirit of the Romantic era, and as the "Pearl of the Ardennes" lost its luster, they quickly outshined the original Spa.

Teutonic Gambling Spas

German spa towns date to the Roman era. Most German towns with "Bad" in their names were, at one point, best known for their "baths." One such town, Baden-Baden, on the Oos River in the western foothills of the Black Forest, was famous as a health retreat as long ago as the early third century A.D. Ruins of Roman baths, long forgotten, would be discovered in the 19th century, when Baden-Baden was approaching the zenith of its Romantic renown.

Though the original Roman baths had been lost, Baden-Baden had managed to recover from the destruction of the Thirty Years' War by the middle of the 18th century. At that time, Baden was a small market town still encircled with walls. The chief business was the breeding and slaughter of pigs, whose carcasses were cleaned in the steaming hot spring waters, lending the village a distinctly unpleasant odor in the summer. All in all, it was an unlikely spot to take a vacation. Still, by the beginning of the next century, at Margrave Karl Friedrich's behest, a bathing commission had made serious progress towards establishing Baden as a legitimate resort.

Licensed gambling in the town was first recorded in 1748, though it may have been going on for years previously. Gambling was then authorized only in the backrooms of inns, suggesting that the town was more of a stop-over than destination resort. Later, efforts to establish more grandiose gambling facilities commenced. In 1765, a building called the Promenade House opened; in it, the town granted a Frenchman named Chevilly a gambling concession. By 1801, several local hotels had gambling rooms; commissioners of the Margrave observed the proceedings and collected a tax, which financed improvements to the baths. A second salon opened in a former Jesuit college in 1809. The operator paid a fee of 700 louis for the right to run games from May to October. These two stand-alone gambling houses, together with the gambling rooms in hotels, paid concession money into a special fund dedicated to new construction at Baden.

The resort received a boost in 1810, when author Johann Peter Hebel, one of the most popular German poets of the early 19th century, recuperated from his ill health at Baden-Baden. He wrote widely distributed descriptions of the attractions at the spa: gustatory extravagance, pleasant small talk with distinguished fellow health-seekers, and the exhilaration of roulette. Hebel wrote in a letter that "one lives in a completely different world" in Baden, surrounded by "glamour, high living, laziness, gambling for money, professors, along with comedians." The food and refreshments, prepared in the latest French style, were both excellent and inexpensive, and the service was impeccable. Hebel concluded that, while everything might not have been princely, it was at least "ala Paris."

Hebel's rhapsodies convinced many to take the cure at Baden. So did diplomatic exigencies. As the map of Europe was redrawn in 1814, Europe's top diplomats and kingmakers met at the Congress of Vienna. Baden-Baden stood about halfway between Vienna and Paris, Napoleon's just-conquered capital, and was a frequent stop for those shuttling between the two cities. Thanks to its central location, the resort was easily accessible to France, Scandinavia, and even Russia. The old town walls were torn down and villas and chalets sprung up across the Oos Valley. The last of the pig-breeders exchanged their hogpens for hostelries. Suddenly, Baden-Baden was the most fashionable spa in Europe.

In 1824, another gambling salon, the Conversation House, replaced the Promenade House. Antoine Chabert, who had formerly owned a club in Paris's Palais Royale, received the concession in return for an annual rent of 27,000 gulden. Chabert directed both the casino and its restaurant and presided over Baden-Baden's chief gambling house until 1837, by which time he had succeeded in doubling the town's annual visitation to a still-small 16,000. Chabert parlayed his limited success at Baden-Baden into the management of casinos in Weisbaden, Ems, Schlangenbad, and Schwalbach.

A French Connection

Meanwhile, another wily operator had been making his mark in Paris. Born in 1778, Jacques Benazet worked as a court clerk before becoming a lawyer, and also managed a Lyons theater. Asked in 1824 to adjudicate a dispute between the two supervisors of Paris licensed gambling, Boursault and Chalabre, Benazet did more than simply split the difference: he slid himself into a share of the lucrative office. Three years later, he claimed the sole proprietorship of the right to oversee the legal, licensed gambling conducted in seven clubs throughout Paris. In 1835, Benazet's concession was renewed. By this time, he had acquired ownership shares in two of the city's most fashionable gaming rooms, Frascati and the Cercle des Etrangers. Nothing, it seemed, could stop him.

However, as adroit as Benazet had proven himself in monopolizing the supervision of legal Paris gaming, he was no match for the resolve of the French Chamber of Deputies. The seven legal casinos of Paris had been incredibly profitable for Benazet and the French government, earning between six and nine million francs a year. The downside of this success was the fact that many prominent fortunes were lost on the green baize. As part of a worldwide turn away from legal gambling, whose echoes were felt as far away as the United States, the French deputies resolved on June 17, 1836, that the gambling clubs of France would close on December 31, 1837.

French gamblers manically plunged into the clubs during the last days of 1837, hoping to get one final shot at beating the *trente-et-quarante* and roulette tables. The clubs opened one last time on December 31 in near pandemonium. Benazet, fearing a robbery or riot, had already dispatched detachments of the police and National Guard to maintain order; he doubled the force on the final day. At 3 P.M., he began letting in gamblers intent on one last fling; three hours later, he had to prematurely shutter the most popular Palais Royale club after a workman committed suicide there. At ten that evening, another gambler, distraught that he would be denied the chance to win back his previous losses, shot himself outside Benazet's Frascati, which was then closed only after the police, with great difficulty, cleared the rooms. Finally, at midnight, Bezanet ordered the police to sweep the crowds from the other clubs and, locking the doors, ended the French regime of legal gaming clubs. In the streets, assembled crowds jeered, hooted, and jubilantly screamed at the swarms of ejected gamblers, prostitutes, and adventurers. It was the end of an era.

Bezanet, however, was too clever to be left out in the cold himself. In October 1838, he purchased the Baden-Baden gambling conces-

sion for a 40,000 franc annual lease and an additional yearly levy of
75,000 florins for the upkeep of the surrounding grounds. Previously, Baden-Baden had been a well-regarded, if somewhat quiet,
resort. No more. Owing to the sudden dearth of legal gambling in
France and aided by Bezanet's astute stewardship, Baden-Baden's
popularity—and revenues—exploded. By 1872, the casinos' annual
payments to the town had increased to 550,000 francs, not a hard
thing to do when the estimated take was 2.5 million francs a year.

Baden-Baden was so successful because Benazet knew his market.
Aware that most gamblers preferred the French language (a Frenchman, he was by no means unbiased), he ensured that, in his small
corner of the Black Forest at least, French was the lingua franca, and
Baden-Baden became, quite by design, a virtual suburb of Paris. The
latest Parisian fashions and hairstyles were seen, restaurant menus
appeared in French, and Benazet ensured that Parisians could come
to Baden without having completely left Paris behind. Masquerades,
chic evening parties, and piano recitals occupied the guests when
they were not gambling.

The shrewd Frenchman did quite well for himself, residing in
a palatial villa, surrounded by all of the trappings of wealth. After
Benazet died in 1848 at the age of 70, his son Edward took his place
as Baden-Baden's gambling czar. Under him, a longtime dealer and
supervisor known as old father Martin continued to oversee the day-
to-day casino operations. Martin became something of an institution in French gambling. Originally a dealer at Paris's Frascati from
the early years of the 19th century, Martin continued his supervisory
role at Baden-Baden (Bezanet had brought him along in 1838) into
the 1860s, recounting tales of past gamblers for all who would listen,
unimpressed by current celebrity. In 1860, for example, all of Baden-
Baden turned out for the arrival of French Emperor Napoleon III,
whom the Prussian prince regent William was feting in a three-day
state visit. When asked why he was not hurrying to the train station to see the emperor's formal reception by an assembly of German nobles, Martin groused that he was already familiar with the
leader: "Napoleon...Napoleon... Wait a minute... Bonaparte, isn't
that right? Ah yes, I remember him from Paris—he still owes the
bank 25 louis."

Edward did more than preserve the venerable Martin in his role as supervisor: he actively added to the offerings at Baden-Baden. In 1855 he expanded the Conversation House, adding four elegant new rooms. Three years later, he opened a racecourse at Iffezheim, a town seven miles west of Baden-Baden. With three grandstands catering to visiting nobles, track officials and members of the local Jockey Club, and the general public, the course was an immediate success. When races began each year at the end of August, Baden-Baden was filled to capacity with eager followers of the turf, who remained throughout September.

Benazet the younger, like his father, masterfully promoted his gambling destination. He ensured favorable press coverage of Baden-Baden and its races as far away as the United States and plied visitors with voluminous tracts that expostulated the grandeur of the small resort. Newspapers and magazines in French, German, and English spread the word that, for those who wanted healthy relaxation or the excitement of betting at *trente-et-quarante* or on the horses, Baden-Baden was not to be missed.

Generally speaking, the *kurzeit*, or cure season, ran from May to October. During these months, the restaurants, promenades, and gaming rooms were filled with vacationing merchants, idling nobility, professional sharpers, and assorted hopefuls. All of Europe was equally represented, with English, Spanish, Italian, Dutch, French, German, Russian, and Scandinavian visitors outdoing other each in fashion and better in the gaming salons. A visiting Englishman described the resort in 1840 as surpassing the famous Crockford's in renown and embracing "all bearing the semblance of gentility and conducting themselves with propriety." Patrons only had to remove their hats and extinguish their pipes and cigars. Amid the dazzling chandeliers and golden pillars, players orbited the roulette and *trente-et-quarante* tables, laying siege to the casino's fortune with alternating moods of patient determination and passionate excitement.

Though most players were men, several women distinguished themselves as particularly ardent gamblers. Some became celebrities. A Russian princess, for example, was noted for her large bets though (a chronicler noted with disapproval) she had the ill-breeding to actually look anxious when luck turned against her and she lost thousands. The wife of an Ital-

From the 1830s until the 1870s, under the leadership of Jacques Benazet and his son Edward, Baden-Baden was perhaps Europe's most popular gambling spa. This image of the main gambling room dates from the 1930s.

ian ex-minister, however, exhibited model deportment, "smirking when she wins, and smirking when she loses." Her dress matched her play, and women gathered around to see what outrageous gown she would wear next. The most famous Baden-Baden female gambler, though, was Leonie Leblanc. Crowds gathered simply to watch her bet the house maximum, 6,000 francs, on each hand of trente-et-quarante.

Most of those who crowded into the Conversation House simply enjoyed the plush surroundings and took their chances at the tables as best they could. Some were not so easily satisfied. Henri Rochefort, a French politico and journalist, lost heavily at *trente-et-quarante* while visiting Baden-Baden in 1866, and he noted, with acid pen, that the opulence of the gaming salons indicated that the odds were stacked against the player:

> If the public were not such simpletons people would make the mental comment that the luxury flaunted in these casinos, the percentage paid to the political authorities who tolerate them, and the expensive theatrical performances given in them are proof positive that the player has not the slightest chance of winning a single penny.

If the proprietors of these highly ornate ogres' dens were not so certain of their clients' gullibility, they would house their croupiers in roughly white-washed barns and appear in the gambling rooms with clothes in tatters. This would at least be an attempt to persuade passers-by that the players win so heavily as to reduce the staff at the casino to the direst poverty. But the flaunting of this daily outlay…can mean but one thing: "What a lot of money we must get from you, if we can spend all this and yet have ten times as much left for ourselves."

Rochefort realized that the inherent mathematical imbalance in mercantile games gave the house a sizeable advantage. So did most other players, but few cared.

Perhaps some players plunged so recklessly with the odds against them because their wealth had not been particularly hard-earned. Of the many fortunes squandered at Baden-Baden, few are as famous as that of Hesse-Kassel, the northern part of the medieval German-speaking earldom of Hesse. In a less than a century, its landgraves acquired vast sums from mercenary expeditions, then lost their prosperity and ultimately their land—chiefly because of the tables at Baden-Baden.

The tale began with Friedrich II, who became Landgrave of Hesse-Kassel in 1760. Hesse-Kassel, a rocky land dominated by mountains and forests, was perpetually undeveloped. Beginning in the 17th century, its landgraves began to hire out their army as a way of gaining revenue that could not be wrung from the uncooperative land. Friedrich II, with no less a desire to live in style, continued the practice. Famously, he rented about 17,000 of his soldiers to Britain's George III in the momentous year 1776. George promptly sent them to the rebellious American colonies, where, along with other German forces, they made up one-third of the crown's troops. Though despised by Patriots as mercenaries, the soldiers themselves saw little of George's lucre. Usually victims of impressment, petty criminals, or debtors forced into army service, they fought to suppress the American Revolution for little or no pay. While the Hessian troops suffered and died in America, the landgrave pocketed millions and lived in extravagance.

Wilhelm IX succeeded Friedrich as landgrave on the latter's death in 1784. If anything, he was even more despised than his father. Not content with the "blood money" garnered from his father's Hessian regiments, Wilhelm was nothing if not inventive in looking for a profit. He made thousands from cornering the grain market, but simple speculation was just a start. Despised as "hard, haughty, egotistical, tyrannical, and sordidly avaricious," he went so far as to turn his own castle at Wilhemsbad into a hotel and casino.

Wilhelm was just as narcissistic as he was greedy. Believing his grandeur to eclipse that of a garden-variety landgrave, he sought to be named a king. At an 1803 German congress, Wilhelm ridiculously achieved his ambition for advancement; though not made a king, the gathering did give him a promotion, declaring him Wilhelm I, Elector of Hesse. Wilhelm joined three other newly-minted electors, including the margrave of Baden. Prince-electors of the Holy Roman Empire had once formed the electoral college that selected the Holy Roman Emperor. By the time that Wilhelm ascended to the office, however, it had become largely ceremonial, and the chief perquisite was that he could now style himself "Most Serene Highness," to distinguish himself from lesser princes, who were only Serene Highnesses.

Wilhelm's triumph was short-lived. The Holy Roman Empire was abolished in 1806 after Napoleon's victories, and he never got to cast a vote. Though he didn't do any real electing, he obviously enjoyed the prestige of his title. Unable to elevate himself into a kingship, he remained "Elector of Hesse" to get one over on his cousins, the Landgrave of Hesse-Homburg and the Grand Duke of Hesse-Darmstadt. His son, Wilhelm II, succeeded him in 1821. After the excitement of the pan-European uprising of 1830, during which Wilhelm granted his subjects a constitution, he retired from his administrative duties, turning over affairs of state to his son, Friedrich Wilhelm.

In retirement, with an abundance of leisure and money and a dearth of matters to otherwise occupy him, Wilhelm turned to gambling. When Benazet inaugurated his reign at Baden-Baden in 1838, Wilhelm quickly established himself as a regular. He gained a reputation as the most fervent gambler in residence—an honor probably more exalted than that of Elector—and his only disappointment was that the gaming rooms closed in October. Not willing to wait until the start of the cure season in May, he rejoiced when, in 1843, the Landgrave of Hesse-Homburg permitted a year-round casino to open in Bad Homburg, nearly in the elector's backyard. Wilhelm ultimately lost most of his fortune there. To pay back a loan graciously extended to him, he gave the casino's proprietors forty orange trees, then a rare and valuable treasure. He died in 1847, having lost at least 100,000 florins in Homburg alone.

Friedrich Wilhelm, naturally, had a jaundiced view of the Homburg casino; most of his patrimony had ended up in the pockets of its proprietors. He unsuccessfully argued for the return of the orange trees and bided his time. When the casino's owners asked permission to build a railroad to Frankfurt across Friedrich Wilhelm's land he resolutely refused. The railroad was eventually built along a circuitous route that bypassed Friedrich Wilhelm's land and cost considerably more than the direct line originally proposed. The elector further found his revenge by competing against Homburg. In 1849, he connected Hanau to Frankfurt by rail, then extended the track to the castle at Wilhelmsbad, which had long been a watering place and had been a casino during the reign of his grandfather.

Friedrich Wilhelm overhauled the castle, which had fallen into disrepair, and reopened the hotel casino, which had rooms for gambling, reading, and conversation on the castle's ground floor, and undersized guest rooms on the second. Outside, visitors could take the waters, listen to public concerts, or wander about the grounds at their leisure. Despite the elector's efforts, visitation to Wilhelmsbad declined throughout the 1850s, and when the rail line from Frankfurt to Homburg finally opened in 1860, it dropped off sharply. The castle closed in 1865, with Friedrich Wilhelm's effort to regain in his own casino what had been lost in others a failure. The next year, as a consequence of choosing the wrong side (Austria) in the Austro-Prussian war, the elector lost his lands, which were annexed by the victorious Prussia. Since the elector left no heir, the line of Hesse-Kassel ended with his passing in 1875, less than a century after his great-grandfather had profited from the American Revolution. Though the passing of many fortunes into the coffers of the Baden-Baden casinos might be lamented, this was not one of them.

As competition from other Rhine towns mounted, Baden-Baden launched a counter-offensive. In 1862, the town opened a new theater suited for plays, ballet, and opera, and Edward Benazet attracted the brightest stars of the musical world to better lure gamblers to the Conversation House, located conveniently near the theater. Hector Berlioz conducted the premier of his opera *Beatrice and Benedict* to open the theater, and other noted composers followed. Some, like Johannes Brahms, preferred walks in the countryside to the clangor of the Conversation House. Still, he composed some of his best-known pieces while at Baden-Baden, including the Trio for piano, violin, and horn in E flat, op. 40, Sextet Number 2 for two violins, two violas, and two cellos in G major, Op. 32, and parts of many others.

Other performers provided Benazet with a double bonus; engaged at the theater to draw visitors, they also lost a considerable portion of their pay at the tables. Jacques Offenbach, composer of *Orpheus in the Underworld* and *La Vie Parisienne*, directed the Baden-Baden theater in 1868 and 1869, and he was such a successful draw—and prolific loser at roulette—that the rival town of Homburg sought to lure him away. Johann Strauss, paid 2,000 francs a performance, conducted his waltzes in the theater in 1872, and lost not only his Baden-Baden salary but most of his savings from his earlier triumphant American tour.

But the good times did not last forever. In December 1867, Edward Benazet died while on his winter holiday at Nice. At his wife's suggestion, the Baden government appointed Benazet's nephew and brother-in-law Jacques Dupressoir to run the gambling concession. Although Baden enjoyed a boom year in 1869 with over 60,000 visitors, its day was passing. A profound shift in leisure travel was underway: no longer fired by the Romantic visions of Goethe or Shelley, the privileged were forsaking the Black Forest for the French Riviera. The prohibition of gambling by Prussia, effective December 31, 1872, only gave a more dramatic finale to Baden-Baden's first career as a gambling resort. The roulette tables would be stilled until 1933 when, in a quite different world, the Nazi government re-legalized gambling and set the stage for Baden-Baden to re-emerge as a leading German casino town. But for those seeking the cure in the Victorian age, Baden-Baden's day was done.

Notes from Roulettenberg

Russians were among the most celebrated visitors to the Rhine resorts. Countess Sophie Kissileff was long the most notorious. First appearing at Homburg in 1852, a common joke ran that she gambled only once a day: from eleven in the morning until eleven at night. Her husband, unwilling to brook her gambling obsession any longer, divorced her, and not even a papal edict that she cease playing could convince her to give up roulette. All told, she lost an estimated four million dollars at Homburg, a considerable sum then and now.

Not all Russians were as gambling mad as Kissileff; many vacationers and expatriates escaped the Rhine resorts with little more than perfunctory attention to the gaming tables. Others didn't gamble at all. Nicholai Gogol, the writer best known for the novel *Dead Souls*, forswore the gambling tables for soul-searching walks through Baden-Baden's countryside. In Russia itself, the social game of whist became popular for a while. Whist gave late 19th century westernizing Russians a recreation shared by the elites of Europe.

It is usually inadvisable to generalize, but even Russians felt their gambling was distinguished by a peculiarly Slavic fatalism, and most of them tended towards the outrageous betting of Countess Kissileff rather than the quiet introspection of Gogol. Count Leo Tolstoy, on a tour of Europe in the summer of 1857, stopped at Baden-Baden, where he discovered roulette. Playing on the first evening for small sums, he spent the bulk of the next day at the Conversation House vainly trying to conquer the wheel. He lost all of his own money, plus two loans from an obliging Frenchman, and penned desperate letters to several relatives and friends, begging for money. His countess cousin Alexandra Tolstoy sent him money, and the writer Ivan Turgenev became concerned enough to travel to Baden-Baden himself. Upon arriving, he lent Tolstoy even more money, which the count predictably lost at the tables. Shortly after Turgenev departed, Tolstoy himself left Baden-Baden in shame, cursing his inability to control his gambling.

Turgenev was more successful at taming the gaming demon. He divided most of his later life between Paris and Baden-Baden, where he lived in a well-appointed house in generous comfort. Turgenev set his novel *Smoke* in Baden-Baden. In the novel, he described the social milieu of the large Russian community and the mixture of French, Italian, German, and English-speakers that gave Baden its distinctive cosmopolitan character. Turgenev assisted many of the Russian émigrés and travelers who had stayed in the Conversation House longer than they should have. Some were grateful for Turgenev's help—Tolstoy, for example, remained a friend for years, and on his deathbed Turgenev penned a final expression of affection for the count.

Turgenev did not share such warm feelings for another great Russian novelist, Fyodor Dostoyevsky who was obsessed by gambling during what may have been his greatest creative period, 1862-1872. When he was exiled to Siberia in the 1850s, Dostoyevsky gambled often, usually losing. In 1862, he made his first trip to Wiesbaden, where he won a sizeable sum. He visited Baden-Baden and Homburg in 1863, losing back all he had previously won; having lost his last gulden, he was only rescued when his onetime paramour Paulina Suslova pawned her jewelry and sent him cash. Though his bets were never that large, he played in a state of grim agitation, his creative mind exponentially magnifying every win and loss.

In 1864, haunted by the death of his wife and the clamoring creditors of his dead brother (whose debts he had inherited), Dostoyevsky signed a contract to deliver a novel to the publisher Selovski by November 1866. Should he miss the deadline, he would be fined substantially and forfeit the rights to all of his already published books. In early October, the situation looked dire. His masterpiece *Crime and Punishment* was as yet unfinished. The forlorn poverty of the protagonist Raskolnikov likely is rendered so well because the author himself was keenly desperate. To satisfy Selovski, he dictated, in four days, a novel to a young stenographer, Anna Grigorievna Snitkin. Dostoyevsky beat his deadline, soon married the twenty-year-old Snitkin, and left for the ages a classic portrait of the hope and despair of an impetuous slave to chance, *The Gambler*.

Writing *The Gambler* did not solve Dostoyevsky's financial problems or cathartically purge him of his gambling addiction. He fled Russia one step ahead of his creditors and embarked on a European tour which naturally took him along the Rhine. He was soon back at the tables again, losing steadily. On July 4, 1867, he entered Baden-Baden, setting up house with his young wife above a smithy, where the din of business must have been less than relaxing. His wife wrote in her diary that his red face and bloodshot eyes frightened her. She cursed roulette and Baden-Baden for what it had done to him.

Despite his hideous appearance, the novelist enjoyed himself—at least initially. Starting with 100 francs, he had won 4,000 in three days. Ignoring his wife's pleas to content himself with such good fortune, Dostoyevsky held out hope that he could continue to parlay his winnings into financial security. His own success paled in comparison to the winnings of others and, although he logically knew he should leave, he could not:

> Apart from my own gains, I saw every day how the other gamblers won from 20,000 to 30,000 francs (one never sees anyone lose). Why should those others do better than I? I need the money more than they do. I risked again, and lost. I lost not only what I had won, but also my own money down to the last farthing. I got feverishly excited, and lost all the time. Then I began to pawn my garments. Anna Grigorovna pawned her last, her very last possession.

After they had lost everything, including the funds to leave Baden, the Dostoyevskys' landlady raised their rent. Dostoyevsky began writing frantic letters to friends, begging more money to secure passage from the Rhineland.

With no other help forthcoming, Dostoyevsky reluctantly sought to get a loan from his fellow novelist Turgenev, who was enjoying life in his villa, oblivious to Dostoyevsky's suffering above the smithy. Though the pair shared a common language and occupation, political, cultural, and artistic differences made them enemies. Dostoyevsky had been vocal in his critique of Smoke, perhaps because Turgenev might have used him as the model for Bindaseff, a boring ingrate who quadrupled a borrowed stake of 100 rubles and left the Conversation House without repaying his benefactor: he had not forgotten that a few years earlier he had lent Dostoyevsky fifty dollars to play roulette at Wiesbaden, and that the money had never been repaid. Dostoyevsky would later get revenge by satirizing Turgenev in *The Possessed*, but for the moment he had a more pressing need: money.

On the morning of July 10, Dostoyevsky gingerly approached Turgenev at breakfast. The heavyweights warily circled each other, trading verbal jabs and attempting to force the other into a breach of etiquette. Turgenev began to expansively declaim on his contempt for all things Russian (Dostoyevsky was a confirmed nationalist) and the merits of atheism (Dostoyevsky was a devout Christian). The German-loving Turgenev declared that Russians were "bound to crawl in the dust before the Germans," and that any attempt to build a uniquely Russian culture was folly and pig-headedness. Dostoyevsky declared the Germans "swindlers and rogues," and an "evil and dishonest" nation. Turgenev, reminding his visitor that he considered himself an adoptive German, considered the last a personal affront, and the two parted company icily.

Fyodor and Anna finally escaped Baden-Baden on August 23, though he continued to gamble, usually leaving his wife behind and sending her letters which cataloged and bemoaned his losses. Finally, in 1871, after his dead father appeared to him in a nightmare and warned of impending doom, Dostoyevsky repented of his gambling. Writing to his wife, he begged for forgiveness, declaring that he was "not a scoundrel, but only a gambler in the throes of his passion," and that he was now free of the chains of the gambling table: "From now on I shall think only of my work and will not dream of gambling all night as I used to do. Now my work will be better, and God will bless me!" Unlike others who have resolved to stop gambling in vain, Dostoyevsky lived up to his words and never gambled again.

A German Gambling Renaissance

At the beginning of the 19th century, gambling towns were relatively plentiful in German lands: there were 24 of them scattered across Austria, Prussia, Bavaria, Hanover, Saxony, and other principalities. But political consolidation, creeping prohibition, and simple weeding out, reduced the field by about 1840 to four truly successful ones: Baden-Baden, Aachen, Wiesbaden, and Homburg.

Aachen (Aix-la-Chapelle in French), is one of the most historic cities in Europe; the Romans named it Aquis Granum for its hot sulfur springs, and it was well known for its baths in the classical period. Later, Charlemagne was buried there (his tomb is still found at the Aachen cathedral) and kings of the Holy Roman Empire were crowned there for six centuries. The westernmost city in today's Germany, it has long been a tourist destination.

By the second half of the 18th century, Aachen was no longer politically important, though its hot springs continued to pour water into the baths and it remained a popular resort. Consequently, it became a famous haunt for gamblers. The government leased the gambling concession to a chief banker who offered hazard; social games like billiards also saw heavy betting. By the 1860s, the place had a reputation as a place for only the most dedicated of gamblers. A traveler wrote that the town's name brought to mind "cards and dice—sharks and pigeons," and that all of Aachen was suffused with a "professional odour." The gambling was drab and mechanical, as the players moved in "death-like silence…not a sound was heard but the rattle of heaped-up money, as it was passed from one side of the table to the other; nor was the smallest anxiety or emotion visible on any countenance."

Wiesbaden, a Rhine town in central Germany, had a similar history as a bath resort, and was no less attractive to serious gamblers. The reigning prince of Nassau-Usingen granted a gambling concession there as early as 1771. At the time, faro and basset were the dominant games, though by the time that a gaming room opened in the first Kurhaus in 1810, roulette had become the game of choice. As elsewhere, casino profits were channeled into municipal improvements and ancillary entertainment venues like theaters and restaurants.

During the resort's 19th century glory years, visitors to the more than twenty baths usually ended their day at the casino. Often, they began it there as well. An account from the 1860s describes visitors to Wiesbaden, frustrated by the Prussian government's recent edict that closed the casino in observance of the Sabbath, clamoring to begin play on Monday at 11 A.M., the customary opening hour for

French and German gambling houses. Visitors of both sexes crowded forward to place their bets on roulette and trente-et-quarante. At times patronized by the wealthy and high-born, by 1868 Wiesbaden had acquired something of a down-market reputation. That year, London's Daily Telegraph reported that most visitors were of the lower and middle classes, with a few celebrities slumming it. With rampant gambling and opportunistic socializing, Wiesbaden was, in the author's words "naturally a Paradise…turned into a seventh hell by the uncontrolled rioting of human passions."

Worse yet, according to the Daily Telegraph, Wiesbaden had become the autumn rendezvous for "all the aged, broken-down courtesans of Paris, Vienna, and Berlin," who, with painted faces and dyed hair, sought to fasten themselves onto younger and richer men in attendance. The author described them as "ghastly creatures, hideous caricatures of youth and beauty," who wheedled every meal and gambling stipend from gullible men, young and old.

In the "Countess C.," the Daily Telegraph reporter found a metonym for the decline of Wiesbaden. The aged countess, possessor of a huge fortune, was long a fixture in the town's gaming rooms. Even in her old age, she insisted on playing at least eight hours a day. Accompanied by eight servants, she tipped them paltry sums if she won, and gave them nothing when she lost. Crying at the tables over her losses, she was more pitiable than contemptible:

> An edifying sight is this venerable dame, bearing an exalted title, as she mopes and mouths over her varying luck…. She is very intimate with one or two antediluvian diplomats and warriors, who are here striving to bolster themselves up for another year with the waters, and may be heard crowing out lamentations over her fatal passion for play, interspersed with bits of moss-grown scandal, disinterred from the social ruins of an age long past….She has outlived all human friendships or affections, and exists only for the chink of the gold as it jingles on the gaming table. I cannot help but fancy that her last words will be "Rien ne va plus!" [no more bets]

The countess might have represented the decaying past, but Wiesbaden, like other German spa towns, remained fairly vibrant into the 1860s. Drawing visitors from far and wide for their baths and idyllic settings, the spa towns were pre-eminent locales for casinos which, as local authorities discovered, were quite lucrative. All of Europe, it seemed, mixed at the roulette tables, and shared a common language of ill-fortune afterwards.

Twilight of the (German) Odds

One Rhine resort in particular bridged the era of gambling dominated by German spas with the coming age of Monte Carlo: Bad Homburg. Homburg did not boast an antique reputation as a Roman bath, but was the very modern invention of a financially-strapped landgrave and a pair of French gamblers, Louis and Francois Blanc.

The Blanc brothers' origins were less than auspicious. The posthumous twin sons of a penniless tax collector, they came into the world in 1806 in a small town north of Avignon, France. Receiving little formal education, they cast about France trying their hand at various enterprises, mostly in the area of finance. They won a great deal of money playing *ecarte* (a trick-taking game similar to euchre) and baccarat, and accumulated a sufficient capital reserve to open a small bank in Bordeux in 1834.

The Blanc bank chiefly speculated in French government securities. Investors with advance notice of fluctuations in stock prices had a decided advantage, and the Blancs hit upon the idea of using the French government's optical telegraph or *telegraphe aerien* to receive advance information. Rival speculators used methods ranging from carrier pigeons to windmill signaling, so they imagined that co-opting the government's system, which involved visual signals between telescope-equipped stations rather than electric transmission, was fair game.

The government, however, prohibited use of the system for such messages, so the brothers set about buying the cooperation of telegraph officials. For two years, the scheme worked perfectly; the Blancs received news of price fluctuations ahead of the curve and invested accordingly. In 1836, one of the administrators involved confessed to the scheme on his deathbed and implicated the others involved. The Blancs were tried and convicted in March 1837 of corrupting government officials. Since their crime was not seen as particularly heinous, they received no prison sentence and only

Francois Blanc, who transformed Bad Homburg into a leading spa resort and later did the same in Monaco.

minimal fines, and were thus left with the bulk of the 100,000 franc fortune they had accumulated over the previous two years. For the enterprising twins, crime apparently did pay.

Having paid their debt to society, the Blancs were chary at remaining in Bordeaux, feeling that prospective business partners might be less forgiving than the court. So they journeyed to Paris, where they met with Jacques Benazet. The gaming supervisor informed them of the huge profits possible in the casino business but noted that, as legal French gambling was due to expire in a few short months, he was himself relocating to pursue his luck in the Rhine. The Blancs decided to follow suit. They settled on the Grand Duchy of Luxembourg as the best location for their gaming salon, and headed north to try their luck.

The military governor was a Prussian army general who happened to be Ludwig, the reigning Landgrave of Hesse-Homburg, one of the smallest principalities of the house of Hesse. Its capital, Homburg, had fewer than 3,000 residents and the court was hopelessly sunk in debt. Past attempts to open a casino/spa, had come to

nothing; in 1830, promoters had been foiled by the confusion resulting from the revolutionary ferment of that year, and an 1836 proposal was scuttled when the Rothschild bankers refused to loan the
operators start-up capital. The next year, Ludwig himself denied four
applications from prospective concessionaires, citing the impending
French gambling prohibition and the previous failures.

But then Ludwig learned that, before the tables had been closed,
the French exchequer had raked off more than 4.5 million francs
in taxes. Other Rhine operators, including Benazet, reinforced the
landgrave's hunch that a casino might not be so bad after all. In
August 1838, the landgrave opened the bidding for the casino and
concession anew. Rejecting all the applicants as unsuitable, he built
a small pump room himself, modestly promoted the medical benefits of the local springs, and hoped for the best. Few visitors came,
though, without a casino. The Blancs, upon meeting the landgrave,
seemed to be the answer to his problems; though the resort would,
at first, appeal primarily to residents of nearby Frankfurt, they envisioned bigger and better things for themselves and the landgrave.

This happy future, however, would be denied to Ludwig. The
landgrave died on January 19, 1839, after suffering a severe chill,
ironically the very thing that might have been forestalled by a warm
bath in a therapeutic spring. His heir, his brother Phillip, approved
of the casino enterprise, and began negotiations with the Blancs. By
July 1840, sufficient progress had been made for Louis Blanc to gain
a personal audience with the landgrave., where he offered to build a
suitable pump room in return for the annual lease on the gambling
concession, which was to run until 1871. In return for the right to
remain open year round, Blanc agreed to bar all subjects of the landgrave from the casino. The contract was ratified by August, and the
brothers eagerly began building their pleasure hall.

By the next May, construction of the casino formally began with
the ceremonial ground-laying of the foundation stone after a pro-
cession that attracted curious spectators from as far as Frankfurt.
The march ended at the site of the future casino with the performance of a specially-written song. Afterwards, a time capsule containing spring water, a rolled parchment declaration, coins, and wine
(presumably to augur a pleasant and profitable future) was sealed

by those in attendance, who took turns striking the capstone with a silver hammer. Following this ceremony was a banquet and ball, at which, for the first time, gambling began in Homburg.

Visitors, mostly from Frankfurt, played in a temporary casino. Here, the Blancs faced the reality that, all things being equal, Bad Homburg could simply not compete with established spa casinos in Baden-Baden, Ems, and Wiesbaden. The Blancs knew they could not offer the social prominence of elegant Baden-Baden, or the natural beauty of Wiesbaden. Though the springs weren't any healthier than those of any other middling spa on the Rhine or elsewhere, they engaged the services of a group of Sorbonne professors, who publicly proclaimed the superiority of the waters of Homburg.

Used to changing the rules to suit themselves, the Blancs literally did just that. While roulette tables throughout Europe had two zeros, theirs would have only one. This gave the players a noticeably better chance of winning. Since then, single-zero roulette has become standard throughout most of the world, while the only casinos to stubbornly retain the second zero are in the United States. The second Blanc innovation allowed them to shave the player's disadvantage at trente-et-quarante, already slight, even slimmer: on ties of 31, the house only won if the last card in the row was black.

The Blancs knew that their profit margins would be slimmer but realized that, in the long run, they couldn't lose: the house advantage inherent in their games, even though reduced, would triumph in the end. Like factories using mass production, they relied on economy of scale—more gamblers leaving less money each—for success. Still, needing security in the event of an unexpectedly lucky run by a big bettor, they secured a reserve loan from the Homburg authorities themselves.

Thus fortified, they were amply prepared for the opening of their main casino building, the Kursaal, on August 16 and 17, 1843. The Blancs feted their esteemed guests, including the landgrave himself, in an opening dinner and ball, and watched with anticipation as the guests began playing. Casino employees had been carefully instructed in the regulation of gaming: they were to quietly remove any locals, badly-dressed guests, workmen, or peasants who managed to find their way into the opulent gaming salon, at the same time deferentially finding room at the tables for those deemed to be meritorious players.

The Kursaal was a stately red granite and chocolate-trim two-story building that fronted Lewis Street, Homburg's main thoroughfare. In the back was a large park laid out by the King of Prussia's own landscape gardener. Exhausted gamblers or their impatient companions could wander through its tree-lined walks and over bridges spanning a series of small lakes. Inside, the Kursaal housed a dining hall, theater, reading rooms (Blanc received all of Europe's newspapers, allowing visitors to remain in contact with their home countries), and the obligatory gaming room, which had two roulette and two *trente-et-quarante* tables.

Croupiers started the betting by gently intoning, "Faites le jeu," (make your game), and closed it by announcing "Rien ne va plus." Betting went on in comparative dignity. Outward expressions of emotion were rare, as both winners and losers barely spoke above a whisper, and surrounding bystanders kept their conversations politely quiet. The dominant sounds were the calm announcements of the croupiers, clink of gold coins, the sweeping of croupiers' rakes, and the ticking of highly ornate French clocks that decorated the gaming salon. The casino employees were renowned for their composure. An apocryphal story held that, after a disappointed loser put a gun to his head and splattered his brains across a Kursaal roulette table, the croupier merely announced "triple zero" before declaring the bank closed and throwing a cloth over the gore. The tale was too outrageous to be true, but it spoke to the higher truth of the imperturbable cool of Homburg dealers.

The ballroom was lavishly furnished with marble pillars and a gilded, frescoed ceiling. Red velvet couches lined the walls. Other rooms, framed by archways, were decorated various gentle colors, and smartly-patterned parquet floored the entire building. Outside, a glass-enclosed colonnade with about one hundred tables provided a sweeping view of the gardens below. In the attached restaurant, famous for its fine cuisine, visitors could enjoy an elegant brunch before taking on the tables, or relax after gambling over an uncommonly delicious dinner. Hotels in the vicinity of the Kursaal housed guests, where they lounged on porches, smoking and relaxing while attired in white sports coats and Panama hats. For the large numbers of British visitors (second only to the Russians), the Blancs provided two essential institutions: an Anglican church and a fully-equipped cricket pitch.

The inducements to prospective visitors, from improved odds to the comforts of home, were fantastically successful. British writer George Augustus Sala described Homburg in the 1850s as "overflowing with life," noting the fashionably-dressed men and women who flitted through the halls of the Kursaal. The gaming rooms, just short of overcrowding, overflowed with the usual suspects, "the same calculating old fogies, the same supercilious-looking young men, the same young girls and full-blown women, with a nervous quavering about the lips, the same old sinners of both sexes one has known at these places the last ten or fifteen years, busily engaged at trente-et-quarante." The roulette tables had a similar assortment, with French marquises, nervous young Englishmen, and professional gamblers, "well and ill-dressed, with sharply-defined Mephistophelean features, quick, restless eyes, and villainously compressed lips," and prostitutes of all nations. Circling the players were "watchful old women and Germans of hang-dog look" who stood ready to pounce any unwatched coins.

Originally, most of the upper-crust health-seekers remained at the established spas. Yet as word of Homburg's favorable odds spread, and the Blanc's press agents proved their worth, wealthier visitors became more common. By the 1850s, the Blancs' casino manager Trittler was writing to Francois that the casino had succeeded in bringing in high-end play, but only at great cost. In doing so, he might have coined a lasting term for such big spenders, noting that in order to attract the wealthy Ossokin to Homburg they had to change his Russian money at such an unfavorable rate as to lose no less than ten thousand francs. "We are throwing sprats [sardines] to catch whales," the manager wrote, "and trusting to the goddess Fortune; such proceedings can only be justified by results."

Sometimes the results were so unfavorable that the goddess Fortune could not be held solely culpable. Beginning in the late summer of 1851, profits began to shrink, though more people were visiting the Kursaal. Specifically, the *trente-et-quarante* tables were becoming

Both male and female gamblers eagerly await the fall of the ball in this rendering of a Bad Homburg roulette table.

less and less profitable, while roulette remained safely in the black. The Blanc brothers were for once at a loss. Francois was recovering from exhaustion and Louis was slowly dying in a convalescent home. By this point, his brother had taken over the supervision of the family business. Francois directed Trittler to closely analyze table performance data and investigate the croupiers—was anyone spending more money than he should have been? Blanc never identified the double-dealer(s), though the increased attention forced an end to the scheme; *trente-et-quarante* profits quickly regained their previous levels.

Francois Blanc knew quite well that, while the odds were bound to favor the house in the long run, a single, lucky, high-betting player might get the better of him in the interim. This happened most famously in 1852, when the Prince of Canino methodically assaulted the bank at Homburg. Charles Lucien Bonaparte, the eldest son of Napoleon's youngest brother Lucien, had become Prince of Canino in 1840, and he already had a reputation as a gambler.

Blanc was overjoyed when the prince arrived on September 26, 1852; he wanted to attract rich and powerful visitors, and Charles Lucien was the cousin of the man who would, in a few short weeks, become the Emperor of France. Arriving in the Kursaal, he immediately began playing roulette, betting nothing less than the house maximums. Playing at roulette and *trente-et-quarante* over the next four days, he won 180,000 francs. The Kursaal could only cover these losses because other players lost heavily that week.

After a day's break, the prince returned to the tables, this time losing most of his house maximum bets. Trittler began to relax, but by ten in the evening Bonaparte had weathered the storm, and he returned to his hotel triumphantly with 560,000 of Blanc's francs. As a committee of shareholders debated whether to lower the maximum bets and return the second zero to the roulette tables, Bonaparte packed his bags and left town. Though the Kursaal would have no chance of winning its money back from the prince, at least it did not have to face the prospect of losing any more to him. Gradually, the losses of other players compensated for the prince's plunder. Blanc even turned the situation to his advantage, instructing his press agents to emblazon news of Bonaparte's exploits across the newspapers of Europe. As a result, all the continent was soon abuzz with talk of how easy it was to win a fortune from Francois Blanc's Kursaal. Over the next few months, visitors flocked to the casino, which enjoyed its most successful year yet.

Blanc could bear the prince's success with equanimity because he knew that over time the house would prevail. He often said that "red sometimes wins; black sometimes wins, but white always," punning on his name. In the years after the prince's raid on Homburg, Blanc turned his attention to long-term business and personal matters. He had already scuttled attempts to legalize casinos in Turin, Savoy, Nice, and Paris, and he continued to be wary of any efforts to introduce potentially ruinous competition. Blanc also secured his own flank, turning aside German legislative proposals to ban gambling. He married Marie Hensel, the charming, though uneducated, daughter of a local cobbler, sending her to finishing school before tying the knot. She proved to be a more than capable mate, and became perhaps his most trusted business advisor. By the end of the 1850s, the casino was enjoying record profits, and with the completion of the direct Frankfurt/Homburg rail line imminent, the future looked rosy.

Then, in August of 1860, he met another challenge: Thomas Garcia, a Spaniard who threatened to repeat the success of the Prince of Canino. Garcia, though physically unassuming, arrived with a retinue that included his young German mistress, who remained by his side as he played. He had already developed a reputation in the illegal casinos of Paris as a bold and crafty gambler who confined himself to *trente-et-quarante*, with its more favorable odds. Along with his confederates he bet the absolute table maximum of 30,000 francs on play. He won over 100,000 francs several days in succession, and though he had losing spells as well, still acquitted himself admirably, once winning 260,000 francs in a single hour. Garcia then left Homburg with his pockets substantially heavier.

He returned in early September, though, and drew a crowd as he won, then lost, then won again. He finally left on September 12 with nearly 800,000 francs of the casino's reserve capital. Garcia's winnings forced a reduction of the stockholders' dividends, and some employees and shareholders began to express discontent with Blanc's administration. The asthmatic Blanc, who spent much of 1861 and 1862 trying to regain his health in Loeche-les-Bains Switzerland, was not on hand to personally supervise the casino. The Kursaal achieved at least a symbolic victory over the intrepid Garcia when he returned in October 1861. Armed with a much smaller bankroll, he quickly lost everything, despite several emergency loans, including one from the pianist Anton Rubenstein, another confirmed gambler who had earlier borrowed money from Garcia. Garcia's partial defeat gave Blanc at least an appearance of triumph which he was able to parlay into a consolidation of his power. Returning to Homburg late in 1862, he successfully quelled the shareholders' rebellion and staved off attempts by the landgrave's government to extract more wealth from the casino. Though victorious in his latest struggles and richer than ever, he began to feel misgivings of his own about the security of his Homburg money machine, and began to consider diversification.

Blanc was right to be nervous. Even before the landgrave's government had begun grumbling for a larger cut of the profits, Blanc had stared down a full-fledged attempt to close his casino. As a consequence of the liberal revolution of February 1848, a pan-German parliament with real legislative powers was formed to bring some order to the loose German confederation. This National Assembly, headquartered in Frankfurt, began debating that the newly-cohesive German central government follow the lead of France in abolishing gambling. All Germans, the ban's proponents asserted, clamored for the closure of the parasitical Rhine casinos. Certainly the landgraves and princes enriched by casinos in the principalities disagreed, but the assembly resolved in January 1849 that, effective May 1, 1849, all gambling would cease.

The reigning landgrave of Hesse-Homburg refused to accede to the closure and permitted the Kursaal to remain open after May Day had passed. The Central Government dispatched infantry and cavalry regiments to Homburg, where under protest the Blancs closed the Kursaal to the public. But they soon re-opened as a private club, to which only card-carrying members, along with their entire family and any acquaintances they might wish to bring along, were admitted. Even this evasion was not necessary for long. Unable to enforce its edicts anywhere else, the National Assembly collapsed after Prussia withdrew its support. By the end of the summer, the casino was once again open to all.

Though it didn't last, the National Assembly's edict showed that many German people disapproved of casinos, whatever their benefits for the spa towns. It was this kind of publicity that led Dostoyevsky to declare that the press expiated on the splendor of Rhine resorts and the huge sums of money waiting to be won there. Such appeals may have been crass, but they were effective. As it became increasingly clear that much of Germany would be united during the 1860s, Blanc hoped that it would be under the aegis of Austria rather than Prussia. The Prussian government, which closed the casino at Aachen in 1854, was resolutely opposed to gambling.

Landgrave Ferdinand's death on March 24, 1866, was equally distressing. Since neither the landgrave nor any of his brothers had any sons, the Hesse-Homburg dynasty was at an end. Luckily for Blanc, the Grand-Duke of Hesse-Darmstadt, who absorbed the electorate, approved of the Kursaal just as much as his cousins. And for good reason: the past two decades had seen soaring visitation rates, economic development, and prosperity. But the Grand-

Duke's support proved a dead letter when he backed Austria (along with fellow gambling haven Baden) in the quick Austro-Prussian War, fought in the summer of 1866. The efficient Prussian army's crushing of the Austrians at Koniggratz on July 12 paved the way for the immediate annexation of the German states that had supported Austria.

This was bad news for Blanc, though it was cushioned by his recent acquisition of the gambling monopoly in a still-obscure Riviera principality called Monaco. In December 1867, the Prussian legislature began debating the cessation of gambling. Blanc did himself few favors by offering a large sum for disaster relief in East Prussia, which legislators correctly interpreted as a bribe. Furthermore, as a native Frenchman he was the object of dislike and suspicion during the run-up to the Franco-Prussian War of 1870. Blanc published a pamphlet stressing the tremendous prosperity of Homburg and its likely poverty without gambling, but his earlier mastery of the press deserted him; the Prussian Chamber passed, by a large majority, a law in February 1868 that ordered all gambling stopped, effective 11 P.M. on December 31, 1872.

The law immediately changed the remaining Rhine casinos, chiefly Wiesbaden, Ems, Baden-Baden, and Homburg. They were to plow two-fifths of their profits back into the development of their host towns, presumably to build tourist facilities to give the resorts a life after gambling, and they were to close the casinos on Sundays and holidays. The first Sunday without gambling in Homburg, March 29, 1868, was a dark day, as the streets were nearly deserted—a grim taste of the looming desolation.

Blanc began developing his interests in Monaco in earnest, though gamblers continued to crowd into the Rhine towns six days of the week. Most Homburg residents continued blithely entertaining visitors, imagining that, once again, Blanc would prevail. But the Prussian government was implacable. In October 1872 the gambling stopped in Wiesbaden and Ems. Homburg's Kursaal remained open, and visitors forced themselves to brave an exceptionally cold winter to enjoy its last days. Finally, in the standing-room only casino, it was five to eleven on December 31, and the croupier called out for the final bets to be placed. With a final spin of the roulette wheel (the winning number was twenty, black), Francois Blanc's three decades of casino ownership in Homburg were ended.

Playing at roulette and *trente-et-quarante* was now illegal throughout nearly all of Europe. The casino at Spa had already closed, and legal gambling in France had ended in 1837. The casino at Saxon-les-Bains, nestled amid the Swiss Alps, remained open, but only until 1877, when it too was closed. The spa towns tried to encourage playing for fun at games like billiards and dominoes in the place of serious wagering on casino games, but to little avail. Visitation dropped off dramatically, and one can imagine tumbleweeds blowing through deserted streets.

The end of German gambling, though, did not leave Blanc destitute. He still enjoyed a personal fortune of more than 60 million francs. Stubborn to the last, he at first refused to surrender the Kursaal keys to the city authorities, and only released them after a Prussian government commissioner compelled him to do so. Blanc quickly liquidated his remaining holdings in Homburg (chiefly a theater, restaurant, bathhouse, and offices), and looked to a brighter future along the Mediterranean coast, where he was already building his masterpiece in an impoverished Riviera principality whose name would soon become synonymous with style and sophistication, thanks to gambling.

3

A Sunny Place for Shady People

Gambling on the French Riviera

A Safe Haven on the Cote d'Azur

Francois Blanc had been preparing for his departure from Homburg for more than a decade, amassing a considerable fortune and securing a new site on which to develop a gambling resort within the tiny principality of Monaco. This was a sunny but isolated spot on the Cote d'Azur (Blue Coast) or French Riviera, located midway between Nice and San Remo. Monaco had been ruled by the Grimaldi family since 1297, when Francesco Grimaldi, disguised as a monk, stealthily entered the town's fortress and, opening the doors for his Guelph followers who had fled Genoa with him, overwhelmed the fortifications and seized the enclave for himself. The family has retained control of the town ever since, (with the exception of brief periods when it was under Genoese and, later, French occupation). In the 14th century the Grimaldis added the neighboring districts of Roquebrune and Menton to their holdings, and by the 16th the independence of Monaco had been recognized by France. With the masterful rule of Honore II, the Grimaldi court of Monaco became renowned for its art collection, and Honore gave himself the title of Prince (earlier rulers had been "Lord"), which is still used today. The Grimaldi family owned extensive estates in France and, coupled with the income from the agricultural produce of Menton and Roquebrune, this income subsidized a generous lifestyle.

The good times ended with the French Revolution. Prince Honore III was deposed, the Grimaldi estates confiscated, Monaco itself annexed to France, and royal family imprisoned. After the fall of Napoleon, the Grimaldis were restored to their sovereign rule of Monaco. During the reign of the reactionary Honore V (1819-1841), the first proposal to turn Monaco into a resort was floated. With its healthy climate and the addition of good lodging, fine food, and "distractions" (i.e., gambling), proponents believed it would become a popular resort. But Honore, pre-occupied with a futile struggle to return things to the way they had been in 1789, demurred.

Meanwhile, the restive districts of Menton and Roquebrune chafed under Grimaldi rule and taxation. During the revolutions of 1848, they proclaimed themselves free cities. Occupied though not formally annexed by Sardinia (they would be incorporated into France in 1861 with a treaty that guaranteed Monaco's continued independence), their income was lost to Monaco, which was now one-twentieth of its original size. Prince Florestan I, or more accurately his able wife Princess Caroline, began searching for any way to wring a decent income from the rocky soil they still possessed. Distilling alcohol from a local plant, lace-making, and the production of perfume all failed.

Caroline refused to give up, and with the help of the Parisian lawyer A. Eynaud began to reconsider the possibilities of a bathing and gambling resort. In 1854, they vaguely proposed forming a company that would build a bathing place, sanatorium, hotel, and casino, but could not get financing. A group of Nice investors volunteered to build the casino themselves, but they lacked money to actually start construction and were dismissed. At Caroline's urging, Eynaud journeyed to Baden-Baden to investigate the casino there, operated by Edward Benazet. He learned that the Grand Duke directly earned 350,000 thousand francs a year from his share of the casino proceeds. On top of this already handsome sum, he derived an additional economic benefit from the estimated 200,000 wealthy visitors who thronged Baden each year in search of health and good fortune.

Inspired by Eynaud's findings, Caroline resolved to secure an effective operator who could build a resort and turn a gambling concession into a cash machine for the Royal Family. Caroline and Eynaud heard many proposals, but none of the operators seemed to have the savvy or finances to build and run a first-rate resort. One group was dissuaded from pursuing the franchise by their hired consultant, Francois Blanc, who, not surprisingly, told them that Monaco had few prospects as a gambling resort—he, after all, owned the casino at Homburg and had actively campaigned against any new casinos for years. He had earlier written to his manager Trittler that it was doubtful that anyone would be so foolish as to develop a casino at Monaco.

Blanc was dubious because the site was so isolated. Monaco could only be reached by a narrow mountain road, whose passage was dangerous, dirty, and time-consuming, or a steamer that sailed irregularly from Nice. Matters were complicated by occupation of Menton and Roquebrune by Sardinia, which had opposed a casino in Nice and might preempt the rule of the Grimaldis if they flouted Sardinian morality by opening one themselves. Still, Eynaud persisted in searching for a builder. Finally, he was approached by the pair of Napoleon Langlois, a Parisian businessman, and Albert Aubert, a journalist, who lacked experience but not enthusiasm. Aubert was particularly expansive in his descriptions of the stately facilities and charming villas which they would build. All he needed was the money to start.

Despite considerable uncertainty about Langlois's capital resources, on April 26, 1856, Florestan I, in one of his final acts (he was to die and be succeeded by his son Charles III in June), granted the pair a concession to build and run a "bathing establishment." To be open year-round, the resort was to include a hotel, gardens, and regular omnibus service to and from Nice. The order specified the "amusements" which the operators could provide for bathers: "balls, concerts, fetes, games such as whist, ecarte, picquet, faro, boston (a whist variant), and reversi, as well as roulette with either one or two zeroes, and *trente-et-quarante* with the *refait* or *demi-refait*." The casino could thus compete head-to-head against Blanc's Kursaal by offering similar odds. The edict further specified government regulation: the gaming could take place only under the supervision of one or more inspectors appointed by His Serene Highness, the Prince of Monaco.

Despite shaky finances, Langlois and Aubert immediately set to work, quickly acquiring land on the rocky peninsula across the harbor from Monaco proper—a section of the district known as Les Spelugues, or "the caves"—for their permanent casino. They neglected to build the actual bathhouse, hotels, or streets, or institute regular transportation from Nice, and other than issuing a wildly boastful prospectus, the operators did little else but set up tables in a temporary site, the Villa Bellevue.

Play began at the Villa Bellevue on December 14, 1856, though the villa was scarcely ready to accommodate even the least demanding of visitors. Prince Charles III's chief commissioner, Henri de Payan, had to demand of the casino's manager that they clear the building's environs of hazards that might "offend the eyes or nose." With limited table reserves, the new casino could not afford high-end play. Few gamblers made the more than four-hour land journey from Nice to Monaco.

Those who did arrive frequently were petty swindlers and rogues who passed forged banknotes and otherwise tried to cheat the house and other players. Someone tampered with the roulette wheel, either in an effort to defraud the company or to discredit it. Langlois and Aubert, unable to finance new buildings or even deep enough cash reserves to put the gambling on a solid footing, were forced to sell their company in December 1857 to Pierre Auguste Daval, a landowner from Charente in central France whose finances were reputedly beyond reproach. Daval, however, proved to have no more money than his predecessors. Francois Blanc, sensing an opportunity, "fired" some of his most trusted employees, who then found work in Monaco, from where they kept him well informed of the ongoing saga. Although Daval began construction of the permanent casino in May 1858, he paid no money to the Prince, nor did he begin transportation improvements. Within a year, steadily losing money, he was forced to sell his ownership of the concession to a newly-formed Paris company.

The new owners, whose most prominent name was that of the Duc de Valmy, the wealthy and influential grandson of the French military hero Francois Kellerman, took possession of the concession on May 29, 1859. The company was to be run by Francois Lefebrve on behalf of its directors. Though they had considerably more solid finances than the previous owners, the new proprietors still found their bankroll lacking. Complicating matters, the outbreak of the Austro-Sardinian war had forced a closure of the casino. Though this war ultimately resulted in the broad international recognition of Monaco's independence and the end of the Sardinian threat, it hardly marked an auspicious beginning for the new owners.

When the war ended, Lefebvre did not re-open the previous facilities, but instead commenced play in a new location in the heart of Monaco itself. Despite the complete lack of hotel facilities, the tables showed a decent average profit—a thousand francs per day. Visitors, if they could reach the casino at all, had no place to stay overnight, and had to leave in the early evening. Lefebvre was not the right man to rise to the challenge of building a new gambling resort; he was afraid to even enter the gambling room, lest he be accosted by an unhappy loser. He refused to spend money to improve the facilities, and, as it became clear that he could not meet the Prince's deadline for completing the permanent casino by January 1, 1863, he resigned.

The Duc de Valmy now openly sought to sell the resort franchise to an established Rhine operator. Wary of the political climate in Homburg, Francois Blanc was well disposed to listen. Eynaud's heart leapt at the chance of Blanc duplicating his success in Homburg and had confidence in his large fortune and sagacious management. He wrote to Charles III that Blanc was a wizard, a "master in the art of dissimulating the green cloth of the gaming tables behind a veil of luxury, elegance, and pleasure."

Meanwhile, the new casino, poorly furnished and half-finished, opened in February. Blanc's Homburg nemesis, Thomas Garcia, terrified the stockholders when he arrived and quickly won 45,000 francs at the tables. In their desperation, they hastily agreed to sell to Blanc. In March 1863, Blanc signed a contract giving him, in return for a cash payment of 1.5 million francs, complete ownership of the gaming concession until April 1, 1913. A new day had dawned in Monaco, and Blanc promised that though he had served his apprenticeship in Homburg, he would create his masterpiece for Charles III.

Blanc formed the Societe des Bains de Mer et Cercle des Etrangers (Society of Sea Bathers and Circle of Foreigners) as an operating company for the casino and the related facilities. He immediately refurbished and completed the casino and adjoining Hotel de Paris, dispatching his Homburg architect Jacobi to bring to the project the expected excellence. Blanc demanded that the hotel be among the finest in the world, and Jacobi did not disappoint. To lure serious gamblers, he immediately raised the table reserves and deposited enough money in a Nice bank to raise public confidence in the casino's solvency. Meanwhile, Blanc advanced improvements in land transport, including the establishment of a rail line, and purchased four boats to provide regular service from Nice and Genoa. He turned his army of press agents and captive journalists onto the single-minded promotion of Monaco as an elegant resort in which gold was simply waiting to be plucked from the tables. Selling a favorable building site to the owner/editor of Le Figaro, the populist, scandal-loving Hippolyte de Villemessant ensured that yet another French media outlet would unabashedly promote the happiness to be found in Monaco. Blanc's efforts paid off immediately, as the number of visitors more than doubled.

Blanc began to promote a scheme of "Homburg in the summer, Monaco in the winter," and though he kept both casinos open year-round, encouraged seasonal play at both. He abolished the second zero at roulette in 1864, making sure that the change was duly promoted in the newspapers. By 1866, Blanc had spent more than 2 million francs improving the roads and harbor and building gardens around his casino. Yet something of a cloud still hung over the enterprise. The Italian and German cognates of "spelugues," translated loosely as "disreputable haunts," and a place named Les Spelugues was hardly a fitting site for a gambling house, no matter how elegant. Blanc campaigned with Prince Charles III to change the district's name, and on July 1, 1866, he got his wish, when the prince humbly declared that, henceforth, the area surrounding the casino was to be known as the quartier de Monte Carlo.

After the railway opened in 1868, the casino could scarcely contain the crowds, and during the winter, Monaco became Europe's chief gambling resort. The Hotel de Paris was fully booked months in advance; tired of turning away prospective gamblers, Blanc ordered its expansion. In 1864, 70,000 people visited the casino; by 1870, the figure stood at 120,000. Yet all was not golden. Blanc wanted to improve the "quality" of visitors as well as their quantity, and an extortion attempt forced a solution. Two amateur "journalists" published a hate-filled pamphlet denouncing the casino; demanding 20,000 francs from one of Blanc's managers, they were arrested for blackmail. Learning that the pair had, in fact, patronized the casino, Blanc developed a system whereby prospective gamblers had to fill out entrance cards, and the casino reserved the right to exclude anyone it wished. Far from lowering the number of visitors, this actually helped to raise it, as entry into the casino became a mark of good bearing. Still, Monaco charged no outright visitors tax, as did competing bathing resorts, and entry to the casino remained free. It was a place where the newly rich could jostle those with century-old wealth, and obsessed gamblers were free to test their luck. In the words of Somerset Maugham, it was "a sunny place for shady people."

By 1872, the final year for Rhine casinos, Monte Carlo was firmly established as the jewel of the Riviera. With its new monopoly on roulette and trente-et-quarante, Monte Carlo could not help but be successful. The next year, on the close of the fashionable winter season in February, the *London Times* reported that Blanc had worked a miracle: a visitor from Nice arriving at an hour when the casino and its surrounding terrace were lit by "a thousand globes of fire" could not help but conclude that he had "left ordinary life and the countries of reality to enter into that brilliant region where all passions combine to obliterate the mind and obscure the reason." Further, the correspondent--who most likely enjoyed Blanc's largesse—declared that the casino master had created "the most luxurious, most beautiful, most enervating place in the world." Accessed by newly-paved roads, surrounded by graceful gardens, the casino was the centerpiece of a wonderland where fine food could be had for a small price, perfumes wafted through the air along with charming music, and a thousand seductions awaited the unwary. For those devoted to chasing the black and the red in a refined setting, it was nothing less than an earthly paradise.

Blanc wanted to forestall any prohibition movement (and avoid a repeat of his Homburg humiliation) by accumulating political debts. He therefore made himself a friend of the French government by becoming its banker: in 1874 he gave the Minister of Public Works a 4.8 million-franc loan to rebuild the Paris Opera House. He thereafter enjoyed rich relations with a variety of government officials, who generously facilitated the improvement of rail connections between Monaco and France. The opera house's architect, Charles Garnier, showed his appreciation by designing a theater for Blanc that adjoined the casino and provided it with its landmark two towers, which soon became an emblem of Monte Carlo.

Blanc enjoyed another triumph when his daughter Louise married a poor but noble Polish aristocrat, Prince Constance Radziwill, in 1876. His rise to wealth and power was complete, though his declining health gave him little opportunity to enjoy it. Ill with bronchitis, he died at the age of 71 in Loeche les Bains on July 27, 1877, leaving a fortune of more than 88 million francs ($17.5 million in 1877 dollars) to his family. His funeral was the most extravagant that Paris had seen for years, and his charitable bequests were duly noted in his obituaries. He had outlived the far-sighted Eynaud, who had served as an apt mediator between Blanc and Charles III for years, by only a few weeks. Princess Caroline, who had guided her husband and son toward her vision of a prosperous Monaco, passed away two years later. It was the end of an era.

Marie Blanc, 43 years old at the time of Blanc's death, succeeded her husband in overseeing the Monte Carlo enterprise, and Bertora, formerly Francois's secretary, assumed the role of casino manager. Since 1863, Blanc had worked wonders at Monaco. Where it once had no serviceable hotels, it now had 19, as well as an assortment of villas and apartments to house long-term visitors. Once nearly bereft of industry, Monaco now boasted shops, restaurants, banks, and support services for the burgeoning hospitality industry that provided work for Monaco citizens who, thanks to the tremendous sums the casino brought the government, paid no taxes.

Visitors to Monte Carlo wagered virtually any currency they wished. French five-franc coins were the most common, but lire, drachma, and even American dollars were common. Particularly large wagers were made using counters or plaques. Usually made from mother-of-pearl or ivory, the first rectangular gambling plaques were made in China in the early 18th century. Brought to Europe by 1720, they were usually bought by individuals for use in private games. Disc-shaped counters were used in Ancient Rome for everything from arena admissions to gambling: these are the true ancestors of today's chips. Metal "whist markers" were used to play that game in the early 19th century in Europe and North America.

Monte Carlo was a bit slow in adopting chips; perhaps its more sophisticated guests preferred to wager real money. Americans, who wanted money to change hands with the greatest efficiency, were among the earliest to gamble with chips. Around the middle of the 19th century, ivory chips became popular with poker and faro players. In the 1880s, "composition" chips, manufactured with clay and shellac, became popular. But there was a problem: since the chips were made without designs in only in a few colors, it was easy to buy one's own chips, then surreptitiously slip them into a game. As a result, manufacturers began making engraved and inlaid litho chips, which featured hard-to-copy designs. Regular inlaid chips, featuring an inlaid color set into a differently-colored chip, became common in the 1890s, and, though chips are now made of high-tech composites and sometimes embedded with radio frequency identification tags, they look similar to inlaid chips of a century ago. Monte Carlo, though, still uses the oversized plaques, continuing a tradition started generations ago.

Marie Blanc presided over the triumphant opening of the Charles Garnier-designed theater, which provided a venue for performances by Europe's finest musicians and actors. Still, she shrank from active involvement in the casino, tiring of the constant stream of letters begging for help and threatening blackmail. The croupiers were on the constant watch for cheating, and discreet detectives roamed the casino, on the lookout for pickpockets and hustlers. Sometimes the threat was more direct. At 10 P.M. on April 24, 1880, a bomb smuggled into one of the gaming salons exploded. Timed to go off just as the theater crowds filled the casino, the explosion was intended to create enough confusion to permit its planters to carry off the wealth on the tables.

The attackers had not counted on the stoic professionalism of the casino's guardians. Though the bomb caused considerable mayhem—windows were shattered, the gas lights extinguished, and scores of gamblers wounded by flying glass—the croupiers remained coolly intent at their positions, refusing to take their eyes off the gold and banknotes heaped before them. This incident only strengthened Marie's distaste for the casino, and though she triumphantly saw the marriage of her second daughter to Prince Roland Bonaparte (a nephew of the Prince of Canino who had nearly broken her husband at Homburg), she did not live long after that, dying quite suddenly at the age of 47 in 1881.

Upon her death her stepson Camille Blanc took control of the casino, after having served a long apprenticeship under his father and step-mother. Encouraging his brother Edmond to pursue his love of the turf in far-off Paris and limiting Bertora's authority, he emerged as the managing director of the Societe des Bains de Mer (SBM). He was praised as a sharp-eyed charming figure who brought Monte Carlo into a new age by renewing its commitment to providing excellent food and lodging and by adding new attractions, including a seaside bathing facility and various sporting events.

In 1898, Camille Blanc renegotiated his father's original pact with Monaco's prince. SBM was charged with financing improvements to the harbor and roads and agreed to subsidize the opera. Prince Albert also extracted the promise of a minimum payment of 50,000 pounds a year from the casino, as well as eight percent of the gross revenues in excess of 1 million pounds. By this time, the casino's internal structure had been divided into three departments underneath the SBM umbrella. Camille Blanc, as chief director, primarily devoted himself to the company's finances and charged the director-general with overseeing the activities of the directors who headed each of the casino's departments. The Interior Department saw to purchasing, maintenance, expansion, and human resources. Exterior handled legal and accounting matters as well as entertainment, utilities, and the gardens. The Games Department was composed of surveillance officers, croupiers, and their supervisors.

The croupiers were trained on site at a six-month school that mercilessly drilled applicants in the science of dexterously handling the roulette wheel and sorting, recognizing, and paying bets. This last was no mean feat. Most casinos today have players "buy" chips of a certain color at the roulette table; matching a bet to a player is as simple as identifying whose color is whose. But as Monte Carlo roulette tables accepted all manner of gold, silver, and paper currency as live wagers, it was essential for dealers not only to remain aware of the position of bets both before and after the ball dropped but to remember which piles belonged to which hands. Generally speaking, SBM hired only those already employed with the firm in some other capacity as croupiers, and held its school at night, after their regular shift. While on duty, croupiers were watched by Chef de Parties, who sat on high chairs overlooking the tables; they were the ancestors of today's pit bosses and floor-people. Surveillance officials also circulated, but the croupiers enforced honor amongst themselves by means of a peer disciplinary council that ruled on serious allegations of fraud or stealing. For those found guilty, the penalties could be severe, including not only termination but forcible expulsion from the principality.

In the late 1860s, Blanc's casino had only four rooms. By 1910, it had been expanded countless times in a patchwork of architectural styles: Greek, Moorish, and French Second Empire. The erstwhile casino became an atrium that connected the Charles Garnier theater and the Schmit Room, the first gaming room. From the atrium, guests passed through a vestibule decorated in the Louis XVI style into the Schmit Room, which was Louis XIV. Like all the gaming salons, it had a parquet floor. The Schmit room was distinguished by its Corinthian columns and onyx pilasters, paintings inspired by the four seasons, four immense Art Nouveau chandeliers, and a ceiling vault topped with a circular skylight. The other gaming salons were a mix of styles, but were similarly lavish. From the outside, two semi-detached Moorish towers were the most distinctive feature of off-white Beaux-Arts exterior, which was capped by green copper vaults.

Though, like his father, Camille took great pains to accommodate the press, attacks on Monte Carlo continued to circulate in the newspapers, ironically often the same ones that scant weeks before had blazoned their pages with glowing praise of the remarkable resort. (One senses that editors and/or correspondents, believing their own hyperbole, had succumbed to temptation and bet more than they should have before turning their venom against the casino.) In 1878, for example, the previously sanguine *New York Times* reported that, the resort was "a sorry substitute for Baden-Baden." As most people

The Monte Carlo casino's twin towers gave it a distinctive appearance, as this late nineteenth century postcard captures.

of worth stayed at villas in Monte Carlo, hoteliers made no efforts to treat their guests with courtesy, though they charged rapacious room rates; at least the Badenites were polite. While the Baden-Baden croupiers had excelled in treating all guests with an aristocratic deference, their Monte Carlo counterparts had "the manners of cavalrymen" and rudely lectured the players, even giving them orders. The gamblers, of a lower class than those who once graced Baden-Baden, glumly suffered such abuse. Finally, petty thefts and squabbles over stakes were common, as were scenes that would be considered disgraceful in the meanest American faro bank.

Still, many wealthy and well-known visitors poured into the principality. One son of an unnamed American railroad millionaire had quite a spree in 1882. Losing all of his ready money at trente-et-quarante, he telegraphed his mother for more, temporizing that he had lost his pocketbook. Before he could hear back, a friend loaned him some money with which he reclaimed his losses from the tables. He then telegraphed that his mother need not send anything, as his pocketbook had been found. Unwilling to quit while ahead, he returned to the tables and lost everything, whereupon he dejectedly telegraphed a third time, imploring his mother: "Do send money. Pocketbook found as stated, but with nothing in it."

This was not the only mother-son pair to make news at Monte Carlo. The Prince of Wales, who would in 1901 become King Edward VII, had long frequented the casino at Homburg, and easily followed the elder Blanc to Monte Carlo. Because it was considered unseemly for the heir apparent to publicly gamble, he adopted several pseudonyms, including "Captain White" and "Baron Renfrew," which gave him a cloak of social invisibility; he flirted, gambled, and carried on his affairs in full view of the public, officially anonymous. His mother, Queen Victoria, had no more patience for the insouciance of Monaco than for her son's playboy antics. She wrote to her prime minister, William Gladstone (himself an occasional gambler), that she approved of a subscription to a British anti-Monaco association, and made her hostility to the principality crystal clear in 1882 when, while passing through en route to Menton, disdained an official presentation of flowers and spurned Charles III's offer of hospitality. This deliberate affront devastated the prince and dismayed Francois Blanc, who remarked that, had the Queen taken up the invitation, it would have provided 2 million francs worth of publicity.

Gamblers at Monte Carlo developed a set of bizarre and sometimes contradictory suspicions. Many supplicants to fortune brought religious icons with them. One woman even had a five-franc coin surreptitiously blessed by the Pope (she had hidden it amongst a group of rosaries) and, though she successfully channeled this papal benefice, she lost the amulet when a friend accidentally staked and lost the holy coin. Anglican church-goers found similar inspiration when one of them staked heavily and won on that Sunday's hymn, numbered 36. From then on, pious English eagerly anticipated the selection of the hymnal, barely waiting for the service to conclude so they could rush into the casino. The pastor, suspecting something was up, loudly directed his congregants to turn to hymn number 47 the next Sunday. Seeing the disappointment on the faces of his flock and tired of being reduced to a roulette tipster, from then on he chose only hymns numbered above 36.

By contrast, most gamblers considered priests extremely unlucky and hoped that, by curling their fingers into horns at the gaming

The Monte Carlo casino rooms were elegant, as this photo from around the turn of the 20th century shows.

table, they could ward off the churchly spirit. Others descended into theosophical speculation or numerological exegesis, plumbing the mystic significance of the Tarot and Hebrew alphabet for lucky numbers. Some carried charms best described as pagan, including a woman who kept a bat's heart in her purse; as a creature of the night, she believed its sympathetic magic would bring fortune to all silver it touched. Pigs were also believed to bring luck. In the early days gamblers tried to smuggle live pigs into the gaming salons, but as the resort became more sophisticated they confined themselves to the occasional lucky pork chop. A truly bizarre superstition held that it was good luck to rub a hunchback. Other lucky charms included pieces of a hangman's rope, locks of hair, snakeskin, rat's tails, and horseshoes. The last of these, as symbols of fertility, were said to augur the collection of a large harvest. They usually did—for the casino.

By the outbreak of World War I, the casino employed more than 500 people at the height of the winter season, which formally lasted from November to February. Croupiers were given regular salaries and pensions. Originally allowed to keep their own tips, croupiers were eventually barred from the practice. Thereafter, management permitted grateful winners to slip a few coins into "number 37," an added slot at the tables. At the end of the day, all of the tips were collected and divided amongst the employees. Until 1948, managers kept half of the collection for themselves. After a sit-down strike, they consented to give the croupiers 70 percent of the takings.

The Blancs surrounded the casino with a range of other amusements. The theater, which featured in its day names as lofty as Sarah Bernhardt, Enrico Caruso, and Serge Diaghilev, whose Russian Ballet was world renowned, provided a venue for opera, theater, and ballet. For more sporting types, pigeon-shooting was a popular diversion. The harbor hosted all manner of water sports and sailing races, and bicycle races transformed Monaco streets into race tracks. With the spread of the automobile, car-racing rallies became popular, culminating in the Monte Carlo Grand Prix, first run in 1929.

Beating the System

No gambler, except the most willfully perverse, sits down to play with the intention of losing. In social games with some degree of strategy, players can bank on both their skill and luck to help them win. Not so for quick-decision mercantile games like roulette and trente-et-quarante. A player simply placed her bet and hoped for the best. Controlling no element of the game's outcome, he or she could only change the size of her bet. Systems of betting, not refinements of skill, held out the only hope that players could in fact beat the house advantage.

Since the days of pioneering gambling mathematician Girolamo Cardano in the sixteenth century, gamblers had tried to take advantage of the odds. Subsequent innovations made the mathematical basis of gambling clear, but did not help bettors. In fact, they showed that no system can possibly guarantee success. While fortune can swing in either direction over the course of an evening, because of a phenomenon mathematicians describe as "regression to the mean," given enough time the edge house's statistical advantage will devour all players. Yet for centuries, players have enthusiastically embraced sure-fire, can't-lose systems, both borrowed and new, that have ultimately failed.

The earliest known betting system is the Martingale progression, which Casanova, according to his memoirs, employed in the Venice Ridotto in February 1754. The origin of the system's name is unknown, but legend links it to a late 18th century London gambling house proprietor named Henry Martingale. Using this uncomplicated geometric progression, Casanova simply doubled the size of his bet after each loss. After he won, he returned his bet to its original size. In theory, this meant that a player would win twice as much as he had lost on the previous deal, but in practice the limits of the system are clear: unless armed with an infinite bankroll, the player has no safeguard against a bad run wiping him out. The Martingale is the quintessential negative progression system, in which players change their bets following losing hands.

Presume that a roulette player with $100 of chips places $5 bets on black. Losing her first hand, she would double her stake to $10; losing that one would require a $20 bet; etc. If she was unlucky enough to lose four straight times (not that uncommon, as anyone who has watched roulette knows), she will not have enough in reserve for the $80 required for the fifth bet. Even if she had twice the capital, she would sooner or later butt up against the table maximum. There is more chance than science to any anecdotal successes scored with a Martingale progression. Still, some deep-thinking player found a way to elaborate the Martingale progression by devising a system where, after each losing bet, he doubled his stake and then added one betting unit. Known as the Grand Martingale, this method allows for greater returns but also bigger losses.

The opposite of the Martingale is the Paroli, or parlay; and it follows the maxim that the best defense is a good offense. Players following a Paroli progression double their stakes after winning. While this would allow a player to score a tremendous coup with a series of wins, it also means that, should he lose deep into the progression, he might be completely wiped out. Variations of the Paroli include systems where the bet is increased according to a regular pattern: instead of reflexively doubling the stakes, players change the amount of units bet. A 1-3-2-6 progression, for example, has a player triple a winning bet, then stake double the original, and finally six times the base bet.

The Labouchere or cancellation system was invented by the 18th century French mathematician de Cordorcet and popularized by a 19th century member of the British Parliament, Henry Labouchere. In a nutshell, Labouchere devotees begin gambling by writing down a series of numbers, for example 1-2-3-4-5. The first bet is the sum of the first and last numbers, in this case 6. After losing a bet, the player writes that wager at the end of the series; after winning, she crosses out the first and last numbers in the series. Once the bettor has canceled all the numbers, she will have reached a net profit equaling the sum of the original numbers, 15 in the above example. The fatal drawback of this system is, as with the others, if the player is confronted with an unlucky run the necessary bet will soon eclipse either the player's bankroll or the table maximums.

The d'Alembert system is named for 18th century mathematician Jean Le Rond d'Alembert, who edited the groundbreaking Encyclopedie with Denis Diderot. In mathematics, he is best known as the discoverer of d'Alembert's principle, an elaboration of the Newtonian laws of motion. The principle that bears d'Alembert's name stems from his belief that systems tend towards equilibrium: applied to roulette, this means that the more the ball lands on black, the more likely it will be to land on red. Those seeking to use d'Alembert's idea of equilibrium to clean up at the tables add one unit to their bet when losing and subtract one when winning. In theory, at least, this would allow the average bettor to make a profit of one unit per win. In practice, though the d'Alembert system does not lead to the quick disaster possible in the classic Martingale, it is no sounder than any other system, despite the impressive intellectual achievements of its innovator.

A related system, the patience system, fuses the d'Alembert principle of equilibrium with selective betting. Patience bettors perch near the roulette wheel, waiting for a run of, for example, three straight reds. The bettor then steps in and places his money on black in the belief that black is "due" to come up. This is nonsense, as neither the ball nor the wheel feel any obligation towards maintaining the game's equilibrium: random events are not influenced by past outcomes. While the patience system cannot guarantee winning, it does have the benefit of giving the bettor ample time sitting on the sidelines to reconsider the idea of using a system at all.

The Gagnante Marche system, known today as the streak or hot and cold system, turns d'Alembert on his head. According to Gagnante Marche, when you're hot, you're hot, and streaks, rather than a steady quest for equilibrium, define the game. Using this system, bettors put their money on the last side to win: if, arriving at the table, black has just come up, the bettor places her money on black, and leaves it there until red comes up. Thus, if one side or the other begins a streak, the bettor will be able to ride it from the beginning. This system's particular shortcoming is that, while waiting for a lucky wave, the would-be table-surfer will be pecked to death by the lurking piranha of random alternations between black and red. He is no better off than if he had simply left his money on either color and spent his energy thinking about whether to have a quick lunch in the coffee shop or wait in line at the buffet.

Though such gambling systems have existed since the mathematical advances of the 18th century put gambling on a surer theoretical footing, they truly blossomed in the years 1870-1914, years that also saw the greatest glory of Monte Carlo. In a sense, system gamblers were no different from the captains of industry who created business behemoths during this era: they sought to rationally exploit the resources of the casino by finding ways of taking advantage of its governing principles. This was a far cry from the noblesse oblige with which English grandees and continental blue-bloods had once placed their indifferent wagers. In the late 19th century, as fortunes were ready to be made—or lost—in new industries, vacationing peers of the realm often found themselves rudely pushed aside by cigar-chewing industrialists, flush with new wealth. For them, roulette was not so much a leisure activity as an attempted hostile takeover of the casino. The table was a battlefield, and the player was armed only with his or her bankroll. The gambling system provided a plan of battle.

Francois Blanc and the casino managers remained serene in the face of system players' enthusiasm. Blanc often said that his casinos had been built on gambling systems and even circulated a story that seems more figuratively than literally true. Deciding to buy his wife a parasol that cost about one pound, he sought to test one of the most popular systems by trying to win the sum in his casino. He gave up after he found himself 1,000 pounds in the hole. Fortified by experience, he concluded that no system could possibly enable any but the richest bettor to threaten his reserves, and gave quiet encouragement to those who felt they knew better.

Still, gamblers big and small chased after the same dream of breaking the bank at Monte Carlo. Legions of small-betting gamblers thronged to Monte Carlo with the hope of parlaying a modest bankroll into a huge fortune. For the typical systems player, weeks or months of study, calculations, and dreaming culminated in a pilgrimage to the gambler's mecca, Monte Carlo. Though constantly reminded that all other systems had proved futile, each pilgrim to fortune held out the hope that his or her system could not fail.

On the face of it, "breaking the bank" would seem to indicate that the casino's reserves have been exhausted (as nearly happened at Homburg) in the face of a lucky bettor and that the house was bankrupted. But breaking the bank was actually more of a publicity stunt: it happened whenever a bettor won more than the cash reserves of a single table. The table was ceremoniously draped with black crepe and solemnly closed until a fresh infusion from the central cashier arrived. This rite began with Benazet at his Wiesbaden casino and was copied by Blanc. When the bank was "broken," the casino was by no means insolvent, and frequently after the hiatus the player lost back all he had won. But the public spectacle of the black-garbed green cloth allowed players to believe that they had beaten Blanc at his own game, and thus encouraged even more resolute devotion to systems.

The really crafty systems figurers did not invest their own money in proving the truth of their hypotheses: they solicited backers to do so. In 1887 two Parisians developed a system which was sure to break the bank. Rather than simply heading to Monte Carlo and raking in the gold, they published a pamphlet that "demonstrated" the infallibility of the system and advertised for backers to take a share in the 1 million francs that would surely be realized from an initial bankroll of 24,000. After collecting 60,000 francs from various addle-heads foolish enough to send money through the mail, they alighted at Blanc's casino and put their system into practice. After quickly losing 24,000 francs, they lost all faith in their system and returned to Paris, where the police promptly seized the remaining 36,000 francs and arrested the pair as common swindlers. Most systems of the era ended in similar frustration.

Yet there were some success stories, particularly before the science of roulette had been perfected. In 1873, an English engineer named Joseph Jaggers went on holiday at Monte Carlo. He later claimed to have never even seen a roulette wheel before. But, accustomed to exercising his intellect by designing cotton spindles, he became curious about the mechanics of roulette. The wheels, he conjectured, might have slight imperfections that would lead to certain numbers coming up more often than they should. Hiring a staff of clerks (which would seem to indicate that this was no holiday fancy; in fact the newspapers reported he had been backed by a syndicate) to record winning numbers at each of the tables, he gathered a week's worth of data. Poring through it, he noted that on a particular wheel nine numbers—7, 8, 9, 17, 18, 19, 22, 28, and 29—came up with surprising regularity. Jaggers bet accordingly and, within four days, had won 60,000 pounds.

The surveillance officers, always on the lookout for cheating, were perplexed by Jagger's success. They compared Jaggers's betting patterns with all known systems—they were already familiar with over forty of them—and found nothing, as he threw his money on the board with no discernable pattern. In actuality, Jaggers was cunning enough to place random wagers on numbers not favored by his system simply to keep his true methods obscure. Finally, in desperation they switched the roulette wheels. The next day, Jaggers stopped playing after less than thirty spins. Noticing suddenly that the wheel no longer had a characteristic scratch, he wandered the casino as discreetly as possible before spying "his" wheel. Sitting down, he continued his winning ways.

But the casino staff now knew Jaggers's secret. They quickly sent to Paris for spare parts and reconfigured every roulette wheel. Jaggers suspected as much and, after losing 200 pounds in his next outing, he left the casino, packed his bags, and departed Monaco 80,000 pounds richer, never to be seen there again. The casino directors immediately began a policy of testing with a level each table and wheel before the 10 a.m. start of the gambling day to guarantee that this perfectly legal method could never be used against the casino again.

Jaggers's success, of course, was not due to a betting system per se, but rather empirical application of observed inconsistencies in a single roulette wheel. As such, it did not fire the imagination as much as bona fide systems did. The public, hungry for a true system to break the bank, jumped eagerly on the bandwagon of one such claimant in 1891. The Englishman Charles Deville Wells was a poorly-dressed, unremarkable flim-flam artist: he once supposedly painted sparrows yellow and sold them as canaries. He took out more than 200 patents from 1885 to 1890 on devices as varied as an automatic foghorn, a sardine-can opener, and a musical skipping rope. He solicited investors, who generously gave him enough funds to open posh London offices and buy a yacht. With no money realized from his fanciful patents, he concluded that his best hope of satisfying his creditors would be found on the roulette tables.

Wells sailed his yacht into Monte Carlo in July 1891 and in three days had parlayed his original 400 pounds into 40,000. He chalked his success up to his adapted Martingale system. He started with 100 pounds, doubled his bet to the maximum and allowed it to ride for three successful bets, running his winnings up to nearly 2,000 pounds before returning to a 100-pound bet. In the course of his run he broke the bank several times. After putting in three eleven-hour days at the roulette tables, he left the casino, but not before also winning over 6,000 pounds at trente-et-quarante.

Wells became an instant celebrity. A song written about him, prosaically titled "The Man Who Broke the Bank at Monte Carlo," caught the public fancy in Europe and the United States. All this only encouraged more tourists to test their own systems in Monte Carlo, usually unsuccessfully. Wells himself returned in November, won an additional 10,000 pounds in three days, and bought 2,000 pounds worth of SBM stock before leaving. Unable to quit while he was ahead, Wells, cocksure in his own abilities, blinded by his success, or blissfully unaware of regression to the mean, returned in January aboard his new yacht.

To the surprise of no one but himself, he now lost steadily. His past soon caught up with him. His latest invention, he claimed, was a device that would increase the fuel efficiency of coal-burning engines; he was testing it on his yacht. He began to wire his investors that the machine had broken down and he needed money for repairs. Amid mounting suspicion, he confessed that the engine aid was a ruse; he had in fact developed an unshakeable betting system to which his investors were unwitting subscribers. Dissatisfied investors reported Wells's perfidy to the police. He was eventually extradited back to the United Kingdom and imprisoned for eight years after his conviction on fraud charges. He spent the rest of his life in and out of prison and on public relief, his system revealed as nothing more than blind luck and crafty salesmanship.

Debate over systems even spilled over into the newspapers. In 1903, Sir Hiram Maxim, the American inventor of the automatic machine gun (and naturalized British citizen) who had been knighted by Queen Victoria two years before, had a letter to the New York *Herald* published which refuted the "evening-up" system of one Herbert Vivian. Fitzroy Erskine, younger brother of James Francis Harry, the sitting Earl of Rosslyn, joined the battle on Vivian's side, arguing that he himself had a system which could beat the bank, and that in fact anyone possessed with "fair capital, good nerve, and iron constitution" could beat the house advantage at roulette.

In 1908, Fitzroy's brother the earl arrayed himself against Maxim's dogmatic refusal to consider the possibility of a winning system. His own system was simple: bet on a single even-money proposition, such as red, beginning with one unit, and then add one unit until the bank had been broken. Lord Rosslyn formed a syndicate of backers (including actress Lily Langtry) and, with a team of players, put their system into operation at Monte Carlo. Rather quickly, the syndicate lost most of its money, and one of its members even collapsed from exhaustion.

This episode might have taught Rosslyn the futility of his system, but he instead goaded Maxim into a showdown. At stake was both pride and a ten-pound wager. The two shut themselves in a Piccadilly room with a roulette wheel and agreed that, should Rosslyn retain his theoretical 10,000 pounds of capital (they did not use real money for the trial) at the end of two weeks, he would be declared the winner. After one week, Rosslyn was ahead by 500 pounds. At this halfway point, both men hedged their bets. Rosslyn issued a written statement to the effect that while there existed no system absolutely guaranteed to break the bank, his was as close to certainty as was possible; this seemed a retreat from his earlier optimism, and conceded Maxim's original thesis, that there was no such thing as a sure-win system. Maxim was more confident, saying that although the fluctuations were great, and that his bank could be wiped out by a bad run of four consecutive coups, it was his belief that "the second week will not allow such fluctuations, and that a balance in favor of the bank will be restored."

At this point, there was no guarantee that it would. Even Maxim's own wife predicted her husband's defeat. She, Maxim admitted, had invented twenty "winning systems" herself, which explains Maxim's consternation regarding Rosslyn's claims. But both Mrs. Maxim and Lord Rosslyn were soon proven wrong. By the end of 14th day, Lord Rosslyn was 10,340 pounds in the hole. Exhausted, he handed over to Maxim a ten-pound note. Maxim was victorious, though even this well-publicized failure could not dissuade systems devotees. Fresh from his annihilation of Rosslyn, Maxim received another public challenge, this one from a French "lightning calculator" named Jacques Inaudi. Weary of proving his point, Maxim suggested that Inaudi instead test his system at Monte Carlo with real money.

The enthusiasm over systems reached its peak at the turn of the 20th century but continues to this day. The mistaken belief that previous random events somehow dictate future independent ones is known today as the Monte Carlo Fallacy or, more generally, Gambler's Fallacy. Yet it continues. Faith in systems remained unshaken by the spectacular failures of supposed "mathematical masterminds" during the heady 1890s. Even today, books touting various sure-fire "betting management systems" are legion. Sometimes disguised in abstruse terminology or knowing talk of thousands of hours spent in real casinos, they are almost all just copies of the original systems debated in the 1890s. Though the systems makers were rarely successful in breaking the bank at Monte Carlo, they would prove adept at breaking open the wallets of their fellow gamblers for decades to come.

Baccarat Gets Big

The Monte Carlo monopoly on gambling was challenged, when, in 1907, the government of France authorized the public play of "games of skill," which included two games today considered more strictly games of chance: baccarat and chemin-de-fer. In actuality, the two were the same game, with the exception that the first was avowedly mercantile, banked only by the house, while the second had at least the trappings of a social game that pitted player against player.

Baccarat was born in Italy as baccara, and was first reported in France during the long reign of Louis XIV (1643-1715). It became a favored game of the nobility, but by the Napoleonic period could also be found in illegal gambling houses as well. After the prohibition of public gambling in 1837, it survived in private homes, but did not make the jump to the Rhine along with *trente-et-quarante* and roulette.

Mentioned occasionally in the 19th century as a private game, baccarat suddenly burst into prominence in the early 20th century in the new French Riviera casinos. It was already recognized as two games. Chemin-de-fer means "railroad" in French, and in "Chemmy" players pass the *sabot* (shoe) across the table, perhaps in a manner reminiscent of a railroad. In this version of the game, the player with the shoe dealt the game and actually banked it; the privilege of holding bank was disbursed to the highest bidder, whose bid became his bet. The banker placed the amount of his winning bid on the table, and any players wishing to play *ponte* matched his bet, either in whole or in part. If several players backed *ponte*, the one with the highest bet played for all. The banker then dealt four cards facedown from the shoe: the first and third for the ponte, the second and fourth for himself.

To determine the winner, each player totaled his cards, which counted for face value, aces equaling one and face cards zero. If the total was more than ten, i.e., two sixes totaling twelve, the player dropped the first digit, giving him a total of two. The winner was the player with the higher point total. If the *ponte* had 8 or 9, he showed his hand immediately. If dealt cards totaling zero through four, he had to ask for another card. With five, he could draw or stand, and with six and seven he had to stand. Thus, the only real strategy for ponte was whether to draw or stand on five. *Banco* also showed his hand immediately if dealt an eight or nine. If ponte did not show his hand, banco had to draw if his total was zero through two. If ponte showed his hand by asking for a new card, or if *banco* totaled three through six, banco had the option of drawing a fifth card. The greater freedom afforded the banker gave him an advantage over ponte, and those with the cash reserves to withstand the inevitable swings in fortune seemed guaranteed victory if they played long enough.

Chemin-de-fer did not pit players against the casino; rather, the casino only extracted a five percent *cagnotte* or "rake" from winning banker hands, which defrayed the costs of the dealer, equipment, and establishment. Though this game attracted swarms of rich gamblers to the Riviera casinos that sprung up in the 1910s and 1920s, the house did not profit greatly from them. Baccarat, also known as Banque a Deux Tableaux (for the double-table configuration which allowed twelve players to join in) or Baccarat en Banque, was the house-banked version of chemin-de-fer, although in some clubs the right to bank the game was put out to bid, as in chemin-de-fer. The dealer dealt two player hands, one to each half of the table, and players could bet on both simultaneously. The rules were similar to chemin-de-fer, but with less room for player choice: players had only the option of drawing or standing on five, and the house dealer had to scrupulously follow pre-determined rules of play.

Even before its 1907 legalization, the game had spread across southern France. While still Prince of Wales, King Edward VII introduced the game to British society. It made its first American appearance in 1911, and enjoyed a brief vogue in illegal American casinos, particularly in New York City, though it never seriously challenged the dominance of craps, and was forgotten by the 1950s, when it was re-introduced in Las Vegas.

The French clubs in which baccarat had prospered prior to 1907 were formally run by a board of directors and chartered for a specific purpose, though more often than not the boards were assembled by club impresarios who, through flattery and convenient amnesia regarding gentlemanly gambling debts, were able to induce socially prominent citizens to serve as front men. The typical Paris club had a restaurant, conversation saloon, a room for small-stakes social games (poker, ecarte, whist, and piquet) and a room for the major game, baccarat en banque. The day-to-day gambling was overseen by two gaming supervisors, working opposite shifts, who decided all disputes and ensured fair-dealing, of at least the appearance thereof. They directed the activities of the other gaming employees: the croupiers, chip-changers, and cashiers. Croupiers shuffled and dealt the cards, collected the house's cagnotte, and paid winners. In return for these responsibilities, they received a regular salary as well as one-third of all tips given by players. The cashier was not a salaried employee of the casino but rather an independent contractor who lent players money in return for a share of the cagnotte and interest on his loans. The chip changer was a factotum of the croupier whose primary duty was to exchange chips for gold and vice versa, carrying the currency from the table to the cashier and back. As in most casinos today, the lowest-value chips were white and the next-lowest red, but larger denominations were distinguished by their size and shape rather than color.

The club also required the services of a secretary and telephone receptionist, a door porter, a bellboy, footman, a groom, and a host of restaurant employees, including a commissary steward, a headwaiter who oversaw a staff of six, a cook, a saucier, and a dishwasher. The club would stage lavish weekly banquets for its members and their guests, and at all times charged only nominal prices for its meals. Members paid annual dues of about 50 francs, of which the government extracted 20 francs as a tax. The government also placed a 100 percent tax on cards, doubling their total cost from 2 francs 50 centimes to 5 francs, thus deriving a significant income from the clubs, as it was the custom to use a deck only once before discarding it as a safeguard against cheating.

With the new popularity of baccarat, casinos at Cannes, Antibes, Juan-les-Pins, Deauville, and Nice began to cut into Monte Carlo's profits. Since they did not have the bonanza of the lucrative mercantile game of roulette, they adopted a more balanced business plan. Instead of using entertainment and dining as loss leaders, as the Rhine resorts and Monte Carlo had, they derived substantial profits from them. Critical visitors blanched at the high cost of drinks, cigarettes, and dinners, but paid them before losing tremendous sums to each other at chemin-de-fer. Still, they paid—and played—and the Riviera casinos soon rivaled Monte Carlo itself.

The Greek Syndicate

But all was not cream for the new casinos. The French government extracted 60 percent of their gross profits as a tax, on top of which local authorities took another 20 percent or so. With such a heavy tax burden, the French casinos began casting envious glances at Monte Carlo. As early as 1925, they began agitating the French government to lift its ban on roulette and allow them a cut of this profitable game. Still, they had one advantage over Monte Carlo. Under a gentlemen's agreement, SBM had agreed not to allow no-limit baccarat in its public casino, and the game was generally confined to the private salons there. In the French casinos, however, well-financed players could take on virtually any bet, and one syndicate of players became so dominant that, in a few years, they assumed permanent control of most of the Blue Coast's baccarat tables.

This group, known as the Greek Syndicate, made its debut at Deauville in 1922. It was indeed composed entirely of Greeks, and led by Nicolas Zographos, one of the greatest gamblers of all time. He is one of the few people in the annals of gambling history to profit regularly from gambling, despite never owning or being employed by a casino. He died in 1953 with a personal fortune of over 5 million pounds (after he had already given much of it away), all of it earned by playing baccarat. The other charter members included Eli Eliopulo, uncle of Zographos's wife Yola Apolstilides, Zamet Couyoumdjian, and Athanase Vagliano, probably the least-skilled gambler of the quartet (he eventually was forced from the Syndicate for losing precipitously at chemin-de-fer).

The Syndicate coalesced in Paris, where the Greeks pooled their resources. They decided that, rather than plow their accumulated capital into purchasing a casino (in which case they would collect only the 5 percent rake from winning hands), they would form a cooperative that would perpetually bank baccarat. With 50 million francs provided by Vagliano, Zographos proposed that the Syndicate announce "tout va" ("the sky's the limit") to the gambling world. This act of daring, Zographos prophesied, would attract every serious gambler, and a host of millionaire dabblers, each convinced that he could break the Greek bank. The group chose Deauville as the spot to take on the world.

The casino at Deauville, founded in 1912, was run by Francois Andre, a former adventurer and carnival operator, and his erstwhile rival, the elderly Eugene Cornuche. The Syndicate was immediately successful: it soon dominated baccarat play. The group triumphed because, in addition to its sizeable bankroll, it had a unique asset: the near-photographic memory and unflappable cool of Nico Zographos. Baccarat was played with a shoe containing six decks of randomly-shuffled cards—312 in all. Zographos was notorious for being able to remember exactly which cards had already been dealt, and could guess the last few cards with ease. He had also studied the "outs," that is, the permutations of cards that would allow him to win a hand, and knew almost instantly the odds of winning a particular hand at any point in the game.

He was more than a clever card-player: he was a virtuoso. Where Benazet, Blanc, and other casino owners had relied on the steady accrual of the house edge to turn a profit, Zographos needed only his skill as a gambler and the serenity to know when to retire for the night. This was another advantage of the Syndicate: because they did not own the casino, they could simply decide to stop banking the game when things became too heated or they were on a serious losing streak. In these cases, Zographos allowed his intellect, rather than pride, to decide whether to continue or not. Zographos professed to never feel the sway of emotions, and boasted that, even as he was about to draw on a five in a move that would either win or lose him 20 million francs, he was calm. He certainly was able to stop gambling dispassionately. In 1923, for example, when the Chilean finance minister Gustavo Ross beat the Syndicate for 17 million francs and then wanted to play double or nothing, Zographos announced that he could go no further and politely withdrew. Such occasions, though, became exceedingly rare as the Syndicate's bankroll swelled.

Zographos was more of a card technician than a gambler. Though he was willing to wager millions on the turn of a card, he had no patience for other forms of gambling, and stuck strictly with baccarat, which he had analyzed so completely that, with the help of his flawless memory, playing it was hardly a gamble. He offered advice for others: "never bet on a race horse, the spin of a ball, or the toss of the dice." This was hardly disinterested counsel; each of these games competed with his own tables. But it is safe to say that Zographos took his own advice and never strayed from the baccarat tables which, with the world clamoring to challenge his "tout va" policy, gave him all the gambling he needed.

The Deauville Casino, scene of many of Zographos's triumphs, had a theater and restaurant in addition to its gaming rooms. In the atrium, boule tables took the stray francs tossed on them, but the real action took place in the chemin-de-fer room, where about forty tables hosted, at peak hours, dozens of games. Unlike Rhenish casinos but similar to later Nevada casinos, it was famous for having no clocks visible. The Greek Syndicate banked the game in a private room, a holy-of-holies of baccarat. Entrance was not restricted to players, but those who wished to simply watch the games were levied an entrance fee of more than four pounds by the casino. At the room's single table, Nico Zographos sat, a matador of the green felt awaiting his next challenge. The wealthiest men of Europe, the Middle East, and the Americas all tried their best, but in the end none could best him. Zographos treated his game like a business (which for him it was), never drinking, seldom smiling, and rarely speaking.

The Syndicate banked baccarat at Cannes for part of the year and eventually obtained the contract to bank baccarat at Monte Carlo itself. Zographos won money from many of the world's richest men, such as French automobile manufacturer Andre Citroen, who lost no less than 30 million francs to the Greek over a period of seven years.

The Syndicate continued to prosper despite the hard times of the 1930s and even survived the cataclysm of the Second World War. Though some members were replaced, Zographos remained the group's anchor. Even after his death in 1953, the Syndicate continued to accept any bet at its baccarat games, though now none of the founding members remained. The Greek Syndicate's legacy, though, could never be erased.

After the Golden Age

While clubs and casinos proliferated across France, Camille Blanc's luck began to run out. Somewhat infamous as a playboy, as time went on he shrank from reinvesting in Monte Carlo without outside assistance. With the coming of World War I, Blanc was placed in a bind: he had several fixed expenses, including croupier pensions, that he could not diminish, yet with war raging across Europe revenues were down. He asked the reigning Prince Albert to continue a temporary reduction in his taxes. Though he agreed to concessions and extended SBM's contract to manage the casino, Albert quietly resolved to seek a wealthier lessee for his lucrative franchise.

He found a willing partner in Sir Basil Zarahoff, a Turkish-born Greek who became enormously rich in the armaments business (he was associated with Hiram Maxim, who first brought him to Monte Carlo). Zarahoff and Albert bided their time as Blanc proved increasingly unable to cope with the influx of newly-rich war profiteers and other non-aristocratic arrivistes after the end of the war. Interspersed among this new crowd were confidence artists and swindlers whom, in 1920 alone, cashed more than 100,000 pounds in bad checks.

When Prince Albert died in the summer of 1922 and was succeeded by his son Louis, the stage was set for a final resolution. Louis wished to immediately undertake an upgrade to the harbor and bore a tunnel for a new road to Fontevielle, a district being reclaimed from the sea. Blanc insisted on strict economy and sought to delay the projects. With Louis's approval, Zarahoff pushed the balky Blanc aside. While Blanc was preoccupied elsewhere in May 1923, Zarahoff surreptitiously bought a controlling block of Societe des Bains de Mer stock and installed himself as its new potentate. Blanc was quietly pensioned off and died in 1927.

To run the casino, Zarahoff tapped Rene Leon, a technically gifted university graduate in mathematics and a charming, genial host who was equally adept at handling visitors, employees, and the media. Leon, a passable tennis, golf, and polo player, had an eye on improving Monaco's sporting facilities and bettering its entertainment. In an effort to jumpstart roulette, he ordered that zero be declared a dead number, with no money won or lost, for a half-hour each night. While this innovation failed to catch on, he successfully raised table minimums, at Zarahoff's suggestion, and began charging casino admission fees. (Previously, only the Salons Prives, or private rooms, had such a fee.) In 1926, Leon orchestrated, at Zarahoff's request, the sale of his shares of SBM to Dreyfus et Cie, a French banking company, who headed a consortium ostensibly anchored by Prince Leon Radziwill, Francois Blanc's grandson, though Leon in actuality held all of the power.

Leon orchestrated several improvements, including the opening of the Summer Casino, a country club, a beach house, and the Grand Prix, which became an unrivaled automobile racing event. He hoped to give the resort appeal beyond roulette. To an extent these innovations worked, but with the onset of worldwide economic depression, Monte Carlo would face its greatest challenge yet. In 1932, SBM failed to issue a dividend for the first time in its history. Struggling to raise earnings, Leon consented to reduce entrance fees to private salons, permit chemin-de-fer in public rooms, and—to the horror of casino purists—allow the American invention of the slot machine in the atrium.

San Remo, over the Italian border, permitted roulette (after Mussolini found he was unable to suppress gambling and reopened the casino there), but the closest that French casino could come to the game that built Monte Carlo was boule, a nine-number version of roulette at which the house had a steep 11 percent edge. Played with an awkward red rubber ball in place of the gently rolling ivory of roulette, the game was derided as a fool's gambit; that anyone played it, according to a contemporary *New York Times* correspondent, was proof of the innate human inability to resist any game of chance, no matter how ridiculous.

Responding to a decade-long campaign and the financial crisis of the Depression, in 1933 the French government bowed to their casino operators' wishes and allowed them to offer roulette and trente-et-quarante. In response, the SBM instituted no-limit baccarat and chemin-de-fer in its public rooms and testily withdrew its instructors from the dealer training school in Paris. In addition, Monte Carlo waived the 5 percent commission charged on baccarat bankers in an effort that harkened back to Francois Blanc's elimination of roulette's second zero.

Though the baccarat give-back did not entirely erase the gains of the French competitors, Leon was able to right the foundering SBM ship before moving to Hollywood, California, in 1935 to manage the Garden of Allah nightclub. Around this time, the Monte Carlo casino employed 404 croupiers in the summer and 620 in the winter, in addition to 46 dinner-jacketed surveillance officers who quietly walked through the salons with an eye on the gaming tables and an untold number of plain-clothes detectives who kept watch over both employees and guests. Over 100 uniformed security guards stood sentry over the establishment, and an equal number of firemen remained on call at all times lest an unattended cigarette spark a conflagration. In addition, an army of gardeners, facilities maintenance employees, entertainers, cashiers, and accounts filled out the ranks of the nearly 4,000 employees directly working for SBM. Each year, the casino bought 100,000 francs' worth of new playing cards and nearly 5,000 francs in new croupiers' rakes—the old ones, hopefully, worn out by raking in players' money. The Monte Carlo casino had become a big business. World War II slowed, but did not stop, the resurgence of Monaco.

The casino kept pace with changing times. In addition to the slot machines that now lined the atrium, another American invention made its way to Monte Carlo in the 1940s: craps. According to legend, cinematic tough guy Edward G. Robinson was responsible for introducing dice to the rarefied salons of the casino. On a break from the Cannes Film Festival, he ventured into the casino and lost moderately at roulette before remarking that "what this joint needs is a real crap game." With an eye toward broadening their appeal to American tourists, the management visited Reno and imported both tables and games supervisors who instructed the croupiers in the arts of dice dealing. The presence of craps highlighted the creeping American influence on the casino, which was only natural. Moneyed German and Russian aristocrats, thanks to war and revolution, were extinct as a species, so it was natural, in the years after World War II, for SBM to increasingly cater to Americans. The marriage of Monaco's monarch, Prince Rainier III, to the American movie star

Grace Kelly in 1956 may have given impetus to the trend, but it was a natural outgrowth of changes in the world's economic balance.

Perhaps the most dramatic change to Monte Carlo in the 1950s was the purchase of a controlling share of SBM stock by shipping magnate Aristotle Onassis. Holding an extensive fortune, and sharing Prince Rainier's commitment for constant improvement of Monaco, Onassis seemed the perfect savior for SBM, which was once again teetering near the brink of bankruptcy. Under his absentee ownership (he was perfectly content to leave the details of SBM's operation to others) and the guidance of the prince, Monaco continued to change with the times. This was not to everyone's liking. James Bond author Ian Fleming lamented the passing of the Russian Grand Dukes, English dandies, French actresses, and Indian maharajas who had once graced Monte Carlo; he found no romance in the clanging of the slot machines or vigorous dice shooting that had replaced the stately plunging at *trente-et-quarante*. The Onassis era ended in 1966, when Prince Rainier, who was frustrated by the shipping magnate's increasing opposition to new development, orchestrated his ouster as SBM chief.

The new management, hand-picked by the prince, would pursue an ambitious program of modernization, but the casino had become but a minor part of Monaco and, with the rise of Las Vegas, Monte Carlo lost its claim to be the world's leading gambling resort. Still, more than 500,000 visitors a year, chiefly French and Italians (with healthy numbers of Americans and British), came to Monaco through the 1970s, and most of them made at least a perfunctory bet at the tables.

By the 1980s, skyscrapers crowded the whole of the principality, whose economy became increasingly dominated by financial services. Monaco's lack of income taxes and low business taxes made it a popular tax haven for both wealthy retirees and corporations. By 1988, only 4 percent of the government's income came directly from gambling. The principality had come far since the days of Charles III, thanks in large part to the vision of Francois Blanc and the insatiable appetite for gambling in the Victorian age.

4

Baiting John Bull

British Casinos, 1700-1914

A British Bath

The spa craze wasn't confined to the Continent. Many Englishmen and women, worn out by the cares of daily life, chose to recuperate in health spas. A successful health resort in the 18th century absolutely needed one thing: a medicinal hot spring. The Ancient Romans had recognized the therapeutic value of such springs, and starting in the 16th century, Europeans rediscovered them.

Today hot water seems a poor reason to plan a vacation, but in the long cold years before the invention of the Jacuzzi, hot springs offered the fashionably unwell a place to gain some respite from their ailments. The springs attracted wealthy guests with plenty of money, too much spare time, and a pathological dread of boredom. Musicians, entertainers, and professional gamblers flocked to hot springs, eager to help those "seeking the cure" ward off tedium.

There were several notable watering holes in England. One of these, Epsom, endured as a health resort long enough to give its name to "Epsom salts" (magnesium sulfate), from minerals found in its therapeutic waters. Another, Tunbridge Wells, began with the discovery of a hot spring in 1606, and it still flourishes as a resort (with golfing and horseback riding now the advertised attractions). In its early heyday in the 17th and 18th centuries, gaming rooms provided an integral part of the amusements, and helped Tunbridge Wells to become a leading winter destination.

For much of the 18th century, Bath, located in southwest England near the Welsh border, was the most fashionable spa in England, drawing visitors from as far as the Continent. First venerated by the Celts, the town's medicinal springs became the center of a complex of baths and temples under the Roman occupation, as the hot baths were a welcome anodyne to the harsh climate. Even after the Romans abandoned Britain, the hot springs continued to flow and the town's libertine reputation was immortalized in the 14th century by Geoffrey Chaucer's Wife of Bath. After centuries of decline, the town began a revival in the 16th century, and in the next century the town's growth slowly continued.

With the Restoration, the royal court periodically began coming to Bath for recreation; with them they brought increased attention and prestige for the resort. By the start of Queen Anne's reign in 1702, Bath had become a regular summer destination for the royal train. Still, the resort was far from elegant. Townspeople commonly threw their refuse, including carrion from butcher shops, into the street, where they turned their pigs loose to feed and root. Rules of decorum barely contained the anarchy of the place: those who wished danced until morning, men wearing boots and women their aprons (much to the disgrace of more genteel visitors), smoking was permitted indoors, and fervid gamblers played cards until they collapsed from exhaustion. A visitor described the town in 1702 as mean and contemptible, lacking both elegant buildings and open streets.

The chief Bath amusements were dancing and gambling. Originally held outdoors, the dances were moved inside under patronage of the Duke of Beaufort, who also authorized gambling in the town hall. The supervision of both diversions fell to the office of the Master of Ceremonies, a figure without real authority or compensation who was, nevertheless, expected to somehow marshal the townspeople and shepherd the visitors.

Richard "Beau" Nash reigned as master of ceremonies during Bath's glory years. Nash, born to a distinguished but impecunious family, had failed to distinguish himself during a year at Oxford, a stint as an ensign in the Guards, or as a law student. His heart lay in fashionable dressing, fast living, and persistent romancing. He claimed to support himself through his gambling winnings, but rumors persisted that he augmented this income by taking purses on the moonlit highways, until he finally revealed the truth—that he was in fact secretly receiving an allowance from a paramour. At times, Nash's need for money pressed him to accept embarrassing wagers: once, his friends, for unknown stakes, successfully goaded him into riding naked through a village astride a cow.

Despite his erratic income, Nash gained distinction in 1695 as the "master of revels," or social director, of a pageant celebrating William III's sole accession to the throne. Though a great success, it hardly relieved his financial embarrassment, and he cast about for a career that would combine his patrician instincts (his friends had nicknamed him "the Count") with his love for gambling, dancing, and extravagant living. Following the annual royal train to Bath in the summer of 1705 in search of gambling action, he soon found his calling. Over the seven-week season that attended Queen Anne's residence in town, Nash prospered at the tables, winning over one hundred pounds a week. Before the season was up Captain Webster, the reigning Master of Ceremonies, sensing Nash's abilities, had tapped him to serve as his chief of staff. In this capacity Nash supervised construction of a pump room, which would permit indoor appreciation of Bath's waters, kept a handle on the gaming tables, and chaperoned the nightly dances.

Webster cut quite a figure wearing a square-cut coat, a large neckerchief tied in a bow, and dark breeches stuffed into his boots, which, while dancing, he would stomp upon the floor as if crushing his enemies. A professional gambler inordinately fond of spirits, Webster had his share of enemies. One evening, a dispute over a hand of cards, fueled by liquor, escalated into hostilities. Both men wore swords, as was customary then at Bath, and honor demanded that they settle the contretemps with a duel. Meeting in the Grove, a space usually devoted to outdoor bowling (for stakes, of course), the two fatally confronted each other: Webster, run through with his adversary's sword, breathed his last on the Grove.

Chosen by the Corporation of Bath to succeed the fallen Webster, Nash immediately extended the improvements begun by his predecessor. Perhaps mindful of Captain Webster's final quarrel, his first act as master of ceremonies was to ban the wearing of swords, as they not only presented a very real danger of violence, but also snagged and tore the ladies' overabundant dresses. With no real power to

Beau Nash, more than anyone else, was responsible for the rise of Bath in the early 18th century as a gambling resort.

enforce his edicts, he smartly drafted a decree stating that only those not entitled to wear swords elsewhere could wear them at Bath. The nobility (entitled to wear swords throughout the kingdom), not wishing to appear common, immediately gave up swords, while the middle classes, wishing to emulate the true aristocrats, abandoned any pretensions towards carrying them. Slyly manipulating social conventions would become a hallmark of Nash's rule at Bath.

Bath was well served by Nash's sensibilities and his egotism. Establishing Bath as the premier resort in England became his obsession, for only in doing this could he cement his own reputation. So he began immediate reforms. Captain Webster had replaced the resident band—actually a fiddler and clarinetist—with a five-piece local ensemble, a considerable improvement. Nash fired the locals and installed a troupe of seven London musicians. The new orches-

An illustration of Bath's Pump Room, where visitors enjoyed the healthy waters before getting to the serious business of gambling.

tra played outdoors at the Grove and baths during the day, and indoors at the town hall at night. To pay for the upgrade, he levied a one-guinea "music subscription" on all guests.

Nash also mandated improvements in accommodations (the lodging houses were notoriously mangy and ridiculously expensive), introduced a second season from March to June, improved the roads, and got a Parliamentary decree that let him institute a night watch and clean up the filthy streets. In 1708, he encouraged Thomas Harrison's construction of the Assembly House, a space in which visitors might play cards, dance, and take refreshments. He financed the building by combining its subscription charge with that of the orchestra: for two guineas, each family entering Bath got three tickets to balls held at the Assembly House. Wealthy visitors, happy to have a place where they could enjoy continuous entertainment, willingly paid Nash's subscriptions, and Bath became England's finest resort within three years of Nash's accession.

Life at Bath revolved around the waters, gambling, and dancing. Most visitors began their day at the Pump Room where they could watch the bathers below while slowly drinking three glasses of warm mineral water. In the baths, people of both sexes frolicked naked next to the truly infirm and diseased, while rambunctious on-lookers sometimes flung dogs, cats, and other people into the steaming waters. At Harrison's Assembly House, visitors enjoyed elegant strolls in a tree-shaded garden, endless rounds of dancing the minuet, and light refreshments. Harrison eventually charged such high fees for the use of his Assembly House that, in 1728, Nash countenanced the construction of a rival assembly room by Humphrey Thayer. Together, Thayer's and Harrison's houses were known as the Lower Rooms (a pair of Upper Rooms opened later), where Nash invited all those in Bath to join him for daily rounds of entertainment. Additional teas and parties were held in private lodgings, and refreshments offered in coffee houses.

Bath drew an interesting mix of the legitimately ill, bored aristocrats, upwardly-mobile professionals, young girls and widows looking for husbands, handsome fortune hunters seeking moneyed women, and all manner of dealers in amusements. In between all of the parties, dances, teas, and concert breakfasts, visitors to Bath found ample time for gambling. Those interested in striking a quick fortune favored hazard and basset, while those pursuing conversation and leisurely play enjoyed whist. Gambling was everywhere, from raffles held in shops, to bets on horseracing, bowling, and prizefighting.

For decades, Bath's popularity grew, as Nash held court like a divinely appointed sovereign. He even assumed the title of master of ceremonies at the rival spa resort Tunbridge Wells, and ran it as an off-season adjunct to Bath. But a growing national frustration with gambling spelled doom for the resort. In 1739, Parliament moved to abolish gambling by passing a law that forbade the most popular games, all of which were played at Bath: faro, basset, ace of hearts (a roulette precursor), and hazard. Notably, these were all mercantile games (although hazard could be played as a social or ahouse-banked game). Bath's gamblers scurried to substitute other games, such as passage and the roulette ancestor roly-poly, but in the next year Parliament passed an even more stringent law, banning passage, roly-poly, and "any other instrument, engine, or device in the nature of dice having one or more figures or numbers thereon" used for betting.

Further attempts to circumvent the law included the modification of roly-poly into E/O, in which players only guessed whether a ball would fall into a slot marked even or odd, but in 1745 Parliament added this game to the codex of forbidden pleasures and declared that anyone, whether a proprietor or player, connected to a gambling house would be subject to the law. After this, public mercantile gambling ceased. Social games like whist continued to be played in the Lower Rooms, and in private rooms card and dice games, often crooked, continued, but Bath began to decline. Nash, it was discovered, had for years received a portion of the profits from gambling operators at both Bath and Tunbridge Wells, something he had deliberately concealed (in fact, he had disingenuously bemoaned his own losses at the tables). In his old age, he struggled to maintain his once-opulent lifestyle, but with the collapse of gambling he was left in dignified poverty. Behind his back, gossipers mocked him as an aging fool, and two members of White's Club in London went so far as to lay bets on who would die first, Nash or an elderly actor named Cibber (Nash had a final triumph as both bettors committed suicide before either Nash or Cibber shuffled off their mortal coil). Nash finally died on February 12, 1761, at the age of eighty-six, having presided over the glory and decline of his beloved Bath.

Gambling still continued, both in private and on horse races, in the latter part of the 18th century. Nevertheless, Bath's fortunes continued to decline, as a class of newly rich arrivistes disturbed the generations of habit established by the old nobility. King George IV discovered the new fashion of sea bathing and made Brighton the new popular resort. The era of pan-European tranquility augured by the Congress of Vienna in 1815 allowed the British to travel freely throughout the Continent. With the unfolding of the 19th century, moneyed British vacationers sought out the Alps, the Rhine, and the Riviera, all of which boasted thriving gambling and health resorts.

London Gambling Houses

Losing their American empire didn't stop the Brits from gambling. In London, a city of nearly one million in the 18th century, cards and dice were played literally on every corner. Thousands of ordinaries where men gambled assiduously after dinner each night could be found throughout the city. As a consequence, ordinaries became notorious haunts for loud gossip and fraudulent gambling. Specialized gaming houses competed with ordinaries by offering no-nonsense mercantile games.

In 1731, *Gentleman's Magazine* conducted a survey of gaming houses specializing in faro (derided as a "cheating game") that enumerated no less than eighteen classes of employees, yielding the impression that the hells consistently won enough to support such specialization. The commissioner, one of the proprietors, audited the books and supervised the director, who actually ran the gaming room. Operators dealt faro, while croupiers raked in the chips. Puffs and squibs (shills) were given money to play and thus encourage others, under the watchful eye of a clerk. An army of ushers, waiters, and porters catered to the gamblers' needs. Outside, lookouts and runners helped warn against police invasion; in the event they were unsuccessful, most houses retained lawyers, bail, and affadavit men. Players clearly entered at their own risk: many houses retained a captain, whose job was "to fight any gentleman who might be peevish about losing his money," a dunner, who recovered money lost at play, and "ruffians, bravos, and assassins," whose responsibilities can only be imagined.

These clubs offered credit and operated in constant fear of the police, necessitating several additional employees and making them even less apt to give players an honest chance—it would have been impossible to support this army of employees on the slim proceeds guaranteed by the honest house advantage. As the predations of the gaming houses grew more persistent, the public became agitated against them. The Grub Street Journal in 1736 printed a letter warning against puffs who induced new arrivals to London into gambling at crooked houses. Many gaming houses soon closed.

With the decline of the gaming houses, play migrated to taverns and coffeehouses, presumably more refined and intellectually stimulating establishments. In 1740s, as reflected in the burst of anti-gambling legislation that had ended serious gambling at Bath, open gambling came under attack, and urban gambling survived only where it could find protective cover. Coffee houses and chocolate houses, their close cousins, fit the bill perfectly.

Coffee and chocolate houses of this time were more than places to grab quick refreshment or meet for a safe first date. At least two thousand of them could be found in London in the early 18th century, and each was the gathering place for a particular trade, profession, class, party, or nationality. Whigs and Tories, Scotsmen and Frenchmen, insurers and stockjobbers, all had their own coffee house. Once a coffee house established itself with a sufficient number of like-minded customers, it was a small step to turn the place into a club by instituting a membership charge and barring all outsiders. In addition to providing a fine place for jolly fraternization, it also provided a legitimate cover for clandestine gambling among members. The first of these, White's, opened in 1697 on St. James's Street, followed by The Cocoa Tree (just a few doors down) in 1746. In the 1760s, a host of new clubs opened nearby, leading the statesman and author Sir George Otto Trevelyan to liken St. James's Street to one vast casino.

Though no club existed solely as a gambling house, some were better known for gambling than others. In the late 18th century, White's, Almack's (which became Brooke's in the 1760s), Graham's and the Cocoa-Tree Club (all originally chocolate houses) were the most notorious for their gambling. In general, upper-class gambling clubs predominated in and around St. James's Street and Piccadilly in the West End. White's in particular was infamous: faro and hazard could be played there into the late hours. Professional gamblers, provided they were not proven cheats, were happily admitted. Players who indulged in social games like chess, checkers, and backgammon, had to pay a small fee to the club; such fees remained common in houses allowing social gambling. The club's members bet on more than just cards and dice: in the official betting book decades of wagers on everything from birth to death were memorialized. Because of its gambling, White's acquired something of a bad reputation, and was believed to be the haunt of highwaymen, waiting patiently for the night's big winner to leave so that they could harvest his winnings.

According to legend, White's was the birthplace of one of the most widely traveled of England's culinary creations in 1765, when John Montagu, the Fourth Earl of Sandwich, gambled for over twenty-four hours straight. Unable to tear himself from the table for dinner, he commanded a waiter to bring him a piece of meat between two slices of bread, thus letting him derive nourishment to continue playing without leaving the table or sacrificing the cards for utensils. Taking the earl's example, other players began asking for "the same as Sandwich."

Montagu's gambling is well-documented—Horace Walpole wrote that, when out hunting, he brought dice so that he and his companion, the Duke of Cumberland, might throw hazard. The earl himself ambiguously blamed his poor finances on "indiscretions," which certainly might include overheavy gambling. Some dispute whether the famous gambler Montagu first conceived the idea for the quick meal at the gaming table or at his desk, or if he simply emulated other gamblers in supping on bread and meat. In any case, the sandwich soon took on the name of its most famous patron.

Club members had more to worry about than just how to best stuff their faces without soiling their cards. The rules of Almack's, a club second only to White's as a gambling roost, reveal much about the clubs. Members were not permitted to gamble in the eating room, with the exception of flipping a coin to determine who paid the bill. Players also had to keep the table minimum on the table while gambling. The club itself did not provide credit, but moneylenders always lurked nearby, eager to help plungers chase their losses. Though technically illegal, these clubs ran without fear of police intervention, largely because of the political importance of their members.

The explosion of new clubs in the late 18th century inspired deep suspicion. The *Times* described, in 1793, the "evil" of West End clubs in great detail. According to the account, some posh clubs existed primarily to lure and swindle young men of fortune. First, the houses plied their dupes with a fine dinner and plentiful wine, gratis. After losing all of their cash, reluctant gamblers were induced into losing even further on credit, which the fine young chaps usually honored rather than risk a scandal.

Even high-toned clubs offering honest games could drive their players into bankruptcy by the mere nature of mercantile gambling, which steadily leached the house percentage away from players.

"Low hells," meaner houses with no membership requirements and low minimums, were an even dodgier affair: if a player won fairly, he might or might not be paid. One magazine estimated that, in the early 19th century, about thirty hells continuously operated throughout London. These were not the elegantly furnished clubs of the West End; located in obscure corners of the city, with a sham business operated as a front, these hells at night accommodated up to fifty players a night, each desperately playing hazard. These hells required stealth and cunning to remain open, in the absence of the political influence of clubs of higher rank.

Many lower gambling houses were, like their high-toned cousins, bust-out joints that lured in fresh suckers and cheated them as a matter of course. In addition, a veritable fraternity of crooked gamesters, known variously as rooks, sharps, sharpers, blacklegs, Greeks, and gripes operated throughout all levels of society. The sharpers were most typically well-born men with the benefit of a genteel education and an unctuous manner that allowed them to fleece recent acquaintances at cards, dice, billiards, or bowling with equal facility.

Curiously, many gentlemen preferred the risks of playing with sharpers. Lord Chesterfield explained that when he won from sharpers they immediately settled their debts, while gentlemen offered nothing more than genteel apologies and empty promises to pay. But according to their critics, these sharpers were hardly sporting blokes. They profited from the weakness of others, and in contrast to the insouciance of the gaming house maintained a strict sobriety: as "animal food" apparently dimmed the calculating faculties, they fed "chiefly on milk and vegetables." One contemporary writer described them in Mephistophelean terms:

> As profit, not pleasure, was the aim of these knights of darkness, they lay concealed under all shapes and disguises, and followed up their game with all wariness and discretion. Like wise traders, they made it the business of their lives to excel in their calling.
>
> For this end they studied the secret mysteries of their art by night and by day; they improved on the scientific schemes of their profound master, Hoyle, and on his deep doctrines and calculations of chances. They became skillful without a rival

where skill was necessary, and fraudulent without conscience where fraud was safe and advantageous; and while fortune or chance appeared to direct everything, they practiced num-berless devices by which they insured [sic] her ultimate fa-vors to themselves.

This army of darkness used numerous techniques, from altered dice and marked cards to collaborative play and deceptive dealing. De-spite centuries of cautions against them and published exposes of their disguises and deceptions, there was never any shortage of gull-ible victims.

Gambling for profit appealed to both sexes. Well-off women with no other income sometimes allowed their houses to be turned into gambling houses. The two best known at the end of the 18th century, Lady Archer and Lady Buckinghamshire, were only the most prom-inent of a circle of "Faro Ladies" who owned banks in private homes. Buckinghamshire was known for sleeping with a small collection of weapons to protect her bank. Though these ladies claimed their aristocratic birth gave them license to run gambling operations as they saw fit, they were occasionally subject to police harassment and frequently the target of public ridicule—Archer apparently enjoyed makeup a little too much, and after a false report of her death had been dismissed, the Morning Post whimsically noted that London's makeup artists and perfumers were rejoicing.

This ridicule characterized the shift in public opinion against mercantile gambling, signaled by increasingly prominent raids on gambling houses in the late 1790s. In 1795, the *Times* reported that young women no longer played faro, and did not emulate their mothers in seeking to cheat young men. But two years later, the same newspaper noted that students at leading boarding schools now learned whist and casino (like whist, a four-player social game that could, in a pinch, be played by only two or three) as a matter of course. Though mercantile gambling had apparently declined, at least among feminine society, social gambling continued unabated. As in France during the early part of the century, gambling domi-nated even dancing; a gentleman asking a young lady to dance at a ball was promised a terpsichorean whirl only after he had played two rubbers (best of three sets) of casino.

Even among men, faro play dwindled in early 19ᵗʰ century England, though hazard's popularity continued unchecked. Macao, a single-card version of baccarat, enjoyed a brief surge in popularity. One Piccadilly house, Waitters on The Street, was for a time entirely given over to it. One writer estimated that three-quarters of the club's members were ruined by the game. Although it was the favored haunt of many luminaries, it lasted only twelve years before being taken over by a band of blacklegs (professional gambling cheats) and operated as a "bust-out" joint. In other clubs whist, played for high stakes, became increasingly prominent, a harbinger of the soon-to-be universal spread of that game.

Crockford's Sets the Standard

Mercantile gambling, which had diminished early in the 19ᵗʰ century, surged back before mounting pressures against it drove it underground again at mid-century. According to contemporary observers, one man stood responsible for the sudden increase in gambling: William Crockford. Born to modest circumstance, Crockford started his career as a fishmonger but soon profited more from his betting at clubs and the turf. He acquired a share in Wattier's Club, then at an address near Almack's on King Street. A hazard club in which he owned a share on Piccadilly was discovered to use false dice, and Crockford hastily settled with the offended parties out of court. He incessantly quarreled with his partners and, at the age of fifty-one, sought in 1826 to build his own gambling palace on St. James's Street. Already a wealthy and infamous man about town, and despite his humble roots (he always spoke with a thick Cockney accent and mastered only the rudiments of spelling) was both envied and feared.

Construction of the house at 50 St. James's Street caused considerable disruption along the thoroughfare, but when it opened in 1828, it was immediately acclaimed as an astonishingly lavish palace to chance. The house's decorations alone cost 100,000 pounds. Visitors entered a stately vestibule adorned with classical pillars and a domed stained-glass ceiling, from whence they could enter a dining room that rivaled "the most lordly mansion," visit the elegant drawing room, or enter the holy of holies, the handsomely-furnished play

Visitors arrive at Crockford's, seen here in an illustration of its 1830s glory days.

room, dominated by the oval hazard table, the heart of the club. There, they sat in comfortable chairs and, using small hand-rakes, wagered chips valued from one to two hundred pounds.

"Who," one diarist noted during the 1830s, "that ever entered that dangerous little room can ever forget the large green table with the croupiers...with their suave manners, sleek appearance, stiff, white neckcloths, and the almost miraculous ease with which they swept away the money of the unfortunate punters." Close by, Crockford, "snug and sly...watchful as the dragon that guarded the golden apples of the Hesperides," sat at a small writing table, from which he offered loans, settled markers, and resolved all disputes. For those interested in more primal sport, the basement sported a cockfighting pit close to the entrance of a secret passage that, in the chance of a raid, would lead bettors to a safe spot in the direction of Picadilly.

Crockford spared no expense: he reportedly kept 70,000 pounds worth of wine in his cellar, which ran underneath neighboring buildings. Over one thousand wealthy and fashionable members paid Crockford's annual 25-pound dues. Membership bought the low-cost gourmet meals prepared by Louis Eustache Ude, Crockford's virtuoso French chef, a chief attraction of the club. Visiting foreigners "of distinction" were permitted into the club as a courtesy. In the gaming room, hazard and whist prevailed, with Crockford making most of his money on the former, which he banked. Dice play was so heavy that the club reportedly played through 2000 pounds worth of the cubes a year. All the while Crockford vigilantly managed the game and scrupulously granted credit—and collected the inevitable debts. Having the poshest house on St. James's, Crockford's attracted the members of neighboring clubs, who came for dinner but obligingly stayed to play hazard. Within a few years, Crockford had earned 1.2 million pounds and inspired scores of less lavish imitators, and as his club waxed wealthy, "general gaming houses" proliferated throughout the city.

After twelve years of necessarily long hours and the stresses attendant upon the management of a gambling house, Crockford decided to retire. Though he had been able to shield himself from prosecution by exploiting the wealth and influence of his clients, he was now sixty-five years old and eager to give up the hectic life of a gaming house manager. Two former employees took over the club, and though Crockford avowedly surrendered all interest, it is likely that he still maintained a stake in the club that bore his name. With the change in operation came lower table limits and a noticeable decline in service.

Crockford had gotten out just in time. In the 1840s, public agitation against the club and its offspring began to mount. In 1844, a Select Committee of the Commons investigated gambling. At these hearings, members of parliament excoriated police for allowing gaming houses to run unmolested, and the commissioner of police lamented the stealth with which operators evaded raids, making prosecutions difficult. Crockford himself testified before the committee and revealed little, carrying his secrets to the grave; he died almost immediately after his appearance, at the age of 68. As the Committee was concluding its inquiry, the suddenly vigilant police raided seventeen gaming houses in and around St. James's, but did not approach Crockford's, perhaps out of respect for the departed gambler.

These raids marked the beginning of the end for Crockford's and its offspring. In August 1845, Parliament tightened sanctions against professional gaming houses. The public houses soon winked out of existence, though social gambling continued as before in private clubs. Crockford's struggled on for a few years before becoming a social club, then an art gallery, and finally the headquarters of the liberal Devonshire Club. Though mercantile gambling never truly vanished, an era had ended. A later poet wistfully invoked the forgotten good times:

Come and once more let us greet
The long lost pleasures of St. James's Street.

But though the hazard tables were stilled, the spirit of gambling proved to be indomitable, and play continued, though in a decidedly quieter milieu, long after the death of Crockford.

According to Hoyle

Gamblers wildly betting at clubs enjoyed quick, no-nonsense games with little subtlety or analysis. But those with a more cerebral bent desired playing cards at a more leisurely pace. For these players, there was one game that reigned supreme in the 18th and 19th centuries: Whist.

Whist developed from a game based on the Italian tarot game trionfi. Also known as ruff or trump, this game first appeared in England in the early 16th century. The English almost immediately added additional advantages, or honors, to the court cards of the trump suit, transforming the game into ruff and honors. By 1621 the game had been modified and had gained a new name: whisk, which might have derived from a ruffled piece of shoulder apparel, or from a player's admonition to her partner to remain silent. By the 1660s, its name had been altered to whist, and this new appellation stuck.

At this time, whist was considered something of a low recreation. Fashionable gentlemen confined themselves to piquet, while ladies with aristocratic pretensions played ombre or its four-sided derivation, quadrille. In George Farquhar's 1707 comedy *The Beaux Stratagem*, the city-born Mrs. Sullen sneers at "country pleasures" like smoking, drinking, and "playing at whist." Her brother, Sir Charles Freeman, likewise claims ignorance of both whist and all-fours, to which the provincial Squire Sullen snorts, "Where was this man bred?" The irony was not lost on contemporary audiences. As late as 1750, whist was a widespread pastoral recreation, played during the winter break in agriculture by bored farmers and graziers. Gambling contributed considerably to the game's excitement.

By the middle of the 18ᵗʰ century, the game had coalesced into its classic form. Four players sat around a table, with those opposite each other playing as partners. The dealer dealt thirteen cards to each player and turned up his last card, whose suit became the trump, meaning that its cards would triumph over all other. The player to his left then played a card, and other players had to literally follow suit, or play a card of the same suit. Whoever played the highest card, or a trump, out of the four players won the trick and got the right to lead to the next trick. Players unable to follow suit could either play a trump or play a plain suit. To win, a partnership couple had to score a specified number of tricks, ten in the original "long" form of the game, five in the later "short" version; losers might pay off winners after each game, or both sides might keep tally and settle up at the end of the session. In the 1730s, a group of gentlemen who played at the Crown coffeehouse elected to have at go at the previously disregarded country game of whist. Carefully analyzing the game, they found it to hold several complexities. After this, the game began to attract attention from urbane students of the cards.

Whist owes its subsequent popularity to one man, whose name, if not biography, is familiar to most casual card players: Edmund Hoyle, "according to" whom generations of rulebooks were printed. For one who has achieved such fame (two hundred years after his death, he is considered the final authority, even for games not yet invented in his lifetime), his origins are obscure. It is only certain that in the 1730s he began to study whist and, in the guise of protecting the young from the deceits of sharpers, resolved to teach it professionally. To aid his instruction, Hoyle prepared notes on the rules for play. Learning to his distress that his work was circulating throughout London without his approval or remuneration, he secured copyright for it and, in 1742, issued a book with the prolix titling endemic to his age. The title begins, A *Short Treatise on the Game of Whist, containing the Laws of the Game, and also some Rules whereby a Beginner may, with due attention to them, attain to the Playing it well,* and continues for several more sentences. Readers simply called it *Hoyle's Whist* or *Whist According to Hoyle.*

The field of "how-to" gambling books was opened by Cardano, and French instruction books appeared as early as 1647, with English translations crossing the channel in 1651. The English market for instructive gambling books exploded with the gambling boom that followed the Restoration. As early as the second edition of his *Wits Interpreter: the English Parnassus* (1662), John Cotgrave offered a chapter explaining ombre, gleek, cribbage, and picket.

The gambling boom also brought a host of lectures and pamphlets on how to avoid the wiles of sharpers. Charles Cotton subsumed some of these into his 1674 compendium of indoor and outdoor recreations, *The Compleat Gamester*, but also provided advice on billiards, an Italian variant of billiards called trucks, bowling, chess, card games (from picket to beast), backgammon, dicing, horse riding, racing, archery, and his epigone of leisure, cockfighting. Cotton's book in 1739, was merged with Richard Seymour's *The Court Gamester.*

Hoyle's book was vital to the development of whist. With the publication of his *Short Treatise*, players at last had a handy guide to

According to the author of *The Whist Table*, the game provided a leisurely pastime that didn't require heavy stakes. He wrote that "the demon of gambling shrinks abashed before the good genius of Whist, and feels his spirit rebuked, as it is said Mark Anthony's was by Caesar."

the game. Suddenly a literate, genteel pastime, whist became the latest sensation. Within a decade, it received courtly sanction as a royal amusement, and it became the favored recreation of the age. Hoyle was hailed as "a second Newton" and his dictates were universally accepted as authoritative. He then extended his empire by issuing books on backgammon, picket, brag, quadrille, and chess. After his 1769 death, publishers continued to offer "improved" editions of his books, and by the middle of the 19th century, his name became a generic byword for encyclopedic instructive gambling books.

Whist continued to evolve after Hoyle. One particularly avid school of players met at Bath, where in 1804 Thomas Matthews published a guide to whist that promised to educate the reader far better than Hoyle, who according to the author was not fit to sit with even third-rate players of the evolved game. London players also introduced innovations into the game, including the abbreviated form known as short whist, and the game spread throughout the world. Reversing the process that had attended the Restoration influx of gambling from France, the French imported whist (the first translation of Hoyle appeared in 1766), presented at Versailles much as basset had appeared in London a century earlier. From the salons Paris the game spread throughout Europe, finding enthusiastic players from Austria to Russia. British colonists and imperial officials transplanted the game into the farthest reaches of their empire, from Australia to Asia to Africa to the Americas, and their former colonists in the United States took to the game enthusiastically, at least in the more settled East; George Washington was only the most preeminent citizen to fall prey to the game's lure.

From Hoyle, writers on whist had explicitly discussed the calculation of probabilities as one of the elements of skilled play. Hoyle, benefiting from the generations of mathematical interest in probability begun with Girolamo Cardano, even wrote *An Essay towards making the Doctrine of Chances easy to those who understand vulgar Arithmetic*. As whist's popularity grew, the game became a matter of serious speculation. Around 1850, a cohort of Cambridge students systematically studied whist; they continued to meet in London after they had graduated. The Little Whist School's members devoted themselves to playing, calculating, and discussing whist in all of its variations. In 1862 "Cavendish," (an unknown enthusiast's pen name) distilled these ruminations into book form as *The Principles of Whist*. Two years later, *A Treatise on Short Whist*, appended to a new edition of John Loraine Baldwin's *Laws of Whist*, extended the "philosophical" consideration of whist, taking in all elements of the game's strategy and theory. Like the game itself, intellectual analysis of it spread throughout the world. In an age besotten with scientific advance and intellectual collation, whist emerged as the thinking man's game par excellence. In the cosmopolitan Europe of the 19th century, whist served as an international language which all cultured gentlefolk could speak.

Inspiring treatises, plays, and even a twelve-canto epic poem, whist reigned without equal in the world of 19th century card games, and would seem to have been a game for the ages. Yet today, it is nearly forgotten. Were it not for references in works still read today like *Around the World in Eighty Days*, the game might have joined Costly-Colours, Bone-Ace, and Pope Joan in the discard pile of history. But whist is really not that far gone. In the 1890s it would evolve again, becoming bridge whist; subsequent innovations created auction whist and then contract bridge. In this form, bridge became the supreme non-gambling card game of the 20th century. Though it is no longer the lackadaisical recreation of county squires or the philosophical pursuit of Cambridge scholars, whist survives in bridge, its origins as a rustic gamble nearly unremembered.

5

Star-Spangled Gamblers

The birth of American gambling

American Gambling Begins

Gambling in America predated the republic of the United States by several thousand years, and Americans fused several traditions—European, Native American, and African—into a larger gambling culture that, with advances in transportation and communications, would overspread the continent.

Most of the hundreds of tribes, bands, and societies of North America had well-developed gambling traditions before contact with Europeans. Native American cultures incorporated new games discovered through foreign contact into their existing ways of life. In the Southwest, gambling was a serious, even sacred pursuit. The Navajo played certain games in the summer and others in the winter, and considered playing a summer game in January dangerously inappropriate. The *kestice* or moccasin game was a winter game played only at night—according to local belief, any who played during the day would be instantly struck blind. To play, two sides took turns hiding a small pebble or ball in one of eight moccasins half-buried in the sand. After flipping a half-darkened chip to determine which side hid the ball first, the winners lowered a screen over the moccasins and secreted the ball in one of the moccasins. The guesser then struck a moccasin with a stick; if it contained the ball, his team took possession. If not, he was penalized a certain number of points, depending on how far off he was, and his team lost a corresponding number of counters. Special songs were sung during each round of the game, and to repeat a song in a later round was forbidden. Whichever team won all of the counters took the game and the stakes.

This game commemorated, elders said, a time when the animals of the day wished for perpetual light, while the animals of the night wanted perpetual darkness. They met at twilight to parley and decided that they should play the *kesitce* game to determine whether they sun would never rise or never set. The animals set to playing, and though each side's fortunes oscillated during the long night, neither had an advantage at dawn, so the game was considered a push: day and night continued as before. Storytellers also explained the physical characteristics of certain animals well-known to the Navajo, and touched on a theme common to Native American games: that of an eternal competition between opposites light and dark, winter and summer, female and male, etc.

Gamblers and tricksters are staples of Native American myths, and the Navajo told stories of a gambling god, Noqoilpi. According to the Navajo, the Pueblo people had built a temple to Noquilpi at Chaco Canyon (in northern New Mexico), where they constructed a huge center of multistory buildings. Though Noquilpi's story has many variations, the best-known version relates that he won all of the people of the earth and all of their possessions while playing at Chaco Canyon. Noquilpi even stole the sun's turquoise earrings, which prompted the sun to ask another god to train a Navajo man to defeat Noquilpi and return the earrings. With the help of several animals, the Navajo warrior did so. He then shot the defeated gambler god into the heavens, where he met the Carrier of the Moon, who returned him to earth, where he eventually became the God of the Mexicans.

In some versions, the gambling temple was located at Pueblo Alto, a place that many Navajos called "home of the one that wins (you) by gambling." Later archeological investigations of Pueblo Alto have indicated that it was likely a gambling center. Sitting at the juncture of five roads which stretched for hundreds of miles, it was the crux of a huge exchange network. Goods brought there were not redistributed but instead stored in a series of great houses that were otherwise unpopulated. In most pueblos, the large central plaza was used for dancing, and its floor has been compacted by the rhythms of stamping feet. But at Pueblo Alto, the main plaza had been resurfaced with clay several times, suggesting that, whatever people were doing there, they were not dancing. It is quite possible that they were gambling.

In what is now the Eastern United States, the Mound Builders, a culture who built large temples and had fairly complex societies prior to European contact, left behind chungke stones, flat polished disks with hollow centers that were either rolled or used as hoops through which stones were thrown. Travelers through the southeastern woodlands in the 17th century reported that, as a hoop and pole game, chungke was widespread. Even in the 19th century, the Creeks and Cherokees of Carolina lived in villages with large chungke yards, recessed spaces as large as three football fields surrounded by terraces. At the center stood a thirty-foot pole and target, at which players likely aimed spears or rocks. This was clearly a major spectator event.

Native Americans did not play games or bet on them merely for amusement. Gambling contests served as effective mechanism to redistribute trade goods and to encourage interaction among neighbors. Men and women of all classes gambled with seeming recklessness, according to European observers, who often missed the underlying religiosity of Native American gambling. During a marathon week-long dice game, for example, the Iroquois prayed nightly for good luck, and losers often looked for supernatural explanations—offense to a good spirit or sorcery of a bad one—to explain their bad luck.

Gambling even had a role in the Spanish conquest of the Aztecs. When Hernan Cortes arrived in 1519, Montezuma believed him to be the returning god Quetzalcoatl. Montezuma brought Cortes to a ball game, and Cortes found the game interesting enough to later send a team to his emperor in Spain. Cortes soon imprisoned Montezuma and, to keep him occupied during his five-month captivity, played totloque, a dice game played with small gold dice. The Spaniards found a passing similarity to their game of tables, or backgammon, which had been memorialized by their king Alphonso X in his 13th century *Book of the Games of Chance*. On one occasion, Montezuma noted that the Spaniard keeping score for Cortes was cheating; this would be the smallest injustice committed by the invaders against the Aztecs. Even the Spanish soldiers in attendance conceded that Montezuma was a generous winner who gave away everything he won. Unfortunately, Cortes was not so magnanimous, and when Montezuma surrendered his treasures to the Spanish, Cortes ordered the gold melted down. The soldiers, using playing cards improvised from parchment, immediately began gambling amongst themselves for their shares. Within six months, Montezuma was dead, and after finally taking his capital city of Tenochtitlan, Cortes affirmed his new power by promulgating a law that outlawed all gambling. Having won an empire, he was determined not to lose it back.

The Montezuma story reveals much about the fate of gambling among Native Americans. Though sacred gambling ceremonies did not stop the onslaught of the invaders, games allowed Native Americans to preserve many of their ritual observances. Tribes throughout North America continued playing traditional games into the late 19th century, and, borrowing European imports like playing cards, incorporated them into traditional gambling practices.

With the forced pacification of most tribes in the late 19th century, gambling often became a vehicle for cultural regeneration and a surrogate for open aggression. Among the Pawnee, the Ghost Dance revival movement of the 1890s also saw a renewed passion for traditional games; both the hoop and pole game and a traditional hand guessing game were incorporated into ceremonial dances. Even after defeat and subjugation, tribes continued to battle through the medium of gambling; before beginning a match, players would pantomime many old combat rituals, and even declared, "We've come on the warpath for the hand game." Even as settlers took over Native American lands, they could not destroy tribal cultures or erase thousands of years of gambling tradition.

Gambling on a New World

Like the Spaniards who preceded them, the first British settlers in the New World were looking for redemption, either financial or spiritual, and sometimes both. The Virginia Company, which founded a colony at Jamestown, made a series of losing gambles on its prospects in the New World. Governors railed against colonists' "bowling in the streets" while serious work remained to be done, many settlers preferred playing and gambling to work, and it was only the discovery (after the Company had lost its charter) that tobacco could be profitably marketed in Britain that the colony became a success—poetic justice for the company's director, who had delayed awarding prizes to lottery winners.

The subsequent tobacco boom hardly made Virginia less of a gamble; prices bounced from low to high and back again with astonishing volatility, and speculators in land and tobacco sought to wring a quick profit from their holdings. In such an atmosphere, gambling was omnipresent, but it was especially cherished among the new elite of tidewater Virginia: the plantation-owning gentry who styled themselves as cavaliers and relished lives filled with hearty food, elegant clothes, bold flirtation, and relentless high-stakes gambling.

In fact, gambling, whether at cards, dice, backgammon, billiards, became a hallmark of elite Virginian culture. As early as 1686, a visiting Frenchman reported that after dinner his Virginian hosts began gambling. By midnight, when the traveler's impatience was finally noticed by one of the absorbed card-players, he was advised to retire to his bed, as the game was just getting good. The next morning, the Frenchman awoke to find the gentlemen still intent at their game. Sometimes the urge to gamble was uncontrollable. After a particularly rough night playing dice in a coffeehouse (he lost 12 pounds) in November 1711 William Byrd II, one of the wealthiest planters in the colony, solemnly vowed in his diary to never lose more than 50 shillings and to "spend less time in gaming." Within two weeks, he reported a loss of 4 pounds at piquet, making no comment about his earlier pledge.

The Puritan settlers of Massachusetts Bay, despite their sanctimonious reputations, often played cards. Puritan dogma held that gambling was bad not because of anything inherently sinful or immoral in it (the Bible, after all, was shot through with lot-casting) but because it was an idle waste of time: godly men and women should, instead of chatting over cards, be preparing themselves to enter heaven's kingdom. In 1646, Massachusetts passed a law that banned gambling in public houses—the first such law in the colonies—but enforcement was lax, with few church members actually fined for gambling. But, for decades, ministers sternly reminded their flocks that to waste time at gambling was, in clergyman Increase Mather's words, "heinously sinful."

Throughout New England, colonists' ardor for fun was hardly chilled by strict Calvinist doctrine. The first Boston "ordinary" (tavern), opened in 1630, and others soon appeared throughout the region; the Connecticut government even ordered three towns to open ordinaries for the sake of travelers who were in need of entertainment. In Rhode Island, strict regulations made ordinaries subject to strict licensure and forbade both drunkenness and card and dice play, but as the 17th century progressed, the number of ordinaries increased throughout New England, and government control over them waned. Ultimately, taverns became havens for all sorts of illegal gambling games, from cards to shuffleboard. They also offered a wide variety of entertainment and leisure activities: guests ate, drank, smoked, and gambled while watching animal attractions such as trained walruses and performing pigs.

Horseracing became common in 18th century New England, but it was never as popular as in the South. Though races were not as regular as in the South, betting was just as common, albeit on a much smaller scale. Blood sports like bear-bating, dog-fighting, and cockfighting, long popular in England, never become widespread in New England, where colonists generally shunned physically violent sports. Officially, Puritan leaders discouraged competitive sports because they inevitably led to gambling. All five New England colonies passed early laws against gambling, though the penalties for breaking the law were usually slight.

Opposition to the perceived debauchery of the Restoration had hardened many Puritan souls against gambling in the late 17th century, and ministers preached sermons inveighing mightily against the sins of playing cards, but gambling refused to go away. Many towns gave out land based on lotteries, and proponents of card playing argued that it was an inexpensive form of recreation that encouraged the development of math skills and did not necessarily need to be bet upon. As a result, whist positively thrived, as college students, professionals, merchants, and even ministers began playing it. All fours, cribbage, and quadrille, a four-player version of the old favorite ombre, were also popular. Piquet, which combined the melding features of modern rummy with the trick-taking of whist, was often condemned as a purely gambling game, though it was a actually social game played among peers. Mercantile games like faro and hazard, so popular on the other side of the Atlantic, never took root.

Colonies in the Cards

Pennsylvania may have owed its very existence to gambling. Quaker William Penn founded the colony as a democratic, religiously tolerant haven after receiving a charter from King Charles II in1681. Exactly why the king would grant an unpopular, socially radical religious sect a lucrative charter to prime lands in America still remains open to debate. The answer may lie in the relationship between Sir William Penn, the young Quaker's father, and King Charles. Although he had first sided with Parliament in the Civil War, Sir William became a favorite of Charles after the Restoration, commanding the English Navy during a war with the Dutch. On his deathbed, Sir William secured a royal promise to care for his sons. It was also rumored that the inveterate gambler Charles never paid the elder Penn for a gambling debt of £16,000, and that his granting of Pennsylvania to William Penn satisfied this debt. If true, the birthplace of American liberty was the largest marker (gambling debt) payment ever.

In his "Great Law" of 1682, William Penn, perhaps unmindful of his father's success at cards, prohibited gambling and prescribed a fine or imprisonment for those who flouted the law. Quakers remained steadfast in their opposition to all gambling, but, as elsewhere, prohibition was never effective, and card-playing, horseracing, and dicing continued. Card-playing was so prevalent that, by 1765, playing cards were used as admission tickets for lectures at the College of Philadelphia. After paying tuition, a student received a playing card on which was written his name and the lectures which he was entitled to attend. Today, the registrar at the University of Pennsylvania (which the College of Philadelphia eventually became) use more sophisticated systems to monitor enrollment, but the use of playing cards as admission tickets in the 18th century demonstrates the wide acceptance of cards in Philadelphia.

Throughout all of the colonies, gambling was a common indoor recreation. As was the case among Native Americans, male and female British colonists of all social standings played cards, tossed dice, and otherwise wagered. But because the taverns and clubs that permitted gambling, were largely male preserves, most heavy betting went on among men. Backgammon was often played for high stakes, was. Billiards proved a popular tavern game and, for wealthy Americans, a showy home amusement—a man needed great wealth to afford to dedicate an entire room to the game. Consequently, home billiards tables were common among merchants and Southern plantation owners who wanted to enjoy the pleasant company a table provided and show off their wealth to friends, business relations, and rivals.

Some card-playing colonists simply imitated the prevailing British fashions. Thus whist enjoyed a great popularity in 18th century colonial British North America. Many non-English games also flourished. Euchre, which may have entered North America through French Louisiana, became a perennial favorite. This four-player trick-based game was the first to feature the American innovation of the joker (two wild cards included with each deck), and it became popular throughout the United States, particularly the north and Midwest, and Canada. Another French game, piquet, was just as popular among less refined gamblers in all the colonies as it was in New England. Mercantile games seem to be nearly unknown in taverns, and there were, as yet, no specialized "gambling houses," though play may have commenced at private clubs in imitation of those in the West End.

In general, thanks to wide-open play in taverns, public gambling was available to all men regardless of background. Taverns catering to apprentices, indentured servants, and slaves gave these men a chance for recreation, and black Americans gambled just as did whites, though in the South they usually gambled separately. Outside of moralizing laws seeking to banish games from the colonies as idle frivolities, there was little opposition to gambling as such, although some colonies passed laws forbidding Sunday play or cheating, fighting, and other offenses related to the gaming table. Cockfighting was just as widespread as tavern gaming, particularly in the South, and remained popular with less wealthy Americans through the 18th century.

Revolutionary Gamblers

The American Revolution was a milestone event in human history. In 1765, the Stamp Act had galvanized colonial opposition to British rule and provided a flashpoint for growing pro-independence sentiment. The act was not a tax on stamps, but rather required the purchase of government stamps to make various documents official, from commercial contracts to newspapers. Among the items needing a stamp were playing cards, which required a one-shilling stamp, and dice, which were to carry a ten-shilling stamp. Colonists, enraged by this intrusion on their liberty, did not care that playing cards had long carried a royal tax stamp in Britain. The Stamp Act was quickly repealed after massive public disturbances. The tax on gambling was hardly the most onerous levy in the Act (the stamp on newspapers and legal papers effectively agitated influential colonial publishers and lawyers), but it was yet another reminder of the power that the crown held over its American subjects.

During the Revolutionary War, soldiers on both sides gambled. The orderly book of the British general Sir William Howe, who oversaw the siege of Boston in 1775 and 1776, contained the following communication, dated July 8, 1775: "Some soldiers of the different corps have observed gaming. The commissioned and non-commissioned officers are desired to be attentive that for the future nothing of this sort happens among the men. Such instances of idleness and depravity are always (and particularly at this time) to be prevented and suppressed." These orders, however, did not curb the gambling habits of the soldiers or officers. Instead, in cities occupied by the British, military men had a ball—literally—drinking, dancing, gambling, and flirting with sympathetic Loyalist women. Tavern owners allowed British soldiers to freely play cards, and horse races were a popular entertainment.

On the other side of the lines, General George Washington had similar concerns about gambling in his ranks. Washington often said that gambling was "the child of avarice, the brother of iniquity and the father of mischief." But he got himself into a fair share of mischief. From the years 1772 to 1775, he kept detailed records of his record at the card table. Though he lost more games than he won, he knew when to fold 'em—he never lost more than six pounds in one day, but took home more than thirteen pounds from an Annapolis card game in October 1772. Washington's gambling strategy carried over to the battlefield: though he lost more battles than he won, British commander Lord Cornwallis surrendered his sword to Washington at Yorktown, and not vice versa.

Despite his fondness for gambling (he recorded gambling, on average once every two weeks) he demanded that his troops put down their cards for the good of the nation. "All officers, non-commissioned officers, and soldiers," he ordered in 1776, "are positively forbid playing at cards, or other games of chance. At this time of public distress, men may find enough to do, in the service of their God and their country, without abandoning themselves to vice and immorality." But this missal was no more effective than General Howe's and the following year he jogged his troops' memories by gravely informing them that all forms of gaming were expressly forbidden, "as being the foundation of evil, and the cause of many a brave and gallant officer's ruin." But all need not be toil: "Games of exercise, for amusement, may not only be permitted, but encouraged." Still, most officers and soldiers found ample exercise and amusement in their cards.

When they were not debating matters of state, delegates to the Continental Congress often gambled. Thomas Jefferson, during the two June weeks he spent writing a draft of the Declaration of Independence, found time to play a little. He recorded winning and losing in moderation at backgammon, cross and pile (heads or tails), lotto, and cards during the time. Jefferson held it to be a self-evident truth that men like himself, working hard to protect the liberty of their country, deserved some time to roll dice, flip coins, and play cards. In this way, at least, he had much in common with his British brethren across the Atlantic.

Gambling in the New Republic

The British army band may have played "The World Turned Upside Down" as General Cornwallis surrendered to the Continentals at Yorktown in 1781, but the establishment of the new United States of America did not mean quick changes in its citizens' gambling habits. Although the king's rule had been thrown off, Americans continued to use traditional cards depicting royalty in their games.

During the 1790s, neither plague nor the threat of eternal damnation could tear city-dwellers from their cards. In 1793 a yellow fever epidemic struck Philadelphia, killing 5000 people (about 10 percent of the population); during the course of the decade, repeated outbreaks in Philadelphia and New York City were equally disastrous. Those who could, fled for the safety of the countryside. Ministers remaining in the cities thundered from their pulpits that the yellow fever was an angry God's retribution on Sabbath-breaking, high-living sinners, and they implored the sporting masses to give up gambling and dissolution. Their pleas fell on deaf ears, as tavern-goers began to bet on comparative mortality rates: Philadelphians bet that a third more New Yorkers would be carried off by the disease, while in New York bettors wagered on the opposite proposition. Even a devastating plague could become an excuse for a friendly bet in the young republic.

Gambling was equally difficult to contain on the frontier, which pushed steadily westward from the end of the Revolutionary War. Settlers were eager for any amusement; gambling was a common diversion, particularly cards (loo, brag, and all fours in the earliest days), dice, and horse racing. Frontier Tennessee, Kentucky, Ohio, and western New York were notorious for their gambling, which provided a rare chance for inhabitants of far-flung farms to congregate. Horse races and cockfights were held on public holidays or became an excuse for a holiday of their own. Travelers often noted the ravenous gambling appetites of westerners. Inns and taverns catering to travelers gave over most of their tables, and sometime even their floors, to card games. Gambling was so rampant that one Congressman, supporting the improvement of the western transportation infrastructure, insisted that it was the only way to stem the tide of gambling. Western lands were so rich, he argued, that farmers without access to Eastern markets only worked part-time to raise enough for subsistence and spent the bulk of their time gambling. (Opening up the rivers, ironically, only increased the scope of gambling by bringing more money into the hinterlands and by permitting easier travel.)

As the market economy pushed westward, the first professional gamblers appeared. Known as blacklegs and officially reviled, people never seemed to tire of playing with them. Some states passed laws that criminalized the business of gambling, but most left the activity itself intact. Thanks to young Kentucky legislator Henry Clay's intervention, an 1804 state law "to suppress the practice of gaming" condoned social games by explicitly banning only bank games "in which one player is continually opposed to all the others." This split between social and mercantile gaming was symptomatic of the fundamental ambiguity most Americans have had towards gambling: even during the low ebb of professional mercantile games, few states dared touch the actual playing of games, something that led to the continued survival of illegal gambling organizations.

Henry Clay had good reason to keep friendly card games legal: he was one of the most renowned players of his day, winning and losing as much as $60,000 in a single night. As Clay rose to leadership as a champion of Western expansion, he claimed to like playing cards more than legislating, and, through luck, boldness, or skill, won more than he lost. Many of his fellow statesmen shared his love for cards, including Massachusetts's Daniel Webster. Clay and Webster's foil, Andrew Jackson, was no less enthusiastic a gambler. In one card game, he staked his horse against two hundred dollars and won.

Faro's importance to American gambling is largely forgotten today, but in the 19th century it was the national game. Where London clubs of the period devoted themselves to hazard and the European resorts specialized in roulette, American professional gamblers, both itinerant and in residence at gambling houses, were infamous for faro. It was so widespread on the frontier that it was called "the game that won the West." In the 1830s, a well-traveled professional dealer kept his faro layout in a mahogany box decorated with a Bengal tiger, and his chips and layout were similarly emblazoned. The tiger became a symbol of faro, as gambling houses displayed paintings of tigers, and "bucking the tiger" became a widely-known slang term for playing faro. Today, Chinese gamblers refer to slot machines as "hungry tigers" that inevitably devour the player; subconsciously, perhaps, American gamblers were saying the same thing when they bucked the tiger against a seasoned dealer.

The game had evolved from its Venetian origins. Usually, a faro dealer used two assistants. One, on his right, collected bets, paid winners, and watched the players for cheating, while the other, on his left, kept track of which cards had been played in the hand with a small abacus-like device. Between the players and dealer stood the game layout, which had spaces for each of the thirteen value cards, usually indicated by spades. To the left, the seven occupied the farthest space, and two rows of cards—eight to king on the bottom, six through ace on the top—ran from left to right.

To play, the dealer shuffled and placed the cards face-up in a dealing box. He "burned" or discarded the top card, and then began placing cards into two piles, one for the player, the other for the bank. Each draw of two cards was called a "turn," and each game consisted of 25 turns: the final card in the deck was, like the first, a dead card. Players placed their bets, either on single numbers or anyone of several combinations, after the deck had been shuffled and placed in the box. Players could also "go paroli" and parlay their winnings, as in basset; if the player's card won on its first appearance, he could

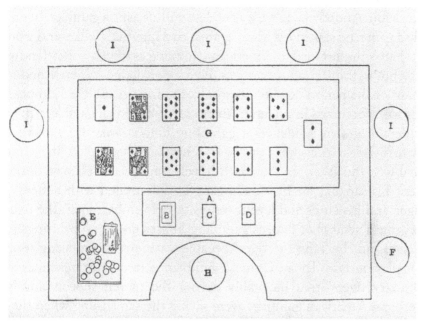

A typical faro layout, featuring *a*, the shuffling board; *b*, the faro box; *c*, the pile of dealer cards; *d*, the pile of player cards; *e*, check (chip) tray; *f*, the case keeper, who kept track of the cards in play with an abacus-like device; *g*, the layout; *h*, the dealer; *i*, the players.

let his winnings ride. When only three cards remained in the deck, players could "call the turn," or bet on their predicted order; if they guessed right, they were paid at 4 to 1. On "splits" (when two cards of the same value were played), the bank took half the wager.

There were fortunes to be made by exploiting the Southern love of faro. Elijah Skaggs, raised in the Kentucky backwoods amid card-playing, cockfighting, and horseracing, made this his life's goal. By his 21st birthday (around 1830) he was a proficient cardsharp, and could nonchalantly stack the deck, deal from the bottom, and otherwise eliminate the element of luck from the game. After winning $2000 from his family and friends, he set out for greatness.

Skaggs made an immediate impact in Nashville, where he arrived wearing a black frock coat and broadcloth suit more suited to an itinerant minister than a gambler. New acquaintances were shocked when the solemn young man produced a faro layout from his grip instead of a bible, and he soon acquired the sobriquet "the preaching faro dealer." People made jokes at his expense, but he had the last laugh: Skaggs became so proficient at faro trickery that, by the 1830s, he had traveled throughout the country playing faro and made himself a wealthy man. His only regret was that he could only cheat one sucker at a time.

Skaggs soon figured a way around this obstacle. He began training a crew of faro artists whom he dispatched in pairs across the country. He sent a member of his large extended family along with each team to keep a strict accounting of its conduct. The dealers received one fourth of all profits, after expenses, and if luck ran against them and they somehow lost their bankroll, they returned to Skaggs for replenishment and re-assignment. Skaggs's teams efficiently plucked pigeons for two decades, but eventually "Skaggs patent dealers" became notorious for dishonest play. In the late 1850s Skaggs retired from gambling and settled into a life of luxury on a plantation purchased with his faro profits. But his inopportune investment of most of his fortune in Confederate bonds during the Civil War impoverished him. He would die destitute in Texas in 1870, just rewards, perhaps, for his decades of faro deceit.

Skaggs's organization was one of the earliest professional gambling combines, though it was not the only one. As the American economy became increasingly sophisticated, gambling houses, often modeled on the West End clubs of London, began to appear. Gambling still flourished in inns and taverns, but the new gambling houses provided the most visible places to gamble in the growing cities, though they did so while remaining legally invisible. Almost always operating in contravention to the law, they only continued to run with the acquiescence of the authorities, usually purchased outright with cash.

These houses appeared in major Southern cities like New Orleans, Charleston, and Mobile by the 1810s, and quickly spread northward. Within a few years, they could be found in New York and especially Washington, DC. Though professional gamblers, newly arrived from Charleston, had filtered among the lobbyists and politicos crowding the new capital as early as 1800, the first true gambling houses did not appear until the Era of Good Feelings, those balmy years after the War of 1812 when party divisions temporarily dissolved. Congressmen were among the best customers of the dozen or so houses that by 1825 lined northern Pennsylvania Avenue and offered faro, brag, ecarte, and all-fours. Often, during race meets, Congress lacked the quorum to conduct its business, and when in session many legislators shamelessly bet on elections. While serving as a senator in 1826, future president Martin Van Buren wagered $10,000 and his evening clothes on one contest.

Although gambling was common in the nation's capital, it could still stir up a scandal. The alleged purchase of "gambling equipment" with public funds added fire to the first truly contentious presidential elections, those of 1828. After he moved into the White House in 1825, new President John Quincy Adams bought second-hand billiard table to entertain guests. After he had it re-upholstered, and bought a new set of balls and cues, controversy erupted. Adams had barely triumphed over Andrew Jackson, despite having fewer popular and electoral votes: the contest was decided in the Congress, where Jacksonians charged that a "corrupt bargain" between Adams and Henry Clay had given the presidency to the New Englander. Jackson supporters formed the Democratic Party and almost immediately began campaigning again for "Old Hickory." Their eyes glittered at the prospect of a scandal in the White House.

When an inventory of expenses at the White House was published the next year, Jacksonians eagerly publicized the erroneous "fact" that public funds had been spent to buy the billiard table. A Jackson supporter in Congress decried the use of tax money to buy "gaming tables and gambling equipment" and expressed dismay at the specter of gambling in the White House, declaring that it would "shock and alarm the religious, the moral, and reflecting part of the community." Lambasting Adams for encouraging dissolute gambling was a curious tactic; the earthy Jackson was notoriously "adept at billiards, cards, dice, horse-racing, cockfighting, and tavern brawls," as Adams loyalists reminded the public, and backwoods Jackson supporters had previously mocked Adams as an effete puritan.

Adams's friends did not help the cause when they argued that, as the aristocratic diplomats of Europe enjoyed billiards, it was a virtual necessity for the nation's leader. Jackson partisans responded by accusing Adams of royal extravagance. Adams himself only clarified "Billardsgate" a year later, when he finally issued a public statement averring that he did not gamble at the table and had purchased it with his own money. Still, the matter kicked off one of the dirtiest campaigns in American history, as Adams supporters counterattacked by branding Jackson a murderer and both he and his wife adulterers. Jackson would go on to trounce Adams in the election of 1828.

Despite the furor over Adams' alleged purchase of gambling equipment, gambling remained incredibly popular, even at the highest levels. An author writing in the 1890s claimed that every president since Van Buren (who was elected in 1836), with the exception of Rutherford B. Hayes, was a known poker player. Members of Congress were similarly fond of cards, and a culture of gambling predominated in Washington. The most famous Washington gambling house was opened in 1832 by Edward Pendleton, a suave, elegant, generous Virginian who sometimes gave back in the form of a consolation loan what he had swindled at the faro table. Pendleton opened his house, which he called the Palace of Fortune on Pennsylvania Avenue near 14th Street; faro players nicknamed it the Hall of the Bleeding Heart.

Like Crockford's house on St. James's Street (which was already booming when Pendleton opened his doors), Pendelton's was decorated with an eye towards lavish detail, stocked with the finest wines, and supplied with victuals by an accomplished chef. Presidents, cabinet members, senators, representatives, editors, and army officers all soon found themselves smoking, drinking, and gambling at the Hall of the Bleeding Heart.

The Hall became a haunt of lobbyists, not because they loved to gamble, but because they knew that members of Congress did. When congressmen needed a quick loan to continue playing, these lobbyists were eager to help out; favorable votes meant that the IOUs could be forgotten. Pendleton himself was a sought-after lobbyist, and many a government official who took the time to advocate a bill on his behalf was rewarded with a complimentary night at the faro table.

But Pendleton's was above all else a gambling house—it employed an army of ropers who brought in prospects. Dealers were only as honest as their players were influential; presidential candidates and cabinet members were allowed to test their luck fairly, but obscure congressmen found themselves on the losing end more often than not as Pendleton instructed his dealers to "protect the house" more assiduously against them. Dozens of congressmen, particularly from the South and West, were believed to have played their salaries away at Pendelton's.

Pendleton offered only faro, though for particularly distinguished guests he allowed facilities for playing social games like brag, whist, and poker. His faro tables used white chips for one dollar bets and red ones for five dollar bets, a practice followed by today's casinos. Pendelton's dealers were skilled enough to bring in rolls of cash that enabled him to enjoy the high life. As tensions began to mount between Northern and Southern congressmen, his house remained one place where all of Washington united in pursuit of faro. Pendleton prospered, becoming one of Washington's most influential men. On his death in 1858, several Democratic congressmen served as pall bearers, and President James Buchanan even attended the funeral. The capital was divided by issues of slavery and states' rights, but nearly everyone could agree that a little gambling among gentlemen was an un-disputed right.

And that sentiment would guide the young republic as it struggled and grew. From coast to coast, whatever the adversities and whatever their internal disagreements, gambling Americans remained united in their pursuit of action.

6

Wild Cards

Gambling moves West

The Nation's First Gambling Capital

Chronicling during his travels in the 1830s among the king-less peoples of the growing United States, Alexis de Toqueville was struck by the equality of conditions there and the enterprise of the hustling Americans. For them, all of life was a gamble. "Those who live in the midst of democratic fluctuations," he wrote, "have always before their eyes the image of chance; and they end by liking all undertakings in which chance plays a part." Though his words were true for all the nation, the West (itself a moving frontier) has always been particularly attractive to gamblers.

When Thomas Jefferson bought Louisiana from Napoleon in 1803, New Orleans became the gambling capital of the United States overnight, and it would hold the title for most of the first half of the 19th century. The three most popular games in the United States over the next hundred and fifty years each began or were introduced to Americans in New Orleans. A century later, the city would be the birthplace of the uniquely American music, jazz; but even in the first years of the 19th century, New Orleans gamblers were improvising and innovating with cards and dice.

In most of the country, gambling was ostensibly illegal. Not so in New Orleans. The Crescent City was known as a gambling center from its 1718 founding. The territory itself was the centerpiece of John Law's infamous speculative scheme that almost bankrupted the French royal government in 1720, so it isn't surprising that those who actually lived in the province felt no compunctions about gambling. Under French and Spanish administration, gambling in taverns and coffeehouses was common, and despite draconian penalties for infraction, including whipping, time in the stocks, and branding, laws against gambling were usually ignored. With the American acquisition of the Louisiana Territory in 1803, New Orleans became the terminus for thousands of square miles of hinterland. Farmers and merchants from throughout the American interior swarmed into New Orleans to sell and buy goods; flush with money, many of them lost some of it at the gambling houses which soon sprouted. With such thriving trade, New Orleans quickly had more gambling per capita than any city in the union.

In preparation for its incorporation into the United States, the Louisiana territorial legislature outlawed gambling throughout the state in 1811. But three years later, with the state safely admitted to the United States, legislators again allowed legal gambling in New Orleans under the supervision of the municipal authorities. They lacked the personnel to properly oversee the houses, and in 1820, the legislature returned to prohibition. Three years later, after concerted lobbying efforts by municipal authorities and prospective operators, the legislature approved an ambitious plan for legal gambling houses that would balance profits with philanthropy.

According to the scheme, the city would license six gambling houses who would pay $5,000 each per year. Four-fifths of the $30,000 raised earmarked for the Charity Hospital, which still operates today, and the remainder was to subsidize the College of Orleans, an institution of higher education that would close in 1826. Within a year of their 1823 opening, the houses thrived, and their operators, demanding the police close down their unlicensed competitors, successfully forced the closure of all the illegal houses (except those in the rough river districts, where the police feared to tread). But these small houses provided no entertainment, no meals, and no refreshments other than hard liquor. Though they did a booming business among rugged merchants and river workers on a spree, these houses didn't attract the really wealthy gamblers.

John Davis, though, set a new standard when he opened a West End-style gambling palace. Born in Saint-Domingue (he relocated to New Orleans after the Haitian Revolution in the 1790s), Davis was a French-educated man of considerable wealth and social standing. In 1827 he opened his club next to his Orleans Ballroom at Orleans and Bourbon streets. Nothing like it had ever been seen before in America: its players, who were free to help themselves to a delectable buffet, were awed by its luxury. Davis's selection of wines and liquors was renowned. Players found they didn't mind losing, so long as they found a comfortable chair in the opulent salons afterward. Davis soon opened a satellite operation on Bayou St. John to handle the weekend overflow. Within two years, his rivals realized that Davis's magnificent gambling palace was far more profitable than their humble faro dens, and they hurried to open their own high-class operations. In 1832, the legislature removed the cap on the number of licenses and raised the annual fee to $7500. Suddenly, there were a score of legal gambling houses where high-stakes betting on faro, roulette, and, to a lesser extent, twenty-one flourished with the happy acquiescence of the law.

Davis offered the French favorite, roulette, and even a few tables for the under-appreciated twenty-one, but most of his customers were intent on losing their money at one game: faro. Davis's ingenuity and cunning provided an advantage that the mathematics of the game did not. His dealers, like most others, often used perfidy to sway the odds in their favor. He also provided guests with the facilities for a number of social games, including ecarte, boston, brag, and a newcomer known as poker, and American an adaptation of a French game.

Those who invented the game were, unfortunately, too busy playing to keep records of its birth, but card historian David Parlett believes that poker traces its roots to earlier vying games. Some claim poker descended from an ancient Persian game known as *as nas*, but *as nas* itself is not that old, and was probably inspired by the same vying games that preceded poker. As early as the 16th century, games like the French *brelan* and the Italian *primero* had vying elements in them. Poker's more obvious ancestor is the German game *pochen*, which consisted of three different phases: in one of them, players bet as to who had the best combination of cards. The game migrated to France in the late 16th century, where it became known as *poque*. By the time it reached the United States in the late 18th century, it was played with a 20-card deck (A-K-Q-J-10) that allowed four players five cards each. There was only one round of betting, and no discarding or drawing of new cards.

Poque was introduced to North America via the French colony at Louisiana and became poker thanks to casual American pronunciation of the French original sometime between 1810 and 1825. As it was played then, the winning combinations were one pair, two pair, triplets, a full house (a triplet with a pair), and four of a kind. Two hands were absolutely unbeatable: four aces, and four kings with one ace. Between 1830 and 1850, poker players started using the full 52-card deck, and both straights (a consecutive sequence of cards) and flushes (cards matching in suit) became winning combinations.

In the second half of the 19th century, two innovations put decidedly American twists on the game. The introduction of the draw meant that, after the cards were dealt, players could discard those they didn't want and replace them with (hopefully) better cards. It was a fitting addition in the democratic republic, particularly out West, where many Americans went to start over. Around the same time jackpots were added to the game: this rule prohibited players from opening unless they had paired jacks or better, while mandating that they bet if they held jacks. This rule was often unpopular, as it took away from the cherished unruliness of the game, by which someone holding no cards of value could bluff his way to victory. But, with these rule changes, poker became the American social game par exellence, and it continued to evolve into various forms to take into account changing tastes.

Craps, another New Orleans innovation, took longer to become popular, but would become a leading casino game. It originated as hazard, the medieval dice game which remained a British favorite. In Europe, the game originally pitted caster against setter at fairly even odds, and most houses that featured hazard profited only by collecting a box fee; when a player hit three mains in a row, he paid the croupier his minimum bet. London gaming houses that banked hazard themselves (a variation called French Hazard), turned it into a straight-up mercantile game. The game was known to French settlers in New Orleans under the name "crabs" or "craps" (from the "crabs" roll). In 1804 the wealthy planter Bernard de Marginy lost so much of his money to the game that he was forced to sell his land.

He wistfully named a street carved from his property the Rue de Craps, perhaps the earliest mention of the game in America.

Sometime before 1840, anonymous Americans streamlined the game by removing the dice caster's "chance" from the game. Now the caster, more properly called the shooter, had to follow a simple rule: if, when coming out, he rolled 7 or 11, he automatically won, and if he got 2, 3, or 12, he automatically lost, or "crapped out." Any other roll became his point, and he had to roll it before 7 in order to win. African-Americans were among the first players, and likely the inventors, of American craps. Black roustabouts and other river workers up and down the Mississippi were for years the most eager players of "African dominoes," which was played as a social game. Gambling houses commercialized the game by charging a flat fee—usually between five and twenty-five cents—each time a shooter made two passes. This variation, called "Take-off craps," wasn't that lucrative, so gaming operators continued to innovate, and by World War I, "bank craps," played on a layout with pass, don't pass, come, don't come, proposition, and field bets, was well known. Players spread it beyond the inner cities during World War I and World War II, when it was a common game among soldiers. By the close of World War II, it had entirely displaced faro in the legal gambling halls of Nevada, and was, until the rise of blackjack in the 1960s, the pre-eminent American casino game.

Faro and craps were joined by chuck-a-luck, also known as sweat or sweatcloth and later birdcage (for the implement used to spin its dice), a game in which players bet on the outcome of a single roll of three dice. Other games were not so much gambling as they were out-and-out swindles. Thimble-rig, or the shell game, involved a player trying to guess under which of three thimbles the operator had hidden a ball or pea. It was inevitably crooked. Three-card monte (not related to the Mexican card game of monte) used cards to achieve the same ends. The later variation banco, also known as bunko and bunco, was first played in San Francisco in the 1850s, and it was so notoriously dishonest that "bunco" became a synonym for any confidence game. Yet, in New Orleans and elsewhere in the growing United States, gamblers never failed to find fresh victims willing to take their chances on these swindles.

New Orleans remained the nation's gambling capital into the 1830s, though Mobile, Alabama ran a close second. From New Orleans, professional gamblers fanned the length of the Mississippi and Ohio rivers, and nearly every river town had a red-light district where gamblers, thieves, assassins, and prostitutes waited to entertain—and, if necessary, intimidate or even murder—gullible travelers for profit. Desperados and professional gamblers were allowed to work with impunity in underworld districts like New Orleans's Swamp, Memphis's Pinch Gut, Vicksburg's Landing, and Natchez-under-the-Hill. Local lawmen were frankly too afraid to venture into these districts.

Vigilantes in Vicksburg

The underground confraternity of gamblers was a loose group that never had any real organization. But in 1835, a white bandit named John A. Murrell began organizing gamblers and garden variety ruffians in a murderous cabal known as the Clan of the Mystic Confederation. Inspired by the fears aroused by Denmark Vesey's earlier attempted insurrection, Murrell organized 2000 outlaws and began encouraging the black slaves of Louisiana and Mississippi to revolt on Christmas Day, 1835. Unlike Vesey, Murrell's men were not motivated by the injustice of slavery. Rather, they planned to use the rebellion as a cover for their brigandage: while most of the citizens hurried to quash the uprising, the Clan would attack and loot the defenseless Natchez, Vicksburg (Mississippi), and New Orleans. But news of the plan leaked out; several black leaders of the planned uprising were executed (though Murrell remained at large), and rumors circulated that the uprising would now occur on July 4.

When the holiday rolled around, white citizens throughout Mississippi and Louisiana were understandably nervous and none too well-disposed towards gamblers, whom they now saw as an enemy within even more disturbing than abolitionists. In nearly every vice district, mobs of gamblers, thugs, and prostitutes milled drunkenly about the streets. Though most of their leaders had fled, they were still restively menacing. Memphis saw some minor looting, but the hooligans quickly became so distracted by their own carousing that the threat quickly subsided. But in Vicksburg, long a gambling center, the day began in fear and ended in murder.

The Vicksburg Volunteers, a local militia, had chosen to celebrate the nation's independence with a barbecue and speeches. In the midst of what was no doubt a particularly stirring bit of oratory, about six of the city's most notorious gamblers, boisterously intoxicated, intruded. One of them, a brawler named Francis Cabler, made his way to the rostrum, overturning tables and chairs along the way. He insulted and struck a militia officer attempting to stop him, whereupon the Volunteers bodily ejected him. Near the end of the event, word arrived that Cabler was returning, ready to kill the officer he had hit earlier and any who stood in his way. Staggering around the town's main square brandishing a pistol and knife, he was quickly disarmed and placed under arrest. The Volunteers, without resorting to the nicety of a trial, tied Cabler to a tree, administered 32 lashes, tarred and feathered him, and ordered him to leave town within 48 hours.

Outraged by this abuse of one of their number, two other gamblers, James Hoard and Henry Wyatt, drew together a band of followers and began marching on the city's hill (where most respectable citizens lived), pledging to burn down its fine houses. They were quickly repulsed, but a hastily-called town meeting passed an ordinance giving all professional gamblers 24 hours to leave town. Most of the blacklegs melted away, but a small gang of gamblers remained. On July 6, the Volunteers made good on the town's resolve, and began a search of every suspected faro house in Vicksburg, confiscating all of the gambling equipment they found. When reaching a tavern where several of the gamblers had holed up, they met with resistance. Shots fired from the second floor killed Dr. Hugh Bodley, a popular local physician. With this, the Volunteers, assisted by enraged fellow citizens, stormed the house and seized the gamblers inside. They then marched the five ruffians they had found to the grove where all of the trouble had begun at the barbecue two days earlier, and without a trial hanged each of them. All of the faro tables and roulette wheels discovered were burned and the money found in the houses returned to citizens who could prove that they had lost it. Neither Hoard, the leader of the gamblers, nor Cabler, whose drunken antics had started the uproar, were among those hanged.

The Vicksburg lynching and lingering fears over Murrell's conspiracy forced a violent reaction against gamblers throughout the region. In cities like Lexington, Mobile, Natchez, and Cincinnati, townspeople formed anti-gambling societies and demanded the enforcement of laws against mercantile games. Louisiana renewed its prohibition on gambling houses, ending, at least temporarily, its experiment with legal gaming. In New Orleans, gambling houses remained strictly suppressed for about ten years, but with the 1846 mobilization for the Mexican-American War, for which the port was a major nexus, several houses opened. The houses boomed two years later with the excitement of the California Gold Rush (New Orleans was a popular port for California-bound steamers), and by 1850 it was estimated that 500 gambling houses were in operation. By the middle of the decade, some even rivaled Davis's in splendor, but they all would disappear—for a time—with the coming of the Civil War.

Rolling on the River

By the time that the Vicksburg Volunteers declared war on gambling in their town, it was estimated that between 1000 and 1500 professionals worked the steamboats that plied the Mississippi and Ohio between New Orleans and Louisville. When the winds of reform blew down the gambling dens of their city haunts, the blacklegs there simply joined their brethren on the river, starting the golden age of the riverboat gambler.

Steamboats, which could navigate both up- and down-river, were a distinct improvement over the earlier flatboats that had previously floated goods only downriver, and after 1820, they dominated river transportation. As boats got faster, betting men began to lay stakes on which of two boats was the faster. Sometimes, captains bet as well, with frequently tragic results: throwing safety aside, they overloaded their boat's boilers, which could win the race but might trigger a deadly explosion. In 1838 alone nearly five hundred people perished in such blasts. This major public safety issue of the day led Congress to pass its first major regulatory act when in 1852 it set standards for boiler construction and steamboat licensing.

A uniquely mixed bunch, from English lords to backwoods farmers, passed the time convivially in the upper deck's main saloon, which sported a bar at one end and tables throughout. Striking up a conversation and beginning a friendly game of cards was not difficult, and the anonymity of the riverboat gave the professional gambler a cloak of respectability. With his handsome clothes and genteel affectations, he might be anyone: a plantation owner, a merchant, a salesman—even a minister.

In the earliest days of steamboat travel, professional gamblers were rarely tolerated; if discovered, they were usually put ashore immediately. But by 1830 gamblers were such a regular presence that they were practically crew members. Some captains claimed it was bad luck to sail without a gambler and refused to leave the docks until a member of the fraternity had come on board. This new tolerance of gamblers was aided by the fact that gamblers had begun cutting in the captain and crew, in effect paying a license fee for permission to operate aboard freely. Only those who perpetrated the most outrageous (or maladroit) of frauds, or those who had chosen a victim whose political or social connections demanded action, suffered any chastisement from the crew.

The archetypal riverboat gambler cut a striking figure, with his knee-length broadcloth coat, exquisitely tailored black or soft gray pants, loose-collared, ruffled white shirt, and characteristic dark hats. Even their boots were imported from Paris. They decorated their vests with intricate designs and ornate buttons, wore a variety of ruby and gold rings, but reserved their greatest extravagance for a single signature piece: a glittering stickpin or a massive gold watch. These showboaters found there their ornaments had a practical value: they were expensive, easily transportable, and quickly negotiable, and could thus be wagered when their money ran out, or pawned if in a desperate pinch.

Blacklegs happily played social games like brag, euchre, whist, boston, all-fours, and poker, and mercantile ones like faro, twenty-one, and chuck-a-luck. In all games, though, they had an absolutely ironclad advantage: cheating. When, for some reason, they couldn't use gimmicked cards or slick dealing to help themselves, blacklegs used confederates who signaled their opponents' cards by a series of pre-arranged gestures, from hand movements to smoke puffs and cane twirls.

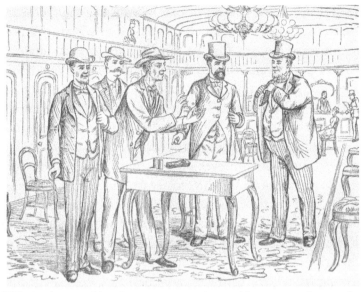

Wily riverboat gamblers dupe an unsuspecting wealthy grocer at three-card monte in an elegantly outfitted upper-deck saloon.

These professionals victimized anyone willing to play, but had particularly sharp knives waiting for wealthy plantation owners and naïve young men with family fortunes to lose. They usually worked in groups of between three and six and played out a recurring social drama. Pretending to be a stranger to the dealer, a roper would steer a fresh victim to him, while a capper joined in the betting, winning big, making the dealer appear to be inexpert, and cajoling the dupe into playing for high stakes. The victim was then efficiently cleaned out.

George Devol, born in 1829, had a long career on the riverboats; in 1887 he published the autobiography *Forty Years a Gambler on the Mississippi*, which recounted a life of adventure that began when, at the age of ten, he became a cabin boy aboard the steamer *Wacousta*. He became yet another blackleg that cheated unwary travelers mercilessly, leaving a trail of empty pockets in their wake.

But Devol shows that the Mississippi gambler was not thoroughly despicable. Often, he used his dark arts to benefit those in need. Once in Natchez Devol helped a few elderly ladies trying to raise $100 for their church by raffling an embroidered lap-robe. Though he had no need for such an article, Devol bought up $50 worth of chances and rigged the contest so that he won. He then returned the lap-robe to the ladies, who raffled it again; after winning it a second time, he returned it again. On the third try he allowed someone else to win the lap-robe, and the ladies had made $400. While he made no money from orchestrating the lottery thus, he was not being entirely altruistic: "I think that money spent did me more good than any that I ever squandered," he wrote, "for I was the recipient of the thanks as well as the prayers of the ladies." Devol also took pleasure in cheating known thieves out of stolen money, though in his memoirs he mentioned no efforts to return the money to its rightful owners. He may not have given up gambling in deference to the fire-and-brimstone preaching ministers he met (he recounted that even men of the cloth were eager, often gullible, gamblers), but he wasn't above hedging his bets.

Cheating riverboat travelers was best accomplished through teamwork, and there was plenty of wealth to go around. But sometimes gamblers bilked their own, just for the fun of it. Devol described one such occasion when a gambler, thinking he was the captain, asked his permission to open a faro game. Devol assented, then had his partner keep the gambler occupied while Devol broke into his room, opened his suitcase, and secretly marked all of his cards. The crafty Devol then replaced the cards as they were and returned to the deck. After supper, his new friend brought out his cards and started a game. The would-be sharper found that he had uncommonly bad luck that night, as Devol and his partner quickly broke him, even winning his gaming tools. Looking for new sport, Devol then fleeced the other passengers at three-card monte (his specialty), winning all of their money, as well as their watches and pistols. All told, the pair made $3600 that night.

Gambling during the Civil War

Devol lived through the golden age of the riverboat gambler, roughly 1830 to 1860. The Civil War, which lasted from 1861 to 1865, ruptured the trade between North and South that was the reason for most of the travelers to take riverboats in the first place. As war raged across the land, riverboat gamblers continued to bilk army officers and others who traveled over the rivers, and gambling continued in the cities.

When Union troops took control of New Orleans in May 1862, the city's new commander, General Benjamin F. Butler, immediately closed all gambling houses. He then began issuing licenses, allowing houses to reopen on the condition that they pay the license fee and take his brother in as a partner. George Devol, remembering the General's administration of the city, allowed that he had kept the city clean, but noted that his share of the gambling houses had made Butler "independently rich."

Soldiers who took up the banner of union and fought for the North, if not already familiar with gambling, soon learned all about it. Soldiers' letters home are filled with references to the universality of gambling. One solider wrote in his diary that 9 out of 10 men in his unit played cards for money and remembered that after the Battle of Fredericksburg he had played in a marathon 24-hour poker game. Indeed, poker was the most prevalent game, followed by twenty-one, euchre, faro, and all fours, also called seven-up or sledge. Cards were popular because they were easily portable and didn't require much level ground to play; dice were considerably less convenient, and, craps was rare, though chuck-a-luck was fairly common. Soldiers also raffled items from watches to horses and bet on impromptu horse races and cockfights. Companies often maintained their esprit de corps by adopting a fighting bird as a mascot and matching it against rival troops' champions.

Gambling was pervasive, but the stakes were paltry—not because soldiers showed much restraint, but because their pay was generally low. Some intrepid gamblers played poker during artillery bombardments, oblivious to the carnage around them. Others, remembering that many at home considered gambling a sin, repented of it on the march to battle and cast aside their cards. If they survived the battle, they never took long to rediscover the joys of gambling, sometimes searching through the mounds of cast-off cards to pick up enough strays to build a full deck. Though some blacklegs made the rounds of army camps on payday and mercilessly stripped soldiers of their cash, for the most part northern soldiers played social games amongst each other for small stakes, a common enough phenomenon in virtually every military force since the Roman legions.

In this pen-and-ink rendering, a Civil War correspondent depicts soldiers playing the dice game chuck-a-luck in 1865.

Confederates played even more than their Union enemies. Southern troops had been gambling from the war's start, but by November 1862 it reached epidemic proportions. General Robert E. Lee issued an order in which he declared himself to be "pained to learn that the vice of gambling exists, and is becoming common in this army." Like their counterparts to the north, rebel soldiers raffled off items without limit, and betting on horse races, particularly in cavalry units, became so common that it threatened army discipline. A Texas regiment in 1863 threatened court martial for any officer caught betting on a horse race.

Cards, particularly poker, were just as common as in the north, along with dice. In a gambling den called Devil's Half-Acre near Fredericksburg, soldiers ran chuck-a-luck games nearly non-stop during the winter of 1862-63. Officers often threatened gamblers, but players showed their Confederate patriotism by using cards adorned with Jefferson Davis or leading generals. As the South's fortunes fell, playing cards became scarcer, and gamblers could only get new decks from Union prisoners or from the haversacks of the dead. When the cards were no longer usable, the rebel soldiers continued improvising games, including paper boat races and louse fights. Despite the disapproval of leaders, including the quietly virtuous General Stonewall Jackson, Southern soldiers were, for the most part, incurable gamblers.

Some Confederates, like the Union soldiers they fought, substituted Bibles for the cards they usually carried as they marched into battle. But those tempted into discarding their "sinful" gambling tools were given pause by a cautionary tale. An inveterate rebel gambler, it was said, carried a pack of cards into combat. During the fight, a bullet hit him, but struck the cards and was deflected; he survived to play again. A soldier fighting alongside him, who carried a Bible, was also struck in the pocket, but the Bible failed to block the bullet and he died instantly. Whatever their merits as body armor, men thought twice about throwing away their cards, particularly when they knew they would be retrieving them soon after battle, anyway.

Despite the animosity between North and South, gambling sometimes brought soldiers from enemy camps together. At nights, soldiers crossed the pickets and, finding a suitably neutral site, enjoyed a quick drink and game of cards together. One Southern officer, inspecting his lines late one night during the Petersburg campaign (1864-5), found them to be nearly empty; he learned that the men charged with protecting the rebel flank were in fact playing cards in the Union trenches. Gambling was impossible to suppress on either side of the lines.

There was even a semi-legendary gamblers' brigade, the Wilson Rangers, of Louisiana. A group of New Orleans gamblers, caught up in the patriotic rush to enlist at the Civil War's outbreak, formed a cavalry company of their own with George Devol as a member. They bought themselves the finest apparel, equipment, and horses to be had and made an immediate impression. "The ladies said we were the finest looking set of men in the army," Devol wrote. They drilled strenuously: Devol recalled that they would assemble, mount their horses, and ceremoniously gallop out of the city. Upon their return, the residents cheered them, thinking that they had spent all day preparing to defend the city. But, Devol wrote, that was not exactly true:

> The first orders we would receive from our commanding officer would be: "Dismount! Hitch horses! March! Hunt shade! Begin playing!" There was not a company of cavalry in the Southern army that obeyed orders more promptly than we

did; for in less than ten minutes from the time the order was given, there would not be a man in the sun. They were all in the shade, seated on the ground in little groups…and in each group could be seen a little book of tactics (or at least it looked something like a book from a distance). We would remain in the shade until the cool of the evening, when the orders would be given: "Cease playing! Put up books! Prepare to mount! Mount! March!"

The Wilson Rangers dreaded the possibility of actually fighting. When the Union army began marching on New Orleans, the cavalry rode out to defend the town with little heart, and, at the first warning shot, promptly broke ranks and raced each other back to the city, where they removed the military insignia from their coats, buried their sabers, and tried to pass themselves off as men of peace for, as Devol wrote, "we had enough of military glory, and were tired of war." His compatriots were smart enough to know that, when the game was played with cannonshot and bullets, they were green suckers, and they had no illusions about it.

After the Civil War, railroads supplanted riverboats as the nation's transportation. With the completion of the transcontinental railroad in 1869, the Rubicon had been crossed, and, until overtaken by the automobile about a half-century later, trains represented the new cutting edge. Not as picturesque as quietly gliding riverboats, they nevertheless allowed Americans to travel farther and quicker than they had before. Aboard them, gamblers worked the smoking cars with the same ingenuity they had shown on the riverboats, bilking suckers mercilessly.

With the expansion of the American economy in the postwar years, gambling houses became far more common. Soon every major city had at least one house dedicated to cards and dice, and the colorful figure of the artful blackleg gave way to the mercilessly efficient gambling syndicate, who bankrolled the major houses of the new age. In the West, though, the gambler became forever enshrined in the romantic mythology of the wild frontier. The true story of Western gambling, of course, was often just as fantastic as the tall tales it inspired, but it was, in many ways, simply an adjustment of the riverboat gambler to a new milieu: the cowtowns, mining camps, and boomtowns of the Wild West.

Way out West

Throughout the 19th century, both the law and conventional morality seemed to have a weaker hold on the western frontier than in the more settled East. As a result, gambling flourished. While every major American city from the 1840s on had a thriving gambling underworld, in the West gambling went on in full view of the public much of the time. "Wide-open" regimes, in which local law enforcement tolerated, and even supported professional gamblers were common. Blacklegs who had learned their craft on the riverboats followed the cowboys, prospectors, and cattle barons west; as always, they went where there was money to be made. They left in their wake a colorful legacy of anecdote, myth, and legend that remains a living part of American memory.

Anglo-Americans moving into the previously-Mexican regions of the West found that existing Mexican towns had one or more *salas* (gambling halls). Newly-settled areas also had plenty of gambling: on mining and ranching frontiers, most new arrivals were single men who spent most of their hard-earned cash in gambling halls, saloons, and dance halls. Freed from familial restraints, gambling dominated cow towns and mining camps.

Those coming to California in the frenzied days of the Gold Rush did not wait for their arrival "in the diggings" to begin gambling. Gaming, particularly poker, ran day and night on the steamers that took men to the jumping-off points for the overland trail. As companies of men made their way to the goldfields with their wagons, they broke up the tedium of camp life with games of cards by the fire. When lucky enough to spend the night in town, faro and roulette were popular for those who had the ready money. In Independence, Missouri, two gambling houses ran around the clock; their windows, kept permanently open, attracted scores of customers with the jingling of coin and excited chatter. Gambling was just as dangerous a diversion for those who took the isthmus route, by which Argonauts sailed from an eastern port or New Orleans, landed at Charges on the Atlantic Coast of Panama, hacked through the jungle for 2 or 3 days to reach the Pacific port of Panama City, and caught another steamboat to San Francisco. Unfortunately, there was often a long wait for ships to California, and faro throwers, thimble-riggers, and monte dealers, had a field day with unwary gold-seekers. Many a quest for gold ended at the faro tables.

Once at the mining camps, the lust for gambling, if anything, was even less restrained. Life in the camps was hard: all day was spent panning in rivers and picking at rocks for gold. In the evenings and on Sundays, professional gamblers were more than happy to help the weary miners relax by playing cards or roulette. One of the first businesses to open in any new settlement was invariably a gaming house in a makeshift tent. Even miners who had not gambled at home now did so without hesitation. One letter-writer spoke in 1850 of a Methodist minister who spent his days mining and his nights playing monte and other games. Many miners did not wait to get back to camp to gamble, and card games in the mines themselves, with stakes of hundreds of dollars, became common.

In the boomtowns, gambling houses were, with saloons and brothels, often the most lavish structures built, and the action was intense. A visitor to Aurora, Nevada, one of these meteoric settlements, lamented the overabundance of liquor and gambling, and the miners' predilection for both: "where men are congregated and living uncomfortably, where there are no home ties or social checks, no churches, no religions—one sees gambling and vice in all its horrible realities." The typical saloon was a one-stop shop for late-night revelers: one wall offered the bar, another a chop stand, where patrons could get fried steaks and meat, and in the rear or in a separate room stood the gambling tables, where hundreds or thousands of dollars worth of gold and silver was staked, joined in more upscale establishments by a billiard table.

Gambling was so common throughout the mining frontier, from California to Montana, that dog fights, bear-fights, and bear-baiting were rampant. One man even proclaimed his "killer duck" an interspecies champion and pitted it against all canine challengers. It is no wonder that most who came to the goldfields in search of wealth returned home empty-handed. Running a gambling house was the easiest way to mine for gold.

San Francisco stood at the center of this mining mania, and, in the years after the 1848 discovery of gold at Sutter's Fort, had more

"Sunday amusements" in the White Pine Mining District, Nevada, 1869. The game is faro.

gambling per capita than any other city in America. The gambling houses of San Francisco became renowned, and, during the heady boom years, gambling was the chief recreation of San Franciscans.

The first gambling house was the El Dorado, which opened in the spring of 1848 in a canvas tent at Washington and Kearny streets. The tent was soon replaced by a hastily-constructed wood building whose proprietors rented out to Thomas Chambers, the El Dorado's operator, for the princely sum of $40,000 a month (at the time, a ten-room house could be built in the East for $2000). Unlike the gambling palaces of John Davis, this resort had little luxury to it. With a monopoly, though, gamblers flocked in, hundreds each night. The El Dorado was so fantastically lucrative that, soon, a host of other gambling houses sprang up; by 1850, there were at least one thousand of them in San Francisco.

The most successful establishments were centered on Portsmouth Square, where they took up all of the eastern side, three-fourths of the northern, and much of the south. The El Dorado was king of the square, while other famous names included Dennison's Exchange, the Empire, the Mazourka, the Arcade, the Varsouvienne, the Ward House, the Parker House, the Fontinem House, La Souciedad, the Alhambra, and the Aguila de Oro. Fire regularly swept through the wood shanties and ramshackle structures of San Francisco of this era, and most gambling houses were rebuilt regularly; few, therefore, had any luxurious furnishings, for they were more likely to be incinerated than not. Most were built along a similar plan: a large room with a long bar on one side, a main floor packed with tables, and an elevated stage, on which bands performed.

There were no sumptuous complimentary buffets (food and liquor were prohibitively expensive), but demure-looking girls selling refreshments flitted through most houses. One of the most popular games was monte, a game invented and usually dealt by Mexicans. It was not related to the three-card version of the thimblerig swindle, but rather was played with a 40-card deck (the standard minus eights through tens). Like faro, the object of monte was to guess the position of a drawn card. To play, the dealer accepted bets, shuffled, cut, and then drew two cards off for the bottom layout and two more for the top layout. He then drew the "gate," and if the card matched one in the top or bottom layout, he paid the winners accordingly.

Gambling among the Chinese immigrants in San Francisco was believed to be inestimable. As soon as the authorities succeeded in suppressing one gambling den, two more would sprout up elsewhere. They offered games familiar in Chinatowns around the world: fan tan, the "white pigeon ticket" pakapoo lottery, and mah jong. As elsewhere, the Chinese disdained all Western games, not giving a whit for the charms of faro, poker, or roulette, though whites flocked to play pakapoo.

San Francisco gambling houses were uniformly lucrative operations. The El Dorado averaged profits of between $100,000 and $200,000 a month during its peak years. These establishments made their profits from hundreds of small fry who bet between 50¢ and $10 a hand. Cumulatively, the turnover was enormous. Initially, these profits could be enjoyed openly as Golden State gambling was at first completely legal. Gamblers were nevertheless linked to political corruption, and in 1856 a series of lynchings persuaded many operators to leave for greener pastures. State laws began criminalizing specific games, but wily operators simply renamed them and continued dealing. In 1860, an ironclad statute banned all bank games, thus ending legal mercantile gambling. The legislature first targeted only professional gambling operators, but in 1885 it criminalized the very act of gambling, and by 1891 the penalties for owning and playing in a game were equalized.

After vigilantes and the law pushed them out of San Francisco professional gamblers filtered eastward. Denver, founded in 1858, became a gambling center almost immediately. In the first years, most play went on at the Denver House, a hotel made from logs which, along with its rustic charm, boasted a drinking and gambling saloon. Men bet money, real estate, and even their revolvers. Monte, faro, and three-card monte were the most common games. Though opposed by the burgeoning town's more upright citizens, professional gamblers nevertheless played, barring intermittent periods of reform closure, more or less wide open into the 1920s. The gambling in mining towns like Cripple Creek, Creede, and Leadville was similarly public. Farther to the north, with the discovery of gold in the Black Hills, Deadwood, South Dakota, became a notorious gambling center, as did Tombstone, Arizona, to the south.

The popular stereotype of the Western American gambler of this era is a rangy, mustachioed, ambling Anglo-American of Southern descent, but gamblers came from every part of the United States and the world. The Chinese, Peruvians, and Australians who flooded into California with the Gold Rush (Mexicans had, of course, been there for decades already) each brought distinctive gambling habits with them. Native Americans continued their games of chance, and new arrivals, it seemed, competed with them to see who could wager the most. Wherever there was a population center, one was sure to find gamblers. In the 1870s, for example, between 30 and 40 gambling houses ran in Kansas City, Missouri, though many professionals were chased across the river into Kansas City, Kansas after the enactment of an anti-gambling law in 1881. Santa Fe was the unofficial gambling capital of the southwest for much of the 19th century.

In the cowtowns that sprouted at the juncture of railroads and cattle trails, gambling was notorious. Licentious Cheyenne, Wyoming, known as "Hell on Wheels" for most of the 1870s, saw virtually unrestricted gambling, as did a series of cow towns: Abilene, Wichita, Newton, Caldwell, Hays, Ellsworth, and the largest and westernmost, Dodge City. These towns catered to cowboys flush with money after long months on the trail, buffalo hunters, railroad workers, and soldiers. Gambling was the chief business there: Abilene had thirty gambling dens and saloons, and only three other businesses, on one of its major streets. Gambling houses helped establish the new settlements as wild hubs of mayhem.

In its heyday as a gambling nirvana, roughly 1850 to 1910, the American West produced some of the most imfamous figures in the history of gambling. These fast-dealing gambling entrepreneurs of the land were cut from a different cloth than the bankers, managers, and croupiers of Baden-Baden and Monte Carlo. Some were impetuous hotheads, bluffing wildly on a hunch, while others were serenely philosophical, like Bret Harte's fictional hero John Oakhurst, who seldom lost his cool. "He was too much of a gambler not to accept Fate," Harte wrote of the black-garbed Oakhurst. "With him life was at best an uncertain game, and he recognized the usual percentage in favor of the dealer."

Real-life gamblers were no less colorful. Perhaps the best-remembered is James Butler "Wild Bill" Hickok, whose death is associated to this day with a certain poker hand. Born in Illinois in 1837, Hickok was an excellent gunslinger: his fame is chiefly due to an 1868 *Harper's Magazine* article about his exploits, real and embellished, and his tour in Buffalo Bill Cody's Wild West show. His reputation helped him prevail over defter card mechanics at the gaming table. In the course of one game, a player periodically dropped cards into his hat; when satisfied with his hand, he pushed $200 into the pot. Hickok drew a pistol and declared that he was calling the hand in the hat. No one objected when he swept the pot. In another game, he was outmatched against a crew of cheaters. After going all-in and losing to a superior hand, Hickok pulled two revolvers as the winner was about to sweep the pot. Fixing his guns on the sharpers, he calmly announced that "I have a pair of sixes and they beat anything." The other gamblers made no outward protest as Hickok took the pot.

In 1876, Hickok's travels took him to Deadwood. Hickok had had a premonition that he would not leave the grimly-named town alive; he was right. On August 2, 1876, he was playing poker in Saloon Number Six with his back to the door. Jack McCall, a saloon journeyman with no known quarrel or connection with Hickok, sneaked up behind the famed gunslinger and shot him in the back of the head. Hickok died instantly, clutching two black aces and two black eights. Ever since then, black aces and eights have been known as "the dead man's hand." (There has been considerable speculation about the fifth card; some say that, as the deal was in progress, Hickok hadn't yet picked it up, while others say that it was the nine, jack or queen of diamonds, and others insist it was the queen of hearts.)

Doc Holliday was equally notorious. Born John Henry Holliday to a wealthy family in Georgia, Holliday was diagnosed with tuberculosis shortly after he completed his studies at the Dental College of Philadelphia (today part of the University of Pennsylvania) and began to practice dentistry. Like many tubercular patients of his generation, he moved to the arid West for relief from the disease. He settled in Dallas, Texas, where he opened a dental practice, though his persistent cough scared off most patients. Holliday started supplementing his income with gambling, and soon abandoned his practice altogether. After killing a man in a dispute over a $500 pot, he moved, one step ahead of the law, to Jacksonborough, Texas. A magnet for trouble (and a crack shot), Holliday roamed through Denver and Wyoming, sweeping pots and finding trouble, before heading back to Texas. In Fort Griffin, he met "Big-Nosed" Kate Fisher, the dance hall girl who was to remain his chief paramour, and Wyatt Earp, the famed lawman, gambler, and saloon keeper.

After killing a man in yet another gambling dispute and only escaping jail under the cover of a fire set by Fisher, a mean gambler herself, Holliday fled to Dodge City, where his friend Earp was marshal. Holliday further followed Earp and his brothers Jim and Virgil to Tombstone, where he supported the Earps against the McLaury and Clanton brothers in the infamous gunfight at the O.K. Corral on October 26, 1881. After being acquitted of murder alongside the Earps after the gun battle, Holliday wandered to Colorado, where he spent the next few years growing progressively more ill (his tuberculosis was slowly killing him) and winning card games in mining camps throughout the state. On November 8, 1887, lying peacefully in bed with bottle of bourbon and a pack of cards, Holliday looked down at his bare feet and murmured "This is funny." He had promised Kate Fisher he would not die with his boots on, and he was right: he breathed his last shortly thereafter, a legendary gambler and gunfighter.

Another friend of Earp's, William Barclay "Bat" Masterson (who Holliday never liked), called himself "the Genius" and related tales of his own glory to all who would listen. After a childhood in Illinois, he moved to Kansas, where he established himself as a buffalo hunter. He then tried his luck as a gambler, with little to show in Dodge but better returns in Cheyenne. Masterson was in Tombstone shortly before the legendary O.K. Corral shootout, dealing faro at the Oriental gambling house (in which Wyatt Earp owned a share and served as an enforcer). From there he returned to Denver and managed a series of gambling rooms in Colorado. He was better known for his gunplay than his dealing (though there is some confusion over exactly how many men he killed, anywhere from one to twenty-six).

In 1902, Masterson surfaced in New York, where he was arrested for carrying a concealed gun and running a crooked faro game before establishing himself as a sports writer and editor, covering boxing and baseball for the *New York Morning Telegraph*. He spent the next two decades embroidering his legend and enjoying a polite infamy; President Theodore Roosevelt, who invited the gambler to the White House regularly, appointed him a United States Marshall. He died in 1921, and would later be fictionalized by Damon Runyon's as Sky Masterson of the popular musical *Guys and Dolls*.

Women of the West

Despite the reputation of the mining frontier as an all-male preserve, women were present in many gambling halls. Since men with money could be found in saloons and gambling halls, both were obvious places for prostitutes to cruise for customers. Saloon owners often employed women as waitresses: they found that men were far more likely to remain drinking and gambling when they could share the company of a friendly female. Beginning in San Francisco, many gambling houses hired woman dealers, on the theory that the rough miners would protest less if they lost their hard-earned gold dust to a vixenish croupier. Many women banked their own games and worked throughout the west as independent gaming entrepreneurs.

In the Mexican salas (gambling halls) of the Southwest, female dealers were common. The most famous was Dona Maria Gertrudis Barcelo, better known as La Tules (a diminutive of Gertrudis). She was born south of Santa Fe (in today's New Mexico) in 1823 and began dealing in a sala at a young age. She was soon renowned for her beauty and grace. Men stormed the doors to lose money to her. Soon she opened her own Santa Fe sala, to which she attracted an upscale clientele, including most of the city's major figures. She outfitted it lavishly with Spanish furniture and Turkish carpets, and the cuisine of her chefs was roundly admired. She outfitted herself extravagantly, wearing an overabundance of golden jewelry. After the American takeover of Santa Fe, she continued to prosper, and died a wealthy woman in 1852.

Other women came to the West for fresh starts. Lurline Monte Verde was one of the most famous and most captivating to reinvent herself there. Born to a wealthy slaveowning Missouri family as Belle Siddons, she spent the first years of the Civil War in Missouri drawing out war secrets from Union officers bedazzled by her beauty. She was arrested as a spy in 1862, but released after four months by the pliant governor. After the war, she married a doctor, who died of yellow fever, before marrying a gambler, who also soon perished, but not before teaching her the mysteries of cards. She then moved to Wichita and became Kansas's best twenty-one dealer, then opened her own houses in Fort Hays, Ellsworth, and Cheyenne.

Siddons next appeared in Denver in 1876 as Madame Vestal, the proprietor of a Denver gambling establishment. She felt that her family background precluded her from hiring girls of easy virtue, so instead she offered gamblers free drinks and a (purportedly) honest game. When gold was discovered in the Black Hills, she relocated to Deadwood where, as Lurline Monte Verde, she arrived to great fanfare: the newspaper made her debut a front-page story, trumpeting the advent of a sultry, sensuous "flawlessly-groomed beauty." Though she soon owned one of the town's leading gambling houses, she was unlucky in love. She fell for Archie McLaughlin, a stagecoach robber who was ultimately captured and hung by vigilantes. Monte Verde would survive a suicide attempt, though she spent her final years wandering around the West, a disconsolate alcoholic and lost soul.

An even more notorious female gambler had a similarly sad end. Eleanore Dumont, dressed in the latest Paris styles, appeared in the mining boomtown of Nevada City, California, one magic morning in 1854; not bad looking at all (despite a downy fuzz on her upper lip), Madame Dumont caused heads to turn from the moment of her arrival. She remained aloof from all gentleman callers but opened a club called the Vingt-Et-Un, and rather appropriately dealt blackjack there. She insisted on strict decorum (no spitting or cursing) in her place, and those who defied the rules faced a disapproving stare from the proprietor and the wrath of her numerous customers, who stood in line, patiently waiting to lose to Dumont. Things went so well that she took on a partner, gambler Dave Tobin, who helped her expand into faro, chuck-a-luck, and roulette.

Their new house, called the Dumont Palace, proved a goldmine for two years, as miners continued to lose steadily to the alluring Frenchwoman. After a falling out with Tobin, she began a peripatetic life, moving from boomtown to boomtown with the sweeping tide of ready money. She maintained a lavish house no matter where she was, but outdid herself in Virginia City, Nevada, where a string orchestra gave consolation to the losers, who enjoyed gratis champagne. She traveled all the way to Montana and Idaho, but as the years went on her luck began to run out. The soft fuzz on her upper lip became more noticeable, leading one wag to nickname her "Madame Mustache," a taunt which followed her for the rest of her life. She would commit suicide near the mining camp of Bodie, California, in 1879, twenty-five years after her triumphant entrance into the Golden State.

Scores of other women earned fame and considerable wealth from gambling, including Texans Kitty "the Schemer" Leroy and Lottie Deno (born Carlotta Thompkins near Lexington, Kentucky), but few were more interesting than Alice Ivers, born in Sudbury, England in 1851, to a respectably middle-class family. She went to school in a female seminary before her family emigrated to the United States, where they ultimately settled in Colorado. There, Ivers married mining engineer Frank Duffield, whom she insisted on accompanying during his visits to gambling saloons. After he died in a mining accident, she decided to support herself by gambling.

Though she played faro as well, someone gave her the name "Poker Alice," by which she was known for the rest of her life.

Poker Alice worked her way across the West in the 1870s and 1880s, dealing in many of the most celebrated gambling dens of the era. She considered herself more than the equal of any man and drank her liquor straight, smoked thick cigars, carried a revolver, and cursed with irreverent impunity. She has one rule, though, which she refused to relax, the residue of her seminary education: she never worked on Sunday, which was the busiest day of the week in most boomtown saloons. After marrying a fellow dealer named W.C. Tubbs, Poker Alice retired from the game and lived in an isolated cabin with her mate north of Deadwood until the winter of 1910, when Tubbs died of pneumonia. Ivers loaded his body into a wagon and drove a team of horses nearly fifty windy, snowy miles to Sturgis, where she pawned her wedding ring for $25, with which she paid for his burial.

After the funeral obsequies, she ambled into a gambling hall and asked for a job. She retrieved her wedding ring with the first $25 she earned, and continued working at the gambling hall. When Prohibition started in 1920, she ran a roadhouse catering to soldiers near Fort Meade, offering servicemen liquor, girls, and gambling six days a week (she remained steadfast in her commitment to Sabbatarianism). One night, during a disturbance, the septuagenarian shot and killed a cavalry trooper. Though acquitted of murder, her roadhouse days were over, and she retired to a rocking chair on her front porch, where she serenely smoked her black cigars until her death in 1930. With her death, an era in gambling ended. The past might have been the province of colorful personalities, but the future already belonged to syndicates and machines that would transform the arts of chance into a business.

7

Fools of Fortune

American gambling becomes urban

Big City Gambling Starts

Western gambling was the stuff of legend, but Eastern gambling was already big business by the end of the Civil War. Two kinds of gambling dens and clubs flourished then: the no-frills "low den" or "skinning house," and the posh "first-class hell." The low dens developed from taverns, while the first-class houses followed exclusive West End clubs such as Crockford's.

Houses dedicated to gambling began to emerge in the 1830s, spurred by the expansion of the American economy, the growth of cities, and the migration of professional gamblers from the South. From the colonial days, gambling had been found in taverns throughout the land, but standalone gambling houses were rare—when a group of New Englanders opened one in New York City in 1732, it closed almost immediately, having attracted too few customers and too much attention from the authorities. At the turn of the 19th century, however, professional gamblers became more numerous in the northern cities, and by the 1820s specialized gambling houses began to appear. Popular games included the old tavern favorite of backgammon and various social card games. The first successful New York gambling house, which opened in 1825 near Wall and Water Streets, was a popular gathering place for clerks, artisans, and volunteer firemen. It was a rough-hewn, democratic imitation of a London club, and it inspired several imitators.

By 1830, about a dozen gambling houses ran in New York City, where professional gamblers, armed with little more than their gambling equipment and bankroll, offered bank games. They usually set up shop in houses that primarily offered social games—quite unlike

Crockford's or the spa resorts, where a single proprietor (backed by investors), offered customers a chance to bet against the house at mercantile games. Professionals roved about the city, looked for opportunities wherever they might find them.

The "wolf-trap" provided the evolutionary link between peripatetic professionals and true gambling houses. The wolf-trap, also known as a snap house, deadfall, or ten-percent house, was born in Cincinnati in the late 1820s and grew to dominance after 1835, as refuges from Mississippi and Louisiana river haunts streamed into town. Any dealer could set up shop in a wolf-trap with little capital, save his bankroll. A dealer who wished to "start a snap" (as banking a game was known), bought a stack of chips from the house manager; this became his bankroll for the game. Snaps ranged from $1 to $500, though most were in the $20 to $50 range. Chips could be valued at anywhere from 1 cent to 50 cents each, though they usually "cost" between five and twenty-five cents.

Wolf-trap dealers generally offered faro, though some played twenty-one or chuck-a-luck. The house provided a table for play and all necessary equipment and a surveillance officer who kept an eye on both the dealer and the players, ensuring that neither tried to defraud the house by introducing counterfeit chips. When the game ended, any players lucky enough to win chips redeemed them from the house bank. If they broke the dealer's bank, the house charged him nothing for use of its premises; if the dealer won, the house took ten percent of his profits as its compensation. Most wolf-trap games were honest, chiefly because most rough patrons would have thought nothing of beating a cheater senseless. But while the games themselves were usually honest, dealers frequently tried to short-change players when changing chips for cash, and players often "dropped a bet," a practice today known as "past-posting," when they surreptitiously slid a wager onto a bet that had just won. Sometimes, raucous troublemakers took the direct approach and simply "bonneted" the dealer: they threw a blanket over his head and made off with his cash while he struggled to free himself. In the wolf-trap, men on both sides of the table remained constantly vigilant.

In the late 1830s, the typical Cincinnati wolf-trap had a single long, narrow room, teeming with dirt, carpeted in straw mats, and amply furnished with shabby chairs, ratty tables, and spittoons improvised from sawdust-filled boxes. The only amenity (besides a series of penny pictures of various sporting scenes tacked to the walls) was a pail of water with a dipper, from which thirsty patrons were welcome to drink. Conversation ran to the topics of racehorses, steamboats, and loose women, and was generously punctuated by jovial obscenities. Most wolf trap patrons worked on steamboats as cooks, stewards, mates, pilots, and engineers, though they were often joined by the local rowdies. The professional gamblers who "opened a snap," or banked a faro game could be easily spotted in the crowd wearing delicately embroidered shirts and bedecked in showy jewels.

Dealers liked wolf-traps for the straight equipment and constant business, notwithstanding the dangers of bonneting. Players liked being able to easily find an honest game. As in other gambling rooms, segregation was common; some wolf-traps catered primarily to black players (though whites frequented these as well), while most white traps were off-limits to blacks. By the 1840s, wolf-traps had spread from the Queen City to St. Louis, Pittsburgh, Philadelphia, Baltimore, New York, and Boston. Still, they were largely a transitional institution.

Though the games dealt in the wolf-traps were generally honest, most faro professionals needed to cheat to consistently win. When a particularly rich sucker wandered in, dealers might ask the wolf-trap's owner to introduce a gaffed deck; in such a case, the owner took a 25 percent share of the profit. The second-class skinning house or brace room, by contrast, was entirely dedicated to cheating. Their uniformly dishonest operators usually preyed upon new arrivals to the city. Some of them superficially resembled the first-class houses known for their fine food, flowing wines, and honest games. But most only gave players cigars and liquor, and seldom allowed the player an even chance. They were open to the public, and generally stayed in business by attracting casual visitors who did not know or did not care that the games were crooked. Apparently, quite a few people fell into one of the categories, because by mid-century, there were about 100 second-class houses in New York City alone.

Other second-class houses did not even pretend to be legitimate gaming resorts; they were plainly (to all except the sucker) brace rooms, where the victim had no hope of leaving with a penny. These were more fronts for an elaborate con game than gambling rooms: they operated for the express purpose of skinning a single mark. Ropers (also known as steerers) searched the railroad stations, saloons, and hotels of the city, looking for an easy mark. Befriending the mark over a drink, the roper then extended an invitation to visit his club. The oblivious mark followed him to his doom.

Meanwhile, back at the brace room, a gaggle of cappers (shills) was lazily playing cards and swapping tales until the ringing of the door bell. The cappers suddenly transformed themselves into bankers, merchants, and lawyers, and the owner/dealer, with the help of an assistant, started losing money to them at faro as the sucker was led to the slaughter. In some brace rooms, a table was set elaborately under the pretense that a fine dinner would be served in an hour or two; by that time, the sucker would be cleaned out and long gone, and the silverware would continue to gather dust. As the mark walked in, he heard incredible stories of the dealer's bad luck, as players spoke of winning thousands. He would join in the game enthusiastically but soon be tapped out.

When he was safely deposited back on the street by the roper, the crew divided the spoils: forty-five percent for the roper, forty-five percent for the owner, and ten percent for his assistant. From his cut, the owner paid rent and incidental expenses and the cappers, who generally got between $1 and $4 per game. Houses running only roped games became common in the 1850s and as late as the 1870s over one hundred could be found throughout the nation: 15 in New York, 6 in Philadelphia, between 1 and 4 in major cities like Boston, Baltimore, and Chicago, and at least one in burgs as small as Omaha, Leavenworth, and Providence. When Congress was in session, the District of Columbia boasted several, and in state capitals such rooms opened when the legislature sat, a sad commentary on the gullibility of the people's representatives.

Respectable marks might wander into a second-class house, mistaking it for a gentlemen's club, but no one was under any such delusions in the penny poker dens that proliferated in slum districts throughout the country, such as New York's infamous Five Points. There were no burnished chandeliers or ample sideboards here: a tallow candle jammed into a bottle provided the light, and a rough plank thrown over a pair of empty whisky barrels the table. In 1849, a *New York Tribune* writer described "the various grades of small thieves and pickpockets" huddling over a table, dealing greasy, worn-out cards, drinking rotgut whiskey, swearing, and fighting. "At these dens men and women are indiscriminately mingled: such men! But more especially, such women!" As in the wolf-traps, these rough establishments were generally as honest as the visitors were fierce.

A more refined recreation could be found at the first-class houses which modeled themselves, with varying degrees of success, on the London clubs. Though public gambling on card and dice was illegal, the proprietors of first-class houses smoothed over this legality with generous gifts to politicians, judges, and police. Many directly employed police as steerers. The dealers might play honestly for locally-known patrons, but out-of-towners steered to a first-class house could usually expect to be cheated. When victims tried to press charges, the wheels of justice—greased by the house proprietors—quickly spun against them. A querulous mark demanding satisfaction from a judge might find himself jailed as a material witness while the offending gamblers continued to walk free. Usually his only play was to drop charges and leave town. In 1850, Horace Greeley estimated in his New York Tribune that more than $5 million a year was lost to professional gamblers in New York, mostly at first-class houses.

These houses were open to the general public and, like the contemporary Rhine casinos, offered chiefly mercantile games: faro, preeminent above all, but also roulette, twenty-one, and rarely *trente-et-quarante* or dice games. Managers passed themselves off as gentlemen and provided a range of comforts to their guests; in every city there could be found at least one house, and often more than a dozen, that might rival Pendleton's Washington palace or John Davis's gilded New Orleans club. Free dinners were de rigeur and seldom disappointed. The finest wines were poured freely, and a man could eat and drink to his heart's content, so long as he repaired to the faro table after he was done. Just as with the second-class dives, first-class houses employed genteel-looking ropers who delivered fresh victims each evening. Sometimes, players lost merely because of the inherently unfavorable odds of mercantile games, but most houses relied on skilled dealers to cheat their way to a profit. Players seldom knew whether they were gambling or being fleeced, and many, in the excitement of the first-class house, did not initially care.

New York City Bets Big

After Louisiana outlawed gambling houses in 1835, New Orleans gambling declined. At the same time, New York City's was booming. By 1850, it was apparent that the thriving commercial hub had become the nation's new gambling capital. In that year, the New York Association for the Suppression of Gambling reckoned that there were no less than 6000 establishments in the city that permitted gambling. About two-thirds of these were primarily gambling businesses (as opposed to taverns that incidentally permitted card games), and the nearly-incredible figure of 25,000 people (nearly 5 percent of a total population of 515,000) reportedly worked in them. Though the houses were ostensibly illegal under New York's anti-gambling statutes, complaisant authorities allowed them to run virtually wide-open.

Most of New York's fifty or so first-class houses were owned by a small group of proprietors. Because of the inherently risky nature of honest gambling, particularly faro, syndicate ownership made sense, as it allowed owners to pool their resources and thus allow higher betting limits. Joining together also helped proprietors coordinate and pay for the corruption of the municipal, judicial, and police authorities whose forbearance was necessary for continued operation. By 1850, the syndicate structure that would dominate organized gambling (and hence organized crime) for the next century was slowly coalescing.

Though ownership of the houses was shared among limited partnerships, several operators distinguished themselves. Reuben Parsons, an enigmatic New Englander who, owned shares in most of New York's poshest first-class houses. It was said that he had been a silent partner in a few New Orleans houses before he appeared in New York in the 1830s, though on his arrival he first tried to make a fortune by playing faro. After losing for about two years, he decided that the only way to make money from bucking the tiger was on the banker's side, and he bought a share in a Manhattan gambling house. He eventually parlayed this into a controlling interest in as many as ten first-class houses. He also invested successfully in the illegal lottery or "policy" games of New York, and became fantastically rich man in a few years.

The wealthy Parsons was a walking contradiction. Though he banked several of the city's most flamboyant gambling houses, he dressed austerely and spoke softly. Considering himself a businessman, he seldom deigned to speak to mere gamblers, and maintained a surveillance and reporting network that kept him constantly informed of his investments' progress. He put his faro and policy profits into real estate, and by the outbreak of the Civil War had retired a millionaire from the gambling business. Not content with his sizeable fortune, he strayed onto Wall Street, where stock market speculation, at which he was a rank amateur, ruined him. He would die destitute in 1875.

During his years as a gambling house owner, Parsons had a number of partners, the closest of which was Henry Colton, with whom Parsons had a lifelong friendship. Together they owned one

This 1867 rendering of a New York City faro bank depicts the tense moment as players await "the turn," the dealing of the last set of cards. On the right, the casekeeper tracks cards in play.

of New York's most celebrated houses, on Barclay Street. Colton had a reputation for rectitude; even his enemies admitted that if he had pursued a "respectable" business, Colton would have been a success. He schooled himself in the mathematics and procedures of games becoming a respected solon of the table whose judgments took the force of law amongst the gambling fraternity. He avoided his friend Parsons' financial reverses by cunningly transferring all of his property to his wife's name in the 1870s when he was threatened by lawsuits.

Patrick Herne was as renowned for his suavity and charm as Colton was for his intelligence. Herne claimed to be an Irish aristocrat who, touring the United States in the 1830s, was cleaned out by New Orleans faro artists and then he took a job in a faro house. Whatever his origins, his true talents lay not in dealing but in roping new customers; he soon began receiving a cut of the profits. With the exodus of gamblers from New Orleans after 1835, Herne moved to New York, where he partnered with Parsons and Colton in several gambling houses before opening his own at 587 Broadway.

Here, Herne allowed his personality to shine, and the former roper used his exquisite charm to draw players and keep them coming back. Though most of them lost in fixed games, Herne helped them to see the bright side—even men considering suicide, it was said, could be perked up by a short chat with the genial gambler. Herne gave pikers (small-stakes bettors) and hustlers a similar treatment, greeting them affably and, during a short walk, begging them to do him the favor of not patronizing his resort for a while. It usually worked. With the authorities, he used more substantial means, sending presents and cash disbursements to his numerous friends among the police. Safe from raids, his house prospered, but Herne spent money as fast as he made it—he was indeed a terrible sucker for faro—and died nearly penniless in 1850.

There were other notable operators in mid-century New York. Sam Sudyam, a former member of the Bowery Boy gang, had gambled on a trip to the South before learning the art of the deal from Reuben Parsons. He eventually owned his own establishment with former house painter Joe Hall, who later sold his share to Sudyam and opened houses in Philadelphia and Washington. "Shell" Burrell honestly took on all comers at roulette, while Jim Bartolf ran a refined trap on Park Place where gamblers had no chance of winning. Most of these houses opened after dark, but there was one, run by Sherlock Hillman on Liberty Street, that was open only from 11 am to 7 pm and catered to businessmen seeking relief from the tedium of the office.

While each of these operators was famous or, at least, infamous, they would soon be eclipsed by a true heavyweight: John Morrissey. Born in Templemore, Ireland in 1831, Morrissey emigrated to the United States at the age of three with his parents, who settled in Troy, New York. There, Morrissey distinguished himself early on as a world-class rowdy and a ferocious brawler and soon made a name for himself in Troy, becoming the unofficial no-holds-barred champion of that city. At the age of 18, he set off for New York City with the ambition of gaining similar prestige in the metropolis. Searching for the accomplished pugilist Dutch Charlie Duane, the young Morrissey entered the Empire Club, a gambling establishment owned by Captain Isaiah Rynders, a powerful, politically influential gambler. Upon being told that neither Duane nor any other prizefighters were in the club, Morrissey declared that he could lick any man present, whereupon he was set upon six toughs, who attacked him with a variety of weapons, including fists, chairs, and bottles. Morrissey held his ground until dropped by a brass spittoon. Rynders was so impressed that he took the young man under his wing. Morrissey returned to Troy for a year, but in 1850 found himself back in New York, where Rynders put him to work as a shoulder-hitter.

Professional gamblers, gangs, and politicians of this era shared a growing affinity that ultimately led to the creation of gambling syndicates. Gambling house operators needed protection from both the law and the lawless: zealous police could enforce anti-gambling ordinances and judges might impose harsh penalties for running a gambling house, while gangs of rowdies might rob or terrorize the house and its patrons. Thus, professional gamblers reached out to the law with graft and employed the outlaws as bouncers.

Criminal gangs were often more powerful than the police, whom they frequently intimidated, and as early as the 1840s freely ran protection rackets and engaged in arson and robbery for profit. The

The first professional gambler elected to Congress, John Morrissey (1831-1878) parlayed the profits from his faro houses into something close to respectability.

more astute gang leaders allied themselves with ward heelers, men who channeled gang violence into political channels: by sending out groups of shoulder-hitters (like young Morrissey) on election day, they ensured that voters picked the right candidates. Ward heelers emerged as political power brokers, and usually controlled the elected machine politicians who in turn appointed the police. Professional gamblers like Captain Rynders, with access to large sums of money and growing influence among criminal gangs, were uniquely qualified as ward heelers. Under Rynder's tutelage, Morrissey began to rise through the ranks of Tammany Hall, New York's Democratic political machine.

Morrissey had ventured far and wide in his quest for pugilistic fame, hitting San Francisco in 1851. In that boomtown, he teamed up with a faro dealer and, becoming wealthy, gained a lasting respect for gambling profits. He had a forceful approach to customer relations. When one of his players declared he had been cheated and insulted by Morrissey, he challenged the brawler to a duel, giving him the choice of weapons. Seeing Morrissey saunter up to the appointed spot with a butcher's cleaver tucked under each arm, he took fright and wisely ran. If Morrissey cheated anyone after this, they had the sense not to complain. After besting George Thompson in August 1852, he declared himself the Champion of America, but that title was not generally recognized until he defeated Yankee Sullivan on his return to New York the next year. He continued fighting until October 1858 when, after knocking out John C. Heenan, he announced that, as he wished to devote himself to his family and society, he was retiring from the ring.

Morrissey earned a fearsome reputation: his nickname "Old Smoke" was inspired by a fight during which he was rolled onto a patch of burning coals but, with his flesh burning, refused to submit; he later beat his opponent senseless. He was not a huge man, standing under six feet tall and never weighing more than 180 pounds, but he was powerful and possessed of a dogged stamina; he never stopped fighting until he was the victor. One of Morrissey's natural rivals was Butcher Bill Poole, a Whig and nativist who beat the Democratic Morrissey in an 1854 fight so intense that one onlooker, later attempting to recreate the battle for a rapt audience, mortally fractured his skull while demonstrating how strongly Poole had thrown Morrissey. The next year, one of Morrissey's partisans shot and killed Poole, whose final words, "I die a true American," reflected the animosity between the native-born Poole and the immigrant Morrissey.

Morrissey had already begun his career as a gambling house operator, using his boxing purses to buy a series of houses, eventually taking over the longest-lived gambling house in New York City's history, the establishment at 8 Barclay Street, which ran continuously from 1859 to 1902 (though not under the same ownership). Morrissey established 8 Barclay as the choice destination for politicians and sporting men before selling it and opening other houses. He took on a variety of partners, and his houses were always successful: thanks to his powerful Tammany connections, the police never dared to interfere with his houses. Morrissey even established satellite operations in the upstate health resort of Saratoga, which he would help to transform into a gambling center, and his name became synonymous with first-class gambling.

Morrissey's political stock rose along with his gambling profits. Tammany Hall chief William "Boss" Tweed recognized Morrissey as the finest vote-getter in the city, no mean feat in wards dominated by thugs, repeat voters, and outright fraud. Tweed rewarded Morrissey with the machine's support for a seat in the United States Congress, where he was elected in 1866 and 1868, becoming the first professional gambler to serve there. After an 1870 rift with Tweed, Morrissey was expelled from Tammany, and on his own captured a seat in the New York State Senate.

Successful as a businessman and politician, by 1868 Morrissey was a millionaire, though the following year, when he took the advice of Cornelius Vanderbilt and invested heavily on Wall Street, he lost much of his fortune. He never succeeded in his ambitions to be recognized as a gentleman by high society, though he remained politically potent and at least modestly wealthy until his death in 1878 from pneumonia. Still, his legacy was powerful: because of his political might, he had been at the center of New York's gambling for more than twenty years, and his vision of Saratoga as a posh resort would eventually be realized by another famous operator, Richard Canfield.

The immigrant/nativist animus exemplified by the Poole/Morrissey feud underscored a multicultural, polyglot city. Immigrants from around the world poured into the United States in the 19th century, and in New York City they quickly established distinctive communities with salient gambling subcultures. Perhaps the most notorious such neighborhood was New York's Chinatown which, like Chinatowns throughout the world at the time, was fairly dominated by fan-tan parlors and lottery shops. Though far from home, it seems, the games seldom changed.

Midwestern Gambling Houses

During the years that New York gamblers thronged to Morrissey's houses and faro was "winning the West," many accomplished gamblers made names for themselves in the Midwest. In Cincinnati, wolf-traps split gamblers with rondo houses and keno parlors. Rondo was a simplified form of billiards that could be played as a house-banked mercantile game. To play, players shot nine balls from one corner onto the opposite pocket. To win, a player had to guess whether there would be an even or odd number of balls remaining.

This uncomplicated game may have originated as a cross between the numerous Native American odd/even games still played in the 19th century and billiards. Rondo was found throughout the American South (including gaming centers like New Orleans and Hot Springs, Arkansas), the Midwest, and even as far west as Arizona and California, where it appeared as a forbidden game in the section of each state's respective penal code that outlawed mercantile games. It was played through the early years of the 20th century.

Keno parlors also proliferated throughout the South at this time. This game was markedly different from the keno played today. Players bought pre-printed cards, with spaces divided into from 3 to 5 rows and the unique ticket number printed in the middle row in large red type. Each row had 5 numbers, taken from a pool of 1 to 90, on it. No two cards were the same. To play, the roller placed 90 balls into a wooden sphere called a goose, shook it, and started drawing numbers. The first player to cover five numbers in a row shouted "keno," and won the prize. This game was also known as lotto, and it was likely descended from lotto-style lotteries. It is more recognizable as a bingo ancestor than a forerunner of today's keno, and was popular among small-stakes gamblers wherever it appeared.

Wolf-traps, rondo rooms, and keno halls kept the populace of Cincinnati enthralled until around 1850, when a growing number of first-class house operators demanded that the police, to whom they paid protection money, close these rival attractions. During the years before and after the Civil War, many riverboat gamblers would retire to Cincinnati to open gambling houses; as long as payoffs to the authorities continued, the Ohio River town was a quite friendly place to do business.

Throughout the region, just about every city of prominence sheltered at least a few members of the gambling fraternity: St. Louis, Milwaukee, Indianapolis, Cleveland, Fort Wayne, St. Paul, and Minneapolis all had significant reputations as gambling centers. Even small towns had their share of the action. In a typical burg, sporting gentlemen declared themselves a "club" and met weekly in the back of some shop where they played the popular games of the day, including the social diversions of poker and its forebears, brag, euchre, and all-hours, whist, and the mercantile games of twenty-one and faro. Layouts were crude, and the proprietor's chief sources of profit were the sale of cards and a percentage of the pot (known as a "rake") from poker and brag. In return, the housekeeper provided a clandestine meeting place (for gambling was invariably illegal), alcohol, and cigars.

When they tired of playing against each other, townspeople welcomed nattily-attired professional gamblers, usually professed gentlemen from the South with languorous accents and seemingly generous dispositions. Upon blowing into town they would usually lose steadily at faro while treating fellow players to round after round of drinks, cigars, and tales from the outside. Later in the evening, as the stakes were raised, they turned the tables, taking the townspeople for all they could bear, and usually left town only a few steps ahead of the suddenly-aroused simple folk. But the small town would instantly forget its anger when the next charming stranger with a real mahogany faro box strolled into town.

In larger cities, permanent gambling houses were common where proprietors could persuade the powers that be to turn a beneficially blind eye. The history of Milwaukee, a city not today renowned for its gambling, is instructive. The first faro house opened in 1843, when the city had fewer than 3000 residents. Its owner, Martin Curtis, became wealthy enough from its receipts that he invested in residential real estate and helped finance the Kirby House, the young city's most prominent hotel.

Curtis was succeeded as the city's dominant faro operator in 1848, when newcomer Tom Wicks opened a house. Wicks would reign over Milwaukee gambling for most of the next three decades. Any operator who did not work directly for him needed, at the very least, his permission to operate without interference, and his influence was so great that he ran his gambling operations from a building owned by the governor of Wisconsin. Wicks operated houses throughout the state and even opened branches in Chicago. At the height of his power, though, he made a ruinous misstep: in 1872 he sought to parlay his gambling wealth into a more "legitimate" windfall and invested heavily in the wheat market. Like most other expert gamblers who traded their cards for stocks, he soon saw his fortunes annihilated, and had to sell everything he owned just to pay his debts.

Instead of rebuilding his fortune through his expert management of faro houses, Wicks turned venomously against all gambling. He publicly denounced all gamblers as frauds and promised to rid Milwaukee of them. His high-profile campaign soon faltered, but not before proving to the police that it might be just as politically expedient to close the houses as to accept their graft: they soon moved against the city's six remaining first-class houses and also instituted a crackdown on backroom gambling on rondo and poker. Predictably, gambling returned to Milwaukee soon enough, though not as openly as before.

Cities like Milwaukee might tolerate a Tom Wicks and his first-class faro houses, but they paled in comparison to the rampant illegal gambling that thrived in Chicago. Even when it was only a town, it boasted the kind of gambling subculture befitting a 19th century city. The town of Chicago was incorporated in August 1833, and by December of that year a letter to the local newspaper was already complaining that authorities were lax in the enforcement of anti-gambling laws. Ten years later, a committee resolved to "root out" the vice of gambling and "hunt down those who gain by it an infamous subsistence." The committee urged Chicagoans to abstain from gambling with professionals and deny them social intercourse; but the games continued.

As Chicago grew in the 1840s and 1850s, it became the undisputed center of Midwestern gambling. A hustling coterie of operators ran the early gaming houses, the most exceptional of which was John Sears. Unlike others, who took on all comers in brag, seven-up, or whist, Sears played only poker, and he was such a prodigy that it was said he had no need to ever cheat. He was also renowned for his sartorial snap and was, for years, described as Chicago's most handsome man. Where most gamblers were content to recount tales of debauchery larded with obscene oaths at the table, Sears was an oddity: possessed of an almost mystical affection for the work of Shakespeare and Robert Burns, he sometimes burst into verse while playing. Respected by his fellows, admired by nearly all, Sears remained a scrupulously honest gambler, and as a result died in poverty. Though other Chicago gamblers might have admired his well-groomed good looks, few emulated his candid dealing.

Sears's honest ways were quickly becoming an anachronism. In the 1850s, the old style gambling houses, which featured primarily social games, a modest ten percent house rake, and square dealers, began to disappear. Houses now specialized in faro, whose popularity surged, and mercantile games such as roulette, chuck-a-luck, and keno, all of which were introduced by veterans of the New Orleans and New York gambling houses. Initially, these adventurers worked their magic in the existing ten-percent houses, but as they became settled in Chicago, they opened their own houses, which were unabashedly skinning operations. By the latter part of the decade, virtually every gambling house was crooked.

The more refined skinning houses were located in the heart of the city on State and Lake Streets, but the more desperate gamblers headed, almost instinctively, for a squalid quarter of town known as the Sands. Attempts to clean up this den of thieves, prostitutes, and professional gamblers were generally fruitless until the 1857 election of "Long" John Wentworth as mayor. Wentworth conceived a brilliant stratagem: he ordered the local papers to print an advertisement for a dog-fight in a distant part of the city. With the most formidable rowdies thus far from the Sands, the mayor then orchestrated the organized demolition of the most ramshackle houses in the quarter. Wentworth was applauded for destroying a gamblers' vipers' nest, but the Sands' resident sharpers simply relocated. The mayor was not content with merely disrupting the gamblers, and pledged to continue the fight against them wherever they might surface. After raiding a prominent house, Wentworth succeeded in forcing the closure of the public gambling houses, though gambling continued. Instead of confidently dealing out of lavishly-appointed houses, faro dealers now moved furtively throughout the city, one step ahead of the police, creating an American urban institution, the floating game.

During the Civil War, Wentworth relaxed his zealous prosecution of the gambling underworld, and hundreds of desperate characters streamed into Chicago. These were not only professional gamblers, eager to rake off a portion of the city's burgeoning wealth, but also prostitutes, pickpockets, thieves, and confidence men. Pre-occupied with maintaining the law in a rapidly expanding city (the population nearly tripled from 1860 to 1870), Chicago police did little to hamper the illicit trade in gambling or prostitution. Chicago gained repute as the nation's roughest city, thanks in part to the numerous saloons that boasted both free-flowing alcohol and wide-open games of chance (each of which, in its own way, contributed to violent quarrels). By 1870 the number of gambling houses was estimated in the hundreds, no mean feat in a city of less than 300,000. Rough-and-tumble low dens were scattered throughout the city's slums, but most of the city's first-class houses—which might or might not be honest—were found in two clusters. The first was on Randolph Street between Clark and State, a stretch of the city so violent that it was known as Hairtrigger Block. Another section, Clark Street from Randolph to Monroe, was dubbed Gamblers' Row. On these blocks, gambling houses predominated, sharing space only with a few saloons and brothels.

Initially, one of the best known houses, at 167 Randolph Street, run by "Colonel" Wat Cameron, a polite and generous Southerner, was known for its honest play. Patrons, drawn in by his fair dealing, flocked to his house. The odds of the game, alas, did not guarantee Cameron enough of a profit to cover his overhead expenses (which naturally included protection payments to the police), so in 1863, Cameron took in two partners from St. Louis who quickly ran him off and converted his resort into one of the city's most infamous skinning houses.

Out of the mass of sharpers who ran gambling houses in this new era, George Trussell was one of the most dishonest and wealthiest. Trussell was a Vermont Yankee who worked as a bookkeeper in Chicago for several years before deciding that he could not maintain his extravagant lifestyle on an accountant's salary and migrated into the employ of gambling houses, first as a roper and capper but soon as an owner. By 1862 he and three partners owned several houses. His group occasioned much ill-will among its rivals by its aggressive "marketing." Trussell employed groups of ropers who weren't content to trawl the train stations and hotel lobbies for suckers. Rather, they would invade the foyers of the few gambling houses known for their square dealing, snuff out its gas lamps, and inform any arrival that, while the house was unfortunately closed, there was an excellent place nearby that the house's proprietors would like the would-be gambler to visit—one of Trussell's skinning dens. Trussell became so wealthy that he was able to pay exorbitant amounts for police protection, and enjoyed both the freedom to run his houses without fear of the law and the connivance of police in raiding anyone who attempted to challenge his dominance.

Trussell also had an interest in the turf, and a fascination for the horses—one in particular—that would prove tragic in 1866. Trussell had made a mistress of (and, some say, secretly married) a prostitute named Mollie, who he set up as the madam of a luxuriant Fourth Avenue brothel. He refused to allow any woman to come between himself and Mollie, and he showered her with expensive gifts, including sparkling jewels and artfully-tailored clothes. But her place in his life was challenged by Dexter, a champion trotter in which Trusell had acquired a part-ownership. Suddenly, he spent all of his spare time down at the stables marveling at his great horse and boasting of him with his race track cronies. When Trussell neglected to ask Mollie to escort him to the festive grand opening of a new racetrack, Driving Park (at which Dexter was to race), she decided that she had had enough. The next evening, dressed in a flawless white dress whose folds concealed a pistol, she went searching for Trussell on Hairtrigger Block. Finding him in a saloon, his glass raised in a toast to the fabulous Dexter, she accosted him. As he dragged her towards the door, she drew her gun and shot her horse-mad lover to death. She immediately screamed her regret for having killed "her George." At her trial, the jury acquitted her of murder, despite the overwhelming evidence of her guilt.

Trussell's downfall may have been a penny-opera tragedy, but the entire city endured devastation with the Great Chicago Fire, which raged from October 8 to 10, 1871. Although popular legend attributed the fire to a lantern kicked over by a cow in the DeKoven Street barn of Kate O'Leary, the fire's actual cause remains a mystery. Daniel "Pegleg" Sullivan, shortly before his death, confessed to starting the fire with embers from a pipe, but it is more likely that dice were the cause of the blaze. Louis Cohn, who died in 1942 at the age of eighty-nine, revealed that he, Mrs. O'Leary's sons, and other local youths were busy shooting dice when one of them (most likely

Sullivan) knocked over a lantern. The story has the ring of truth because one of Mrs. O'Leary's sons, Jim, later enjoyed a career as a leading gambling-house operator in Chicago. Getting an early start in the trade, he may have contributed to one of the worst disasters in American history.

The fire did not dampen Chicagoans' enthusiasm for gambling, and in the years after the cataclysm a new boss gambler emerged: Mike McDonald, a Chicago native (b. 1839) who got his start as a professional gambler in his teens. When Mayor Wentworth closed the city's gambling houses, McDonald journeyed down to New Orleans, where he refined his skills and adopted what would become his characteristic attire of black suits with white shirts. He returned to Chicago committed to becoming the city's greatest gambler, and showed real promise: by the time of the Civil War, he was well-known as a gambler throughout the city.

McDonald furthered his ambitions in 1873 when he backed the hands-off Harvey Colvin for mayor. Colvin reversed the policies of his predecessors, who had ordered the police to conduct perfunctory raids on known gambling houses, and allowed all manner of gambling to flourish without even the shadow of a threat. One downcast reformer wrote that "the town was literally handed over to the criminal class who held high carnival by day as well as by night." McDonald thrived, opening a new gambling house, attached to a hotel and saloon, called "The Store" at Clark and Monroe Streets. This resort soon became the leading gambling house of the entire Midwest. To outward appearances, it was a square joint whose 12 faro tables, six roulette wheels, and six chuck-a-luck tables were all honestly run. But in actuality, McDonald instructed his dealers to use a sliding scale: they were to be as honest as the player was politically influential.

Monroe Heath, who succeeded Colvin as mayor in 1876, cracked down on the gambling houses, but his successor, Carter Harrison, was so lenient that the gamblers referred to him as "Our Carter." The Store remained the city's largest gambling house, and would reign over the prairies into the 1890s. It had a number of Chicago rivals, among whom the Clark Street establishment of the Hankins brothers was preeminent. In 1890, it had about 40 fulltime employees and earned for the brothers an estimated $20,000 a month in profit. The operators refused to admit professionals, instead courting a wealthy but inexpert body of gamblers known collectively as the "dinner pail brigade." The rivalry with McDonald was a relatively friendly one, as he joined with the Hankins brothers in a bookmaking syndicate—a sign of the growing move towards cross-ownership of gambling operations that was to define the coming century.

McDonald owned a piece of, or extracted tribute from, virtually every Chicago gambling operation by 1880. By this time he had already become a millionaire, and during the 1880s diversified into downtown real estate, ownership of the Chicago Globe newspaper, and large shares in several transit companies. All the while, his gambling operations reaped millions. But even he was unprepared for the rush brought by the 1893 World Columbian Exposition, which unleashed a "gambling orgy." Amid the carnival atmosphere, faro dealers, dice throwers, and bust-out artists had a field day.

But the good times did not last. Three days before the fair closed, the gamblers' euphoria was dimmed by the assassination of their beloved Carter Harrison by a disgruntled office-seeker. After his death, a Civic Federation comprised of clergy and business professionals demanded that his successor, John Patrick Hopkins, more strenuously combat the gambling element. Many of the best-known houses closed, and McDonald retired from active gambling and, until his death in 1908, enjoyed his vast fortune, though he came to grief when his young wife killed a man with whom she had become infatuated, though she was not imprisoned thanks to McDonald's hiring eminent legal counsel to defend her. After McDonald's retirement, many of the gambling houses reopened. In the early 20th century, struggles over gambling houses and bookmaking monopolies would contribute to the violence of the Windy City.

Perfidious Professionals

Several thousand Americans made their livings from gambling, sometimes honestly but usually not. These professionals formed, by the 1840s, a distinct subculture in most cities. Writer Edgar Allen Poe, whose gambling debts complicated his already gloomy life, de-

scribed the gamblers—by which he meant professional sharpers—to
be found in any American city:

> They wore every variety of dress, from that of the desperate
> thimble-rig bully, with velvet waistcoat, fancy neckerchief,
> gilt chains, and filigreed buttons, to that of the scrupulously
> inornate clergyman, than which nothing could be less liable
> to suspicion. Still all were distinguished by a certain sodden
> swarthiness of complexion, a filmy dimness of eye, and pallor
> and compression of lip. There were two other traits, more-
> over, by which I could always detect them: a guarded lowness
> of tone in conversation, and a more than ordinary extension
> of the thumb in a direction at right angles with the fingers.

These men populated the low dens and skinning houses of the cities,
quick to pluck any unwary enough to play their games.

Urban professionals had country cousins as well, itinerant vaga-
bonds known as "fakirs" who toured the nation in carnivals, running crooked games, often strolling into town to separate the yokels
from their money using incredible feats of prestidigitation. Often,
the fakirs cajoled the operators of legitimate county fairs, ostensibly
dedicated to education and entertainment, to allow them to practice
their trade on the fairgrounds. Sometimes, fair associations sold the
franchise cheaply, for a bribe of as little as $50; other times, directors
insisted that the fakir first submit to a show arrest and pay a fine to
the local authorities. Most fakirs considered the cost of "sugaring,"
or bribing the local sheriff and prosecutor, a necessary business expense, and there were few local potentates whose wrath against the
fakir's trickery could not be sweetened with a present of cash.

The fakirs employed a variety of crooked games. The needle wheel
was one of the most ingeniously constructed and ubiquitous of attractions. This device consisted of two wheels: a raised center rimmed
with a sloping wheel with 32 compartments. On the wheel's table
stood a box, numbered from 1 to 32, which contained 16 blanks and
16 prizes. A player bought, for $1 or so, the right to place a marble
in the upper wheel, which was then set into motion, just as the lower
wheel was spun in the opposite direction. As the wheels slowed, the
ball would drop into a slot on the lower wheel; if played fairly, the
marble would have an equal chance of dropping into a winning and

losing slot. But the fakir hid, beneath the wheels, an apparatus that allowed him to raise nearly-invisible needles at the top of the winning slots as the wheel spun, thus blocking the marble and cheating the player.

The fakir usually employed a capper who placed a bet and won a prize. Sometimes, this capper would place his own money down and ask an on-looker to spin the wheel. Naturally eager for a free turn, the on-looker usually assented, and after losing was convinced to go "double or nothing," multiple times, sometimes losing as much as $1000 in this manner. Other wheel devices included the jenny wheel, a scaled-down needle wheel, and the corona or mascot, which used a pointer on a wheel numbered from 1 to 60. Players bought tickets, which were placed in a box, and the wheel was then spun. The only winners were usually cappers, as the fakir could control where the needle stopped and thus ensure that no prizes were actually awarded. The squeeze spindle, a similar device, was used to defraud fair-goers for generations.

Another wheel, called the wheel of fortune, can be found today in many casinos, though its odds (with a nearly 20 percent house advantage and an average hold approaching 50 percent) make it one of the worst bets in the house. Yet those who play the game in today's casinos at least have a chance of winning, whereas those who spun the wheel on the fairgrounds never had an even break. The typical wheel has numbered spaces painted on the rim, separated by tabs. A large cloth or painted table allows players to place bets or bids for prizes won if a certain number comes up. The wheel operator, by using a foot-operated lever running through the wheel, was able to stop the turn on a non-winning number, and as always the only ones to win large prizes were confederates of the fakir. Another variant of the game, called the "Board of Trade Wheel," was often popular in rural districts, and used instead of numbers representations of various commodities: pork, lard, wheat, oats, and barley.

By their nature, most fakirs slid between the cracks of history, as they hardly would have enjoyed prosperous careers if they revealed their secrets to a scribe or left detailed records of their swindles. Yet one member of this curious tribe left his story for prosperity. "Honest" John Kelly, a quintessential small-time grifter, gambler, and con artist (and one of several gamblers to share the nickname), when near his death, charged his wife with delivering his "diary" (actually little more than a set of notes) to a newspaper editor he had once taken into his confidence. The resulting biography shows a man evilly adept at fleecing others, yet naïve and unfortunate enough to be forever chasing one last big score.

Kelly, born in 1878 in sleepy Marshalltown, Iowa, was an adept pool hustler and dice mechanic by the age of 15. Using homemade crooked dice, he delighted in taking hard-earned money from local farmboys until, one step ahead of an unfriendly police officer, he joined up with a pair of "big-shot" gamblers—actually small fry con artists—who, in their first adventure with Kelly, used all of their guile to evade a police dragnet and con a train conductor into taking a worthless watch in lieu of their ticket fare. Kelly and his mentors then joined a traveling carnival, where he was initiated into the "knife game," a predictably gaffed carny attraction.

The carnival was a fitting introduction to the peripatetic life that Kelly was to follow. The proprietor, one Colonel McNudder, was "a fine, bluff-looking gentleman until one got close enough to see his shifty eyes." There was not a single game of skill that did not have two modes of play: the fair game, allowed only to the cappers who stimulated yokel interest, and the crooked game, which predominated. Kelly eventually exposed the Colonel's cheating in the crew's nightly poker sessions and soon lit out for greener pastures, his appetite barely whetted by what he had learned of crooked games and cheating devices.

Kelly thought that he was about to emerge into the big time, but twenty years later, he was still working the carnival circuit, supplementing his income by cheating at poker against fellow carnies and the local rubes. Throughout his life, just as he had gotten achingly close to establishing himself as a true "big shot," the cruel hand of fate snatched away his wealth. Flush with four thousand dollars from a crooked card game in which the local sheriff and his deputy were the chief victims, he barely escaped a police roust and fled to Canada without his bankroll. From Vancouver, Kelly and an accomplice took a steamer to Yokohama; while at sea, they bilked several passengers and succeeded in both fleecing and publicly humiliating a powerful Canadian industrialist. After arriving back ashore in Los Angeles with three thousand dollars, Kelly was rolled by his former partner-in-crime and was forced, hat in hand, to beg the "big-time" Angeleno gambling boss Harry Carey for a job.

After being hired as a roulette operator on Carey's offshore casino, Kelly (in the author's rendering, anyway), had a moment of self-reflection, telling himself that this "was the guy that was going to come back a big shot, buy Mr. Shannon, his retired minister father-in-law, a little farm out in the country" and support his wife decently. Instead, he realized that he was nothing more than "a fifty-dollar-a-week cheater in a gambling house, living with his wife's folks and choking on every mouthful they fed him because he knew they hated him for having their daughter when he was a gambler, an outcast." Clad in a newly-bought tuxedo, Kelly went to work on the boat, fleecing the wealthy gamblers aboard until one night a police raid forced him to jump overboard; though captured by the Coast Guard, he escaped when his skiff approached the shore and snuck off.

Since Los Angeles was now too hot for him, Kelly made his way towards Denver, but was waylaid by a lonely, bearded miner who, in Kelly's account, forced him to pass counterfeit gold coins in poker games. His fraud was discovered and he spent about a year in Leavenworth federal prison. Vowing to go straight after his release, he nonetheless was ensnared by a pair of cheaters in a scam familiar to anyone who has seen The Sting. Kelly played his part expertly before ruining the con by cheating a boy out of five dollars with crooked dice drawing police attention. Kelly had to skip town minus the $190,000 he had "legitimately" earned by the scam, a typical outcome for the putative big shot. Kelly then worked a legal gambling house in Agua Caliente, Mexico and had a nice stake until it was taken by bandits taking advantage of the confusion of Mexican Revolution. Kelly then served in the United States Army for three years and saw combat in the First World War before returning to the states, where he worked in a "boiler room" selling bogus stocks and played a small role the Arnold Rothstein's famous fixing of the 1919 World Series.

Kelly made one last try at the big time, buying an illegal casino near Canton, Ohio, but was forced to sell to a bootlegging syndicate,

who had at least the courtesy to hire him back as a poker dealer at
$50 a week. He spent the rest of his life working the fakir circuit,
and, while running a knife game (his first scam) at the 1933 Chicago
World's Fair, collapsed. His dying words to his wife distilled a half-
century of frustration at never having made the big time: "I almost
was a big shot," he told her, "I'm sorry I didn't turn out better." That
was as fitting a memorial as any for the life of a small-time grifter.

Kelly wasn't the only professional to suffer regret; the confession-
al autobiography of the "reformed gambler" is common enough that
it is virtually its own genre. Many professional gamblers, through
naivety or greed, never enjoyed the riches they fleeced from others.
John Philip Quinn, an erstwhile St. Louis gambler who was brought
to the side of anti-gambling, characterized the "downward career
of a gambler" as beginning with high hopes at the prospect of a life
made easy by the ruin of others, progressing to the silent villainy of
a midnight prowler, and ending with the ragged garb of a tramp.
Quinn felt the blackleg "enslaved by his own degraded instincts" to
be as much as a "fool of fortune" as those who dissipated their wealth
in his crooked games.

Still, gambling remained a popular career, particularly for those
who liked the world of plush houses and midnight card games. Even
those with pedestrian lives jumped at the chance to profit from
chance; store owners throughout the nation used a variety of tools,
some straight, some crooked, but all unfavorable to the player, to
perk up their bottom lines. Like the lotteries of 16th century Flan-
ders and Italy, these were essentially glorified raffles for overstocked
merchandise. Tobacconists and candy-store owners used a variety of
"trade stimulators," as they were politely called; each was unabashedly a gambling game. The "star pointer," for example, was a wheel of
fortune fitted up to raffle off prizes.

There seemed no limit to the contraptions that could be turned
into a gambling medium: one game, popular with children, involved
an artificial fish pond filled with bobbing wooden fish. Paying a
dime, players were allowed to use a rod to reel in a fish, from whose
ventral region was pulled a slide which indicated whether the player
won a corresponding prize, whose value was usually less than one
cent. The most popular trade stimulator was the cigar wheel, basi-

cally a wheel of fortune that ostensibly paid out in cigars but whose operator could choose to offer a cash equivalent. In this fashion, even the proprietor of a small tobacco shop could become a small-time gambling boss, scooping up the nickels of his patrons.

Though cigar wheels, fish ponds, and other trade stimulators were popular, a related genre of retail aids reigned supreme over late 19th century American shops, surviving even the onslaught of slot machines in the 1890s and 1900s. Game cards and punchboards allowed merchants to raffle off merchandise using an easily-disposable medium: paper. The typical game card cost 5 cents to play and featured 255 poker hands concealed behind seals. If a player uncovered a four of a kind, he won 80 cents' worth of merchandise; full house,

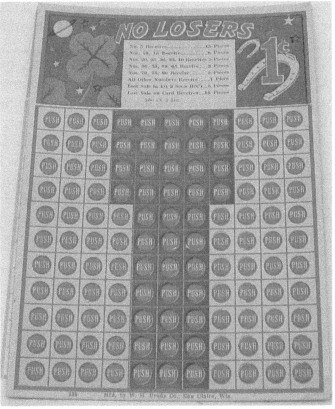

This punchboard was typical of the thousands that could be found throughout small-town America in the late 19th and 20th centuries. Customers paid a penny for a chance at a prize. Taking in $1.21, it paid out 49 cents in prizes, leaving the owner a respectable 72 cents profit.

50 cents; straight, 40 cents; three of a kind, 20 cents; two pair, 10 cents; jacks or better, 5 cents. If he uncovered a lower hand, he naturally received nothing. The game cards were forerunners of today's "scratchers," instant-play games authorized by many lotteries. Store proprietors could expect a profit between $2.20 and $7.00 for each card, an impressive return.

Punchboards operated on the same principle, but were larger and somewhat more substantial, and were popular in a variety of retail shops, from druggists to dry goods emporia. Players paid a stake to punch out a slot in the board, which might reveal a prize. A very popular advertising medium, punchboards came adorned with the images of a variety of products, and themed punchboards, decorated with the colors of sports teams, were also common. Punchboards were so ubiquitous that most Americans did not consider them to be a form of gambling, and even church elders often livened up trips to the store with a quick "pick-out game."

Like all other gambling devices, punchboards had both a fair and a crooked side: one of Honest John Kelly's many adventures saw him travel across the land as a punchboard salesman who provided a confederate with the "key" to the boards. The confederate would then visit the stores Kelly had stocked with punchboards and win all of the valuable prizes. But even those who didn't enjoy this kind of inside information delighted in punchboards, which for decades was one of the most widespread gambling games in the United States. This appetite for gambling fed a sizeable population of roving grifters, crooked gamblers, and con artists, each taking advantage of the suckers' hopes to get something for nothing.

8

Wise Guys and One-Armed Bandits

◇◇◇◇◇◇◇◇◇◇

Big city gambling in the gangster age

Saratoga Springs Makes a Few Fortunes

At the turn of the 20th century, American gambling belonged to machines—both the coin-in-the-slot variety and the urban combinations that facilitated corruption. But at Saratoga Springs, the nation's most famous gambling spot, one man held sway: Richard Canfield. When his reign ended in 1907, syndicates had made gambling crime big business, and technology—from telegraphs to slots—had brought gambling into the machine age.

Settled in the late 17th century, Saratoga initially balanced whatever gaiety might be found at the springs with morality; in its earliest years, it had a reputation as a "moral resort" where Bible-reading and hymn singing punctuated bouts of drinking the area's healthful waters. By the 1830s, though, sporty Southerners had brought public dancing, billiards, and card-playing. In Saratoga's stately hotels, like Congress Hall and the United States Hotel, private card games frequently kept guests up until dawn. Later in the decade, billiards halls began allowing faro and chuck-a-luck operators to set up shop. A professional gambler named Ben Scribner opened the first genuine gambling house in 1842 in an alley convenient to both the United States Hotel and the railroad terminal. Others soon followed, and by the late 1840s "the gamblers of Park Row" had become notorious. In addition to the playing at faro houses, Saratoga's visitors could bet on trotting races, first organized in 1847.

John Morrissey, always looking to expand his Gotham faro empire, opened up a Saratoga house in 1862. Accustomed to the diverse amusements of the metropolis, he conceded that while his tables might provide ample evening recreation, there was still not much for sporting types to do during the days in Saratoga. He decided that a racecourse would fill the afternoon void well, and, having no real experience running a track himself, reached out to a troika of well-known New Yorker sportsmen to build and operate the facility. John Hunter, Leonard Jerome, and William Travers bought land near an existing track and constructed a new track named the Saratoga Race Course. The course was astonishingly successful from its 1863 opening; in the next year, its operators ran the first Travers Stakes, which is the oldest thoroughbred stakes race still run in the United States.

The Civil War had proven a double-edged sword: though it prevented Southerners from taking their relaxation up north, it also cut off Northerners from the competing springs of Virginia. After the war, Saratoga became a leading summer destination. Most of New York's society set filled the stands during the brief racing season. As in his New York faro houses, Morrissey profited from these swells' wishes to gamble. He did not act as a bookmaker, setting odds and taking all comers, but instead served as stakeholder for large bets, taking a commission of between 5 and 15 percent, and ran calcuttas, from which he took a healthy consideration.

Morrissey expanded his gambling operations in 1867, opening a new red brick gambling palace called Morrissey's Club House in a reclaimed swamp on Broadway, Saratoga's main thoroughfare. Hailed as America's finest gambling club, it was the capstone of Morrissey's distinguished gambling career. Some considered it to be superior to even Benazet's Kursaal at Baden-Baden. The handsomely-decorated Club House had two rules Morrissey's staff enforced with iron resolution: no women and no Saratoga residents were permitted in the gambling rooms. Morrissey might have intended to protect Saratoga's vacationing ladies of substance from the evils of gaming, or to ensure that, away from the prudent oversight and disapproving glances of their wives, men might be induced to gamble more freely. Women were welcome to lounge in the salons and drawing rooms while their menfolk gambled, and many of them did.

Already a millionaire, Morrisey expanded the clubhouse in 1871 and the operation soon grossed over $250,000 a year. In 1872 he reportedly turned down an offer to sell the facility for a half-million dollars. By the next year, about a dozen imitators had sprung up, despite the fact that Saratoga Springs' charter specifically forbade gambling (a nicety which Morrissey overcame by unparalleled generosity to local charities and causes). Other gamblers followed suit, and the townspeople became firmly convinced that Saratoga was a far better place with gambling than without.

Others sought to emulate Morrissey's success. The North Jersey shore town of Long Branch served as the summer home of President Ulysses S. Grant (six other presidents have famously enjoyed its hospitality). Its gambling was energetically promoted by Johnny Chamberlin, a New York partner, then rival, of Morrissey's. In 1869, Chamberlin opened an ornate gambling clubhouse and then a racetrack, Monmouth Park, which drew thousands of spectators but closed its doors in 1873. Chamblerlin's Monmouth Club House cost $90,000 to build, and was an exceedingly profitable investment, though Chamberlin ruined himself in the 1870s after excessive betting on his stable of thoroughbreds.

Despite the competition, play at Saratoga remained strong. A pair of New York gambling house operators, Charles Reed and Albert Spencer, took over Morrissey's Club House, renaming it the Saratoga Club House. Spencer, who was frugal and abstemious, retired from his gambling interests to collect art and broaden his cultural horizons, while Reed took Richard Canfield on as a partner in 1893, and in the next year Canfield assumed sole possession of the Club House, as Reed sold his share to concentrate on breeding and racing horses.

Like Morrissey, Spencer, and Reed, Canfield had already become wealthy by owning New York gambling houses. Born in New Bedford, Massachusetts in 1855, Canfield traced his lineage back to the Mayflower and made up for his lack of formal education by becoming a voracious autodidact and patron of the arts who could converse with equal facility on the subjects of art and the Latin classics. Canfield had gotten his start in his teens with an interest in a Providence poker room and, after success at local faro houses, parlayed his winnings into a $20,000 bankroll with which he toured Europe in 1876, spending considerable time at Monte Carlo. He lost most of his money there, but learned much about gambling house management, particularly that the only way to consistently profit was to bank the game.

Canfield split the next five years between wintertime poker operations in Pawtucket and summertime work in hotels in New York and the Jersey Shore. Canfield then moved back to Providence, where he partnered in a gambling house until an unfortunate 1884 raid landed him in jail. After serving a six-month prison sentence, he decided that he would make a stab at the big-time gambling scene, and relocated to New York City, where he unsuccessfully applied to deal at the famous 818 Broadway gambling house. In 1887, with the backing of a Providence gambler, he opened a Broadway poker room with fifty-cent limit games and a comfortable profit of $300 a week. That was more than an average workman's annual salary then, but Canfield, still ambitious, grabbed for the brass ring: his own faro house. Partnered with David Duff, a dealer at one of Charles Reed's houses, in 1888 Canfield opened the Madison Square Club in a brownstone at 22 W. 26th Street. The club, whose entire second floor was soon devoted to faro and roulette, was uniformly successful, and in 1890 Canfield bought out Duff, whose own gambling had become a liability, and became the Madison Square Club's sole proprietor.

Canfield became the nation's most celebrated "prince of gamblers." His cultured mien concealed a character paradoxically shot through with steely restraint and wild impulse. Inordinately fond of good, rich foods, he struggled with his weight throughout his life, drank large amounts of wine, and smoked cigars incessantly. Yet he was also something of an ascetic, at least in the gambling underworld: though he spent much of his time overseeing his luxury houses, he seldom entered the actual gambling rooms, and he never played himself nor allowed any of his employees to gamble, though he did become wealthy through stock market speculation. He dressed conservatively, avoiding the flashy clothes and glittering jewelry that many of his fellow professionals affected. In contrast to ropers who promised their suckers sure wins, Canfield was disarmingly honest, plainly telling all who would listen that it was impossible to win against the bank and that they should never gamble more than they could afford to lose.

Canfield was even more successful in Saratoga than Manhattan, recouping his $250,000 investment in his first season there. In 1902, he added the Italian Gardens, and in the next year he built a sumptuous dining room with exquisitely-detailed stained glass windows that depicted the signs of the zodiac. Owing perhaps to his own enormous appetite, Canfield placed a tremendous emphasis on the club's restaurant, which was praised as the finest in the nation and possibly one of the best in the world. Canfield hired a French chef named Columbin for $5000 a summer, and paid him to travel across Europe during the ten-month offseason in search of new gastronomic delights.

Under Canfield, as under Morrissey, the gambling room featured about 10 roulette wheels and 4 faro tables, with private rooms for particularly heavy betting. The customary betting limits on roulette were $50 for any single number (which would pay $1750 if it hit) and $50,000 on even-money bets (odd, even, red, black, low, and high), twice those in Monte Carlo. Faro limits were $500 for regular numbers and $1000 for specials. Canfield used uniform chips which were transferable between his varied gambling establishments (in addition to his Saratoga and New York clubs, he briefly ran the Nautilus Club in Newport, Rhode Island), and he paid all big winners via check, though he kept as much as $1 million on hand at Saratoga to satisfy any players who demanded cash.

Canfield took on all of the leading gamblers of the day, in an era when betting was, proportionally, at its highest levels in American history. Assorted princes of Wall Street and captains of industry won and lost thousands on each deal—be it cards or business. Though Canfield's New York clubs were select (there were usually only a half-dozen or so well-heeled visitors playing on any given evening), their take was enormous; players often lost $100,000 in a single night. Canfield cornered the market on high-end play.

Most of Canfield's visitors were famous for their betting, but one was absolutely infamous: John "Bet-a-Million" Gates, whose speculations in the stock market had made him a multimillionaire. He would play poker for stakes of $1 or $50,000 a hand with equal relish. When bored, he bet on coin flips. On an 1897 Chicago-Pittsburgh train trip, he won $22,000 betting on which of two raindrops would reach the bottom of a window first. He enjoyed limits as high as $5000 per card at Canfield's where he played for upwards of three days at a time with scant interruptions for food.

One evening in 1902, Gates played what might have been the biggest faro game ever. He lost $375,000 before dinner, after which his luck remained bad, and by 10 P.M. he was down $525,000. He then asked Canfield to double his limit and, betting as much as $10,000 a card, won back a much of his previous losses, finishing the day out "only" $225,000. Poker games among his Chicago and New York intimates were high stakes, even by today's standards; typical pot sizes were over $50,000, and sometimes ranged as high as $1 million. Cleaned out in the Wall Street panic of 1907, Gates continued to bet heavily in private, though he no longer speculated on stocks, and in one of his final appearances, at a conference of the Southern Methodist Church, he implored his listeners to never bet on cards, dice, horses, or stocks: "once a gambler, always a gambler," he cautioned. Yet he remains notorious as perhaps the biggest big-money gambler of history.

Gates's public turn against gambling mirrored a larger reaction against the speculative excesses of the unregulated stock market and public distaste of stock-market millionaires who flaunted their wealth by losing thousands at card games. Several Progressives who championed clean government and sober work (increased regulation, prohibition of alcohol, and the passage of a national income tax were three progressive victories) also took up the fight against gambling, and pressure forced many public gaming houses to close their doors. In 1907, Canfield closed his Saratoga resort and soon retired from gambling. The City of Saratoga Springs bought the building at a tremendous discount, turned over the top floor to a museum, and allowed card games (but not gambling), smoking, and reading in the former casino.

To this day, the erstwhile casino can be rented out for weddings or other special occasions. Canfield's legacy has been no less durable. Worth more than $13 million at the turn of the century, he was, until the explosion of corporate casino ownership in the 1970s and 1980s, the richest casino promoter in American history.

Gambling's Industrial Revolution

With the emphasis on streamlined production and mechaniza-
tion that came with the Second Industrial Revolution in the late
19th century, it was only a matter of time before someone invented a
machine that could help people gamble faster and more efficiently.
Since the early 1870s, early gambling machines—really mechanical
versions of punchboards—known first as "coin in the slot machines"
and then simply "slot machines," dispensed credits for cigars, candy,
gum, or simply the chance to win more.

Many early slot machines mingled elements of chance and skill.
A "reward-paying punching bag" let players relieve their frustrations
for a nickel a punch; if they hit the bag just hard enough to drive
a pointer to a designated spot on the dial, they won a prize. The
"manila" required players to use a pistol to shoot a nickel into one
of four slots; a successful shot won some prize, usually of dubious
value. Games of chance based on dice or roulette were also common.
In order to skirt restrictions on gambling, some machines gave at
least token prizes, like gum or candy, for all who inserted coins, but
promised bigger prizes for especially lucky players who could land
a coin into the right slot. Other machines were rigged to pay off in
cigars. Many slot machines, even though they clearly offered players
a chance to win a prize, were fitted out with stern placards declaring "This is not a gaming device," (losers doubtless agreed), which
sometimes kept the authorities from enforcing anti-gambling laws.

The national poker craze of the 1880s inspired the invention of
a poker-playing machine. A Brooklyn company sold the first such
device in 1891, and within two years the machines were available
throughout the country. On many early machines, players put in a
coin, after which the machine randomly flipped through five sets
of cards which displayed in a window. Lucky players won a prize in
proportion to the strength of their hand: two pair might garner only
one "cigar" (or its cash equivalent, a nickel), while a full house might
win four.

The machines were particularly popular in poker-infatuated San
Francisco. In that city three German mechanics, Charles Fey, Gus-
tav Schultze, and Theodore Holtz, revolutionized slot machine de-

sign. Schultze began with a machine called "Horseshoes" that paid a player two nickels if the game's wheel landed on one of ten horse-shoes (out of twenty-five objects). Fey and Holtz opened an electrical shop that supplied parts for Schultze's slot factory, and Fey took to designing machines himself. One early try, the 4-11-44, was based on a policy combination popular among African-Americans; it allowed a player to spin three dials, which paid when they hit certain combinations such as the eponymous 4-11-44. Fey then went into the slot business fulltime, and in 1898 built a machine called the "Card Bell," which was the first poker machine that automatically paid out coins. Because Fey could not engineer an automatic-payer with five reels, he reduced the number of cards to three. The reel slot machine was born.

In the next year, Fey reworked the Card Bell, renaming it the Liberty Bell. The machine had three reels; a combination of three bells won 20 coins, and the remaining symbols, mostly card suits and horse-shoes, won lesser prizes. Little could slow down San Francisco's growing slot industry, not even the catastrophic 1906 earthquake, until a 1909 law made slots unambiguously illegal. By then, city authorities had gotten nearly $200,000 each year in taxes on the city's 3,200 slots.

Even when slot machines didn't get the complete approval of the law, they often thrived in a grey zone. Machines that supposedly dis-

This five-cent Liberty Bell (pirated from Fey's original design) was one of many "authentic money makers" the Mills Novelty Company touted in its catalog. The accompanying pay table reveals just how small jackpots were. Slots paid off "in trade" rather than cash to skirt anti-gambling laws, though Mills brazenly advertised that its machines would accept and pay off in coins as well as tokens.

pensed gum used symbols of fruit rather than playing cards, on their reels; hence the appearance of cherries, oranges, and plums on slot reels, which supposedly represented the flavors of gum a player could win. Often, even this evasion was unnecessary. A friendly payoff to the local police or judge almost always guaranteed that a slot route operator could place machines in public places with little fear of official interference. Cheating, theft, and hijacking by criminal gangs were the biggest obstacles operators faced. The first two problems were addressed by a series of mechanical improvements, as slot owners sought to keep one step ahead of ingenious tricksters who used plugged nickels or coins with strings. The third was mitigated by cutting in the gangs for a slice of the profits. As a bonus, this muscle could then be directed against competitors.

Slot machines quickly became ubiquitous throughout most American cities, and became popular with women and children. During Prohibition, when many Americans furtively snuck off to speakeasies for forbidden pleasures, slots positively exploded, and slot routes became lucrative enterprises for Al Capone, Frank Costello, and other underworld bosses. In 1931, Costello controlled over 25,000 New York slot machines that reportedly took in more than $25 million a year. Once touted as the next generation of "trade stimulators" for bars, cigar stores, and candy shops, slot machines suffered from their links with organized crime. Most states would look askance at legalizing the virally popular gambling devices in the next half-century, and they only survived with the law's blessing in a single maverick state.

Syndicates Take Over

As Richard Canfield stood astride New York's gambling world at the turn of the century, his contemporaries knew that he was without equal. Hailed as the last of a breed because he owned his gambling houses outright rather than as part of a syndicate, he was actually one of a kind. For decades, syndicate ownership of gambling houses had been the norm rather than the exception, both in the United States and in Europe.

Syndicated ownership made sense because of the inherently unpredictable nature of gambling. From the beginning, sharing the risk of running a faro bank made sense. Despite the romantic image of the lone wolf gambler, gambling, whether crooked or straight, was almost always a group proposition. In addition to the help a dealer needed from ropers, shills, case-keepers, and lookouts, more partners meant a deeper bankroll. So most gamblers worked in teams and shared ownership of houses.

Gambling evolved alongside mainstream American businesses. In the 1870s and 1880s, as American industrial ownership became more sophisticated, full-scale gaming syndicates became far more common. Consciously or not, these syndicates were modeled on the trusts that increasingly dominated American business. Syndicates were, in essence, small corporations that owned a house or houses. Usually, a syndicate member served as on-site manager. Members enjoyed a modicum of security in an inherently volatile business. In addition, syndicate members pooled their resources and contacts to arrange payoffs to police, judges, and politicians, buying wholesale protection for their games. Non-members who wished to run games were forced to take on the syndicate as a partner or face police raids.

Just as it led the nation in business, New York City had the best-developed gambling syndicate of the late 19th century. Though gambling was illegal, a "Gambling Commission" composed of a commissioner (head of an undisclosed city department), two state senators, and the city's leading pool room organizer levied monthly fees on all illicit gambling operations and purportedly disbursed the riches (minus a commission) to New York's political and police elites. A 1900 *New York Times* investigation revealed that each of the city's 400 pool rooms paid $300 a month to the Commission. Crap games, usually run in the back of taverns or billiards halls, paid $150, while each of the city's 20 luxury gaming houses paid $1000 a month for protection. Policy writers paid a simple lump sum, and smaller gambling houses (there were 200 of them in 1900) paid according to a sliding scale that averaged about $150 a month.

The syndicate mimicked any "legitimate" club or business organization. Prospective gaming entrepreneurs went to their police precinct captain, who forwarded membership applications to the Commission. The applicant was investigated (chiefly for his ability to pay and his "reliability") by the precinct captain, who, for his troubles, was paid a $300 initiation fee by the applicant. If the Commission, who met weekly, approved the applicant's bid to run a gaming business, they notified him and began collecting their monthly tribute; if for some reason they rejected his application, the captain was instructed to return the initiation fee. The system was an effective way to line the Commission's pockets and ensure that only "approved" operators stayed in business, as all those who defied the commission found the full fury of the police directed against them.

When confronted with evidence of the Commission's existence, the President of the Police Board and the department's commissioner both insisted that they would be the first to wipe out any vice whose existence they were informed of. Unfortunately, they explained, crap games used little more than dice and boards and therefore left little physical evidence; even pool rooms could be quickly disassembled before the police could take decisive action. When asked about why no action had been taken against Canfield's 44th Street gambling palace, which was anything but clandestine, the commissioner admitted that it might exist, but protested that it was a "private club" and thus "hard to get at."

Chicago also had a large syndicate. In 1890, John Phillip Quinn wrote that the city's "gamblers' trust," had all of the hallmarks of a syndicate: it was a "combination of sporting men" who contributed each week to a common fund whose exact purpose was known only to its superintendents, but, Quinn imagined, somehow accounted for the fact that trust members enjoyed "practical immunity from police interference." The Windy City's gamblers were not alone. Minneapolis had "the combination" in the 1870s; this syndicate ran the city's two first-class houses and a host of lesser resorts. As the American business and politics became increasingly well organized in the late 19th century, the groups that ran that nation's gambling palaces became likewise consolidated.

Syndicates didn't confine themselves to the biggest urban areas: slot machines, dice rooms, and bookmakers were common in even the smallest cities. San Bernardino, for example, was dubbed "California's Casbah" and, in the late 1940s, was a serious rival to growing Las Vegas. When reform shuttered many of the gambling dens there, Southern Californians flocked to Bobby Garcia's Double O

Ranch, a Morongo Valley resort that aspired to country-club elegance. Even after a police raid forced Garcia to substitute bridge and bingo tables for craps and roulette, selected guests continued to play casino games in a back room.

A range of other cities, from Galveston, Texas to Buffalo, New York, had thriving illegal casinos. In San Francisco, the illegal "Chinese Lottery" was just as popular as Nevada's keno, its legal counterpart. No section of the country was without its secret gambling: Butte, Montana had action just as wild as that in Wheeling, Oklahoma City, Chicago, Boston, or Miami. But some illegal clubs were recognized as the truly elite. After Mayor Fiorello La Guardia's 1934 crackdown on illegal gambling, gambling bosses moved to the suburbs. Across the Hudson River, New Jersey's Bergen County soon boasted a string of "gambling resorts" that earned as much as $10 million a year for their proprietors, members of illegal gambling syndicates. The first such resort opened in a back room of Ben Marden's Riviera, a popular nightclub whose lavish floor shows rivaled anything that would later be found on the Las Vegas Strip. Further south, Atlantic City hosted an even wider selection of illegal gambling clubs (more on those in chapter 12).

During the late 1930s, a host of illegal casinos opened throughout the county. Typically, gambling operators secured police protection before converting former warehouses into lavishly-decorated gambling and entertainment resorts. Guests were ferried from New York via Cadillac, wined, and dined before being escorted to the gaming tables. Towns such as Clifton, Leonia, Linden, Lodi, East Paterson, Little Ferry, Cliffside, Caldwell, and Canfield had, at different times, elegant illegal resorts. With public attention suddenly directed against illegal gambling with the Kefauver Committee hearings in 1950, the Bergen County casinos closed. Many of the dealers and patrons, though, moved on to Las Vegas, where they could play legally.

To the south, the Sunshine State had a similar wide-open streak. Miami and Miami Beach were both renowned for their gambling dens, but for years Edward Riley Bradley's Beach Club made Palm Beach the toniest gambling spot in the state. The club had opened in 1898 as a members-only, men-only club with few games. The following year, Bradley liberalized the entrance policy and watched the cash begin to pour in. Though housed in a simple white frame house that hardly rivaled Canfield's sumptuous clubs, Bradley insisted in providing only the finest food for his guests, who soon included many of the nation's wealthiest men and women.

Bradley put his profits from the Beach Club to good use: he bought a horse farm near Lexington, Kentucky, and became renowned as a "turfman." Between dodging sporadic anti-gambling drives in Palm Beach, he found the time to own four Kentucky Derby winners. He also gave back to the community—apparently a believer in Andrew Carnegie's Social Gospel, he sincerely tried to give away his fortune before he died. When a 1928 hurricane cut a swath of destruction through Palm Beach, he reportedly financed the rebuilding of all the area's churches. He also donated huge sums to Florida and Kentucky orphanages. Though he profited well from gambling, he came to believe it was a sin; before he died in 1946, he left instructions in his will that the Beach Club be donated to the city for use as a park and its gambling equipment be sent to sleep with the fishes. This hardly stopped gambling in Palm Beach, though the Beach Club's closing marked the end of a lustrous era.

On Florida's West Coast, Tampa was a thriving gambling center. American bolita originated in the city's Ybor City district, and the city was a gambling hotspot into the 1960s. The Southern climate remained hospitable to gamblers long after the last riverboats had cruised the Mississippi. In Biloxi, Mississippi, which flourished as a tourist town before and after the Civil War, gambling never passed from the scene. As in Atlantic City, it took on a new vigor during Prohibition; an elegant but small casino opened on the Isle of Caprice, a tiny barrier island which, before its development, was known as Dog Key. Though beach erosion caused the Isle to vanish by 1932, no force of nature could stop the gambling that continued on the mainland. In both Biloxi and neighboring Gulfport, slot machines, high-stakes poker, and casino games were a natural part of life.

Though Biloxi's gambling flourished in the 1950s, a group of local reformers, following the lead of the Kefauver Committee, forced authorities to clamp down on the most blatant gambling offenders. Gambling continued in the backrooms for a while longer but increased pressure, combined with declining numbers of tourists and the destruction of 1969's Hurricane Camille, eventually choked Biloxi's once-thriving gambling subculture into submission.

Beaches weren't a prerequisite for a gambling haven. Hot Springs, Arkansas, developed as a health resort in the early 19th century but, much like Saratoga, became famous for its gambling. This was a thriving business by the 1880s, and eventually fell under the sway of "Big" Jim O'Leary, the former Chicago gambling kingpin whose name is inextricably linked with that city's disastrous 1871 fire. Hot Springs became a major gambling center and rest haven for gangsters, and remained so until it fell victim to a national drive against illegal gambling led by Attorney General Robert F. Kennedy in the early 1960s.

Some of the most notorious illegal casinos in the nation were found in northern Kentucky. Covington and Newport were, in the middle of the 20th century, major gambling centers. In the state of Kentucky, casino gambling was avowedly illegal, but was, for years, a de facto local option. Though gambling was a part of Kentucky culture since its frontier days, illegal casinos dated only to Prohibition, when, it is alleged, Cleveland syndicate members "organized" the gambling action. In Newport, clubs like the Alibi, Sportsman's 316, and Tin Shack had varying degrees of squareness. Though some ran honest games, others were bust-out joints where unfortunate visitors had no chance of winning. These illegal casinos ran virtually without interference until 1961, when a local vigilance effort rode the coattails of Kennedy's national anti-gambling campaign and drove out gambling. This hardly meant a public renunciation of gambling as a fun pastime: the winds of reform, as in Arkansas, New Jersey, and elsewhere, blew gambling operators and their patrons straight to Las Vegas.

American-style gaming was not confined to the United States. Cuba was the pre-eminent Caribbean casino destination. On April 15, 1951, a full-page advertisement in the *New York Times* welcomed Americans to holiday in Cuba. It offered them "a never to-be-forgotten chapter" in their lives, and the "gayest, most glamorous, most glorious vacation ever!" The advertisement extolled the glories of Havana: "Modern hotels...delightful restaurants...fabulous night clubs…racetrack thrills and other sports…beach bathing and pleasure…all these and more will fill your stay with pleasure." In addition to sparkling beaches and carefree shopping, the advertisement also highlighted "Cuba's glorious temple of the Goddess of Chance—the Grand National Casino." In the middle of the decade, tourism boosters consciously promoted Cuba as the "Las Vegas of the Caribbean," aware that the combination of vacation sunshine and gambling offered there was markedly similar to Las Vegas's action. It seemed that Cuba would become a new international gambling center.

But the best hopes of Cuban casino operators were dashed on New Year's Eve 1958/1959 when rebels led by Fidel Castro chased Fulgencio Batista, the country's ruler, into exile. As Batista fled to the Dominican Republic, Castro's forces consolidated their hold over major cities like Santiago and Santa Clara. Batista's flight inspired rioting in Havana, as hated symbols of the Batista regime, from parking meters to hotels, were targeted by looters and vandals. Casinos, connected in the public mind with foreign gangsters and Batista's proclivities for American business, were also branded as anti-revolutionary. Mobs looted casinos, though the venerable Hotel National was not damaged. The Plaza Hotel's recently completed casino, however, was completely destroyed, and others gaming rooms suffered damages. Although Fidel Castro initially seemed willing to regulate rather than prohibit casino gambling, smart operators realized that casinos had no real future in Cuba. On September 29, 1961, Fidel Castro announced that casino gambling would henceforth be illegal in Havana and the last remaining casino was unceremoniously closed.

Agua Caliente, a golf course and hotel complex near Tijuana, Mexico, opened in 1928 with a luxurious casino and several restaurants. Two years later, a racetrack opened, and the resort drew Hollywood stars and wealthy Americans until President Lazaro Cardenas ordered an end to all gambling in 1935. The racetrack reopened two years later, but never recaptured its former popularity.

North of the border, Montreal was a center for horse racing thanks to telegraph betting. Illegal casinos featured games like roulette and craps but also barbotte, a dice game unique to Montreal which was far and away the local favorite.

Urban gambling, from bookmakers to slot machines, became so widespread that, by the 1940s, it could no longer be hidden. The voting public demanded that their elected officials do something about "syndicate crime," seemingly oblivious to the fact that, if they themselves stopped gambling illegally, the syndicates would crumble. Nevertheless, public animosity towards "boss gamblers" became a potent political issue in the late 1940s. In 1950 the ambitious Tennessee Senator Estes Kefauver capitalized on the anti-gambling furor by chairing a special Senate committee that investigated "organized crime in interstate commerce." Known as the Kefauver Committee, its televised hearings (in which reputed gangsters invoking their Fifth Amendment rights when asked even the most basic questions) introduced a shocked public to the idea that local gambling was a big business controlled by murderous national crime syndicates.

Though Kefauver's investigations often missed the mark, the wave of reform he provoked succeeded in closing many illegal gambling centers. This time, though, state governments didn't just force gamblers to lay low until the reform impulse had passed; by and large, they moved into the lucrative gambling business themselves, under the guide of public interest gaming. Outrage at the profits secured by gambling racketeers had given way to unabashed envy. When Attorney General Robert F. Kennedy mounted an even more concerted federal drive against "organized gambling" in 1961, he legitimately wished to purge the nation of corrupt "boss gamblers."

These anti-gambling drives would, paradoxically, help a growing gambling resort solidify its presence. With Americans no longer able to play close to home, many of them began considering a trip to the desert to indulge their yen for gambling. Managers and dealers who'd learned their trade in underworld casinos likewise headed west, to a city where they'd be free to practice their craft.

In the end, Kefauver and Kennedy did more to help Las Vegas than its most ardent boosters ever did.

Hard to Resist

Nevada becomes America's gambling oasis

Nevada's First Gamble on Gambling *gambling illegal*
When the first California miners spilled eastward over the Sierra Nevadas in search of gold in the late 1850s, they brought their gambling with them. California had only banned mercantile bank games four years earlier, and social gambling was still legal there. But Nevada's territorial governor, James Nye, a New Yorker appointed by the Lincoln Administration to oversee the transition to statehood, inveighed mightily against gambling in his message to the newly assembled territorial legislature in 1861. Reminding the gathered solons of their duty to legislate against vice (including carrying concealed weapons, drinking, and Sabbath-breaking), he paused before exhorting them to be particularly vigilant against gambling: "Of all the seductive vices extant, I regard that of gambling as the worst," he declared. "It holds out allurements hard to resist."

The legislators heeded Nye's admonitions and later that year proscribed stiff penalties for running a game of chance: a maximum $5,000 fine and two-year prison sentence. Even playing a game of chance was a misdemeanor with penalties of six months in jail and a $500 fine. Enforcement was left to local authorities, who balked at enforcing an unpopular law. To stimulate prosecutions, the legislature offered a $100 bounty—to be paid by defendants—for every conviction. Still, this measure was not much of a success and when Nevada became a state in 1864 members of its new legislature attempted to legalize and regulate gambling. They failed. At the urging of new governor Henry Blasdel, who was even more staunchly opposed to gambling than Nye, the legislature passed in 1865 a new law that was less harsh than the original—gaming operators were punished more mildly and players not at all—but still made gambling illegal, and garnered no revenues for the state.

Governor Blasdel continued to fight ferociously against any tolerance of gambling, which he declared an "intolerable and inexcusable vice." In 1867 he turned aside a proposal to legalize it, but in 1869 gambling supporters succeeded in passing—over the governor's veto—an act to decriminalize gambling in the Silver State. To legally offer games of chance, a proprietor had to pay a quarterly license fee of $400 in Storey County (then the state's most populous county and home of its biggest city, Virginia City) and $250 in all other counties. The county sheriff collected the fee, half of which went to the county and half to the state. There were few regulations: the gambling age was set at 17, and conducting a game in the front room of a building's bottom story was forbidden.

Nevada's gaming laws would change over the next forty years with little rhyme or reason. In 1871, the legislature lowered license fees, but in the next legislative session debated a bill to adopt California's ban on gambling. Though that ban was defeated, the legislature began to take a harder line on gambling. In 1875 it raised the minimum age to 21, demanded a $400 quarterly fee—paid in advance—for all operations, and prohibited gambling parlors from advertising. It also passed an act to "prohibit cheating and unlawful games" which outlawed three-card monte and similar hustles and made cheating a felony. This measure was not designed to protect the gambling halls, as Nevada's later anti-cheating laws would be, but rather to safeguard the public from con artists like Honest John Kelly who duped gullible travelers. The law specifically empowered railroads to arrest suspected offenders.

This law protected the public from sharpers, but not those who gambled too much at honest games. The 1877 legislature came to the rescue of these unfortunates with an "act to prohibit the winning of money from persons who have no right to gamble it away." Under this law, any family or creditor could give a gambling proprietor notice that a particular father or debtor should not be permitted to gamble. Anyone who accepted a wager from someone thus identified was guilty of a misdemeanor. Men were hardly thrilled at the prospect of being forbidden from gambling by their wives, but the law was rarely invoked.

Throughout the remainder of the century, Nevada continued to tinker with legal gaming, changing the provisions for first-floor gaming, hours of operations, and permitted games. The new mechanical slot machines became legal in 1905 with the proviso that they not be visible from the street and their owner paid a $20 per machine quarterly license fee. Swimming against the anti-bookmaking tide, Nevada in 1903 legalized bookmaking on horseracing.

The legalization of bookmaking suggested that Nevada could profit by permitting what other states forbade. Yet this sentiment was hardly universal, and many citizens of Reno, now the state's leading city, felt that legal vice was more an embarrassment than an opportunity. Although attempts to outlaw gambling in Reno failed in the first years of the 20th century, legislators statewide became increasingly attuned to the small but vocal anti-gambling minority, most of whom were swept up in the self-improvement and anti-vice principles of the burgeoning Progressive movement. In 1909 the anti-gamblers triumphed at last when they succeeded in gaining the support of enough lawmakers to pass a law (signed into law by Governor Denver Dickerson) that made it unlawful to deal or play a range of social (poker, bridge, whist) and mercantile (fan tan, faro, craps) games, to maintain a slot machine, or to make book on horse races. Those who violated the law could be sentenced to as many as five years in prison. Nevada's days as a wide-open gambling haven were, it seemed, over.

But gamblers kept at least a foot in the door. Two years later, the legislature relaxed the prohibition on social games such as whist and bridge (keeping poker on the forbidden list), though it kept the ban on bank games, slots, and bookmaking. In 1913 the state's lawmakers went even further and allowed all social games and "nickel-in-the-slot machines" played for drinks, cigars, or sums less than two dollars. In 1915 pari-mutuel betting was legalized, though only at tracks where races were being run. By 1919, cities and counties throughout the state were licensing card rooms that permitted social games.

While mercantile games were prohibited, another "outlaw" diversion, boxing, remained. Though other states refused to sanction prizefights, Nevada often did, and promoters staged the bouts more for the betting action than the gate receipts. Tex Rickard (who had parlayed a share in a Goldfield, Nevada, gambling hall into a career as a boxing promoter, builder of Madison Square Gardens and first owner of the New York Rangers) and others staged bouts in Goldfield and other towns in the early 20th century, but the most famous fight he promoted—the July 4, 1910, contest between the black heavyweight champion Jack Johnson and his white challenger Jim Jeffries—almost didn't take place in Nevada. It was only after the governor of California strenuously objected to the fight being held in his state that its location was moved to Reno. While training for the fight, Johnson got into the Nevada spirit by politely inviting in fans who came to watch him work out at a resort near Reno to have a few drinks, play some poker, and listen to a jazz band he had hired. This generosity did not offset the white public's largely hostile view of Johnson, and when the rugged fighter demolished the "Great White Hope" Jeffries at his leisure, the Reno crowd sat in stunned silence (though the news of the fight sparked race riots in other cities).

Nevada Rolls the Dice Again

In 1920s, Reno was home to numerous legal card rooms. Clubs that allowed forbidden games flourished, often with the knowledge of the police. The leaders of Reno's gambling underworld were James McKay and William Graham, who also controlled much of the illegal trade in liquor and narcotics and prostitution (Reno's infamous Stockade, a sort of Wal-Mart for the sex trade, was theirs). Under the aegis of George Wingfield, a former cowboy and gambler who had parlayed his steely resolve into a Nevada banking and commercial empire, McKay, Graham, and their associates dominated Reno. As speakeasies and houses of prostitution already abounded in certain areas of Reno, adding a faro table or roulette wheel in a bar that already had slot machines and poker games was hardly a capital offense. Though the official licenses did not reflect it, Reno's gaming industry was booming.

In the roaring 1920s, as Americans drank bootlegged liquor in defiance of Prohibition, pro- and anti-gambling forces fought in

Nevada. No one, it seemed, was satisfied with the halfway covenant that allowed gambling but deprived legitimate business the opportunity to profit from it. Reform groups, chambers of commerce, and politicians with their ears to the electoral ground debated the merits of expanding the state's approval of social games into "wide-open" gambling and embracing protective legislation that would ban gambling entirely. At first, the antis had the upper hand; wide-open proposals died on the legislature floor in 1925 and 1927 and backers didn't even bother to introduce one in 1929. With the smaller operators of existing card rooms, moral reformers, and many business elements opposed to wide-open gaming, the chances for further progress seemed slim.

In the end, money talked. The economic malaise brought on by the Great Depression led prominent Nevadans, including big gambling operators, businesspeople, and business groups, to increasingly embrace wide-open gambling. Las Vegas real estate developer Tom Carroll bought newspaper advertisements that touted wide-open gambling and horseracing as the center of a strategy to make Nevada the nation's playground. Many found the idea laughable, but others listened. By the time that freshman assemblyman Phil Tobin, a Humboldt County rancher with no known gambling connections, introduced Assembly Bill 98 on February 13, 1931, it was clear that this year, there would be a real fight for wide-open gambling.

After extensive debate, the gaming interests carried the day: the bill passed the House and Senate. Governor Fred Balzar signed it into law on March 19, 1931. Nevadans were now free to gamble at a number of games: faro, monte, roulette, keno, fan tan, twenty-one, black jack (listed as separate games), seven-and-a-half, big injun, klondyke, craps, stud poker, draw poker, "or any banking or percentage game" played with cards, dice, or a machine, provided they did so at a licensed establishment. Licenses for social games (poker, bridge, and whist) cost $25 per table per month, mercantile games $50 each, and slot machines $10 each. Licenses were to be approved by city commissioners and issued by county auditors, and the county sheriff was to collect all license fees. Their disposition reflects the scattered nature of the licensing and taxing process: one-half of all fees went to the city or town, one-quarter to the county, and one-quarter to the state.

This law placed a few restrictions on gambling: it prohibited "thieving games" and cheating with marked cards or other devices, and it set the legal gaming age at twenty-one. In addition, it barred aliens from even applying for licenses, no doubt a reflection of the anti-immigrant (more particularly, anti-Asian) sentiment that was still strong in the 1930s. But, fitting its promotion as a wide-open gambling law, it gave cities tremendous latitude in licensing new gambling establishments. Along with a successful bill to cut the state's three-month residency requirement for "quickie" divorces to six weeks, the wide-open gambling act created the possibility that Nevada might indeed prosper by permitting what others forbade.

Reno Makes a Splash

Right away, Reno profited more than any other Nevada city from the liberalization of divorce and gambling laws. Reno "wide-open" gambling got its coming out with the Max Baer-Paolino Uzcudun fight on July 4, 1931 (promoted by Graham and McKay). It was an economic awakening. McKay and Graham had moved quickly to take advantage of legal gaming: they installed slot machines at the venue of the Baer-Uzcudun fight and built a temporary casino at the racetrack they controlled. With the passage of the six-week divorce bill, dude ranches catering to hopeful divorcees rapidly proliferated, and gambling halls were just as quick to sprout up. They offered a variety of games, including faro, panguingue, roulette, twenty-one, craps, monte, fan tan, klondike, chuck-a-luck, hazard, rouge-et-noir, and several kinds of poker. As the industry became more established, though, the selection of games narrowed appreciably.

Monte, hazard, and klondike (a now-obscure dice game unrelated to solitare) began appearing less frequently on license applications, and even the once-great faro was rarely found after the 1930s, either because it was too open to cheating or too even a game. Popular wisdom holds that both reasons contributed to its downfall, though mathematicians have pointed out that honest faro, as usually dealt, has a house edge comparable to that in craps, which in the 1930s became the pre-eminent Nevada casino game. Another game, panguingue, was occasionally found in Nevada casinos after 1931's legalization. Pan was a rummy-like game that came to the United States from the Philippines, where it is said to have originated among the Tagalog peoples in the early 20th century. Popular on the West Coast, many early gambling halls and even later casinos offered it.

In Reno, gambling halls were not formally restricted to any single part of town—at first—but the stretch of Center Street between Commercial Row and Second Street soon became the town's de facto casino district. McKay and Graham owned several gambling properties (including the out-of-the-way Willows, which had a reputation as a posh retreat as early as the 1920s) at various times, but the jewel of their holdings was Reno's most prominent casino of the 1930s, the Bank Club. The property began as a second-story room in which the pair ran illegal games, including a race book. With legalization, they moved to the ground floor of the building next door. With as many as twenty table games running at peak hours and about sixty employees, it was the biggest club in town. McKay and Graham were not above using strong-arm tactics against promising rivals; they were believed to have sent confederates to sabotage the Monte Carlo, an elegant resort that closed soon after its 1931 opening. They also used their possession of the local race wire franchise to intimidate and punish those who would not meet their demands. It was widely rumored that McKay and Graham laundered money for several notorious bank robbers and criminals. Despite its unsavory reputation, the Bank Club weathered several scandals, including Graham's fatal shooting of a professional gambler in another club (as Graham had been shot at first, it was later ruled to be self-defense).

Another murder, that of bank cashier Roy Frisch, was not so easily shrugged off. Frisch had been scheduled to testify against McKay and Graham at one of their fraud trials before he mysteriously disappeared. It was alleged, but never proved, that notorious gangster Baby Face Nelson, who was a friend of the pair, had killed Frisch. Finally, the law caught up with the Bank Club when its principles, McKay and Graham, were convicted of mail fraud (on their third trial) in 1938. Though the pair continued to operate the Bank Club through managers, it began to fade, and eventually closed.

Their first serious rival was the Palace Club, begun by a former partner of McKay and Graham, John Petricianni. Petricianni successfully raised a legal challenge to McKay and Graham's monopoly of the race wire by threatening to ask the federal authorities to more closely examine the business's legality. The Palace never quite eclipsed the Bank Club in popularity, but ran a strong second for much of the 1930s. The club was regarded as the best place for gamblers to indulge in high-stakes play, and famous gamblers like Nick "the Greek" Dandalos played at the club while in town.

The Palace Club, like most other major clubs of Commercial Street, did not hire women dealers, and non-whites, though not legally barred, were usually not welcome. But several clubs off the main drag welcomed blacks, Native Americans, and Asians. Smaller clubs usually opened their doors to anyone with money; many of these were found on Lake Street, which had been the site of Reno's Chinatown (before municipal authorities burned it to the ground in 1908). Some of them, like the New Star Club and Henry's Club, were operated by Chinese-Americans. Freddie Aoyama, a Japanese-American, managed the Reno Club, a gambling/bingo hall, in the 1930s, though he left when anti-Japanese sentiment after Pearl Harbor forced the Reno Club's Japanese-American owners to sell. Although there were not many African-Americans in Reno, the city eventually had a black-owned gambling club, the Peavine, a nightclub to which owner Harry Wright added several table games in the early 1940s. Though most major clubs adopted segregationist polices, there remained possibilities for minority players and owners in Reno.

Reno gamblers of all backgrounds shared a love for bingo and its many variations. Bingo took America by storm in the gloomy 1930s. In Reno, the game was often called tango. The gambling district boasted several tango parlors in the early 1930s, and many gambling halls had two rooms, one reserved for tango and the other for casino games. Unlike today's bingo, tango had an apparent element of skill; instead of drawing numbers from a hopper, operators had players toss balls at a target. Tango had two competitors: the game of keno, which was still played in its original form, and the Chinese lottery, easily recognizable as the pakapoo or White Pigeon Ticket lottery. The former was so similar to bingo that it soon lost its identity, and the latter had two disadvantages: it was traditionally drawn twice a day, far too rarely to generate action in the bustling gambling district, and it was held by authorities to be a lottery, and therefore illegal in Nevada.

John Petricianni of the Palace Club introduced a variant of the pakapoo lottery that became an enduring casino game. He found a version of the game being legally run in Montana (where it may have been brought by peripatetic Chinese laborers) that used a punch board with hidden capsules containing numbers rather than an urn from which slips of paper were drawn. Petricianni hired Warren Nelson to run the game in his Palace Club. Before taking bets, he convinced Nevada governor Richard Kirman that the game was not a lottery but actually "racehorse keno," where players bet on horse names, not numbers. All winners were to be paid off at the end of a game, and winners were paid by the house at fixed odds rather than out of a pool of bets; this made it a bank game and, therefore, not a lottery. Racehorse keno debuted at the Palace in June 1936 and was wildly successful, with several draws drawn each hour. Nelson soon substituted numbered balls for the punch board, and the modern game of keno achieved its present form. The game was so successful that it forced the New Star, which still offered the traditional twice-a-day pakapoo game, out of business.

Another Reno icon that would soon be nationally famous debuted a year earlier when Harolds Club opened its doors. The club was owned by Harold Smith (though it was spelled without the apostrophe) whose father Raymond I. "Pappy" Smith had begun roving the country running carnival games in his teens. Pappy ultimately settled in Northern California, where he ran games of chance at an amusement park near San Francisco and bingo games at Rio Nido in Sonoma County. With a local crackdown on bingo and related games, Pappy decided that he'd best move his operation to Reno, where his son Harold bought a floundering Virginia Street bingo parlor.

The Smiths put their carnival background to good use and introduced many innovations that eventually became standard. They started humbly, with only a roulette wheel they had salvaged from a broken-up Modesto operation and some slot machines, but soon had a variety of games. As there were already several bingo parlors in the vicinity, the Smiths did not open a bingo parlor. Still, they used their knowledge of gambling to their benefit. While most clubs had dark and forbidding interiors, Harolds was brightly-lit and its employees were deliberately friendly. The Smiths also offered free lessons on how to play, something that successfully lured many heretofore novices.

Observing potential female players balking at braving the aggressively masculine gambling hall, Pappy decided to hire woman dealers after the club opened. Pappy got the idea when a prospective woman gambler, after a few tentative steps inside the club, looked around, exclaimed, "There are no women here!" and ran out. Other club owners at first laughed at the idea (seemingly, they had no knowledge that women had been expert dealers for years throughout the Old West), but when they saw how female dealers brought in new customers, they soon emulated the practice. Harolds was also the first club to remain open twenty-four hours a day and the first to enjoy the luxury of air conditioning. Some of Pappy's ideas, such as a roulette game that used a live mouse, fizzled, but even when he failed, the patriarch was not defeated. The mouse game was a disaster and only lasted a week, but got the upstart club plenty of free publicity. The slogan "Harolds Club or Bust" became known worldwide as it was posted by American servicemen abroad who had appreciated Pappy's hospitality while in Reno. Domestically, the Smiths placed 2300 signs on the nation's busiest roadways. The club was a smashing success, drawing on smaller bettors, curious tourists, and women. Though Harolds had its roots in the shady carnival past, it pointed the way towards the future of Nevada gaming: brightly-lit, loudly-promoted, and customer-friendly. Once an outcast (the Smiths were blocked from purchasing a location on the city's main casino street, Center), Harolds helped shift the center of gravity to Virginia Street, which soon boasted most of the city's successful casinos.

Another Virginia Street upstart founded a gambling empire that would become the world's largest casino corporation. William Fisk Harrah started in the business in 1933 by taking over a Venice, California, bingo-like game from his father. Harrah stood conventional wisdom on its head by firing the shills, reasoning that players would find a smaller game more attractive, since they would actually have a greater chance to win. He was right. He also insisted on giving the

In 1937, Bill Harrah opened his first bingo parlor in bustling downtown Reno, not far from friendly rival Raymond Smith's Harolds Club.

customer comfortable surroundings (in this case, more comfortably padded stools). When Harrah found himself on the wrong side of a local reform fight, he elected to try his luck in Reno.

Arriving in town in May 1937, Harrah bought a failing Center Street bingo parlor, the Silver Tango, and renamed it Harrah's Club Bingo. A marginal location, combined with keen competition, drove Harrah out of business within a matter of weeks. Harrah doggedly resolved to try again, leasing a new location on Commercial Row in July 1938 as Harrah's Plaza Tango. Harrah soon abandoned the location when he bought out a failing Virginia Street parlor, Howe's Heart Tango, renaming it Harrah's Heart Tango. This new location proved a lucky one, and Harrah quickly gained traction in the competitive bingo wars of the late 1930s. He then branched out by buying a bar in which he and a partner ran twenty-one, roulette, and slot machines, and eventually built Harrah's Club—later Harrah's Casino—on Virginia Street.

Harrah built his reputation on attention to operational detail and tireless customer service. The classic story, that he demanded an immediate explanation for any burned-out light bulb, illustrates the emphasis that Harrah's managers placed on consistently presenting the best image possible. Working at Harrah's Reno gambling hall (or, starting in 1955, his Reno property) meant that an employee was thoroughly indoctrinated in the Harrah's way. In fact, those who learned their trade in Las Vegas were often told to look elsewhere when they applied for jobs at Harrah's: managers complained that they brought bad habits—shortcuts and shoddy work—with them.

Harrah had a simple philosophy: provide a pleasant atmosphere for middle-income gamblers and let the house advantage take care of the rest. He was among the first to begin a bus marketing program, bringing Greyhounds with visitors from San Francisco to his Tahoe property. To draw players he also engaged top-quality entertainers. An intensely introverted man, he only felt comfortable speaking with celebrities, who were often just as shy as he, or "car guys" with whom he could share his love of classic automobiles. Despite his aloofness (he seldom walked through the public areas of his own casino), Harrah brought the idea of mass production to the casino floor by creating a uniformly satisfying experience for all patrons.

While Harolds and Harrah's pursued the everyman (and everywoman) bettor, other Reno clubs harked back to the elegantly-appointed casinos of Europe. The Deauville, which opened in 1931, catered to the wealthy set and styled itself as one of the world's most luxurious gambling houses. Unable to meet its high overhead, however, it lasted only two years. Yet others jumped to fill its meticulously-shined shoes—Club Fortune, which opened in 1937, was the most successful of these. It was a combination casino-nightclub-restaurant that was aggressively promoted as the city's finest "palatial new gambling and dining spot." Though the image of patrons tossing baseballs into a moving cart to determine tango winners hardly suggests sophistication to today's readers, the club nevertheless developed a reputation as a leading nightspot. In addition to the tango salon, the Club Fortune also had a carpeted gaming room with twenty-one, craps, and roulette, the trio of games that were fast becoming the standard throughout Nevada. Touted as the ultimate Reno luxury nightspot, it suggested an alternative to Harolds and Harrah's path, though it would be Southern Nevada operators who ultimately continued on this course.

Renoites did not have to go to the large gambling houses to indulge their desires for games of chance. Virtually every public place, from bars and restaurants to hotels, bowling alleys, cigar stores, hotel lobbies, and drug stores had slot machines. Soon after the legalization of slots in 1931, a Nevada tradition started when four Reno-area Piggly Wigglies installed slot machines. Slots in convenience stores and supermarkets remain a peculiar institution of Nevada today. Eventually slots disappeared from some of the more outrageous sites, such as soda fountains, but they remained part of many establishments, and a cadre of slot route operators, who owned small clusters of machines in several locations, soon sprung up.

As World War II approached, the Reno city council drew a red line around what had become its casino district in midtown and

In his Reno club, Bill Harrah pioneered in providing a uniformly customer-oriented gambling experience. This 1959 photo shows the inside of the club that is today Harrah's Reno.

refused to license any gambling halls (excepting "luxury" hotels with at least 100 rooms) outside of it. This decision pleased Renoites still opposed to gambling, existing gambling interests who had less competition to fear, and business owners in the surrounding areas who were now safe from losing their leases to lucrative casinos. Though the red line ultimately fell, it would slow the development of Reno's casino business in the crucial 1940s and 1950s.

Other areas of Nevada had a diversity of gambling clubs. At Lake Tahoe, where South Shore and North Shore clubs soon began entertaining travelers on the California-Nevada state line, gambling houses were largely seasonal, closing for the snowbound winter months until the area became a popular ski attraction. For years the pre-eminent Tahoe club was the Cal-Neva Lodge, which had first operated during the 1920s by straddling the border; when Nevada authorities raided, all gambling equipment was moved to the California side of the property, and when California troopers threatened, it was shifted back to Nevada. Because it was owned by the infamous partnership of McKay and Graham, though, it was seldom disturbed. In the 1930s, the Lodge attracted a range of guests, including socialites in evening dresses, wealthy gambling habitués, and notorious gangsters like Baby Face Nelson and Pretty Boy Floyd. Though it burned to the ground in May 1937, it was quickly rebuilt and reopened in July of that year. In the 1960s, it was for a time partially owned by Frank Sinatra, who surrendered his Nevada gaming license and sold his interest after allegations that he had hosted alleged mobster Sam Giancana at the casino.

Elsewhere, small communities, usually along important highways or at state borders, had a few gambling operations. They typically offered none of the frills of Reno clubs, but sometimes they pushed ahead of their big-city brethren. Ely-area gambling clubs competed more intensely than those in Reno and few smaller cities lacked their own gambling houses. Elko, a chief town in northeastern Nevada, boasted the Commercial Hotel, which was the most prominent of several bars, clubs, and hotels. Not letting their remote location or small size deter them, Elko's gambling proprietors sought to promote their town. In 1941 the Commercial's manager, Newton Crumley, Jr., scored a coup when he brought in Ted Lewis, then a popular bandleader, to star in the hotel's new showroom; this was the first major headliner to play an American casino. Lewis was followed by a parade of notables, including Ray Noble, Chico Marx, Paul Whiteman, and Sophie Tucker. Crumley set a trend in Nevada gaming; over the next several decades, casino entertainment would develop into a multi-million dollar business in its own right.

Though many of these small-town gambling halls had enterprising owners and enthusiastic patrons, they would soon be outshone by a bright neon glare coming from the state's southern reaches. Though it was initially as obscure as Yerington, Pioche, Eureka, or Winnemucca, Las Vegas would grow to challenge and then supplant mighty Reno as the state's gaming center. Within a half-century of gaming legalization, it would be considered the world's premiere gambling destination.

Las Vegas, Pre-Viva

The future "gambling and entertainment capital of the world" had an inauspicious origin. Begun by the Salt Lake, Los Angeles, and San Pedro Railroad with a land auction in 1905, the town was still confused with Las Vegas, New Mexico, a generation after its founding. Even though Las Vegas grew rapidly in the 1920s, it still had barely 5,000 residents by 1930. But at the time of the 1931 gambling decriminalization, Las Vegas residents were already giddy with anticipation over a completely unrelated development: the federal government's construction of Hoover Dam southeast of the town on the Colorado River. The dam brought federal dollars and a modicum of publicity to the formerly-sleepy railroad stopover. The gambling dam, however, was just about to burst, because within fifteen years legal gaming would transform the area far more than the massive engineering project to the south.

Like Reno, Las Vegas was no stranger to gambling. In the town's original master plan, the notorious Block 16 (First and Second Street between Stewart and Ogden) was designated a red light district in which saloons and brothels could operate without interference. Fremont Street, the town's original main thoroughfare (it radiated eastward from the foot of the rail depot) was dotted with legal card rooms where prohibited games could often be found after the 1909 gambling ban.

When the state legalized gaming, cities and counties split the authority to issue licenses; their powers were mutually exclusive, so that if an establishment was in the city of Las Vegas, its owner went to the five-member City Commission, but if it was outside the city, its owner petitioned the then three-member County Commission. This would have tremendous ramifications for the future of Clark County gaming.

The City Commission acted quickly, first discussing potential Fremont Street clubs on March 25, 1931, less than a week after the legislature had approved legal gaming. Two weeks later, the Commission issued the first four licenses, and legal gambling began. This quick action was a far cry from today's ponderous licensing process though: licenses were screened by the commissioners and, if no one objected and everything seemed in order, they were promptly approved. There was no background investigation, environmental impact statement, or vetting of project finances.

The first licenses went to a cluster of downtown clubs: the Boulder Club, at 118 Fremont; the Las Vegas Club, at 21 and 23 Fremont (across the street from its present location); the Exchange Club, at 123 S. First Street; and the Northern Club, at 15 Fremont Street. After granting these licenses, the Commission resolved not to grant any licenses to new establishments until after it had established a gambling zone—a formality it never pursued. Within a month, it had granted two more licenses and issued several slot machine permits, both in established clubs and for restaurants and retail establishments. The Vegas Sweet Shoppe, for example, got 17 machines on June 29, by far the largest number (more than double the runner-up, the Boulder Drug store). Given that gambling was restricted to those over 21, it was curious that a candy store would receive so many slots. By the next year, the Commission would issue more than a dozen licenses.

Las Vegas clubs, like those in Reno, were mostly owned by limited partnerships, in which a small group of owners, one of whom was usually an on-site manager, pooled their capital and split the profits, a pattern long established in illegal casinos throughout the nation. Proprietors had diverse backgrounds: some had long careers in vice, while others did not. J. Kell Houssels, principal owner of the

Las Vegas Club, was a trained mining engineer who found gambling more lucrative than metallurgy. He began running the Las Vegas Club as a card room, and parlayed his role as a full gaming operator into interests in several downtown casinos, a successful stable of racehorses, and ownership of the Strip's Tropicana. His son, J. Kell Houssels, Jr., followed him into the business.

Women played key roles in a few of the early clubs, and a woman was among those granted the first four licenses. Mayme Stocker, along with manager Joe Morgan, received the license for the Northern Club. Her husband and sons all worked for the railroad and maintained an interest in the club, though as railroad employees they were officially barred from owning it. It had initially been a legal card room, but within two years of becoming a full-fledged gambling hall, the Stocker family sold the operation. But she was not the only woman in Las Vegas's nascent gambling industry. The wife of Thomas Rowan, an owner of the Rainbow Club, bought out her husband's partner after his death and remained a proprietor for several years. Joe Morgan went on to open the Silver Club, an establishment which he operated with his wife Helen, who also dealt cards and ran the roulette wheel—an early exception to the city's de facto ban on woman dealers.

These women represented the growing trend of female involvement in gambling. Although Las Vegas clubs at first did not make any special efforts to attract women, they began to admit them. By the end of the 1930s they actively sought to become more hospitable to women, adding new features, particularly dance floors and entertainment. Several specifically bought advertisements that read "ladies welcome." But one prejudice remained: though Reno clubs hired so many women to deal that, by the 1940s, the idea of a woman dealer was cliché, Las Vegas casinos, for the most part, refused to do so, and confined women to a small circle of jobs: shill, waitress, change girl, housekeeper, and entertainer.

The early downtown gambling halls had virtually identical features: a bar, a few table games (usually twenty-one and craps, with roulette and faro often mixed in), a score of slot machines, and sometimes a room for "Tango Derby" (bingo). Mayme Stocker's 1931 application for a keno license was denied, though she received one the next year after she sued the city. After much back and forth, the city finally permitted keno, though it continued to disallow applications for racehorse keno. Soon, several clubs boasted keno parlors with more than a hundred seats.

In their advertisements, Las Vegas clubs shouted "Come one, come all," but from the start, like Reno's establishments, they frequently barred African-Americans. Jim Crow was not, at first, absolute, though race was enough of an issue that in April 1931 the City Commission specifically stated that, despite limiting licenses, they would still consider applications by "a person of the Ethiopian Race for the conduct of a game or games in a place catering exclusively to persons of the same race only." The Commission ultimately granted such a license to a club on Stewart Street, then the site of several black-owned businesses. In the next decade, segregation in Las Vegas would become more rigid, and clubs geared towards a black clientele—though they accepted whites as patrons without prejudice—appeared on the Westside. Some were owned by blacks and others by whites, and clubs like the Alabam, Harlem Club, Brown Derby, and Cotton Club provided virtually the only outlet for black Las Vegas residents or visitors who wished to gamble until the city's unofficial but brutally present policy of segregation crumbled in 1961.

Some club owners spoke of the need to exclude "undesirable elements" from their clubs, but they were blind to a very real danger: affiliates of organized crime who came to Las Vegas in the 1940s. Initially, legal Nevada gaming had little attraction for bootleggers and those who ran organized gambling outfits in the cities of California and the East. With money rolling in already, they had no reason to invest in the comparatively small stakes of Nevada. But a sequence of events forced a change. After the end of Prohibition in 1933, many organized crime groups replaced bootlegging with illegal gambling, which meant new entrants into the business. Next, in the mid- and late-1930s, California authorities began cracking down on illegal games, driving many illegal operators to Nevada, including the relatively clean William Harrah and Raymond Smith, but also convicted criminals and those suspected of links to organized crime.

Gambling inside the Boulder Club, a typical Fremont Street gambling hall of the 1930s and 1940s. Early Las Vegas clubs featured craps, roulette, blackjack, slots, and occasionally older games like faro.

The influx began in earnest in 1941, when the Nevada legislature passed a law that legitimized pool rooms, though they called the facilities race books. The race wire, whose domination by underworld figures could not be contested, powered illegal pool rooms throughout the nation, and through it criminal elements would find a foothold in Nevada. Even before the law, race books had been tolerated, and their history was hardly stellar; Graham and McKay had used their race wire franchise in Northern Nevada to pry their way into the management of several clubs. But with the apparent acquiescence of Nevada authorities to a gambling form universally condemned throughout the nation, even more notorious criminal elements saw opportunities for plunder.

A national war over control of the race wire had been raging. After Mont Tennes's retirement, Moses Annenberg had consolidated the racing information business under his Nationwide News Service. This made the race wire even more lucrative than it had been: his monopoly served an estimated 15,000 bookmakers nationwide, and estimates of its annual profits ran as high as $2 million. Facing a federal legal onslaught that eventually sent him to prison for income tax evasion, he sold off Nationwide in 1939. Two rival factions, the Continental Press Service and Trans-American Publishing, feuded for dominion of the profitable franchise. The Los Angeles representative of Trans-American, Benjamin "Bugsy" Siegel (a reputed member of Murder, Inc.), sought to expand his area of influence to Arizona and Nevada. Before long, he had acquired interests in several downtown racebooks, and he and his associates began planning to buy or build a casino of their own.

Siegel was not the only outlaw to search for riches in the neon oasis of Las Vegas. Guy McAfee had abandoned a career as a Los Angeles Police Department vice-squad commander for one openly dedicated to gaming after he chose to resign from the department rather than face corruption charges (he owned several illegal casinos while supposedly directing the LAPD's war against vice). With the crackdown on illegal Los Angeles gambling in the late 1930s, McAfee set up shop near Las Vegas, where he bought the 91 Club, a small roadhouse-type establishment on the then-neglected Los Angeles Highway. He and his associates bought the downtown Frontier Club in 1939, marking his debut as one of the most influential operators in the city. McAfee subsequently owned shares in several establishments and in 1946 opened the Golden Nugget, a downtown gambling hall that would prove pivotal in the career of the city's most innovative casino developer, Steve Wynn.

Another veteran of Los Angeles's gambling underworld had taken a shot in Las Vegas even earlier. Antonio Cornero Stralla, better known as Tony Cornero, had been a bootlegger during Prohibition, but like many others diversified into gambling, running casino boats off the Southern California coast in the 1930s. In 1931, he jumped at the chance to run games legally in Nevada and opened the Meadows just outside Las Vegas city limits, the first attempt at a "gambling resort" away from downtown. Though the club was officially owned by Cornero's brothers Louis and Frank (Cornero's felony conviction disqualified him), it was primarily Tony's inspiration. Located just over the city limits, where Fremont Street becomes the Boulder Highway, the gambling casino, cabaret, nightclub was designed to be the finest resort in the entire Southwest. It opened with great fanfare, but Cornero soon lost interest, leasing the property to a series of operators, and the resort struggled before closing in 1937. Cornero would return to Las Vegas in 1945 after the California authorities forced his offshore gambling boat the S.S. Rex, to close. He would run a gambling hall named the S.S. Rex on the first floor of the Apache Hotel, which had opened in 1932 as an elegant, three-story hotel and bar. It still operates today as part of Binion's casino.

The clubs of downtown Reno, Las Vegas, and small town Nevada catered chiefly to serious gamblers. They contributed their share to county treasuries, but were not viewed as essential to the state's general economy. Attempts to open more lavish resorts, such as Cornero's Meadows, were typically short-lived. Yet with the arrival of World War II—and the tremendous changes in American life and culture that would follow it—gambling resorts geared to the casual gambler and leisure traveler would transform the Las Vegas Valley. Though these hotels were inspired by European spa resorts, they still owed quite a bit to the original gambling clubs of Nevada, north and south.

10

A Place in the Sun

◇◇◇◇◇◇◇◇◇◇

The Las Vegas Strip is born

The El Rancho Vegas Starts Las Vegas Boulevard

In the 1930s, Las Vegas, Nevada, achieved national prominence. The construction and opening of nearby Hoover Dam early in the decade brought tourists and a must-see attraction. As war clouds darkened the horizon later in the decade, prospects for the city began to look up. The war would bring a jump in the city's population, as the nearby Basic Magnesium plant and Army Air Corps Gunnery School brought jobs and paychecks to the city. But even before the United States had entered World War II, the Las Vegas gambling landscape had been altered.

Though at the time it seemed like the opening of just another gambling hall, the debut of the El Rancho Vegas on April 3, 1941, signified the birth of the Las Vegas Strip, and began the transition from smoky downtown gambling halls to verdant, luxurious suburban resorts. The El Rancho Vegas opened on the Los Angeles Highway (also known as Highway 91), which angled out of Las Vegas and meandered approximately 300 miles, two-lane and unpaved much of the way, southwest towards Los Angeles. Before the El Rancho Vegas, there had been a few road houses and nightclubs along the highway. One, Frank and Angela Detra's Pair-a-Dice, opened in 1930 and later became the 91 Club, while another, the Red Rooster, went through a series of owners. Similarly, there had been a range of road houses along the Boulder Highway (which, true to its name, led to Boulder City and Hoover Dam) during the 1930s. These rough nightspots catered mostly to dam workers and, when construction was complete, most of them folded. Had more visitors driven to Las

Vegas from Arizona than California, the burst of development that took place on the Los Angeles Highway would probably have taken place on Boulder Highway, and Tony Cornero's Meadows would be remembered as a pioneering resort rather than the El Rancho Vegas.

The El Rancho Vegas was built after years of effort by local boosters to attract a genuine resort hotel for the city's downtown. Thomas Hull, a Californian who owned a small chain of El Rancho hotels, built one, but chose a parcel of land on Highway 91 just outside of city limits (San Francisco Street, today's Sahara Avenue) about three miles from downtown—to better attract the Angeleno tourist trade. Hull's complex had little in common with the city's previous hotels, like the Hotel Nevada/Sal Sagev (now the Golden Gate) and the Apache. Instead of bunching its rooms in a two- or three-story building whose ground floor housed a bar and casino—a steadfastly urban design—he built a sprawling complex: 63 rooms arranged in a series of separate bungalows surrounding a central building which had a casino, restaurant, and dinner theater. The casino resort—an isolated vacation palace in which gambling was only one of the attractions—was born.

The first casino built on Las Vegas's Highway 91, the El Rancho Vegas pioneered the integrated design that would become the hallmark of casinos along the Las Vegas Strip.

Visitors to the El Rancho Vegas were not expected to just drop by for a shot of whisky and a roll of the dice. Instead, the property was promoted as a full-service resort in which all of a guest's needs could be met effortlessly. During the day a guest might lounge by the pool or visit the health club for a massage or steam bath; at night, they could enjoy a fine meal and top-notch entertainment, all at a minimal cost. After the show, of course, they would gamble, and their losses would more than equal the casino's outlay on food, drink, and entertainment. The El Rancho Vegas began a Las Vegas tradition with its Chuck Wagon buffet (originally little more than cold cuts, but eventually to evolve into gourmet fare). As traditional urban gambling halls, be they illegal or legal, came to be regarded as hopelessly seedy, the idea of a casino as the centerpiece of a finely-manicured vacation resort would dramatically change American attitudes towards gambling.

Almost immediately, Hull had competition. Later in 1941 a local partnership opened the El Cortez at 600 East Fremont Street, several blocks east of the train station and other gambling halls. Like the El Rancho Vegas, the El Cortez had a restaurant, and though it lacked a full-blown showroom it sported a cocktail lounge which became a popular entertainment venue. Its 90 hotel rooms made it one of the town's larger operations. Another try at a downtown resort, the Nevada Biltmore, was less successful; opening in 1942 about six blocks north of the train station, like the Meadows it had a successful launch but ultimately sank; no other casino or hotel development took place near the Biltmore, and the resort closed in 1949.

The Next-to-Last Frontier

After the Biltmore's failure, there were no other attempts to build big resorts downtown until the 1950s, when the resorts along the Los Angeles Highway had already shifted the center of the city's tourist economy south. Even in 1942, it was becoming apparent that the future lay there, as the El Rancho Vegas was doing tremendous business. That year it got a neighbor: the Hotel Last Frontier opened October 30 on the previous site of the 91 Club, which Griffith had bought from Guy McAfee. Built by R. E. Griffith and his nephew, Bill Moore (the family owned a string of movie theaters and hotels in the Southwest), this was a "luxury" casino resort similar to the El Rancho Vegas, but with a twist: it was a themed resort, Las Vegas's first.

Earlier gambling halls didn't have themes—they were simply bars with a few table games added. The El Rancho Vegas was decorated in a western style, but made little attempt to follow through on the idea, short of throwing a few cowboy hats on the walls. The Last Frontier was an entirely different creature: according to Moore, the architect, it was consciously designed to replicate the Old West, down to antiqued wood ceilings and sandstone patios. Moore transformed the existing 91 Club into the Carillo Room lounge (named for Western movie actor Leo Carillo), and installed the erstwhile bar of the old Arizona Club—one of Block 16's pioneering saloons from earlier in the century—as the centerpiece of the Gay 90s Bar. But this genuine piece of saloon history wasn't authentic enough, so Moore added saddle-shaped barstools: guests could not mistake that they had re-entered the Old West.

The resort had the usual fixings (casino, bar, dinner theater, rooms, pool) but Moore felt it was incomplete. In 1947, he added the Last Frontier Village, a "genuine replica" of an old western town with a drug store, general store, post office, schoolhouse, and jail, a gambling hall (the Silver Slipper, which in 1951 opened as a separate casino within the village), and an assortment of artifacts collected by Robert "Doby Doc" Caudill, a gambler, collector of Western antique, and Las Vegas institution.

Such a thoroughly themed casino was far ahead of its time, but Moore's choice of a theme left him in the past. In the 1930s and 1940s, the city had promoted itself as the "Last Frontier" of the West, often using "the Old West in Modern Splendor" as a marketing catchphrase. Moore made that the resort's motto, though it became apparent, as new resorts pursued luxe rather than lassos, that the public was more interested in a ritzy sun-soaked vacation than reliving the Old West. In 1955, the Last Frontier made way for the space-age New Frontier and the Village eventually closed, though the Little Church of the West, once part of it, was transplanted to the southern end of the Strip and is still a wedding chapel today.

The Fabulous Flamingo

With the end of World War II, the floodgates opened. Tourists began discovering the pleasures of vacations in the resorts just outside Las Vegas, and developers hurried to grab a piece of this lucrative market. The next casino to open, the fabulous Flamingo, is notorious for its supposed founder, Ben Siegel. Some consider Siegel a brilliant visionary who saw limitless potential in a wasteland and successfully built and operated the city's first real casino. But there were already two flourishing casino resorts on the Los Angeles Highway when the Flamingo opened, and the idea for the resort did not come from Siegel, an unabashedly bloodthirsty gangster, but Billy Wilkerson, the suave, well-traveled publisher of the Hollywood Reporter and owner of several Los Angeles nightspots, including Ciro's and LaRue's. Yet Wilkerson was a tragic genius: a brilliant publicist and tireless promoter, he was also, unfortunately, a self-described "degenerate pathological gambler." Urged by his friends, including 20th Century Fox co-founder Joe Schenk, to cure himself by building his own casino, Wilkerson eventually began building the "Flamingo Club" on a piece of land south of the Hotel Last Frontier.

As should have been expected from a man with severe gambling problems, Wilkerson soon ran out of money. Desperate to finish his project, he accepted an emergency infusion of capital from a group of "Eastern investors" who included Siegel. Siegel, though he had little love for Las Vegas and no real experience in actually running a casino, much less building one, demanded a role in the decision-making process. At first deferring to Wilkerson, then merely tolerating him, Siegel eventually tired of the Flamingo's founder and, as the project's completion neared, delivered a chilling ultimatum: Wilkerson must surrender his share of the casino or suffer the consequences. Wilkerson was sufficiently awed by Siegel's reputation for violence that he hurried to the airport, flew to New York and then Paris, and checked into a room at the Hotel George V under a pseudonym. Still apprehensive, he spent the next few weeks reading newspapers and listening nervously to each footstep outside his door.

Back in Las Vegas, Siegel seized total control of the project. He had already moved up Wilkerson's planned March 1, 1947 opening date to December 26, 1946. Though the hotel was not ready for

guests, Siegel, desperate to begin generating a return on his investment, forged ahead with plans to throw open the doors of the casino
and hope for the best. He capriciously changed the opening date to
December 28, a Saturday, and mailed out formal invitations to an
opening gala. Changing his mind again, he moved the date back to
the 26th and ordered his staff to notify guests by phone. The opening was a disaster. A smattering of Hollywood B-listers showed up,
but bad weather, poor timing, and Siegel's noisome reputation kept
most of the stars in Los Angeles. Locals dressed in cowboy hats
and boots made a mockery of Siegel's claims to have opened a chic
cosmopolitan resort, and guests who won money from the tables,
with no rooms at the Flamingo, returned to the accommodations at
the El Rancho Vegas and Last Frontier, where they lost back money
that should have stayed at the Flamingo. After less than a month,
with the casino hemorrhaging cash, Siegel was forced to close the
Flamingo's doors.

More concerned with prolonging his life than recouping the hundreds of thousands of dollars he'd invested in the Flamingo, Wilkerson sold his remaining interest in the property for pennies on the
dollar. He returned to Hollywood, driving a bullet-proof Cadillac
that had once belonged to Tony Cornero. Receiving a tip that his life
was still in danger, Wilkerson hastily returned to Paris to wait out
the storm. Yet it was Siegel whose days were numbered. On June 20,
1947, while sitting in the living room of his mistress Virginia Hill,
he was gunned down. According to popular lore, before the dust had
even settled, Moe Sedway and Gus Greenbaum, representing the
"syndicate" interests, confidently strode through the front doors of
the Flamingo and assumed control of the operation.

The Siegel murder was never solved, triggering rampant speculation about who killed him, and why he was killed. At the time,
the struggle over control of the racing wire had erupted into more
or less open warfare in several cities, and at the time this was the
most popular theory. Others have suggested that his involvement in
a Mexican heroin smuggling ring led to his murder. The possibility
that his partners executed him for skimming construction money
from the Flamingo only became more widespread after the growth
of Las Vegas, and the gangster was enshrined as the mythic godfa-

ther of the Las Vegas, even though he had no vision for the future of the business and was a washout as a casino operator.

Yet the Flamingo was, in the end, a success story. Purged of Siegel's vicious temper and mismanagement, it became a popular resort and one of the mainstays of the 1950s Las Vegas Strip. Underworld influence continued; in 1973 it was proved in federal court that operators had concealed alleged mob kingpin Meyer Lansky's part-ownership of the casino and had been clandestinely funneling profits to him for years. Eventually, Hilton Hotels would buy the property and renovate it beyond recognition into a 3500-room, six-tower colossus. Though Wilkerson has been all but forgotten, the Hollywood operator ultimately found peace; after the birth of a son in 1951, he forswore gambling and, with few regrets, enjoyed a measure of happiness.

From Mayfield Road to the Mojave

In a few years the Flamingo would be surpassed by an even swankier resort, the Desert Inn, a casino that proved to be a true pioneer. Its founder was Wilbur Clark, an affable gambling operator who had worked the national circuit of illegal casinos from Saratoga to San Diego. He had dreams of greatness,and chafing at the newfound intolerance for California gambling, Clark moved to Las Vegas, where he bought into a score of gambling clubs, including the small Player's Club on the Los Angeles Highway. In 1945, he opened the downtown Monte Carlo Club on the site of the original Northern Club, and bought a majority share of the El Rancho Vegas. In 1946 he sold both to begin building a predictably luxurious resort on the Los Angeles Highway.

Clark started with high hopes but soon ran out of funds. Midway through the project in 1949, desperate for capital, and denied loans from traditional avenues, he turned to a group of Cleveland businessmen and gambling operators headed by Moe Dalitz. The group, which grew out of Cleveland's Mayfield Road Gang, also included Ruby Kolod, Morris Kleinman, and Sam Tucker. All of these men had made livings as bootleggers or illegal gambling operators and were rumored to have ties to the criminal underworld. In return for over $1.3 million in capital, the Cleveland group received a 74 percent interest of the casino. Now decades removed from the lawless Prohibition years, the members of the Dalitz syndicate hoped to find in Las Vegas one thing that their various enterprises could not give them in the East: respectability.

When the casino finally opened in 1950, Moe Dalitz was clearly in charge, though Clark's name blazed across the marquee. All-star entertainers graced the Painted Desert room, and gamblers filled the casino. With its 300 guest rooms, a lavish casino, and the third-floor Skyroom lounge, the resort was an immediate hit. Clark proved an affable host, and become the goodwill ambassador not just of the Desert Inn but of Las Vegas itself. Meanwhile, Dalitz and his associates, particularly his manager, Allard Roen, a sharp, college-educated star on the rise, planned to make Las Vegas more than a gambling haunt: they wanted to transform it into one of America's leading vacation resorts. The addition of the Desert Inn golf course in 1952 gave the Strip its first 18-hole golf course, drawing an entirely new class of wealthy vacationers to Las Vegas. The construction of the Desert Inn Estates, country club homes around the course, was an

As can be seen from this photo of the Desert Inn in the early 1950s, Las Vegas Strip casino resorts presented gambling in the context of a relaxing vacation, a far cry from the down-and-dirty illegal urban gambling of the previous generation.

early attempt at residential living on the Strip. The Desert Inn lit the way for the development of a stretch of roadway that would, in a few short years, become truly world famous.

Even more than the Flamingo, the Desert Inn demonstrated the complex connections between the legal casinos of Nevada and organized crime. The relationship between gambling and the mob was, at the time, about a century old. Illegal gambling syndicates first appeared in the 1850s, when serious illicit play—and the police departments that were charged with suppressing it—first appeared.

In the Gilded Age, cities grew bigger—and wealthier—and gambling prospered. Men like John Morrissey, Pat Herne, and Ruben Parsons became wealthy and, often, powerful thanks to their income from gambling halls, though they had a regrettable tendency to squander their ill-gotten gains on faro or the stock market. All the same, corporate ownership—of a type—solidified its grip on the gambling market. Syndicate members owned shares in a variety of illegal houses around town, or in several cities. Lesser shareholders worked as managers, while the top figures merely added their capital and influence with the police and courts. Those who didn't join the syndicate found themselves targeted by the police, who found they could satisfy two masters with one raid: the genteel public, which demanded that "vice" be contained, and the gambling syndicate members, who were happy to feed a competitor to the wolves while their own houses ran undisturbed. This classic "bootlegger and Baptist" coalition kept anti-gambling agitators and wealthy gambling bosses equally happy.

Gambling syndicates, thanks to their access to money and the urban criminal underworld, became politically powerful. But they were soon to change. In the progressive era, legal gambling in the United States reached its lowest ebb—by 1912, all gambling was illegal save betting on horse racing in Maryland and Kentucky. Competition over the race wire (telegraph race betting) franchise led to murder and bombings in several cities. But things were about to get much worse, thanks to another round of prohibitory legislation. National Prohibition, directed against alcohol, created a new breed of syndicate criminal, the bootlegger, who would come to dominate gambling as well. The men who seized opportunity in the wild period were, for the most part, born between 1895 and 1905. As organized crime historian Mark Haller argues, these "wealthy and ambitious upstarts" swiftly overtook the older gambling syndicates, often folding them into their bootlegging operations. Frank Costello, Lucky Luciano, and Dutch Schultz are a few of the more notorious, though they had several less infamous partners and rivals.

After Prohibition's 1933 repeal, some bootleggers stayed in the liquor business and "went legit," while others drifted into other forms of organized crime—prostitution, loan sharking, narcotics, and union racketeering. A large share, however, concentrated on gambling, be it illegal casinos, race and sports betting, or lotteries. Gambling was ideal because it was in demand and, for the most part, socially acceptable, though still illegal. It certainly didn't have the stigma of drug-running or prostitution, and was less messy than taking over unions or loan sharking. For men who wanted to live well off the proceeds of crime, it was an ideal business. They developed a variety of illegal gambling enterprises, including illegal horse-betting (pool rooms), sports betting and book-making, slot machine routes, illegal casinos, and the numbers.

But starting in the 1940s and intensifying in the 1950s, illegal gambling became less acceptable, partly because of the violence between rival criminal enterprises. As investigative journalists and crusading public officials put the pieces of the organized crime picture together, they realized that gambling operations were not innocuous—that they funded other, less savory branches of organized crime. Many "boss gamblers," facing grand juries and newly-aggressive prosecutors at home, decided to head for greener pastures. Around 1950, the most succulent acreage seemed to be a growing resort city in the Nevada desert.

Let's say you're building a new casino in 1957. A man associated with a notorious organized crime family offers to invest substantially in your project. Why on earth would you say yes?

For three reasons: finance, marketing, and debt collection. In each of these, a casino with a mob "affiliation" had a definite advantage over a "clean" casino.

In a lucky coincidence, Nevada needed this influx of talent and capital: mainstream financiers were reluctant to invest in such an inherently risky business. Hospitality businesses are, by their nature, less secure investments than residential or commercial real estate. While banks, pension funds, and insurance companies took the occasional flyer on a hotel, they drew the line at casinos. A new casino cost anywhere between two and ten million dollars to build by the mid-1950s. Few former illegal operators had that kind of cash lying around the house. So they had to turn to other sources: their old friends "back East" who remained in "the rackets" and had substantial sums of illicit, untaxed income that were mostly untapped.

These deep-pocketed mobsters, who had a better understanding of the profit potential in Las Vegas, were more than willing to finance casinos—if they could get a cut. In addition, there was no better training camp for casino managers than illegal operations. So early on, state officials made an uneasy truce with casino men who had checkered pasts. Being accused—or even convicted—of a gambling-related offense wouldn't disqualify an applicant, though being publicly linked to more serious crimes might.

In the 1950s, the Nevada Gaming Control Board was just getting established, and its investigative abilities were not as wide-ranging as they later would become. As long as each of the official investors and principals looked clean, investigators did not look much deeper. So organized criminal figures, some of them quite notorious, became sub rosa investors in many Strip casinos. Meyer Lansky, who had a substantial interest in the Flamingo until it was sold to Kirk Kerkorian in 1967, is the most famous, though countless others had similar arrangements with other casinos.

To deliver "dividends" to these silent partners, casino managers engaged in scrupulously methodical skimming. By systematically under-reporting casino income and diverting the excess cash to organized crime, skimmers both deprived the state of its fare share of gaming revenue taxes and contributed to the growth of organized crime. There are no reliable figures on the exact magnitude of the skim, but anecdotal evidence suggests that, on average, somewhere between 5 and 15 percent of total revenues were not reported, with some of this distributed among employees and the bulk heading off to parts unknown. Forced to choose between a 100 percent share of nothing and an 85 percent share of a prospering business, the rational decision must be the latter one. Advantage to the mob.

Even if a hypothetical casino man had enough money to build his casino, he still needed to fill it with customers. Casino marketing was, in those days, an underdeveloped discipline. National print advertising specifically excluded any reference to gambling, lest it fall afoul of federal or local anti-gambling laws. Casinos had no databases of preferred players, no direct mail promotions, and no way of connecting with potential players. In this period, serious gamblers were responsible for the lion's share of a casino's business. So, without real advertising, how could a casino owner in Las Vegas lure big players to his doorstep?

Junkets were a perfect solution: casinos outsourced their marketing. They let a third party organize a group trip for several "big gamblers" from a city. The junket organizer found the players, arranged credit, and chaperoned the trip.

It sounds perfectly above-board, but there was one problem: who would know the gamblers in a city where gambling was illegal better than the people who ran the illegal games? So many junket operators were drawn from the ranks of gambling entrepreneurs who necessarily had working relationships with local mob bosses. Even a casino in which organized crime figures held no direct interest might choose to work with junket operators with questionable ties. Advantage again to the mob.

The final connection between gambling and the mob, debt collection, owes a debt to the law itself—in this case a piece of English common law codified by the Statute of Anne in 1710. According to this bit of law, debts arising from any wager could not legally be collected. So gamblers owed debts could not sue to ensure their payment.

This made perfect sense when gambling wasn't legal: by their very nature, these debts were not legally accrued. But even after Nevada legalized "wide open" gambling (in both 1869 and 1931), the state did not make gambling debts collectable. So casinos owed money had little legal recourse if a player welshed on his markers: they could deny future credit, but they couldn't recover a penny in the courts.

Imagine now that you're a player with credit lines at two casinos, one "clean" and one "mobbed up." You rack up $100,000 in debt at both, but only have $100,000 in ready cash to satisfy the casinos. Neither casino can legally lay a hand on that $100,000, but the casino with less savory friends willing to collect their debts can exercise a stronger persuasion that the strictly law-abiding one. Advantage yet again to the mob.

The Strip Looks for New Customers

By the time that the Desert Inn Golf Course opened, the Los Angeles Highway was no longer merely a conduit to downtown but a destination in and of itself. Its name was hardly appropriate, and in the early 1950s civic boosters threw around several alternatives. Highway 91, the road's official designation, was even less alluring than "Los Angeles Highway." Others proposed the "Great White Way" or "Gay White Way," referencing the neon signs that now lit the desert sky in abundance. In the mid-1940s, Guy McAfee, nostalgic perhaps for Los Angeles, began facetiously calling the empty stretch of roadway between his 91 Club and downtown the Strip, after the famous Sunset Strip. The name caught on, and as resorts and their brightly-lit signs filled in the once-desolate length of road, people forgot that it was originally a joke. By 1952, "Las Vegas Strip" had become the accepted name for the street. When Highway 91 officially became Las Vegas Boulevard on January 1, 1959, the transformation of the Los Angeles Highway into the Las Vegas Strip was complete.

The Strip would become a constantly-changing landscape as, over the next several decades, casino operators competed to build the biggest, most expensive, and flashiest of everything. Swimming pool wars were followed by competition for star headliners. The Las Vegas Strip became famous as a place where average vacationers could holiday in supreme leisure, enjoying bountiful food and drink, abundant sunshine, and premium entertainment at minimum cost, so long as they gambled for a while. Gambling became a fun and, thanks to a nostalgia for the Wild West, even all-American activity, a far cry from its image elsewhere as a vice-ridden, crooked racket.

The new palatability of gaming was evident as early as 1955, when five new resorts debuted. The Royal Nevada opened on April 19, fol-

Opening in 1955, the Dunes was a typical Strip resort of the period, distinguised only by the oversized genie that dominated its frontage.

lowed by the Riviera the very next day. The Royal Nevada struggled from the start and failed spectacularly; accused of cheating, it closed permanently in 1958. The Riviera, the Strip's first high-rise at nine stories, also ran into immediate money problems (it had vastly over-paid opening headliner Liberace) but weathered the storm, becoming one of the Strip's most enduring properties after being taken over the by the group that owned the Flamingo. Despite fears that the Strip was overcrowded, the openings continued, with the New Frontier, a space-age themed resort, opening on the site of the Last Frontier. The Dunes rose from the desert near the Flamingo, its un-imposing structure festooned with a mammoth paper mache sultan that beckoned ominously. The Dunes collapsed early, and was soon taken over by the managers of the Sands, one of the bedrock proper-ties of the growing Strip.

While the Riviera and Dunes ultimately survived, the real ground-breaking resort of 1955 did not. Following what had be-come a Las Vegas custom so entrenched that many believed it to be the law, Strip resorts did not admit African-Americans as guests and permitted them to work in only a narrow range of low-paying jobs.

(This gave the lie to the promotion of the Strip as a playground for "everyone," and was unfortunately common in a nation then plagued by racial segregation.) Even superstar black entertainers who packed the Strip's showrooms were starkly informed that they could not stay at the hotel or walk through the public areas. Some, like Sammy Davis, Jr. and Lena Horne, challenged this affront, but, steadfast in the belief that it was what their white customers wanted, Strip resorts uniformly refused to accommodate black would-be patrons.

The Moulin Rouge sought to break the Las Vegas color line. Opening in 1955 on West Bonanza Road (far from the Strip and downtown), the Moulin Rouge was primarily owned by whites (though boxer Joe Louis had a nominal share and served as a host) but advertised itself as a "cosmopolitan" resort—a well-known code-word for integrated. A full-service, Strip-style resort, it quickly became one of the city's most popular destinations and musicians, black and white, famously patronized the lounge after finishing their shows on the Strip. Despite its popularity, it was undercapitalized and it closed within a year, and, though it periodically reopened, never again became a signature Las Vegas destination. Despite the Moulin Rouge's popularity, other resorts would not end segregation until 1960, when integration was clearly becoming the law of the land throughout the nation. It was an opportunity missed.

The 1955 financial problems—and the possibility of organized crime control over casinos—caused real anxiety for Nevadans. In 1952, commercial gambling had eclipsed both mining and agriculture to become Nevada's biggest revenue producer. Not only casino owners and employees, but the entire state was tied to the economic well-being of the casinos. Should the industry lose public confidence or trigger federal prohibitory regulation—a very real concern in the 1950s—all would be lost. As early as 1945, the legislature had signaled the increasing importance of gaming by passing for the first time a direct levy on gaming revenue: the state was to receive one percent of gross winnings. The state Tax Commission, rather than local sheriffs, was placed in charge of collecting the new tariff.

The two challenges facing Nevada were to guarantee the fiscal strength of the gaming industry and to promote its image as a clean, honest business. In 1955, the legislature created the Gaming Control

Board, a division of the Tax Commission, which would "eliminate the undesirables in Nevada gaming" and oversee the licensing and operation of casinos. This new board had three full-time members appointed by the Governor and a staff of auditors, investigators, and office workers. The legislature hiked state license fees to pay for the work of this body, which was to research applicants for licenses and ensure that casinos followed all industry regulations and otherwise upheld the good name of the state. In 1959, the legislature moved the Gaming Control Board from the Tax Commission. Under the aegis of a new body, the Gaming Commission (a five-member governor-appointed body that adopted regulations governing the gaming industry), the Control Board issued and revoked licenses, imposed fines and penalties for infractions of gaming regulations, and collected all state gaming fees. The Control Board continued to serve as the state's investigatory and auditing arm.

With the establishment of stronger regulatory oversight, the casino industry was placed on a much more solid political footing. Yet if the crisis of 1955 proved to be permanent, there would be little development. With less than 10,000 guest rooms in resorts, hotels, and motels throughout the region, naysayers began to lament that Las Vegas had been overbuilt. In a sense they were right: the resorts had just about tapped the limits of the available vacation market. The hotels were filled over the weekend, but during the week they were frightfully destitute of guests. It seemed that the growth was at a standstill.

But casino operators realized that the Strip could be more than just a weekend playground, and they worked together to pursue another breed of traveler: the conventioneer. Starting in the late 1950s, resorts began adding convention facilities to attract meetings of professional and fraternal organizations, which were burgeoning with the expanding economy. In 1959, the Las Vegas Convention Center opened. A bond issue paid off by taxes on guest rooms funded this collaboration between the casinos. Its location, just off the Strip on then-vacant Paradise Road, was the final proof of the shift away from downtown. One of the area's biggest visitor attractions, the Las Vegas Convention Center, was not even in the city of Las Vegas but was, like the rest of the Strip resorts, comfortably perched on county land.

Casinos outdid each other in promoting Las Vegas as a place where visitors could "get more done, then have more fun" (the convention center's official slogan). When legal gambling began in the state, few thought that gambling halls would, within thirty years, happily cater to automobile dealers, insurance professionals, Rotarians, or any of the other groups that chose to meet at Strip casinos. But, thanks to the changing perceptions of gambling, the broadening commercial availability of jet travel, and the effervescent promotion of Las Vegas as a safe, fun adult adventure land, the Strip became solidly Middle America. Casinos sponsored bridge tournaments, golf games, and other recreational activities more suited to suburban tract homes than smoky gambling halls.

The successful addition of business travelers allowed resorts to remain filled during the week. As their bottom lines improved, casinos expanded, adding at first new low-rise wings and, by the 1960s, hotel towers. They also pursued star entertainers with greater gusto. Though virtually every casino was famous as the haunt of one celebrity or another, one casino raced to the head of the pack, as it were, and made itself the undisputed cool capital of Las Vegas, if not the world: the Sands.

The Sands, which opened in 1952, was owned by a group of investors who included Texas gambler Jake Freedman and New Yorkers Carl Cohen and Jack Entratter. Entratter, who served as entertainment director of the resort, had owned the Manhattan's Copacabana lounge and used his show business connections to help put the Sands, known as "A Place in the Sun," on the map. The resort owed much of its eminence to its most famous entertainer, Frank Sinatra, who caroused onstage and off with his friends—the press dubbed the group the Rat Pack—and drew throngs of admirers to the casino. Sinatra had long since reestablished himself as one of the music world's top talents, and though his records didn't sell nearly as well as those of Elvis Presley or, later, the Beatles, Entratter was interested in more than the box office receipts. Sinatra drew a relatively affluent, middle-aged crowd with money to spend and a sense of fun—the ideal casino patron.

Together with Dean Martin and Sammy Davis, Jr., Sinatra epitomized cool for legions of fans. Supplemented with Joey Bishop, Peter Lawford and whoever happened to show up, the big three held court at the Sands' Copa Room for much of the early-to-mid 1960s. While filming the quintessential casino heist movie, *Ocean's Eleven*, in 1960, the Rat Packers worked on the film in the afternoon and performed two shows each evening before drinking, gambling, and carousing all night. They defined the Las Vegas Strip for a generation.

The Las Vegas Strip of the Copa Era, the years of the Rat Pack's greatest prominence (all would continue individually as top casino showroom draws for the rest of their careers) was a far different place then it had been just a few years earlier. In 1960, after threatened public protests by the local black leaders, the Strip resort operators agreed to abandon segregationist policies; almost immediately they began organizing events to cater to black visitors. Dr. James McMillan, who as president of the local NAACP had, more than anyone, spearheaded the integration effort, later recalled that the hotels settled for business reasons: fearful that the bad publicity would scare off convention bookings, they quickly gave in. "Money moves the world," McMillan said. "When these fellows realized that they weren't going to lose money, that they might even make more, they were suddenly colorblind." The civil rights leader was right: the

Strip casinos used star entertainers to put themselves on the map. On March 6, 1957, Dean Martin began a solo run in the Sands Hotel's Copa Room; eventually he, Frank Sinatra, and Sammy Davis, Jr. would reign as the unofficial kings of Las Vegas.

Strip casinos prospered in the 1960s by creating a gambling scene where everyone felt welcome and where everyone's money was as good as everyone else's.

Skillful Players Get an Edge

Casino operators on the Las Vegas Strip excelled at promoting their resorts to casual gamblers and neophytes more interested in the dinner theater than the craps odds. But as vacationing receptionists and clerks stepped up to the tables, another breed of visitor often blended with them: the serious gambler. These players could be professionals who made their living by winning games of chance and skill (fairly or not), or they might be amateurs who believed they had found a winning system. Since Francois Blanc, casino managers had scoffed at and even encouraged systems players, knowing that games like roulette and craps, in which each decision was independent of all previous decisions, were ultimately impregnable. But as the Rat Pack was wowing audiences at the Sands, genius gamblers (and those who imitated them) proved a growing concern for casino bosses.

John Scarne was the most celebrated expert gambler of the 20th century. Born to Maria and Fiorangelo Scarnecchia in Niles, Ohio in 1903, he grew up in Fairview, New Jersey. Coming of age during the 1920s, he decided early on that he would use his incredible skills in service of the public good rather than for illicit private gain. So while Tony Cornero and Ben Siegel were bootlegging whiskey and sponsoring illegal casinos, Scarne was perfecting card manipulation. Practicing all of the dark arts of bottom-dealing, false-shuffling, and card-crimping, from the age of 14 Scarne worked six hours a day on improving his game.

Had he wished, he could have been a master cheat. Instead, he worked as a professional magician before finding his true calling: educating the public about crooked gambling. He first became famous during World War II, when he served as a consultant to the American armed forces and lectured GIs on the wiles of fraudulent gamblers. He started by sending letters of advice to friends and neighbors who had been drafted and was soon hired by Special Services to educate servicemen. Scarne's message was one perfect for a nation that was becoming increasingly tolerant of gambling: the activity itself was not bad, but one had to be careful not to be made a sucker. This was the same approach that the state of Nevada adopted towards gambling by regulating it to ensure an honest reputation.

After the war, Scarne's star shone even brighter. He traveled the world, speaking before rapt audiences and helping train casino staffs from Las Vegas to Cuba (he unwillingly witnessed the Cuban Revolution while advising the Habana Hilton about card cheats). His expertise in trickery and sleight of hand helped him become a master debunker, exposing not only card and dice mechanics but all manner of frauds, including those who duped the public with tales of extrasensory perception and mind-reading (he famously exposed "Lady Wonder," a reputed mind-reading horse). He was proudest of his own feats of mental ingenuity: he invented several games (though none became popular). With a reputation as the "Einstein of games," his books on cards, dice, tricks, and gambling sold well, and by educating the public about crooked games, he did a great deal to increase their comfort with square ones.

Scarne was famous for his gambling expertise, but he was not famous as a gambler. Those famous for gambling in the early part of the century, though they styled themselves as "sportsmen," were still viewed as unsavory; with master gambler Arnold Rothstein reportedly fixing the World Series, one can understand why. But with the legitimatization of gambling, famous gamblers became almost heroic figures. Perhaps the most celebrated, and possibly the most tragic gambling legend was Nick "the Greek" Dandolos. Born in 1883 in Crete to a wealthy family, he came to the United States at the age of 18, though he soon moved to Montreal and began to bet on horse races. He later transferred his play to gaming tables and by the 1920s was famous for his betting; it was said that he had broken the bank at Monte Carlo and was the only man who could consistently beat Arnold Rothstein.

Rothstein liked betting but, as his 1919 World Series fix showed, he preferred a sure thing. Dandolos, on the other hand, emerged as a champion of gambling for gambling's sake, often stating that the next best thing to playing and winning was playing and losing. "The play's the thing," he would say, a perfect message as gambling

Nick "the Greek" Dandolos was one of the 20th century's most prolific gamblers. Here he is seen in profile with legendary casino owner Benny Binion.

became less of a vice than a diversion. If measured by sheer dollar amount, Dandolos might have been the biggest gambler in history: he claimed to have had more than $500 million pass through his hands as he won and lost money at the tables and tracks, and estimated he had been gone from wealthy to busted no less than 73 times. He lived for years in a $10 Las Vegas hotel room, becoming something of a local landmark; tourists would point and gawk at the Greek, who gambled for days on end, subsisting on little more than orange juice, chicken sandwiches, and cigars. Though he remained an institution to the end, dazzling fellow players by quoting Plato and Aristotle (he had majored in philosophy), Dandolos eventually found himself losing more than he won, and by his final days he was reduced to playing penny-ante games in Southern California card rooms. Yet at his death in 1966 newspapers recounted his glory years, when he sent suits to the cleaner's with tens of thousands of dollars still hidden in them and was as much of a star at Las Vegas casinos as their headline entertainers.

Dandolos, like another Nick the Greek, the Euopean baccarat-playing Greek Syndicate's Zographos (there have been countless Nick the Greeks, just as there have been innumerable Honest John

Kellys), was celebrated mostly for his endurance and bankroll. He did not claim to have any mathematical knowledge greater than an appreciation for the game odds; he simply bet when the odds against him were at their least and hoped for the best. Unlike Scarne, he was not an "expert gambler" but a notorious one. Scarne, knowing enough of the odds to realize that the percentage always lay with the house, excelled as an ambassador for honest play but was not particularly celebrated as a gambler. Expert opinion and serious gambling, it seemed, did not quite mix.

The mathematical study of blackjack would merge deep thought with high action. Using computer simulations and mathematical theory to unlock the secrets of blackjack—the one casino game uniquely open to system play—in the 1960s a new generation of expert gamblers would elevate the game into the most widely-played table game in the nation.

Blackjack skill play is feasible because the game is played with a finite series of cards. In craps, the previous throw of the dice has absolutely no bearing on the next one, but in blackjack, previous hands have a direct bearing on future draws. If all the aces have been played, for example, the player has no chance of getting a "natural" blackjack (an ace and a 10-value card), which usually pays 3 to 2. For more than a century, blackjack flew under the casino radar. While enthusiasts and dilettantes tried to break the bank at Monte Carlo with roulette betting systems, blackjack remained a relatively unimportant game.

As blackjack became more popular in Nevada gambling halls in the 1930s, bettors started to develop systems to help them track which cards had been played. They were the first card counters. Since the conventional wisdom held that betting systems were doomed to fail given the inexorable house advantage, most casino managers laughed off claims that blackjack could be beaten. Since the mathematics behind early card counting systems was often shaky, the casino bosses were usually right. Through the 1950s, card counting remained something of an occult science, known only to a few initiates and not particularly reliable.

But card counting became a very real threat to casino revenues thanks to the work of a University of California, Los Angles mathematics Ph.D., Edward O. Thorp. Thorp became a blackjack expert by chance: though he was not a gambler, during a break from his teaching duties at UCLA in the late 1950s, he and his wife chose to spend a few days in Las Vegas to enjoy the shows, inexpensive food, and swimming pools. They were like millions of Americans who were increasingly drawn to Las Vegas for more than gambling. Before the trip, a fellow professor directed him to a 1956 article on card counting from the *Journal of the American Statistical Association*. Titled "Optimum Strategy in Blackjack," it claimed to offer a way to limit the house edge, usually assumed to be over 2 percent, to .62 percent. Thorp tested their system "under fire" with lukewarm results (he lost $8.50).

Still, Thorp was intrigued and, upon returning home, used an IBM 704 computer to help him devise a better strategy, one that he christened "basic strategy." Simply by using this guide on when to hit and stand, Thorp found that the house's edge could be shaved to .21 percent. But he went even further: players who could successfully keep track of cards already played could take advantage of "favorable conditions" and actually gain an advantage over the dealer. At last, it seemed, the house would not always win.

Theoretically, Thorp's system was sound: the more high-value cards that remained in the shoe, the higher probability that the dealer, forced to draw to 17, would bust. By keeping a running count of high-value cards, Thorp estimated that he could gain an advantage of up to 15 percent. And he was no armchair strategist: backed by investors, he took $10,000 to Las Vegas and put his system into action. He successfully doubled his bankroll, though casinos, suddenly wary of his winning ways, inaugurated disruptive tactics, including constant re-shuffling and even, in one instance, a cheating dealer.

When Thorp published his system and an account of his winning field test in *Beat the Dealer* (1962), card counting became an instant phenomenon. A variety of systems soon emerged; everyone with access to a computer claimed to have developed a new, improved, guaranteed method for beating casino blackjack. Most of these were variations on Thorp's basic premise, tracking high- and low-value cards. The simplest system requires the player to give low cards (2, 3, 4, 5, 6) a value of +1, ten-value cards and aces a value of -1, and 7s,

8s, and 9s zero value. When the count is high, a player is more likely to win and should bet accordingly.

Though feasible, card counting was not foolproof. Many who tried to master counting simply lacked the concentration and quick recall necessary. In addition, casinos could easily thwart counters by arbitrarily re-shuffling the cards or simply barring suspected "skill" players. Though, as places of public accommodation, casinos are forbidden to discriminate based on race, gender, handicap, or nationality, as private businesses they are allowed to refuse service at will. Thus, even though they might have a foolproof system, the deck was usually stacked against counters.

Despite the unfavorable odds, many would-be casino beaters were entranced by the mathematical certainty of winning the card counting, if done correctly, promised. In order to frustrate casino countermeasures and to allow bigger bets by starting with a larger bankroll, team play emerged in the early 1970s. Its most famous exponent was Ken Uston, a math prodigy, Harvard MBA, and former vice president of the Pacific Stock Exchange, who, like many others, became interested in blackjack after reading *Beat the Dealer.*

In March 1974, Al Francesco, leader of a San Francisco-based blackjack team, recruited Uston. The team made money by a simple division of labor. On a typical night, it sent several card counters into a casino; each of them bet the table minimum and, using an "advanced point count" system, quietly kept track of the table's favorability. When the player's edge was strong enough, using a series of pre-arranged signals the counter would call over the B.P. (Big Player), who would then bet the table limit. The system worked until casino surveillance started to recognize the players' teamwork. Then, players adopted disguises and otherwise attempted to outwit casino managers, surveillance teams, and independent consultants hired to combat skill play. When he went public with his role as a "Big Player," Uston became a blackjack celebrity. Claiming to have made millions from blackjack tables in Nevada in Atlantic City, he was ultimately barred from nearly every casino in the country. He fought unsuccessfully to challenge his banishment before his death in 1987 at the age of 52.

Though blackjack lost a true original with the passing of the flamboyant Uston, the idea of team play remained. The most famous blackjack team since Uston's group is the MIT card-counting team. There have actually been several counting groups affiliated with that prestigious university, but they remained relatively obscure until the 2002 book *Bringing Down the House,* in which Ben Mezrich told the story of "Kevin Lewis," a member of the early-to-mid 1990s edition of the team who spoke of millions in dollars of profits. Though the story was hardly revolutionary, it (as well as *21,* the 2008 film of the book) introduced a new generation of young players to the thrill of team play, and may have contributed to a boom in blackjack play among younger casino patrons.

So, while casinos were built on the idea of an impregnable house edge, the idea of being able—through skill and daring—to beat the house remained a powerful one. Fifty years on, players are still looking for the magic blend of mathematics and good fortune that will let them walk out winners every time. And casinos remain vigilant, guarding against "advantage players." The cat-and-mouse game between skillful players and suspicious casino bosses now unfolds in casinos throughout the world, with a new chapter of gambling history being written every time someone tries out their sure-fire, can't-miss system for beating the dealer.

11

The Sky's the Limit

◇◇◇◇◇◇◇◇◇◇

Las Vegas reaches for the stars

An Emperor Arrives

As the popularity of Las Vegas soared, casinos became paradoxically both more extravagant and more egalitarian. As the booming postwar prosperity gave Americans more free time and discretionary spending, many of them chose to vacation or meet for business at the sunny suburban casino resorts of the Strip. Yet competition for customers remained fierce, and casinos pursued two strategies to lure them in: they spent lavishly on headline entertainers like Frank Sinatra, Liberace, and Nat "King" Cole, and they staged a series of increasingly outrageous publicity stunts.

Despite their reputations as pleasure palaces, the casinos of the 1950s and 1960s were, for the most part, bland, non-descript hotels with nightclubs and casinos simply tacked on: they were comfortable but hardly breath-taking. But something more grandiose was on the horizon. Jay Sarno, an accomplished developer, emerged as a visionary who brought to Las Vegas a resort where every man and woman was a Caesar, surrounded by luxury.

Sarno was already a successful motel operator: his Palo Alto Cabana had been named the most outstanding motel in the United States, and the entire chain of Cabana motels won awards for its design and service. Throughout the 1950s, he refined his architectural ideas, so much so that the Palo Alto Cabana was a scaled-down version of the eventual Caesars Palace. Stopping frequently in Las Vegas to gamble, Sarno was appalled by the blandness of the Strip resorts and, borrowing amply from the Teamsters Central States Pension Fund, started building a hotel and casino that lived up to his standards. He placed water features and statues abundantly throughout the property, and revived the idea of the themed casino, bringing back to life Ancient Rome. Even the stationary had the appearance of slightly burnt parchment. Traversing the long drive-way, passing Greco-Roman-inspired fountains, guests left behind the ordinary world of mortgages and punch-clocks and entered a fantasy world where they could be Caesar, Cleopatra, or whoever they wished. Despite his focus on luxury, Sarno built a solidly busi-ness-friendly resort. Caesars Palace opened in 1966 as a full-service convention resort, and its managers were just as enthused to sign the National Milk Producers as convention guests as they were to land Frank Sinatra in their showroom, the aptly-named Circus Maximus.

Having built the quintessential high-end resort, Sarno was not content. His next project was an attempt to bring the excitement of a circus to the Las Vegas Strip. Circus Circus rejected the well-established model of the integrated casino resort. Sarno hoped that as a stand-alone casino, Circus Circus would be innovative enough to thrive, at least until he had the finances to add hotel rooms. Most other resorts were so unimpressive, Sarno thought, that patrons would be naturally drawn to the unique casino, which was arrayed under a permanent pink-and-white big top.

Other casinos suggested exotic locales with names like "Tropi-cana" and "Riviera" and let their guests' imaginations do the rest; not so for Sarno, who insisted that Circus Circus in fact be a working Circus. He scoured big tops for acts and turned the casino's second floor into a carnival midway, with games and prizes galore. Honest John Kelly would have felt right at home pitching his knife game to passers-by. Circus acts performed above the gaming pits, much to the consternation—and distraction—of players. Tanya, an elephant who could pull slot machine handles and play keno, entertained visi-tors but was an operational liability; for years she stank up the em-ployee dining room, located uncomfortably near her quarters.

Like many other visionaries, not all of Sarno's inspirations were successful. Opening in 1968 without a hotel, Circus Circus strug-gled. It did not help that Sarno actually charged admission to the casino, a common practice in Europe but anathema along the come-as-you-are Strip. Circus Circus was undeniably innovative but often

When it opened in 1966, Caesars Palace took casino design to an entirely new level. It quickly became one of the world's most famous casinos, and would have a profound influence on the next generation of Las Vegas Strip resorts.

unbalanced, much like Sarno. He gambled away millions in the late 1960s and early 1970s and was renowned as a lover of women, much to the chagrin of his wife Joyce, who divorced him in 1974. Despite a rotund physique, he was an avid golfer, though not much of a health nut: his idea of a diet was to breakfast on filet mignon instead of salami.

Sarno was more successful as a casino designer than an operator. He sold Caesars Palace to the Florida-based eatery chain Lum's in 1969; Lum's would eventually discard its restaurant business and rename itself Caesars World. Over the next two decades, Caesars would become one of the most instantly-recognizable names in gaming. In 1974, Sarno finally abandoned Circus Circus, selling it to William Bennett (no relation to the future Secretary of Education) and William Pennington. Bennett and Pennington retained Sarno's general idea of a circus casino but made it more manageable, confining the circus acts to the Midway level (out of sight of the serious gamblers) and eschewing high rollers for middle-market gamblers. Adding several hotel towers and an RV park, they made Circus Circus a top destination for budget-minded family vacationers. Though Sarno's final vision—the Grandissimo, a 6000-room resort replete with waterfalls and roller coasters—was never built, it would brilliantly foreshadow the super-resorts of the 1990s. Sarno was simply ahead of his time.

The Bountiful Billionaire

As Sarno was building Circus Circus, an unlikely benefactor was buying up much of the Las Vegas Strip. Howard Robard Hughes had parlayed his inheritance from a father who invented an essential oil drill bit into careers as an aviator, a Hollywood producer, and speculative businessman. By the fall of 1966, Hughes was flush with $566 million that he had received for selling his TWA stock as part of a court-ordered settlement and looking for a home that would afford him both privacy and shelter from taxes. Nevada fit the bill well; he already owned property there, but decided (possibly in order to avoid process servers; he was still heavily embroiled litigation) that he needed less permanent digs.

Following a cross-country ride in a sealed rail car, Hughes arrived in Las Vegas in the pre-dawn hours of November 27, 1966. Stopping the train outside of town, he was taken by van to the Desert Inn, where he had reserved the entire ninth floor of the St. Andrews tower. Once there, he comfortably took up residence, running his empire through his right hand, Robert Maheu, with whom he communicated only by memo or telephone. By the time New Year's Eve was approaching, Moe Dalitz and the Desert Inn's managers were anxious to see the Hughes party leave; they were by this time taking up two floors that should, by rights, be reserved for gamblers. With plenty of excess cash from the TWA settlement, Hughes instructed Maheu to negotiate for the purchase of the resort. On March 22, 1967, Maheu sealed the deal; at a cost of $13.2 million, Howard Hughes owned one of the Strip's most storied resorts, and could stay put.

Seeing an easy way to convert his taxable TWA settlement cash into non-taxable income-earning properties, Hughes instructed

Maheu to buy indiscriminately: the tally of Strip purchases included the Sands (from which Frank Sinatra soon quit because of personal animosity with Hughes, to take up residence at Caesars Palace), the Frontier (a Western-themed resort that replaced the New Frontier in 1967), the Silver Slipper (part of the old Last Frontier Village), and the Castaways. He also bought the unopened Landmark, which would consistently struggle from its ill-timed 1969 opening to its 1995 implosion. Hughes also bought Harold's Club in Reno, Las Vegas's CBS affiliate KLAS-TV, vast Nevada mining claims that proved to be worthless, and much of the available real estate in and around the Las Vegas Strip. He eventually employed over 8000, making him the state's biggest employer.

Hughes has been hailed by some as "the man who saved Nevada" and brought reputability to the gaming industry by buying out the "mobbed-up" syndicates, but in fact he did little to alter the trajectory of the casino business. None of his acquisitions became particularly successful after his purchase. In fact, in 1969 Hughes's Nevada portfolio produced a net loss of $8.4 million. Although he spent much of 1967 and 1968 planning to build a supersonic jet airport that, he believed, would make Nevada the transportation hub of the American West, the terminal was never built. Much of his energy seems to have been wasted on ultimately unachievable goals. The Landmark, for example, which he bought against the advice of Moe Dalitz, was never profitable. In an age when the boundaries of the casino resort were pushed beyond imagination, he built nothing and changed little in the way his casinos were run. When, on Thanksgiving 1970, he was bundled down the Desert Inn fire escape and into a plane bound for the Bahamas, his Nevada empire continued running on auto-pilot. His Las Vegas real estate empire, which has yielded the master-planned community of Summerlin, much of Green Valley, and several other prominent areas of the growing city, has become his enduring legacy

At the time, the public was largely unaware of his growing personal eccentricities, and he was hailed as one of the most powerful forces in American business; he was still thought of as the dashing aviator of the 1930s. Yet he stood against most of the trends that would soon transform the Strip: he opposed corporate ownership and wrote a letter to Robert Maheu discountenancing the degeneration of Las Vegas into "a freak, or amusement-park category, like Coney Island." He wished to retain an image of the Las Vegas of the 1940s: a small, somewhat exclusive resort town that catered chiefly to gambling habitués and wealthy leisure-seekers. The onrushing democratization of the casino landscape simply disgusted him. And for all his millions, not even Howard Hughes could change the growing accessibility of Las Vegas casinos or the American public's burgeoning love affair with gambling. Las Vegas resorts were now more circus than cocktail party, and people couldn't get enough of them.

The World Series of Poker's Birthplace

As the Strip opened up into America's adult playland, downtown Las Vegas grew as well, though in a profoundly different direction. Home to gambling clubs since the city's founding in 1905, it soon hosted a few full-blown casino hotels as well. The 1932 Apache and 1941 El Cortez had hotel rooms, but they were hardly palatial. With downtown already crowded, if there were to be resorts that could compete with the Strip, they would have to build up. In 1956, the Fremont, a 15-story hotel and casino, did just that. The Mint, which had opened in 1957 as a small gambling club, added a 26-story tower in 1965 and became famous for sponsoring the Mint 400, an epic desert off-road race. The Union Plaza, which opened in 1971 on the former site of the train depot, was even larger, and it made history when in 1975 it opened the first modern casino sportsbook. Despite these advances, though, downtown would become famous as a throwback to a time when the stakes were high and gambling, not showrooms or pools, was the center of action.

This back-to-basics approach of downtown found its purest expression in the World Series of Poker. It was based on a simple concept: get the best poker players in the world, offer them a gigantic purse, and let them ante and fold until only the champion remained. The World Series was hosted by gambling legend Benny Binion. Born in Pilot Grove, Texas in 1904, Binion grew up during Prohibition and developed an early love for gambling. He moved from numbers and policy operations (dabbling along the way in bootlegging) to illegal dice games in the 1930s. Suspected of several murders, Binion backed the wrong side in a 1946 Dallas election and, with his political protection gone, moved to Las Vegas.

Once there, Binion bought an interest in J. Kell Houssells' Las Vegas Club. After Houssells moved the Las Vegas Club across Fremont Street to its current location, Binion opened the Westerner. In 1951 he acquired the Eldorado, which was on the ground floor of the Apache Hotel. He renamed it the Horseshoe, installed a carpet, and set a policy designed to attract diehard gamblers: the Horseshoe would have the highest limits in town. "The Sky's the Limit" became the gambling hall's slogan. Where most casinos had an upper threshold of $50 on craps bets, Binion accepted wagers as high as $500, and would usually waive even this, declaring that a customer's first bet was his limit. This ran entirely against the grain. Generally speaking, casinos prefer lower betting limits; forcing patrons to spread out their bets gives the inherent house edge more chances to work. Binion, a gambler at heart, brooked little talk of percentages, and instead reasoned that, as a gambling hall owner, he was in the business of taking wagers.

With Benny's policy firmly established, the Horseshoe saw some of the largest bets ever recorded. In 1980, William Lee Bergstrom, nicknamed the "Phantom Gambler," staked $777,000 on the "don't pass" line and won. He gathered his winnings and returned to Austin, where he owned an apartment building. Early in 1984, he won $538,000 at a similar bet, and in November of that year he placed $1 million on the "don't pass" line—the biggest single bet in Nevada history—and lost. After a breakup with his male lover in February 1985, he committed suicide and was eulogized by Ted Binion as "the biggest bettor of all time."

Binion's fame as a casino owner did not shield him from ongoing troubles with the law. He was forced to sell the Horseshoe in 1953 to finance his legal battles. After serving three years in Leavenworth federal prison for tax evasion, Binion returned to Las Vegas in 1957 and re-acquired the Horseshoe, though he could not get his license back. Instead, his sons Jack and Ted officially owned and operated the casino, while Binion the Elder was merely listed as a consultant. But with a booth in the basement coffee shop for an office and a handshake for a guarantee, the Horseshoe remained Benny's house.

The inspiration for a poker tournament at Binion's Horseshoe dates back to 1949. Super-gambler Nick "the Greek" Dandolos couldn't find a poker game rich enough for his blood (he wanted a no-limit game against a single opponent), and Binion offered to get him suitable competition on one condition: that the game be played in public. Binion called his old friend Johnny Moss, a well-traveled Texas road gambler (some of his peers included Doyle Brunson, Sailor Roberts, and "Amarillo Slim" Preston) and tough customer—he usually carried a revolver and a shotgun to deter would-be thieves; hijacking was an occupational peril for road gamblers of the era. Moss quickly caught a flight to Las Vegas. Binion placed a table near the entrance to his casino, anticipating hundreds of spectators.

On a Sunday afternoon in January, Moss (a no-limit specialist) and Dandolos greeted each other with a handshake and sat down to play. For the next five months, Binion had an attraction that put all others to shame. The pair played four or five days non-stop, pausing only then for sleep, though Dandolos spent most of his off-time at the craps tables; he was then at the peak of his powers. They started by playing five-card stud, and later switched to low-ball deuce to seven (in which the player with the lowest hand wins) and high-draw poker. At one point, the crowd gaped with awe when Dandolos won a half-million dollar pot by calling Moss's bluff and winning with a jack in the hole—possibly the largest documented single hand of poker ever played in a public game to that point. During five months of marathon play, the irascible Texan gradually wore the cool Greek down. Watching Moss sweep in his last chips, Dandolos politely said, "Mr. Moss, I have to let you go," and rose from the table, an estimated $2 million poorer.

In 1969, Benny, Jack, and Ted were invited by Tom Moore, owner of Reno's Holiday casino, to an event called the Second Annual Gaming Fraternity Convention: it was the country's first major poker tournament. After buying the casino, Moore and his wife Lafayne had decided to invite fifty or so of the country's biggest gamblers to a tournament featuring table games; they hoped to draw attention to their new casino. The following year when they held the "convention" a second time, they switched it to high-stakes poker and invited between twenty and thirty professional poker players and bookmakers

Johnny Moss, left, won the first two World Series of Poker, while Jack Binion, right, is credited with deciding to use a freeze-out no-limit Texas hold'em game to determine the champion. Here they pose with some of Moss's winnings.

to play Texas hold'em, Kansas City lowball draw, razz, stud, and ace-to-five lowball draw. At the end of a week of games, legendary San Antonio poker player Crandell Addington won a silver trophy designating him as "Mr. Outside," a moniker reflecting on his status as a road, or outside player, as opposed to a casino or race book owner.

Though the Horseshoe did not even have a poker room at the time, the family decided to adopt the tournament when Morehead retired, renaming it the World Series of Poker. Moss triumphed at the first Binion's World Series of Poker in 1970. When, in 1971, Jack Binion scrapped the unwieldy election system, a freeze-out, non-limit, Texas Hold'em game determined the champion (Moss won again). Players could win bracelets in a number of different games, but to be world champion, they had to beat the best at a game that had become the Cadillac of poker.

Texas Hold'em is a community-card poker game that is related to Omaha, a game in which each player received four cards of his own

In the 1979 World Series of Poker, the dealer gathers chips while Doyle Brunson and Hal Fowler await the next card. Fowler won the tournament that year (the first nonpro to do so) and took home $270,000.

("hole" cards) and five community cards were dealt to the center of the table—the flop. A player then must use two of his own cards and three of the community cards to make the best hand. Texas Hold'em is similar, but players receive only two cards, which they must use. Some believe that Texas Hold'em split from Omaha in the 1920s, but there is no consensus. Still, most agree that Texas Hold'em emerged in the 1920s and 1930s in the Dallas region, and spread throughout the South after World War II. In Texas Hold'em, players bet once when they view their hole cards—the pre-flop—or fold. After the flop, another round of betting occurs, as after the fourth and fifth community cards are dealt. Typically, most card games have set betting limits, but the World Series of Poker championship was no-limit, meaning that any player, at any stage in the game, could go "all in" and bet all of his chips.

For a $10,000 entry fee, anyone who wished could vie for a championship bracelet. The WSOP merged the growing popular appeal of gambling with the idea of an ultimate gambling championship. Since the game was intended primarily to publicize the casino, the

Binions structured it to yield a relatively quick winner. After losing all his or her chips, a player was out for good. To keep players from playing too conservatively, antes and blinds escalated periodically. Within a few years, the World Series of Poker had become a downtown institution and gave the Horseshoe more publicity than anything, excepting perhaps its horseshoe-shaped display of $1 million in $100 bills.

Downtown Las Vegas Standouts

While Binion's was countering the glamour-soaked Strip resorts with an emphasis on gambling, across the street a young newcomer had his own ideas about how to run a better casino. Stephen A. Wynn was the son of Maryland bingo operator Mike Wynn. In 1963, when his father died shortly after Wynn graduated from the University of Pennsylvania with a degree in English Literature, the young man took over his father's business. Four years later, he jumped at a chance to get into the Las Vegas gambling scene and, with $45,000 saved from his bingo profits, bought a share in the Frontier, where he learned the casino business as a slot manager and assistant credit manager.

Wynn might have remained just one of many ambitious young men if he had not made the acquaintance of E. Parry Thomas, one of the most influential figures in the history of Las Vegas gambling. Thomas was not a casino operator, a slot machine supplier, or a politician. He was a banker and, for years, his Valley Bank was the only legitimate source of capital for Las Vegas casinos. One of the most powerful men in town, he was in a position to help a young man with an eye toward advancement. He guided Wynn into ownership of a liquor distributorship and then, in 1971, helped him score a coup: Wynn bought a small sliver of land adjacent to Caesars Palace from Howard Hughes—the only parcel of land that Hughes sold during his lifetime—and sold it to Caesars for a respectable profit.

Wynn had already begun buying stock in the Golden Nugget, a rather bland downtown gambling hall that had no hotel. Wynn soon accelerated his stock purchase, and in 1973 became president and chairman of the board of the Golden Nugget. Wynn embarked on a massive housecleaning, firing thieving or dishonest employees, and commenced to dramatically remodel the casino and to add the first of several hotel towers. Within a year, Wynn had quadrupled the Golden Nugget's profits. As remarkable as Wynn's transformation of the Golden Nugget seemed, it was just a hint of things to come.

Wynn's recasting of the Golden Nugget may be one of the most dramatic stories of downtown Las Vegas, but he was not the only innovator. John D. "Jackie" Gaughan pioneered many elements of casino marketing that are common today. He'd learned the trade young; his family operated an illegal gambling house near Omaha, Nebraska. Stationed in Tonopah, Nevada, during World War II, Gaughan was convinced that his future lay in the Silver State. In 1946, he bought a share in the Boulder Club, which he followed in 1951 with a 3 percent stake in the Flamingo. Despite this Strip venture, his destiny lay downtown. He bought the Las Vegas Club in 1959 and the El Cortez in 1963. These acquisitions formed the cornerstones of a downtown empire.

In these casinos, along with the Gold Spike, the Western, and the Plaza, Gaughan unleashed a slew of innovations. He invented the casino funbook, a book of coupons for free bets, match play (the casino in effect doubles the player's bet by matching it), two-for-one specials, and the like. Funbooks are now ubiquitous in budget-oriented casinos throughout the nation. Gaughan also started casino giveaways, which he used to perk up otherwise-sluggish holidays; by giving away boxes of candy, he was able to fill his casinos. With these promotions, Gaughan pioneered the mass-marketing of casino gaming—with the increasing popularity of American gambling, it was long overdue.

One of Gaughan's partners in the Plaza built his own casino empire that would ultimately evolve into one of the industry's most successful corporations. Sam Boyd grew up in Depression-era Oklahoma, and when his family moved to Southern California started running carnival games of chance on the Long Beach boardwalk. Boyd later ran bingo games throughout Los Angeles and on gambling ships. From 1935 to 1940 he spread the bingo gospel in Hawaii, where he ran games in Honolulu and Hilo and made several lasting relationships. Moving back to Nevada, Boyd dealt in various casinos before being drafted in 1944. On his 1946 return to Las

Vegas, Boyd worked his way up the career ladder at the El Rancho Vegas and then the Flamingo and the Thunderbird.

In 1952, Boyd borrowed and saved enough to buy a stake in the Sahara, becoming a shift manager at the new casino. When, in 1957, the Sahara's owners built downtown's Mint, Boyd bought a share and was appointed general manager. There he harked back to his carnival roots with promotions that never failed to excite patrons. Annual birthday parties for the casino featured an oversized cake, and free meal giveaways were common. Boyd's generosity made good business sense, but it also revealed a truly charitable nature—he and his family would become renowned for their deep philanthropic efforts within Las Vegas over the ensuing decades. Boyd purchased his own casino, a Henderson, Nevada club that he renamed the Eldorado, in 1962, and left the Mint after Del Webb consolidated its control of the casino in 1966.

Boyd returned to downtown with the Union Plaza, a project whose shareholders included Jackie Gaughan and J. Kell Houssells Jr. Boyd, as the biggest investor, ran the casino. He was the first to hire female dealers in downtown Las Vegas; though the practice had long been commonplace in Reno, Las Vegas dealer's lounges remained men's only clubs until Boyd's 1971 experiment at the Union Plaza, which he opened with a dealing staff composed exclusively of women. After making the Union Plaza a success, Boyd and his son, William, who had followed him into the business after practicing law, sold their shares to Gaughan and moved to their next development, the California. Opening in 1974, the California has become a Las Vegas landmark not for its unique architecture but for its clientele—Boyd used his Hawaiian connections to promote the hotel energetically there, and visitors from the islands soon made the California a winner.

Boyd would add Main Street Station and the Fremont to his stable of downtown gambling halls, but he would solidify his reputation in 1979 with a resort that he put his name on: Sam's Town, which, at Boulder Highway and Nellis Boulevard, catered almost entirely to locals, a market that was then untapped. Over the next two decades, as a sufficient number of competitors opened, the area became known as the Boulder Strip, a down-market version of the glittering Las Vegas Strip. Leadership of the Boyd casinos soon passed to his son William Boyd, who took the company public and expanded it astoundingly, opening casinos in six states and buying the Strip landmark Stardust resort in 1985.

Though developments throughout the rest of Nevada were outshone by the stellar growth of the Strip, gambling continued to grow and thrive elsewhere as well. In Reno, Bill Harrah developed his flagship property into a full-service casino-hotel that featured some of the top entertainment stars of the day; his Tahoe casino was equally lustrous. Ernest Primm successfully challenged the city council's red line, which had kept casinos confined to a few blocks in downtown Reno, and in the 1970s a host of new casino-hotels opened. Though the south grabbed much of the glory, Reno and towns along the state line, like Jackpot, Mesquite, and, later, Primm and Laughlin, rode the gambling wave and soon had casino-hotels of their own.

Changing the Rules, Changing the Game

The growing size of casino resorts in the 1960s forced a crisis in casino finance. In the 1940s and 1950s, casino developers, denied the usual lines of credit, were not particularly discriminating about their pool of investors. Most American companies and individuals found investing in a casino simply too risky, and for good reason: many resorts perpetually teetered on the brink of ruin despite their popularity. Those with a background in illegal gambling (who were by definition criminals) knew that a well-run operation could not help but yield solid profits and eagerly invested, often moving to Las Vegas to work in the industry.

Since 1945, those who wished to own a share in a Nevada casino needed a state license; with the creation of the Gaming Control Board in 1955, licensing procedures were strengthened. Nevada regulatory authorities frequently granted licenses to those who had been convicted of gambling offenses, but drew the line there. Convictions for more serious crimes, ranging from extortion to murder, could disqualify an applicant from ownership. Notorious figures linked to organized crime who wanted to invest in Nevada casinos were barred. Even those who were not convicted of a crime, but merely suspected of connections with organized crime could not be openly involved. Rather, they had to work through dummy share-holders or just give investment capital to the casino's managing principles. In the early boom years of the Strip, this practice was more common than not.

Like any other investor, someone who had illicitly invested in a Strip resort expected a dividend. Above-board investors could receive a share in the profits openly, but the clandestine backers, whose links to organized crime meant a great deal of subterfuge in any business dealing, received their cut of the profits by means of a process known as skimming. Skimming was possible because of loose controls over currency on the casino floor: with thousands of dollars washing through the casino every night, there was ample opportunity for money to disappear. Some skimmed funds were given to employees in a crude attempt at profit sharing; it was considered a mark of a good manager to give his employees "something extra" in return for good work (and to prevent outright theft). But most of it was sent to illicit investors.

For casino managers, skimming was a rational solution to the question of how to capitalize casinos without access to mainstream financial outlets. Yet the public was not so cool-headed about the practice—for good reason. Opponents of Nevada gaming decried a system that let money legally gambled by honest Americans be funneled to organized crime. Skimming scandals persistently dogged Strip resorts, from the Thunderbird and Tropicana in the 1950s to the Flamingo in the 1960s and the Stardust and Aladdin in the 1970s and 1980s. Through skimming, according to the industry's critics, organized crime had become entrenched in Nevada gaming.

But, by the time the Stardust skimming scandal broke in 1983, mob ties were becoming a thing of the past and in 1999 the National Gambling Impact Study Commission found that organized crime had no significant presence in Nevada gaming, (or legal gaming elsewhere). There were two reasons for the turnaround: a profound generational shift within organized crime itself and the increasing professionalization of the casino business. The generation of gamblers who came of age during Prohibition had, as a matter of course, business dealings with criminal elements. When, in their forties and fifties, they wanted to "go straight," many of them moved to Las

Vegas and opened casino resorts. By the 1960s, these men were in their sixties and looking to retire. They had sent their children to college and, when their progeny followed them into gaming, it was armed with business degrees rather than tommy guns. At the same time, organized crime, which once derived much of its profits from illegal gambling, had moved into narcotics and labor racketeering. Gangsters no longer had any specialized business knowledge that would help them better run or invest in casinos. So those raised in legal gaming lacked experience in "the rackets," while those who remained in organized crime soon knew little about the casino business.

At the same time, the resorts of the Strip were making gambling a more mainstream activity. Thanks to the energetic promotion of Las Vegas as a vacation and convention paradise, millions of Americans found nothing particularly unseemly about casinos. Corporate involvement on the Strip began in 1951, when principles of the Del E. Webb Corporation, one of the nation's leading builders and the owner of the New York Yankees (a team fittingly started by gamblers), helped Milton Prell secure financing for his Sahara casino. Del Webb worked with Milton Prell to build the Mint in 1957, and four years later bought both casinos outright.

This seems like a fairly unremarkable business transaction, but it was fraught with difficulty because of Nevada's gaming regulations. According to the law, all investors in casinos had to be investigated before being granted a license. This was a workable procedure for the few dozen shareholders in most casinos, but impossible for a publicly-traded corporation with thousands of constantly shifting stock-owners. Del Webb was only able to buy the Sahara and Mint by skirting the letter of the law: a wholly-owned subsidiary actually owned the properties and hired the Consolidated Casino Corporation, owned by Del Webb and his partners, to run the casino. Its rental fee was set to match the casino's annual revenues. Webb owned casinos for years, only selling its portfolio in the 1980s, but the convoluted administrative acrobatics needed to legally operate Nevada casinos kept other corporations out of the state.

In 1967 and 1969, thanks to the advocacy of Governor Paul Laxalt, the legislature amended the gaming laws to permit full-fledged corporate ownership of gaming properties. Publicly-traded corporations were now permitted to enter the gaming business, provided that they adhered to strict licensing guidelines: all shareholders, directors, and officers of the corporate subsidiary that directly ran the casino had to be licensed. In the publicly-traded company itself, only shareholders with ownership of more than 5 percent of the corporation's stock needed to be licensed. These changes, combined with the public perception of the Hughes purchases as a step towards legitimacy, made Nevada gaming far more palatable to mainstream investors.

Kirk Kerkorian was one of the first to capitalize on gaming's new legitimacy. Growing up in hardscrabble Depression-era central California, he parlayed a love for flying into a charter air service; Las Vegas was one of his most frequent stops. He bought a parcel of Strip land that he later sold to Jay Sarno, demurring on a lucrative rental agreement because, reportedly, he thought the resort had dim prospects.

By 1966, Kerkorian wanted to be more than a landlord: he wanted to own a resort himself. Buying land adjacent to the Las Vegas Convention Center, he hired architect Martin Stern, Jr. (who had previously built high-rise towers at the Sahara and Sands) to construct the world's biggest resort hotel. To ensure that he had a staff worthy of the facility, he hired one of the city's best managers, the Sahara's Alex Shoofey, as his casino's president. Kerkorian bought the underperforming Flamingo in 1967 (it had been notorious for its massive skimming) and Shoofey, bringing over much of his loyal staff from the Sahara, ran the resort in preparation for the opening of his new casino.

Shoofey turned the Flamingo around—turning over $3 million in profits in his first year in charge and $7 million in his second—but this was just a prelude for the debut of Kerkorian's juggernaut resort, the International. Opening on July 2, 1969, the International represented a gigantic leap forward in casino design. With 1,500 rooms, it was the world's largest hotel. It had a golf course across the street, but also a full complement of swimming pools, tennis and badminton courts, ping-pong tables, and a health spa for the athletically inclined, seven restaurants for the hungry, the world's largest casino (at 29,000 square feet, claustrophobic by today's standards), three entertainment venues, including the International Showroom, and spacious convention facilities. A "Youth Hotel" daycare center entertained juvenile guests whose parents were having fun in the casino.

The International, which was the first y-shaped resort on the Strip (this would be the most popular design of the 1990s), marked the start of a new generation of casino design. The first generation Strip resorts were essentially dressed-up motels with nightclubs and restaurants attached. The second-generation International featured a massive hotel tower, sizeable casino, and ample recreation, entertainment, dining, and convention facilities, all in a single integrated structure. The massive showroom (with 2000 seats, it was larger than anything yet built on the Strip) was the perfect venue for superstars like Elvis Presley.

Though the International was mightily successful, Kerkorian, stretched thin by his purchase of MGM Studios and Western Air, sold the casino to Hilton Hotels, who in 1971 acquired a majority stake in Tracinda, Kerkorian's operating company that owned the International and Flamingo. The International became the Las Vegas Hilton; Elvis stayed, and the resort became one of Las Vegas's most recognizable icons. The storied Flamingo became the Flamingo Hilton, a name that it kept until, in 2001, it became simply the Flamingo again. Despite selling his casinos, Kerkorian wasn't done with Las Vegas; in 1973 he built the even-bigger MGM Grand (when it opened it was, with 2,100 rooms, the world's largest hotel). This behemoth stood tall at Flamingo Road and Las Vegas Strip and instantly became one of the Strip's top properties. But Kerkorian was destined for even greater things; he would, in the next phase of the Strip's development, become an increasingly more important player.

Hilton's entrance into Las Vegas brought an internationally-recognized hospitality chain to town, but most gaming corporations had developed out of existing partnerships. The owners of casinos as diverse as Harrah's, Showboat, and Circus Circus took their companies public to finance new acquisitions and expansion. As new capital poured in, high-rise towers blossomed along the Strip; as annual Nevada gaming revenues surpassed the $1 billion mark, the corporate era was dawning. Yet the casino that would one day be the flagship of the world's biggest gaming company had distinctly non-corporate origins. In 1973, Claudine and Shelby Williams opened the Holiday Casino, a small, expertly run casino in front of a north Strip Holiday Inn. The casino was soon one of the Strip's best. It was, in 1983, completely acquired by Holiday Inns (who three years earlier had bought a forty percent stake in it) and, in 1992, became Harrah's Las Vegas.

Though the sky seemed the limit with the opening of the MGM Grand, the 1970s and early 1980s were difficult years for the Strip. Oil shocks and economic malaise translated into stagnation. The November 21, 1980, fire at the MGM Grand, which claimed more than 80 lives, was a tragic symbol of the Strip's new vulnerability: that the newest, most modern casino was the scene of such a disaster only intensified anxieties over the future of the Strip. With competition looming from Atlantic City's new casinos, it seemed that Las Vegas's days as a gaming mecca might be soon over.

12

America's Playground...Again

Atlantic City becomes the casino capital of the East

Backstory on the Boardwalk

By the 1970s, states that embraced horseracing and lotteries found gambling tolerable and even desirable. Yet despite several states' attempts to legalize slot machines—Maryland most prominently—Nevada remained the only state to sanction casino gambling. But as the nation's economic picture darkened, casino proposals floated in a number of states, and the most serious surfaced in New Jersey.

Citizens of Atlantic City had urged the state to legalize casino gaming there since the 1950s. Atlantic City, born as a vacation resort for Philadelphia, emerged as a national destination during the Gilded Age. One of the country's pre-eminent convention and exposition spots, majestic hotels flanked the world-famous Boardwalk, whose piers hosted concerts, conventions, and product displays for companies from Heinz to General Motors, and its streets were immortalized in the Depression-era boardgame Monopoly. The city's nightclubs drew crowds with headline entertainers—and, until the winds of reform picked up in the early 1950s, barely concealed backroom casinos.

Though promoted as a family resort, as early as the 1860s those who knew where to look could have some very adult fun gambling. Under the de facto rule of Enoch "Nucky" Johnson, who rose to power as the sheriff of Atlantic County in 1908, wide-open gambling was viewed as a boon to the tourist trade. Reportedly, Johnson struck a bargain with underworld eminence Charles "Lucky" Luciano in 1923 such that, in exchange for a modest ten percent cut of the proceeds, he would permit bootlegged liquor to be landed on "his beach" and gambling operations to be run by Luciano and his friends—who included gangsters Frank Costello and Joe Adonis. A federal investigation of Johnson's vice empire revealed that there were at least 25 casinos and pool rooms that flourished under his protection in Atlantic City, along with 9 numbers banks; all of these conducted business openly, safe from prosecution, and earned combined profits of well over $10 million a year.

After Johnson was finally sent to prison in 1941, gambling continued, albeit in a less public fashion. Most of the city's world famous nightclubs fronted secret backroom casinos: Paul "Skinny" D'Amato's famous 500 Club, where Frank Sinatra played some of his most famous shows and the comedy team of Dean Martin and Jerry Lewis was born, had a full-service casino that had every table game found in Las Vegas, but no slot machines. The world-famous Boardwalk was a gambling mecca of another sort: bingo and other carnival games of chance were common along the boards, and big-money poker games were common in the private rooms of its ritzy hotels. Those who wanted more casual action could play the numbers or bet on horses. Atlantic City remained a gambler's paradise until the early 1950s, when the exposure brought by the Kefauver Committee's 1951 hearings there forced an end to the wide-open days.

The reform effort, coincidentally or not, succeeded in driving out these illegal casinos just as the city was beginning to decline. The availability of cheap air travel, which facilitated the development of mass-market tourism in Florida and Las Vegas, meant that many who might have spent their vacations "down the shore" now flew to more exotic destinations. When Atlantic City hosted the Democratic National Convention in the summer of 1964, news media from around the country filed stories on the city's alarming decline. With little new investment in hotels or tourist facilities, the once-opulent resort rightfully touted as "America's Playground" became a punchline.

But some far-thinking residents, mindful of Las Vegas's success, reasoned that legal casinos might be the answer. As early as 1956, Skinny D'Amato had publicly urged state legislators to permit him and other nightclub and hotel owners to legally operate casinos. Two years later, Mildred Fox, owner of the Fox Manor Hotel, prompted the Women's Chamber of Commerce to promote an unsuccessful pro-casino drive.

Despite these setbacks, Atlantic City couldn't stop thinking about casinos. As unemployment sky-rocketed and the city decayed even further, locals began to organize more seriously. A December 1968 testimonial dinner thrown in D'Amato's honor at the Shelburne Hotel, according to some, began the concerted effort to bring gambling to Atlantic City. Attended by an assortment of the area's power brokers, talk soon turned to the prospects for legal gaming: all agreed that it was essential to the city's revitalization. In the early 1970s, debate over casinos raged throughout the state, and in 1974, casino backers succeeded in placing a statewide referendum on the November ballot.

This measure, though almost unanimously supported in Atlantic City, had many opponents in the rest of the state. Church leaders denounced gambling as immoral (though the state had, in 1970, turned to a lottery in an unsuccessful attempt to stave off a state income tax), and law-and-order types suggested that organized crime would quickly dominate Garden State casinos. In addition, there were concerns over where casinos would be allowed; Governor Brendan Byrne wanted casinos only in Atlantic City, but the Assembly had approved language allowing them anywhere in the state if a local referendum permitted. That helped to turn the tide against the idea, and voters rejected the measure. Astute political analysts concluded that, with both religious leaders and law enforcement officials stridently urging the populace to reject gambling in the name of morality and law, the prospect of casino gaming had no chance of even returning to the ballot, much less winning.

These pundits ignored the growing national move towards gaming liberalization. New Jersey had already embraced horseracing and a lottery, and with Nevada's booming success, it seemed inevitable that some state would consider legalizing casinos. Thanks to adroit political maneuvering and skillful log-rolling, the measure re-appeared two years later. This time, Catholic leaders roundly supported the measure, which was re-written to authorize casinos in Atlantic City only. Dedicating a portion of casino taxes to fund programs for senior citizens was a masterstroke that added the support of a politically potent group. With strict regulation promised, even law enforcement warmed to Atlantic City casinos. Still, the pro-casino lobby wanted to take no chances, and hired political consultant Sanford Weiner to assist the unfortunately-named CRAC (Committee to Rebuild Atlantic City). Couching the referendum in terms of help for Atlantic City (and money for statewide programs), Weiner marshaled a then-astronomical $1 million warchest and doggedly pushed the issue throughout the state. Anti-casino forces, who raised only $21,000, watched helplessly as, on November 2, 1976, the Atlantic City casino referendum passed.

"CITY REBORN" screamed the headline in the hometown *Atlantic City Press*. From bellmen to bankers, just about everyone in town was jubilant at the chance for a second chance, which all agreed casinos could bring.

But the devil, as always, was in the details. How would the state's new casinos be regulated? Who would keep them free of organized crime? The hard work of deciding these and other vexing questions fell to New Jersey's lawmakers. Meanwhile, construction started on the first of the city's reborn pleasure palaces, a casino that would highlight the growing pains that Atlantic City faced.

Paradise Found

The dice started rolling on May 26, 1978, when Resorts International opened in the erstwhile Haddon Hall, a converted golden-era Boardwalk hotel. Over the previous months, the state legislature had created the regulatory framework for the new industry: a Casino Control Commission would issue licenses and set policies, while the Division of Gaming Enforcement would be the investigatory and enforcement arm of the government. Government officials were particularly concerned with keeping organized crime out of the industry. During the opening festivities at Resorts, New Jersey Governor Brendan Byrne—a supporter of legal casinos—channeled Charlton Heston, warning organized crime: "Keep your filthy hands off Atlantic City! Keep the hell out of our state!" Many chuckled at the notion that the mob might only now be moving into the Garden State.

Resorts International's history shows the potent allure of casino gambling. The company was originally the Mary Carter Paint Company, and it indeed distributed and sold paint. In the 1960s, Florida-based operation became a conglomerate, acquiring several other companies ranging from paint rivals to the Biff Burger fast food chain. Among these acquisitions was Bahamas Developers, Ltd., which had hotel and real estate interests in the Bahamas, including a casino. Finding this to be a much more lucrative trade than paints, the company sold off its paint division in 1968, renaming itself Resorts International.

The company had gambled on Atlantic City in 1976, when it paid $2.4 million for the company that owned Chalfonte-Haddon Hall. Resorts generously funded the pro-casino camp in the run-up to the 1976 referendum, and the moment that it passed, broke out the hammers and started converting the Haddon Hall part of the Chalfonte-Haddon into a serviceable casino hotel.

Resorts had a head start. Nevada-based casinos, seemingly a shoe-in to expand to New Jersey, were not initially permitted to do so. Since casino gaming had been illegal in the rest of the United States until 1976, Nevada's gaming regulations prohibited its licensees from doing business elsewhere. This is why the sentiment from Las Vegas ran from muted resignation to outright hostility on the question of Atlantic City casinos. Yet once the voters spoke and it became clear that casinos were a *fait accompli*, Nevada solons, not wishing like Canute demand that the tide recede, amended their laws in 1977 to permit its casino owners to operate casinos in other jurisdictions where it was legal, provided its regulatory system passed Gaming Control Board muster. New Jersey would clear that bar with room to spare, much to the frustration of several Nevada casino owners who found the doors to Atlantic City closed to them.

Still, Resorts was the only operator even close to being ready to open. With work on its casino on the Boardwalk at North Carolina Avenue proceeding apace, the company in December 1977 submitted its official application for a casino license and a $100,000 ante on its $550,000 application fee to the Division of Gaming Enforcement. In January of the next year, it received $16 million in loans that would allow it to finish its conversion of the aged Haddon Hall, built in the 1920s, into an ultra-modern casino hotel for the disco age.

Getting the money wasn't easy, but it wasn't nearly as taxing as the investigation the company faced. With the Division of Gaming Enforcement itself still being established, there was a definite learning curve. Investigators had to determine the suitability of the company itself, which involved reviewing its Bahamas operations and searching for any possible ties to organized crime; all of this had to be done before the company would be granted a license and allowed to open its casino. They also had to investigate every employee, from the president to the night janitor, for financial suitability, good character, and freedom from association with known mob figures. As can be imagined, this was both costly and time-consuming. Yet, if the industry's regulation was to be as strict as had been promised to voters, this was necessary. It was estimated that it would take the forty agents assigned to investigate Resorts until the fall to finish their work.

At the same time, there was pressure building to allow the casino to open for the summer season. Resorts chairman James Crosby insisted the property could be open by Memorial Day. He opened a school to train the four hundred dealers who would be needed to staff the casino's gaming tables. And it appeared that New Jersey wouldn't have an East Coast monopoly for long. New York, Pennsylvania, and especially Florida, it was feared, might soon approve competing casinos. So while there were solid law enforcement reasons for holding back on issuing licenses until investigators could complete their work, political realities meant that the dice would have to start rolling before the summer season began in May.

So New Jersey's lawmakers passed a measure allowing for temporary licenses; these permits, good for up to nine months, would allow a casino to open before it had been thoroughly vetted. By early May, even without a casino license in hand, the hotel at Resorts International had booked all of its rooms clear through Labor Day. Finally, on May 15, the Casino Control Commission granted Resorts a six-month temporary license. With everything now legal, the casino then opened on May 26.

Resorts saw incredible crowds on its opening weekend, which coincided with the Memorial Day holiday. Lines to get in stretched blocks down the Boardwalk. Steve Lawrence, who along with Eydie Gorme was Resorts' opening headliner, officially placed the first legal bet in Atlantic City when he ceremoniously put $10 on pass. After rolling a five, he sevened out. This didn't dampen the ardor of the thousands of gamblers who filled the casino, standing five deep at tables and even slot machines. In its first six days of operation, Resorts made $2.9 million—a world record. In its first full year, the casino pulled in nearly $225 million. By comparison, Nevada's most lucrative casino at the time, Las Vegas's MGM Grand, brought in about $84 million annually. Suddenly, Las Vegas had a serious rival.

A Boardwalk Regency

Resorts International enjoyed a casino monopoly for the rest of the year; while a host of casino operators, foreign investors, and adventurers scrambled to snatch up real estate and hire architects, Resorts was raking in the chips. And those who were already in the

On May 26, 1978, Resorts International, Atlantic City's first casino hotel, opened in a renovated Haddon Hall. This is the Haddon Hall-Chalfonte complex in 1976, shortly before the casino referendum passed. Resorts demolished the smaller Chalfonte for a hotel expansion that was never built.

business of gambling in Nevada were wasting no time in getting a piece of the action.

Caesars World was primed to be among the first into Atlantic City. Earlier in the decade, it had bought two Poconos honeymoon resorts. These Pennsylvania outposts featured no gambling, but they did plant the Caesars flag on the East Coast, and they were soon joined by a third. The company also bought Sky Lake Country Club in North Miami Beach, Florida, and held 400 acres for future condominium development, and even owned a mid-tier Florida restaurant chain, Steakthing. On the Strip, the company bought the Thunderbird hotel, which it planned to replace with the 2,300-room mid-range Mark Anthony hotel. The company also was planning a Lake Tahoe casino hotel. True to his flagship casino's name, empire was on the mind of Caesars World chairman Clifford Perlman.

It wasn't an easy march to glory, though. By 1977, the company had sold the Poconos resorts and leased them back and disposed of the Thunderbird. It was also in the process of liquidating its Florida real estate holdings after the market there fizzled. Also in that year, as soon as New Jersey lawmakers passed the Casino Control Act and created a regulatory system that would pass Nevada muster, it leased the former site of the Traymore Hotel, an Atlantic City legend that had been imploded.

But developing the planned $115 million Caesars Palace Atlantic City would take time—too much time for Perlman's liking. At the same time, the Jemm Corporation planned to convert its Howard Johnson's Motor Lodge, located several blocks from the Traymore site at Arkansas Avenue and the Boardwalk, into a casino hotel called the Boardwalk Regency. In 1978, Caesars agreed to lease the project from Jemm, giving that company an experienced casino operator and letting Caesars get into the market for the $30 million it would cost to renovate the hotel and add enough rooms to meet New Jersey's statutory minimum of 500 guestrooms for casino hotels. With Resorts International earning over $10 million in monthly revenues over its first year of operation, it seemed like a no-brainer: in a few months, the casino would pay for itself and help to fund construction of the larger Caesars Palace. Eight months after groundbreaking, Caesars World was ready to open Caesars Boardwalk Regency.

But there were problems. Caesars World's real estate empire had connections that New Jersey regulators found unsavory. In particular, it had concerns about Alvin Malnik and Samuel Cohen, from whom Caesars had bought its Florida land in 1974 and to whom it sold its Pennsylvania resorts. Both men had ties to underworld financial power Meyer Lansky; Cohen had pled guilty in 1973 to skimming $36 million from the Flamingo in Las Vegas though Lanksy, brought up on the same charges, was not tried after a judge declared him too ill to withstand the rigors of the court. Despite repeated warnings from Nevada gaming regulators, Caesars continued to do business with the pair. Allowing Caesars to open, New Jersey authorities feared, would give one of the mob's most notorious money men a straight line into the industry.

After Caesars World chairman Clifford Perlman agreed to take an unpaid leave of absence, the Casino Control commission granted Caesars Boardwalk Regency a temporary license. On June 26, 1979, Atlantic City's second casino opened. Like Resorts International, it was incredibly profitable, pulling in $226 million in revenues during its first full year of operation.

New Jersey regulators, however, could not grant Caesars World a permanent license without asking something in return: Clifford Perlman and his brother Stuart would have to completely divest themselves from Caesars World. Atlantic City was such a lucrative market that the Caesars board of directors did just that. Henry Gluck, a retired corporate financier, replaced him as Chairman, and Terry Lanni, a business school graduate who had started his career with the company in 1977 by helping it secure a $60 million loan from Aetna Life Insurance (the first from a mainstream lender to a Strip casino), became President.

That transition was emblematic of the changes casinos would face in that era, signaling both the corporate future and the increased regulatory scrutiny that would drive organized crime from the business. For its part, Caesars Boardwalk Regency expanded several times before and after its 1987 name change to Caesars Atlantic City.

The decline and fall of the Perlman brothers highlighted two facts about Atlantic City's burgeoning casino business. First, its regulators were no push-overs: to say no to the owners of the most famous casino in the world after they'd already invested $30 million meant that New Jersey wasn't all bark and no bite. Second, it showed that companies were so eager to tap into the market, they would even sacrifice their own top management to do so. With Resorts International making over $800,000 a day by July 1979—an unheard of average in Las Vegas—other Vegas operators were willing to pay any price, bear any burden, and wave goodbye to any friend in order to assure access to that kind of money.

Building the Industry

The next several years were noisy ones in Atlantic City, as the sound of old hotels crashing down alternated with the din of pile drivers and new construction. Bally's Park Place, a combination of old and new, exemplified the city's growing pains. The Marlborough hotel had been built in 1901 by noted architect William Lightfoot Price, and, when land in front of it became available, the hotel's owners retained Price to build the Blenheim. This Boardwalk hotel was artistically and architecturally groundbreaking: Thomas Edison helped design the hotel's reinforced concrete, and it was the Boardwalk's first "fireproof" hotel and the first to feature a private bath in each room. The Blenheim's Moorish style presented Boardwalk strollers with a breathtaking display of domes and chimneys, and it stood for decades as the city's architectural centerpiece. When gaming was legalized, locals were cheered when Reese Palley, an active booster of casino gaming, bought the hotels in 1977 and announced plans to preserve the Blenheim half of the hotel and to replace the Marlborough with a modern 750-room casino hotel.

Palley succeeded in having the Blenheim placed on the National Register of Historic Buildings but he soon stepped aside as Bally Manufacturing bought a controlling interest in the project. Bally then switched architects and announced plans to raze the Marlborough, Blenheim, and the adjacent Dennis Hotel to build a sprawling, modern casino hotel with an octagonal 385-foot hotel tower. Preservationists were aghast, but Bally cited the difficulties of bringing the old structures up to code. Ultimately, Bally chose to keep the older, less architecturally significant Dennis while imploding the

Marlborough and Blenheim. In December 1979, Bally's Park Place opened as a 51,000 square-foot casino complex tacked onto the renovated Dennis Hotel. Bally's eventually erected an unabashedly hideous pink tower on top of the casino addition, and later added the Wild Wild West themed casino and bought the neighboring Claridge casino (which had opened in a converted hotel), making Bally's Atlantic City (as the casino was renamed) the island's biggest casino, for a time.

The Brighton hotel-casino, soon renamed the Sands, signified another disturbing trend. Atlantic City had over a century's experience as a world-famous destination resort. Yet, aside from the first wave of casino operators who preserved the past out of expediency (they wanted to get open as quickly as possible, and renovation was faster than new construction), the city's casino resorts paid little mind to the city's rich past, its urban framework, or its pedestrian-friendly Boardwalk. Instead, they sought to scoop the casino resort up from the Nevada desert and transplant it on the Jersey Shore.

In fact, the Casino Control Act (the Atlantic City industry's enabling legislation) specified that casinos had to have at least "500 first class hotel rooms," convention space, live entertainment, 24-hour restaurants, and a host of other conveniences. Even advertising had to be regulated "to insure that it is truthful, in good taste, and that gambling is not the dominant theme," because New Jersey legislators were intent on using casinos to springboard Atlantic City into the destination stratosphere of the Las Vegas Strip. Yet these requirements virtually guaranteed that visitors to Atlantic City casinos would not venture far from the garishly-carpeted casino: all of their needs were already met there.

The renaming of the Brighton symbolized the growing "Las Vegasization" of Atlantic City: its historic hotels would be razed and replaced with second-rate versions of Las Vegas Strip casinos. Atlantic City versions of the MGM Grand, Dunes, and Sahara were proposed but never opened, while the Sands, Caesars, and Harrah's (then only in Reno and Tahoe) Showboat, and Tropicana planted flags of Nevada icons on the dunes of Atlantic City.

The Nevada casino operator to make the biggest impact on Atlantic City wasn't a large hotel operator like Holiday Inns, Inc. (who had bought Bill Harrah's Reno and Tahoe casinos in 1980) or a big name like Caesars. It was Steve Wynn, the forward-thinking owner of downtown Las Vegas's Golden Nugget. Wynn had transformed the Gold Nugget into a full-service casino hotel that was the finest downtown. Seeing true possibility with the opening of Resorts, Wynn unobtrusively flew into Atlantic City in June 1978. Jim Crosby, chairman of Resorts International, obligingly steered Wynn to an available parcel—at the opposite end of the Boardwalk. Wynn, wearing a Willie Nelson t-shirt and draw-string pants, strolled into the Strand Motel, offered owner Manny Solomon $8.5 million and, twenty minutes later, owned a piece of Atlantic City.

Wynn successfully courted Wall Street lenders who, charmed by the casino developer's natural charisma and ambitious vision, financed the construction of a classy white and gold casino hotel. Wynn's magnetic leadership made the Golden Nugget the first choice of virtually every casino employee, and his hands-on approach to player development—like Benny Binion, his downtown neighbor and mentor, he was sure to walk the casino floor, shake hands, and listen—helped the casino become the city's most popular. Signing Frank Sinatra to a then-unprecedented 3 year, $10 million deal as the casino's star headliner in 1983 was only icing on the cake.

Yet for every Steve Wynn who struck gold in Atlantic City with seeming ease, there were others who found it slow going. Ramada Inns might be the poster child for the problems that some found down the shore—and the potential payoffs. In 1978, the company bought the shuttered Ambassador Hotel and the adjacent Deauville at Brighton Avenue and the Boardwalk for $35 million. It initially planned to build a $70 million, 549-room hotel-casino called the Phoenix on the site—an apt image for Atlantic City's revitalization. But then it backpedaled, revealing that instead it would refresh the 60 year-old Ambassador first and then, once its casino was operational and money was flowing into the corporate coffers, build a thousand-room "Phoenix-class" hotel.

This did not make many in New Jersey happy. The construction unions, in particular, were chagrined. Two years earlier, they'd been promised that casino gaming would spark a new round of building, putting their idled members back to work. The politicians, too, had been told that casinos would refresh the city's hotel stock, with new facilities giving the city an edge in attracting more convention business. Instead, both Resorts, which had already opened, and Caesars Boardwalk Regency, which was nearing completion, simply reused existing structures. Yes, they had refurbished them, but this wasn't exactly the jackpot the city had been holding its breath for. So the Casino Control Commission, tired of patch and paint jobs and hungry for some real construction stimulus, ruled *ex cathedra* that the Ambassador would have to be imploded and the Phoenix built entirely anew from its ashes.

Ramada executives volleyed back that they had grandiose plans for the site that included what would have been one of the largest hotels on the East Coast; yet they were being held to a different standard than other operators. So the Casino Control Commission delivered a Solomonic compromise that was completely free of any of Solomon's wisdom: Ramada could strip the Ambassador down to its steel framework and use that as the skeleton for a "new" hotel. Construction finally started in October 1979. Before too much work had been done, Ramada Inns bought the Las Vegas Strip's storied Tropicana, which led the company to rename the Atlantic City project the Tropicana.

After numerous delays and overruns, the Tropicana—whose cost had ballooned nearly 500 percent to $330 million, opened in November 1981. Its casino was smaller than had been planned, and it was swimming upstream in a market that was decidedly more competitive than it had been in 1978, when work on the project started. To pay off the $400 million in debt Ramada Inns had taken on primarily to build the Atlantic City casino, the company sold off many of its hotels. Throughout its first year of operation, it looked like this phoenix was destined to return to the dust.

But the following year, things began to turn around. A new parking garage helped to draw more patrons, and the casino suddenly became one of the city's hotspots; the money started pouring in. Within a few years, Atlantic City's Tropicana was not just one of Ramada's most profitable properties—it was generating a large portion of the hospitality chain's revenues. In 1988, Ramada added a new hotel tower and a two-acre indoor theme park, Tivoli Pier. As part of its new identity, the Tropicana became TropWorld which, executives hoped, would become a resort destination to rival perhaps Disney World. Despite this misperception, TropWorld continued to power the company, which the following year sold off its hotel division—all of those Ramada Inns—and spun its casinos off into Aztar, a company that took its thematic inspiration, if not its business methods, from the Aztec empire. With the Las Vegas Tropicana lagging that market, TropWorld was the centerpiece of the new company

This spoke to the seismic shift that had rocked the American casino business. In the early 1980s, Atlantic City became, arguably, the world's leading casino destination. In 1984, it had more than double the visitors of Las Vegas (28.5 million to 12.8), and, though it had one-sixth the hotel rooms, half the gaming tables, one-fourth the slot machines, and limited hours of operation, it nearly matched Las Vegas's $2 billion annual casino revenue. Almost all of these visitors came by car or bus; nearly 1000 busses daily brought casino patrons, chiefly from New York, Pennsylvania, and New Jersey. Supplemented by a regular parade of international high rollers chauffeured in from Philadelphia and New York airports, bus people provided a stable, unspectacular customer base.

But all was not roses: many operators chafed at overly-strict regulations that involved state bureaucrats in every aspect of casino design, staffing, and operation. Caesars, Hilton, and Playboy's Hugh Hefner sunk millions into casino resorts only to be told that they had been denied permanent casino licenses. The Perlman brothers, chief stockholders in Caesars World, were forced to sell their interest before the corporation could be licensed. The Playboy was the hottest property in town before being sold and renamed the Atlantis, which fittingly sank. Steve Wynn's selling his Golden Nugget to Bally Gaming in 1987 should have been a wake-up call, but regulation continued to slow development. As a result, the city was ill-equipped to handle the explosive growth of casino gaming throughout the nation in the 1990s.

Some, however, found Atlantic City to be the promised land. Caesars, Tropicana, and Harrah's found that their Atlantic City branches far out-performed their original Nevada casinos. By 1984, Harrah's Marina was generating a quarter of the company's revenues. The cash flow from Harrah's Marina enabled the company to dramatically expand during the 1990s.

The Donald Takes The Boardwalk

Long before The Apprentice, long before he mulled a presidential run, Donald Trump was a youngish developer looking to make a mark. What better way to make a splash than to go into the fastest-growing casino city in the world? With only a few operators, his developer's savvy—and marketing touch—could make him a major player. Throughout its history, the casino business has drawn its share of out-sized individuals. Many of them were first attracted by the gaming tables themselves, but a host of others, Trump included, primarily saw casinos as business opportunities.

Trump was first drawn to Atlantic City in 1980, when he planned a hotel and casino on a narrow 4.5 acre plot adjacent to the city's Convention Hall, site of the ill-fated 1964 Democratic convention and the annual Miss America Pageant. Even in booming Atlantic City, this wasn't the easiest time to borrow money; banks' prime rate had soared to over 15 percent. Trump was also hesitant about putting his name—and money, borrowed or not—into a project before having any assurances that he'd actually be given a license. The Perlmans were in the process of being forced out of Caesars World, after all, and while Trump was sure such a thing could never happen to him, it was the principle of the thing.

Other prospective casino owners had come to the Casino Control Commission, hat in hand, politely applying for licenses and then waiting—and building—while the process inexorably dragged out. Trump, however, was so white hot that he was able to deliver an ultimatum to the commissioners: before he would do so much as turn a shovel of dirt, he'd need an official up or down vote from the Commission. The Commission uncharacteristically obliged, and in March 1982 awarded him a license, even though he still had no casino. Now, Trump looked for a partner to take care of the messy business of actually running the casino that he'd build.

At the same time, one of the most trusted names in casinos was looking to expand. After acquiring Bill Harrah's Nevada casinos— Harrah's Reno and Harrah's Lake Tahoe—in 1980, it rebranded

By 1986, a score of new casinos joined converted hotels to create jobs and revenue in Atlantic City. The under-construction Showboat and the project that became the Trump Taj Mahal are at the far bottom; the freshly-painted Resorts International is just above them. While some of the city's classic amusement piers are still languishing in decay, the Million Dollar Pier has been transformed into the Ocean One Mall.

its about-to-open casino hotel in Atlantic City's marina district Harrah's Marina. This casino was successful, and the company wanted a slice of the Boardwalk trade as well. By partnering with Trump, Harrah's could get a foothold on the boards at a fraction of what it would cost them to build on their own. It was to be an expensive bargain, as Trump secured an artful deal: in exchange for providing the land, Harrah's would pay him to build the casino, split all profits with him 50/50 and not hold him liable for any operational losses over the first five years of the partnership. Trump had found a way to foist nearly all of the risks of the ventures to Harrah's while maintaining a healthy percentage of any potential profits.

In May 1984, $210 million later, 39-story Harrah's at Trump Plaza opened with an all-star gala bash. Yet from the start there were tensions between the partners. Harrah's had built itself as a company that catered to the middle-market gambler: it didn't court the high-risk, often low-margin VIP business, but instead looked to cultivate armies of stolidly loyal quarter- and dollar-machine players. Trump refused to build a parking garage, a necessary element of Harrah's marketing strategy. He even forced the official name change, dropping "Harrah's at" from the marquee. This was now simply Trump Plaza.

Across from Harrah's Marina, another saga was unfolding. Hilton Hotels had finished an Atlantic City branch that would, naturally, feature a casino. The company already owned two of Nevada's largest casinos, the Las Vegas Hilton and Flamingo Hilton, and felt that licensure was a mere formality. It wasn't. The Casino Control Commission, suspicious of the company's past ties to Sidney Korshak, a Chicago labor lawyer suspected of being a link to the Windy City criminal underworld despite having never been indicted for so much as a jaywalking violation, denied the hotel giant a license. Hilton, stuck with a $306 million, 624-room casino hotel it now couldn't operate, mulled an appeal but decided to unload the property.

Steve Wynn's Golden Nugget made an offer to buy the unopened casino, but Hilton decided to sell the property to Trump, who became a next-door neighbor and direct competitor to Harrah's, his putative Boardwalk partners. Harrah's sued Trump, charging him with deliberately mismanaging the Boardwalk venture in an effort to lower its value; Trump charged that Harrah's was doing the same. After a federal judge essentially sided with Trump, allowing him to keep his name on both casinos, it became clear that the partnership could not last. In early 1986, Trump signed an agreement to buy out Harrah's. His first order of business? To build a parking garage.

Yet Trump wasn't done yet. Under the leadership of James Crosby, Resorts International had begun building an ambitious 1,250-room casino hotel across Pennsylvania Avenue from its flagship casino. After his 1986 death, work on the project continued, though the company became overwhelmed by the debt load it had taken on to finance it. The following year, Trump bought Resorts International. With the gaming regulations limiting each owner to a maximum of three casinos, Trump planned to close Resorts' gaming area, folding its hotel into the Taj's operations (the two were connected by a covered walkway) and using it primarily for convention space. In 1988, however, Resorts met its unlikely savior: television legend Merv

Griffin, who purchased the balance of Resorts' portfolio (chiefly the Bahamas operations and Resorts International), leaving Trump free to open the Taj Mahal while Resorts remained open.

The Trump Taj Mahal opened in a blaze of glory on April 2, 1990. It was, for a time, the world's largest and most lucrative casino, and it would be the last new casino to open in Atlantic City for more than a decade.

Receding Tide

The Taj Mahal opened at a time when Atlantic City casinos were facing their first real crisis. Casinos had been popping in and out of bankruptcy for years, but never before had the city as a whole faced such a crisis. Indeed, it still has not reclaimed its Reagan-era swagger.

Atlantic City faced several problems, but in short it suffered from a failure of imagination. Casinos competed intensely with each other, and their increased marketing outlays—often in the form of coin given to bus junket arrivals—eroded their bottom lines. Many casinos overleveraged themselves and found themselves, by the early 1990s, in bankruptcy.

Looking back, it is clear that both the myopia of both regulators and casino operators were responsible for the city's failure to transform itself into a truly world class destination. In addition to burdensome regulation, the state also limited the types of games casinos could offer: it was not until the early 1990s, when competition from Connecticut Indian casinos (see chapter 13) had already eroded the city's dominant position on the East Coast, that poker, keno, and race books were allowed in Atlantic City casinos. In addition, casinos were slow to invest in non-gaming attractions. Because players drove to Atlantic City merely for convenience, they inevitably chose closer casinos as they became available.

Gambling on Indian reservations in Connecticut, which started with bingo in 1986 and included full-fledged casino gaming, with table games, by 1992, was just one of the seaside resort's new competitors. Indian casinos in other parts of the nation, a swell of riverboats in the Midwest and South, and slot machines at racetracks—Delaware's started in 1995—progressively shrank Atlantic City's sphere of influence. For much of the 1990s, its casinos made few attempts to reinvent themselves, as the Las Vegas Strip was doing in Nevada.

Some retained hope, and after the turn of the millennium, a wave of development hoped to bring the time-honored vision of re-establishing Atlantic City as a world-famous vacation and business resort closer to reality. The Borgata, the city's first new casino resort since the Trump Taj Mahal, opened in 2003 to nearly universal acclaim. Operated by Boyd Gaming, joint owners with MGM Mirage, the Borgata would not have been out of place on the Las Vegas Strip: it was chic, classy, and, like its Strip counterparts, very profitable. Though its golden glass façade is far removed from the graceful concrete spires of the Marlborough-Blenheim, the Borgata signified that Atlantic City was still in the game.

In preparation for the Borgata, Harrah's Atlantic City (the casino lost the Marina designation in 1990) expanded itself upward with two new towers and an indoor pool/spa expansion. On the Boardwalk, the Tropicana added The Quarter, a retail and dining expansion that was roughly on par (though on a smaller scale) than Las Vegas Strip facilities. By mid-decade, several new projects appeared ready to transform the city: MGM Mirage announced plans to build a $5 billion, three-tower, Las Vegas-sized casino resort adjacent to the Borgata. Pinnacle Gaming, a riverboat operator, purchased the Sands casino and imploded it, planning to build a $2 billion mega-resort. Next to the Showboat, Revel Entertainment planned its own $2 billion resort, to be named Revel.

But fate, in the form of renewed competition from Pennsylvania's new slot machines and the credit-tightening, consumer spending-sapping recession of the latter part of the decade, killed these grandiose plans. By 2012, the results were clear: Pinnacle's Boardwalk plot remained an empty lot; MGM Resorts International (to which MGM Mirage changed its name in 2010) canceled plans for an Atlantic City casino, and Revel, after a few delays and a downsizing, opened to disappointing results. That new casino, and a new tower at the Trump Taj Mahal that opened in 2008, are the most significant new construction that Atlantic City may see for some time.

As Atlantic City's casino market has shrunk (gaming revenues fell from $5.2 billion in 2006 to $3.5 billion in 2010, with no end to the drop in sight), it has seen an ownership shuffle. Landry's Restaurants, owners of the Golden Nugget casinos in Las Vegas and Laughlin, Nevada, bought Trump Marina in 2011 and gave it a $150 million renovation that restored the Golden Nugget name to the city's skyline after a 25-year absence. Resorts changed hands as well, and its believed that, after Revel's opening shakes up the market, other properties may change hands or close outright.

By 2013, Atlantic City might seem destined to a future as a minor sub-regional gaming destination, but it has a true claim to gaming history. Before New Jersey permitted legal casinos there, no state had attempted to replicate Nevada's success with casinos. New Jersey showed that an economically diverse state in the nation's most populous region could create a gaming industry that, on balance, contributed to the economic health of the state.

In addition, Atlantic City represented a turning point for casinos. Before 1976, they had been tolerated in Nevada as a sort of necessary evil—they were already legal and employed thousands of citizens, so there was no use outlawing them, but they weren't, outside of the state, considered model enterprises. Casino proponents in Atlantic City, however, promoted casinos as a positive social good and a necessary ingredient for urban revitalization. Casinos wouldn't bring crime—they would reduce crime by creating jobs and a more robust tourism infrastructure, bringing opportunity to Absecon Island. Voters agreed. This was the first real use of casino gaming as a tool of social and economic policy in the United States, and it would not be the last. In the 1980s those supporting Indian gaming as well as riverboat gambling also spoke the language of economic development.

Atlantic City had changed the casino game. And, while the rest of the country hoped to start playing by those rules, Las Vegas started worrying about how it would catch up.

13

The Burger King Revolution

◇◇◇◇◇◇◇◇◇◇

Las Vegas bounces back for the first time

Gangland Goodbye

As Atlantic City offered Las Vegas its first real competition, the Strip was in the midst of its own transformation. Some changes were visible, like the new hotel towers that signaled the city's turn to mass marketing. But others were kept as low-profile as possible, only occasionally bursting into public view. The gradual though often dramatic exit of organized crime from the operation of Nevada casinos was the most significant of these changes.

In 1960, organized crime seemed to have a stranglehold on Las Vegas gambling. Casinos with mob ties had advantages in financing their construction, recruiting players, and collecting debts. There seemed no reason to expect any of that to change. But in 1999, the National Gambling Impact Study Commission declared that the industry was mob-free. "Effective state regulation, coupled with the takeover of much of the industry by public corporations," the Commission's final report read, "has eliminated organized crime from the direct ownership and operation of casinos."

Nevada regulators had been warring with "undesirables" (the official Nevada code word for "mobbed-up casino guy") since the 1940s. Fears of a federal crackdown, as well as the discovery that mobster Meyer Lansky had owned a covert share in the Thunderbird casino, prompted the state to get more serious about policing its growing casino industry in 1955, when the legislature created the Gaming Control Board as an investigative and enforcement arm of the state government. The Gaming Control Board would investigate all applicants for gaming licenses, and the governing body—at first the

Tax Commission but, after 1959, the Gaming Commission—would use its recommendations to issue (or deny) licenses.

Five years later, the Control Board issued the Black Book, a list of reputed mobsters who, it cautioned casinos, should not be permitted to even enter their premises. Their reputations were so unsavory that the very presence inside a Nevada casino might discredit the entire state (and bring down the wrath of federal agents). After a court challenge, the Black Book was established as the law of the land, and it sent a clear message: Nevada was getting tough with the mob. In 1963, after allegedly hosting reputed Chicago mob kingpin Sam Giancana at his Cal-Nevada casino in Lake Tahoe, Frank Sinatra became the subject of a Gaming Control Board investigation. He subsequently surrendered his gaming license rather than face a formal hearing to defend his right to keep it. The Black Book had teeth.

Yet Nevada's mob-fighters were facing a challenge: the advantages organized crime-affiliated operators held in finance, marketing, and debt collection has allowed them to establish a significant foothold in the Las Vegas casino market. It is likely that nine of the eleven major Strip casinos had some degree of affiliation with organized crime figures in 1960.

Within ten years, however, the mob's hold would begin to weaken, and within a generation, it would be nearly gone. Why?

One reason was generational. Most of the operators who moved to Nevada in the 1950s had started their criminal careers in the 1910s and come of age with Prohibition. Members of that violent generation who weren't killed or imprisoned during Prohibition went on to assume leadership of America's criminal syndicates in the 1930s. But in the 1950s, they were well into middle age and looking for stability and respectability. Many went to Las Vegas to find both, and they brought both financial and human capital to the expansion of the Strip in that decade.

By the 1960s, this ambitious coterie was looking to retire. Even before Moe Daltiz had sold the Desert Inn to Howard Hughes, Wilbur Clark had already sold his interests (and passed away in 1965). Many others who were now in their sixties were doing the same. Their children did not follow them into the business of crime, but instead entered legitimate business. Some pursued business degrees and entered the hotel and casino business via that route, but none gained any significant experience in illegal gambling, and none rose to leadership positions within traditional organized crime families.

At the same time, the mob itself was changing. In the 1960s, organized crime began to focus less on gambling and more on areas like illegal narcotics, prostitution, loan sharking, and labor racketeering. The new criminal leaders poised to take control of the crime "families" of major cities, then, had no real connection with gambling, outside of their personal enthusiasm for it. This did not give them any competitive advantage in financing or managing legal casinos. So on the supply side, there was less reason for organized criminals to seek out investments in the legal casino industry.

The demand side shifted too, as the mob-affiliated casino owners essentially priced themselves out of business, victims of their own success. A new Las Vegas Strip casino hotel cost between $2 to $5 million in the early 1950s. For that price, an ownership group could expect a roughly 10,000 square-foot casino, a respectable dinner theater, about 300 rooms in low-rise motel wings, a swimming pool, and other amenities. The casino, which would look a lot like the Flamingo, Sands, or Dunes, might earn a few million dollars a year in gross revenue.

With the expansion of the convention market in the late 1950s, though, casino executives discovered that, since they could now fill rooms during the week as well, they could expand their casinos considerably. New properties were built to handle the new mass traffic: the Stardust had 800 rooms when it opened in 1958. Statewide gaming revenues jumped thanks to the boom on the Strip and the new business market. In 1955, Nevada casinos earned $94.4 million, and in 1960, they pulled in $162.8 million, a 72 percent increase in a five year stretch punctuated by a national recession.

As a result, new casino hotels had to be larger to take advantage of the new convention trade and to build economies of scale. They were more expensive to build: Caesars Palace cost $19 million in 1966, and Kirk Kerkorian's International cost $50 million. The latter resort had 1,500 rooms, and from then on, every major project built on the Strip would be larger and more expensive.

The old ownership groups couldn't afford a $50 million casino. It was never easy to get financing for casinos, but there were enough shady businessmen with undeclared income to get sub rosa investors to get them built. The Teamsters Central States Pension Fund helped a few casinos, including Caesars Palace, build or expand in the 1960s, but in order to construct the massive new resorts the industry demanded, operators needed to attract mainstream capital—large commercial banks, institutional lenders, and publicly-traded companies.

As a result, those with organized crime connections lost their hold over the casino industry. Since they couldn't procure capital sufficient to build new resorts, they no longer had an advantage over "legitimate" operators. Meanwhile, the more balanced bottom lines of larger casino hotels appeared far more attractive to the mainstream investors who'd earlier passed on casinos. With banks offering loans and national corporations offering to purchase existing hotels, why partner with the mob?

Changes in Nevada law—particularly the 1967 and 1969 Corporate Gaming Acts—facilitated the advent of mainstream capital, but the market itself demanded the actual influx of money from previously uninterested sectors. If the casino business had not been proven profitable, no existing public corporation would have risked shareholder wrath by buying a Nevada casino, and investors would not have chanced buying stock offerings from existing operators. In the final analysis, the successful track record of Nevada casinos attracted mainstream investors, whose larger projects drove the traditional ownership cohort from the market. The mob never dominated new casinos like Kirk Kerkorian's International or MGM Grand, or the pint-sized Holiday Casino that expanded until, in 1992, it became Harrah's Las Vegas.

The area of casino marketing saw another shift. Previously, the junket trade gave an advantage to those who had connections with the illegal gambling scene in target cities—obviously an area where organized crime could dominate.

But with the proliferation of direct marketing, customer databases, and mass audiences for the Strip, old-time junkets became less necessary. William Harrah pioneered with a bus program in Lake Tahoe in the 1960s: simply drive enough low-rolling gamblers to your doorstep, and you don't have to court expensive high rollers. Other casinos followed suit, along the way developing data collection and analysis tools that let them determine, with mathematical precision, who their best players were.

This was a crucial breakthrough for casinos. They could do significantly more player development in house, significantly reducing their reliance on outside junket operators. Furthermore, after the 1950s illegal casino gambling operations around the United States dwindled, the remaining operators became less relevant. At the same time, people who would never dream of placing an illegal bet flocked to Las Vegas casinos. Many of these neophytes would have been quite frightened by marketing representatives with lengthy rap sheets and underworld connections. Again, the advantage fell to the clean regimes.

The law still gave unsavory operators an advantage in extra-legal debt collection: with gambling debts not legally enforceable under Nevada law, those who could "persuade" debtors to make good their IOUs had a definite advantage over those who couldn't. With credit play representing a large portion of many casinos' bottom lines, this was a major consideration.

But new competition forced Nevada to reconsider its ban on debt collection. In 1977, the New Jersey legislature specifically made debts incurred in Atlantic City casinos legally actionable—partially to ensure that all collection remained on the up-and-up. After that state's casinos opened Nevada casino credit offices they noticed a disturbing pattern—players were paying off their Atlantic City markers long before their Las Vegas ones. It was easy to see that this disparity would give Atlantic City casinos a decided advantage; in these years, as Atlantic City revenue numbers soared and Nevada's remained steady, competition from the East Coast was a very real fear.

So in 1983 the Nevada legislature permitted the state's casinos to collect gambling debts by taking advantage of bad check laws. Result: a casino who wanted to get recalcitrant debtors to pay up needed the Clark County District Attorney's bad check unit on speed dial, not a hotline to the goon squad.

These changes in the structure of the Nevada industry, both intended and unintended, worked to remove any competitive advantage organized crime might have in the legal Nevada gaming industry and to bolster the ability of "clean" companies to build and run casinos. It is difficult to say which, if any, of the changes can be isolated as the single most important: would mainstream finance have gotten involved in the industry if organized crime had continued to use illegal gambling operations as training grounds for casinos? If New Jersey had not changed the rules of debt collection, would the Nevada industry have demanded the law be amended anyway?

Whatever process, it is clear that the sum total of the innovations severely undermined the competitive position of those with organized crime affiliations. When combined with the increased law enforcement effort against organized crime, both locally and nationally, these changes gave organized crime affiliates a definite disadvantage in the new market. With the mob cleared out, mainstream finance invested in casinos at unprecedented levels in the 1980s and 1990s, leading to the massive growth of the Las Vegas Strip and the proliferation of gaming throughout the United States.

Knocking Down a Strawman

Those seeking to oust the mob from Nevada casinos saved, it seems, the best for last. As the mob's hold on Las Vegas weakened, the city saw several spectacular scandals erupt. When the smoke cleared, people were speaking about organized crime in casinos in the past tense.

The United States Justice Department had been itching to unroot skimming and other mob connections in Nevada's casinos since 1961, when Attorney General Robert F. Kennedy announced a war on organized crime. He believed that gangsters throughout the country were using Nevada casinos as piggy banks, skimming money lost by honest tourists. For its part, Nevada gaming authorities denied large-scale skimming was taking place. Indeed, nearly a decade of federal efforts resulted in only a handful of convictions: in 1973, Samuel Cohen, Morris Lansburgh, and two others pleaded guilty to skimming income from the Flamingo. Meyer Lansky, the ultimate target of the investigation, ended up not facing trial due to his "ill health."

Those who were skimming the money—and the feds knew they were doing it, thanks to wiretaps that, under Nevada law, were inadmissible in court—were simply too careful to get caught. And sometimes the feds simply couldn't connect the dots. In 1970, FBI agents stormed the casino cage at Caesars Palace as part of a multistate bookmaking sting. Inside, they found $1.5 million in a lock box belonging to Jerry Zarowitz, who had no official position at the casino but who had been running many of its operations since its 1966 opening. But the agents could offer no proof that the cash had been skimmed from Caesars' tables, and weren't even convinced that it wasn't instead the take from a sports betting operation.

Yet later in the decade either law enforcement became more astute or the skimmers became less cautious—perhaps it was a mixture of both. It's believed that skimming operations at casinos like the Sands and Desert Inn had been quietly going on for decades. Those casinos passed from their original syndicate ownership to new corporate bosses (Howard Hughes bought both of them) having never seen an arrest, much less a conviction, for skimming. Yet within the space of about five years, skimming scandals would mar several Las Vegas casinos.

The most sensational skimming case and the one that might have put the nail in the coffin of the mob's sway over the count room, was born from the Strawman investigation. The probe started hundreds of miles from Las Vegas, in Kansas City, Missouri. Thanks to extensive wiretapping (legal in that state) FBI agents learned that thousands of dollars a month was being siphoned from casinos owned by Argent, a real-estate start-up helmed by Allen R. Glick that, thanks to $100 million in Teamster loans, became the owner of four Las Vegas casinos—the Stardust, the Fremont, the Marina, and the Hacienda—nearly overnight. In exchange for their influence in getting the loans approved, mob kingpins insisted on the installation of bookmaker Frank "Lefty" Rosenthal as "Director of Nevada Operations and Special Consultant to the Chairman" of Argent. From that vantage point, he was able to direct a massive skimming operation that diverted millions in casino cash to underworld couriers and thence back to Kansas City, Milwaukee, and Chicago. (If all of this seems familiar, it might be because it was brought to the silver screen in Martin Scorsese's 1995 film *Casino*.)

Because of his unsavory connections and a previous conviction for point shaving, Rosenthal had been denied a license by the Nevada Gaming Commission in 1976. But he still clung to an unofficial position of power, and the skim continued. Despite behind-the-scenes pyrotechnics, including a failed 1982 car bombing attempt on Rosenthal's life, the skim continued until 1983, when a federal indictment sent the house of cards crashing down.

The Gaming Commission acted quickly. It immediately severed those involved with the skimming from running Nevada casinos. It asked the Boyd Group, Sam Boyd's respectable hometown operation, to manage the Stardust on its behalf in 1983, and in 1985 Boyd formally acquired the casino. For many this marks the end of the mob's influence inside Nevada casinos. The casinos that would be built in the coming decade would be financed by mainstream financial institutions. The purging of "undesirables" from the gaming industry, a goal of the Gaming Control Board since 1955, was complete—nearly. Even today, the Board remains vigilant in its investigations of applicants for gaming licenses.

Some glamorize the "good old days" of mob influence as times when the town and its casinos were smaller, friendlier, and more honest. But they forget that organized crime was, well, crime, and while the pit boss might have done a better job of remembering your name and your favorite drink, those who stood behind him also brought murder, robbery, and extortion to the game as part of the bargain. For those who simply like gambling, having a casino industry that's financially accountable and free of criminal interest is a good thing.

Las Vegas Gets Competition

Yet just as feds were flushing the last of the goodfellas from Las Vegas casinos, storm clouds appeared on the horizon. Competition from New Jersey was proving surprisingly stiff. In its first half-year of operation, a lone casino, Resorts International, earned more than $134 million in revenues. This vindicated Resorts chairman James Crosby, who boasted before the casino even opened that it would out-earn the MGM Grand, one of Las Vegas's most profitable casinos, which made about $84 million annually. Despite a nearly fifty-year head start as a casino monopoly, Nevada was suddenly challenged by a powerful upstart.

Worse yet, Atlantic City casino revenues continued to soar despite a dire national economy. In 1979, the city's casinos won $324 million, and in the following year nearly doubled their revenue to just under $650 million. By 1982, annual revenues approached $1.5 billion, and in 1985, with eleven casinos, the rapidly-maturing new gaming industry broke the $2 billion mark.

Las Vegas casino revenues grew much more slowly. In 1985, Atlantic City's landmark year, the Las Vegas Strip's 38 major locations boasted under $2.3 billion in revenues, up barely more than $100 million from the year before. Atlantic City, with less than a third of the Strip's casinos, was within shouting distance of Las Vegas's crown as the world's top casino destination. Atlantic City, nearly everyone agreed, was the city of the future.

The alarming success of Atlantic City sparked anxiety in Las Vegas. More than three thousand new high-end hotel rooms had just come online in the desert resort, and it now seemed that gambling junkets and conventions from the East Coast might not be coming to the party in Las Vegas, but instead might play closer to home. Gamblers were certainly arriving in the seaside city en masse. As early as 1983, only five years after the birth of the industry there, over 26 million visitors enjoyed the new casino experience of Atlantic City—more than double the 12.3 million that flew or drove to Las Vegas.

Even before the first Atlantic City casinos opened, it was clear that the town would bring a new competition to the casino game. "New Jersey, which envisions glamour and glitter returning to the depressed boardwalk town, is the first state to intrude on Nevada's gambling monopoly," the *Las Vegas Sun* announced in an above-the-fold story the day after New Jersey voters approved casino gambling in 1976. Las Vegas news outlets generally gave coverage of Atlantic City a negative slant, betraying an underlying apprehension about the potential rival.

Though the industry's leaders maintained poker faces—Gaming Control Board Chairman Phillip Hannifin boasted that he couldn't see how Atlantic City would catch up with Las Vegas or appreciably cut into its East Coast customer base—there was an undercurrent of anxiety amid the happy faces. As Resorts' opening approached, the knives came out. *Las Vegas Sun* publisher Hank Greenspun, in an appearance on NBC's *Today* show hours before the casino opened, warned that organized crime would "fleece" the city. "If they think it's a devastated area now…just wait until those sharpies get through with it." This was a curious threat from one of the strongest boosters of Las Vegas, a city with a long history of organized crime scandals, from Meyer Lansky's hidden shares in casinos during the 1950s to the still-unfolding Strawman investigation. The next week, a front page *Sun* article announced that gambling in Atlantic City just wasn't as fun as in Las Vegas: blackjack was saddled with cumbersome rules, like not allowing aces to be split, and craps was played at "an almost incredibly slow pace." The author even complained that counting cards was harder in Atlantic City, although Las Vegas casinos had long employed anti-card-counting measures and certainly didn't encourage the practice. While they professed to be unafraid, those with a stake in Nevada gaming protested too much to be entirely relaxed.

Even operators who gave Atlantic City long odds worried about the end result of competition. "God love 'em, let 'em have it," casino owner Michael Gaughan told the *Valley Times* after the momentous election. "They'll find out it's not as easy as it looks. I don't welcome it and I don't fear it….[but] it might open a Pandora's box, lead to gaming in other places that could hurt us more." Atlantic City, Las Vegans agreed, might yet prove a loser; but the idea of competition would probably prove a winner in the long run. That was not good news for a state that had built its reputation around a national monopoly on legal casino gaming, and it augured poorly for Las Vegas's future prospects.

Malaise at the Gambling Tables

Atlantic City was only one of the bugbears facing Las Vegas. As formidable foe as the eastern resort might be, Las Vegas faced an even deadlier enemy within: its own susceptibility to a weakening national economy. The 1970s were not a period of economic growth nationally, though early in the decade Las Vegas had, nevertheless, expanded. By the Carter years, however, the situation had changed. The economic crunch then unfolding, during which the nation charted its decline via the misery index, a combination of inflation and unemployment, reached its peak in 1980, though the adverse effects would sap Las Vegas's gaming economy for years. Early in the 1970s, gaming revenues seemed to defy the generally dismal economic outlook, posting double-digit gains from 1972 to 1975. When adjusted for inflation, these increases are not as impressive, particularly in 1974-1975, but they still represent real gains in revenue during times of widespread economic hardship and uncertainty.

In the latest (2007-10) recession, some analysts discovered for the first time that the casino business isn't recession-proof. Yet this has been apparent for decades. Economist Thomas Cargill had debunked the idea of Las Vegas as a recession-proof haven as early as 1979. In a paper for the University of Nevada Reno's Bureau of Business and Economic Research, he argued that Nevada was not "an island unto itself," but was profoundly influenced by regional, national and global economic events. Since a significant number of Nevada tourists came from California, drops in employment, income, and economic well-being in that state naturally would adversely impact Nevada. Rising fuel costs and gas shortages had severely cut into the drive-in market, and the dismal national economy and a dampening market for air travel similarly restricted traffic at McCarran International Airport—from a high of about 10.6 million passengers in 1979, passenger arrivals dropped slightly in 1980 and more dramatically in the next two years. In 1981 and 1982, less than 9.5 million passengers used McCarran airport.

Gaming revenues in the period reflected this malaise. Earlier in the 1970s, they'd been galloping ahead; now, adjusted for inflation, they began to sink. Visitor totals fell as well. In 1970, nearly 6.8 million visitors a year came to Las Vegas and its environs. Eight years later, the total stood at 11.1 million. But from 1978 to 1980 this remarkable growth slowed—only 11.9 million came to Las Vegas in 1980, a growth of less than 800,000 in three years. Over the next two years, visitor volume declined, slipping to 11.6 million in 1982.

Events far from Nevada conspired to rob Las Vegas of several of its most valued customers. Starting in the 1970s, several casinos had marketed to Mexican high rollers. In 1982, when the peso was dramatically devalued, most of these customers could no longer afford trips to Las Vegas. Worse yet, they were unable to pay off their gambling debts with their devalued currency, leaving Las Vegas casinos with millions of dollars in uncollectable bad debts: from 1980 to 1983, the percentage of casino revenues written off as bad debts on the Strip more than doubled. Similar difficulties in Hong Kong and the Middle East kept big spenders from those locales home as well. With Atlantic City siphoning off a significant portion of the East Coast and their established inroads abroad eroded, Las Vegas casino operators were justly pessimistic.

Yet Las Vegas faced more than just increased competition and a dismal national economy. It also confronted a crisis of confidence and a shattered public image due to a massive, entirely preventable, tragedy.

On November 21, 1980, a deadly fire ripped through the MGM Grand Hotel Casino, then Las Vegas's newest and most modern resort. Eighty-seven people died, and video footage of black smoke billowing from the casino entrance—and trapped guests in the hotel towers desperate for rescue—aired on newscasts around the nation. The fire, which was made far worse by the casino's failure to install sprinklers, was a public relations nightmare for Las Vegas. If guests couldn't be safe in this ultra-modern palace, could they feel comfortable in any Las Vegas hotel? Las Vegas was a tourist town built on certain insouciance and escape from care, and the specter of death—the ultimate reality—understandably reduced its appeal for revelers.

There was more bad news to come. Four months later, a fire at the Las Vegas Hilton—which killed eight people, injured two hundred, and left blackened scorch marks along the tower's façade—compounded the disaster. Retro-fitting the massive casinos of the Strip to mitigate such blazes would be costly, time-consuming, and would make far less impression on the public than the tragic fires. Even if the hotels of Las Vegas were to have perfect safety records for the next five years, millions of potential visitors would not forget the images of fire, death, and destruction, and many of them would decide to vacation elsewhere.

In the early 1980s, then, Las Vegas seemed down on its luck. The MGM Grand fire symbolized a larger loss of confidence in the city's future. With decreasing revenues, increasing competition, and a hotel inventory now viewed as unsafe, the smart money was against the house. In a 1982 *Boston Globe Magazine* article, Connie Page summed up the mood in Las Vegas. In contrast to previous trips to the Strip, when guests freed themselves from their usual restraints…

> this year's visit…was different. Life seemed to have switched into neutral. Snatches of conversation with some of the army of casino workers…soon made the difference clear: local unemployment was higher than ever before, business was off, the prospects for recovery uncertain. The people of Las Vegas, ordinarily carefree, were worried about the future. In short, Las Vegas was in the throes of the Great Recession of 1982.

Behind the tables, the gloom was even more intense. A "recession impact survey" that polled casino managers in 1980 revealed that most respondents felt that the recession had hurt their business. The high-end properties on the Strip felt the pinch far more acutely than the value-oriented downtown hotels because, as one respondent put it, "there are a lot more 'ordinary people' in this world than high rollers." Though most Nevada respondents insisted that the gaming industry still had long-term growth potential, few denied that the state was in a bad position. By contrast, Atlantic City's managers reported that they did not feel any decline in business at all.

But the city's casino operators did not give up or passively wait for business conditions to improve. Rather, they reconsidered their operations and devised a new formula for attracting visitors that they believed would help them adapt to the new challenges of the 1980s.

Welcoming the Masses

The 1980 Laventhol and Horvath survey revealed a troubling consequence of the on-going downturn: the luxury hotels of the Strip were more sensitive to economic fluctuations than the low-roller gambling halls of downtown. The smart money had always said that high rollers were the bread and butter of any first-class casino resort. But the recession was proving this assertion wrong.

The recession and the growth of Atlantic City sparked what was called the "Burger King Revolution": an embrace of middle-class vacationers, bus tourists, and families in campers on the Las Vegas Strip. This was the only way, a variety of industry leaders believed, that Las Vegas could remain viable and continue to grow. The exclusive approach might have worked in the past, but the city had crossed a threshold and now had to market itself to a broader audience. Thus, Rossi Ralenkotter, director of tourism and research for the Las Vegas Visitors and Convention Authority, said that "Now we are into mass marketing. When you've got 53,000 hotel rooms to fill, you'd better appeal to everyone."

The Revolution transformed Strip casinos. Some would keep their baccarat pits tucked off to the back, but they wouldn't be adding many more suites. Instead, slot machines, RV parks, and fast food restaurants would attract customers, and discount coupons would become the coin of the realm. An $800 million expansion of McCarran airport would help speed the arrival of the masses, and a $10 million advertising campaign would let them know that Las Vegas was welcoming new customers.

The "Burger King Revolution" was not just a turn of phrase: this shift centered on an actual Burger King franchise, serving Whoppers and Croissan'Whiches on the Las Vegas Strip. Attorney and certified public accountant Jeffrey Silver, who had earned a reputation as "the Red Adair of Las Vegas" by putting out a proverbial fire and reversing the fortunes of the oft-troubled Landmark casino hotel, brought fast food to the Riviera in 1984 as part of his strategy to revive that troubled Strip landmark. The Riviera had spent decades chasing high rollers only to end up in Chapter 11 bankruptcy while across the street Circus Circus chased low-action players and thrived. Once put in charge of the Riviera, Silver immediately began building an expansion that would house 500 new slot machines, a video game arcade, and a Burger King—the first fast-food franchise in a Strip casino.

The move to the masses was not without controversy. Several Riviera executives opposed Silver's Burger King idea, arguing that it would cheapen the hotel. But Silver was onto something. Directly across the street, a McDonald's did "land office business" even though it was in the shadow of the Circus Circus marquee, which advertised a $2.49 lunch buffet. McDonald's was inexpensive, but couldn't come close to meeting the price/volume quotient of the Circus Circus buffet. Silver concluded that the McDonald's thrived because a significant portion of the Strip's clientele was either uneasy about the quality of food in the casinos or simply liked the security of a familiar setting on their vacation. Even those who opposed the Burger King saw Silver's logic, and the project went forward.

Outside the casino, the opposition was even stronger. The Clark County Planning Commission refused to approve his proposal to erect a Burger King sign outside the hotel, deeming its addition a detriment to the character of the Strip. But, Silver insisted, it was a matter of changing with the times. Only by pursuing a previously-neglected market, he argued, could Las Vegas meet its latest challenger. Atlantic City might be a gambling town, but as a vacation destination, it could never beat Las Vegas. By making it an affordable destination, Las Vegas could rebound...and then some.

Ultimately, Silver won. The Burger King opened a few months later, and was for a long time the most successful franchise in the chain. Other casino operators, who had initially opposed Silver, began sniffing out franchise opportunities of their own.

The Riviera's new eatery did more than prosper; it drove customers to the hotel and gave the casino a safe, friendly image. "We've changed the focus of the hotel," Riviera president Arthur Waltzman proclaimed triumphantly in late 1985. "We're targeting Middle America." Silver's vision of a Burger King Revolution on the Strip came to pass: fast-food restaurants now appear inside most Strip hotels, even upscale ones like the Venetian—and Caesars Palace.

Visitors to town in 1984 encountered several signs of the new order. Checking in for flights, they received for the first time funbooks. These had come a long way since Jackie Gaughan had started using them Downtown. Gaughan had been using them to lure patrons to his no-frills downtown gambling halls for years, but now they were ubiquitous on the formerly proud Strip. Passed out with room keys, at restaurants, and with ticket purchases, they gave the thrifty an excuse to visit casinos that, five years ago, would have given them the cold shoulder.

By the time this photo was taken in 1986, Circus Circus had expanded several times, become the most profitable casino in Nevada and was emulated on the newly budget-conscious Las Vegas Strip.

Silver's Burger King was revolutionary, but he was right to seize the moment and boldly go where no food-and-beverage director had gone before. Already, outside observers noticed a change in the tenor of the desert resort. "Vegas has changed," the *New York Times* concluded in 1984. "It's looking for new customers as it tries to adjust to new competition, a different kind of trade, and new technologies."

This included re-evaluating the city's target customers. In 1985, Mint Casino Hotel general manager Marv Leavitt admitted that previously the "high roller" betting big on table games was the "premier gambler" of Las Vegas. But that was changing. "Now we've recognized that the dollar slot player can be worth more than a $5 table player." Quarter-slot players also proved a valuable market segment; quarter-slot machine inventory on the Strip more than doubled from 1983 to 1989. By 1987, more than half of all of the slot machine on the Strip were quarter machines. The humble quarter slot was suddenly driving the growth of the Las Vegas Strip.

Leavitt's championing of the slot player was emblematic of the Burger King Revolution's impact on the casino floor. The new focus on low rollers speeded the dominance of slot machines. Jay Sarno, with Circus Circus, is believed to have been a pioneer in promoting the slot machine as a major part of the casino revenue picture. He consciously designed this casino, which opened in 1968, to feature slot machines as an important part of the casino floor. Slots-only parlors were already common, but this was the first attempt by a major Strip property to court the slot customer. After assuming management of the casino in 1974, Bill Bennett and Bill Pennington abandoned Sarno's attempts to attract high rollers, eliminated many of his ancillary and competing attraction, and honed a business model that centered on middle-market slots-playing visitors. They had a great deal of success, turning profits that belied the modest bankrolls of their customers.

In turning to slots, the Strip began to converge with downtown Las Vegas, which had weathered the recession comparatively better than the Strip. In 1980, Strip casinos derived more than 65 percent of their income from the table games of the pit, chiefly blackjack, craps, roulette, and baccarat. That percentage steadily fell, until in 1988, for the first time, Strip casinos got less than half of their gross revenue from table games. Even in high-end casinos, slot machines were becoming more important. In 1975, a blackjack or craps table was likely a casino's most important piece of gambling equipment. Ten years later, it was a quarter slot machine.

"Gaming is Growing Again"

Just as Circus Circus had been ahead of the curve in seizing on the primacy of slot machines, it was also one of the first casinos to thrive in the "new Las Vegas" of the 1980s. The casino decided to stop extending credit to players, forgoing $10,000-a-trip high rollers entirely for families whose total annual income was less than $45,000. The casino had no baccarat tables, a clear signal that big spenders were not welcome. By charging between $16 and $36 for a room night, the casino's managers ensured that it would always have plenty of quarter slot players. Its buffet was typical of the Circus Circus approach: with an all-you-can-eat breakfast at $1.99, lunch at $2.49, and dinner at a mind-boggling $3.49, the eatery was a bona fide loss leader. Yet, as analyst Dan Lee explained to USA Today, the company was happy to lose money on the meals because, "first you have to go though the casino to get to the buffet. I defy anyone to get there without spending at least that much on a slot machine."

Loss leaders had been a staple of the Las Vegas Strip since the 1940s, yet Circus Circus was applying them to the grind business with brutal efficiency—and prospering. The managing partners opened a Reno casino in 1978, bought the next-door slot mart Slots-A-Fun in 1979, and acquired the Silver City, a small casino across the Strip from Circus Circus, in 1981. These properties helped Circus Circus Enterprises become the Cinderella story of early 1980s Las Vegas. While other casinos were reeling from the recession in 1980, Circus Circus turned an $7.9 million profit, a slight drop-off from its 1979 haul of $8.1 million, but stellar compared to the losses other were suffering. After that, the sky truly was the limit: net income edged up to $9.1 million in 1981, then jumped to $15.8 million in 1982, $18.3 million in 1983, and $23 million in 1984—a 23 percent average annual increase over five years in a period when most casinos were struggling to remain solvent. For the rest of the decade, net income grew at even more impressive levels; 1989 saw profits of $81.2 million, a five-year compound growth rate of nearly 29 percent.

It wasn't a question of gambling, as it was one of mass entertainment. Circus Circus touted itself as an "entertainment merchant" whose model was the mega-market or box store, an enormous retailer that sold a variety of goods at bargain prices. "Basically, we are mass merchandisers," Circus Circus Enterprises chairman Bill Bennett declared in 1985. In contemplating a new development on the south Strip that ultimately became Excalibur, the company in 1988 saw Circus Circus, only larger: again, it would cater to "middle-income guests and players," and the new casino therefore would have policies that resembled those at the company's existing properties "with their traditional emphasis on extraordinary value for the price." The world's most profitable casino company believed that it had found the winning formula, and it wasn't going to tamper with it.

Circus Circus prospered because, with its circus acrobats and bargain prices, it was uniquely situated to exploit a market segment that other casinos were only now discovering: families. Driving in, eating

lunch at Burger King, and spending the day at the newly-opened
Wet N' Wild water park, between the Sahara and Riviera casinos,
couples with kids found themselves welcomed in Las Vegas as never
before. Five years before, they had only been welcome under the
pink and white big top of Circus Circus; now they were courted
everywhere.

"For the first time," a 1985 *USA Today* article noted, "casinos along
the Strip are catering to Middle America, a giant class of low rollers known as 'grind players' who bring their families, stay a few days
and spend $500—at most." By way of explanation, Glenn Schaef-
fer, chief financial officer of Circus Circus, enunciated what would
become the city's mantra for the next decade: "Yes, Middle America
is the largest and most dependable segment of the gaming market.
And that market of high-rollers…is very finite. There just aren't a lot
of people who can afford to lose a lot of money."

Refocusing on Middle America proved to be the road to Eldorado for Las Vegas casino operators. Revenues began rising again
in 1983 and maintained their upward trajectory for the rest of the
decade. On the Strip, revenue gains matched those for Clark County, which was boosted by the continuing success of downtown and
the growth of Laughlin, a bargain Vegas on the Colorado River. By
broadening its base, the Strip had effectively increased its total revenue stream, with non-gaming increases keeping pace with the rising gaming win.

In the mid-1980s, Strip operators did more than just take advantage of the recovering national economy. They strategically reposi-
tioned themselves to exploit a mass market of lower-value but higher
volume players, recognizing that the international high-rolling crowd
of the 1970s wouldn't be returning. Those who filled the Strip's coffers
in 1984 and beyond weren't, for the most part, foreign visitors playing
baccarat; they were middle-class Americans playing slot machines. In
this regard, the Strip specifically borrowed from not only downtown
Las Vegas but even its Eastern nemesis Atlantic City: the latter ma-
tured into a destination primarily for day-tripping quarter slots players by the mid-1980s, and the Strip, though it required a longer stay by
necessity, had no problem chasing a similar caliber of player, plus the
bigger gamblers who had long flocked there.

The Burger King Revolution was, then, a resounding success. The pessimism of just a few years earlier dissipated like mist in the desert sun, and casino executives again began thinking about expansion. As early as 1985, *USA Today* noted an ironic reversal: now Atlantic City's growth was slowing, while Las Vegas's was speeding up. Glenn Schaeffer could proclaim that, "Nevada and Las Vegas are in the midst of an up cycle in casino revenues. Gaming is growing again."

Casino revenues skyrocketed, in part, because the casinos that embraced the new mass-marketing strategy added thousands of rooms, letting them welcome more players with smaller bankrolls. Circus Circus added the Skyrise tower, a 1200-room high-rise addition, in 1986. The Tropicana added an 806-room tower as part of a $55 million facelift in the same year.

Ramada Inns gaming group president Paul Rubeli, who oversaw the expansion, explicitly said that he was turning to the "middle-class, the resort-oriented customer," and was happy to see the property's high roller business drop from 50 percent of its total revenue to 30 percent. The low end players had a profit margin of only ten cents on the dollar, and high rollers were too risky and their market too competitive. "But right in the middle," he argued, "is that husband and wife who spend $500. With them, we'll make 70 cents on the dollar." Several other casinos added room expansions, as the city's hotel room inventory rose from 50,270 in 1982 to 61,394 in 1988. This was the total of three 1990s-style mega-resorts, and nearly all of the rooms were geared away from high rollers and towards middle-market, bargain hunting customers.

Casinos also built non-hotel additions that catered even more directly to a modest-spending clientele. Circus Circus added Circusland, a 421-space RV park to its offerings in 1979. The Hacienda and Stardust later built similar, though smaller, on-site RV parks. The following year, while Caesars Palace was showing off its new, outrageously lavish Fantasy Tower, Circus Circus added Circus Circus Manor, an 810-room three-story self-contained motel that was later connected to the casino by a monorail. Back in 1978 Circus executives had forecast that Las Vegas needed RV hookups more than hot tubs. Five years later, they were vindicated.

Success with Middle America bred, if not complacency, a certain restlessness. With the mass market now taken for granted, those at the forefront of the industry began thinking about new horizons. As casino gambling began spreading wider and wider throughout America, Las Vegas would need to strike back. And it did.

14

Runaway American Dream

Gambling in the public interest

By the late 1980s, casino gambling was on the minds of government officials and voters throughout the United States. Las Vegas was booming like never before; casinos seemed to have reversed the fortunes of Atlantic City. Why should these two cities reap the entire bonanza of Americans' expanding appetite for card games and slot machines?

With a now-proven track-record as job creators in Atlantic City, casinos began to appeal to other regions looking to improve their fortunes just as dramatically. Lambasted as hopelessly corrupt scarcely three decades earlier, casinos were now embraced as public policy tools that would promote economic growth, balanced state budgets, and civic improvement. It was an astounding reversal whose full impact has yet to be appreciated.

The New Buffalo

Atlantic City, with its crumbling hotels and depressing spiral of unemployment, crime, and poverty, was in dire need of help, but even that resort was well-off when compared to many Indian reservations. Since the beginnings of European settlement of the Americas in the 16th century, the native inhabitants of the New World found themselves systematically driven onto marginal lands. In the United States, the federal government's policy towards Indians, which at one point embraced the wholesale destruction of Indian polities and culture, had softened by the 1930s. The "Indian New Deal" sought to revitalize tribes as communities and had as its goal tribal self-sufficiency rather than assimilation.

The subsequent decades of well-intentioned government aid did little to improve life on Indian reservations: they still remained remote settlements wracked with poverty and a host of social problems. With gambling an increasingly alluring revenue option for many states, it is perfectly understandable that a few tribal leaders started to look at gambling as a solution for their own problems. The federal government had actually approved tribal government supervision of gaming as early as 1924, when the Bureau of Indian Affairs officially recognized tribal gaming laws, but no tribes opened facilities catering to non-Indians.

In the late 1970s, the Penobscot Indians of Maine moved to offer bingo, followed by the Seminoles of Florida. After all, 34 states allowed charitable organizations to run bingo games, and Indian tribes, sorely in need of money and jobs and not run for profit, certainly qualified as charities. But Indian bingo operators soon argued that they were not subject to state oversight: because they are sovereign political entities, tribes are not subject to the civil laws of the states that surround them. Bingo operators reasoned that if bingo was not absolutely prohibited as an illegal game—a violation of the state's criminal code—then the state had no authority to police tribal bingo games. Tribes began offering bingo games with super-jackpots, sometimes as high as $50,000. Suddenly, bingo players were finding their way to reservations, their bingo nights suddenly much more exciting.

Rival bingo operators were understandably upset at this exercise of tribal sovereignty, as were county officials. Raids against tribal high-stakes bingo operations in California and Florida triggered legal battles that reached the Supreme Court in 1987. The Florida raid, which sparked a successful lawsuit by the Seminole tribe, was a touchstone for shifting American views towards Native Americans. While state authorities argued that the tribe should be kept from violating state laws, many outside observers vocally defended the Indians. After centuries of broken promises and unfair treaties, they argued, allowing tribes to run bingo—at which attendance was not compulsory—seemed like a small concession. Seminole Chairman James Billie believed that the bingo hall gave his people a chance at turning the tables. "It's more than beads for Manhattan," he stated, referencing the story that Dutch colonists had purchased Manhattan in 1626 from its Native inhabitants for $24 in beads.

Echoing Billie's sentiments, many tribes did not wait for the matter to be resolved by the courts. With unemployment as high as 70 percent and sharp cuts in federal assistance, many tribes embraced bingo. In 1983, for example, the Yaqui, an Arizona tribe, opened a $1 million, 1300-seat bingo parlor hailed as the biggest in the West. Able to offer $12,000 jackpots that were three times as large as those presented by church and other nonprofit bingo games, the Yaqui bingo hall drew players from nearby Tucson. The 200 nonprofit bingo halls in that city reported an immediate 10 percent fall-off in business. At the time, between 40 and 60 tribes nationwide had, like the Yaqui, turned to bingo.

Later that year, 2,400 people flocked to North Carolina's remote Cherokee reservation, paying $500 each for a chance at a $200,000 jackpot. In 1984, the Otoe Missouria Indians of north-central Oklahoma opened what it claimed was the world's largest bingo hall, a 6,000-seat acre of bingo called the Red Rock Bingo Palace. Players for hundreds of miles around took buses to the remote reservation and stayed overnight in a nearby hotel, playing from noon to midnight Saturday and Sunday on alternate weekends. Some weekends, they won as much as $400,000 in prizes. The games bordered on the festive; when one of the many Texans in attendance won a game, "Deep in the Heart of Texas" played over the sound system. Yet amid the merriment, some felt lingering apprehension: one player told a reporter that she didn't use her real name when playing because she was a Baptist. Still, they came. Whatever the concerns of existing charitable gaming operations, bingo clearly had the support of players. Even so, with the laws regarding Indian gaming still ambiguous, the legal foundations of this potential goldmine remained shaky.

The Supreme Court soon swept away all doubt of the legality of tribal-run gaming operations. In February 1987, the nation's highest court issued a landmark ruling in California vs. Cabazon Band of Mission Indians: if a state legalized a form of gambling (in California's case bingo and poker), tribes could offer that kind of gambling without any interference from—or regulation by—state, county, or municipal authorities. High-stakes bingo and no-limit card rooms on Indian reservations were now unambiguously legal; tribes could also offer lotteries and perhaps even casino gaming in states that regulated those games. In his decision, Justice Byron White's declared that Indian gaming was actually a welcome opportunity for tribes to develop economically: gambling, a proven winner in Nevada, New Jersey, and most other states, would now be tabbed to end centuries of tribal misfortune.

Even before the Cabazon decision, the federal government had been encouraging the development of Indian gaming. As part of his mission to shrink the federal government, President Ronald Reagan had declared the reduction of tribal dependence on government funding to be a priority of his administration; he cut appropriations to tribes, forcing them to find alternate sources of funding, which could only be accomplished by developing tribal industries. Bingo fit the bill, and the Department of the Interior and Bureau of Indian Affairs approved tribal ordinances that set up high-stakes bingo games. The federal government even helped to finance tribal bingo start-ups through grants and loans.

Dispassionately, the development of tribal government gaming was about tribal sovereignty and economic development. Many states, though, viewed the growth of high-stakes bingo and the Cabazon decision with alarm. They were fearful that full-blown casinos might open within their boundaries and drain money from competing state gambling enterprises. Since the states were clearly powerless to control tribal government-sanctioned gaming, a growing chorus of state governors sought help from the federal government. In 1988 Congress passed the Indian Gaming Regulatory Act. This measure did not "legalize" or "authorize" Indian gaming, which had been flourishing for years, but rather provided rules for its continuing development.

The Act established three classes of Indian gaming. Class I games were traditional games played among tribal members and were to be regulated solely by tribes. Class II games included bingo, lotteries, and non-bank games (poker, etc). Class II operations were to be overseen by the National Indian Gaming Commission, though after a period of successful operation tribes could construct their own regulatory bodies. Class III gaming was, basically, casino gaming: slot machines and mercantile card and dice games.

Congress, wishing to give states some say in the process, declared that to run full-blown casinos, tribes first needed to ink compacts with states. These were essentially treaties between the two sovereign polities that set forth the type and number of games to be played. Though states had no power to tax tribal casinos, most compacts required tribes to pay a fixed sum or a portion of revenues each year to states. The casinos were usually regulated by tribal governments, though some states retained the right and responsibility to conduct background checks on casino employee applicants. In the IGRA, Congress pointedly echoed the sentiments of Justice White, finding that gaming was consonant with the federal goal of promoting tribal self-sufficiency and economic independence.

Even before the Cabazon decision or IGRA, some Indian tribes started full-fledged casinos. With the legal status of tribal gaming in doubt, many opened facilities that were primitive in comparison to the sprawling resorts of the Strip. In 1984, Frederick Dakota opened the nation's first Indian casino in his brother-in-law's converted garage on the L'Anse Indian reservation off Keweenaw Bay in northern Michigan. The erstwhile garage, insulated against the winter with chipboard walls, featured two blackjack tables: a $2 table and, for high rollers, a $5 one, whose dealer's chief experience was having once run a church bingo game. Those tired of playing could relax at the three-seat bar, where well drinks cost 70 cents and high-end libations (Canadian Club whisky) 90 cents. Both state and federal authorities refused to close down Dakota's game. In that two-car garage, the modern Indian casino was born.

Detractors scoffed at the first Indian casinos, arguing that they would never be more than glorified bingo halls. Yet within barely a decade of the passage of the Indian Gaming Regulatory Act, an Indian reservation would host the world's largest casino. Foxwoods Resort Casino in Ledyard, Connecticut, has enabled the Mashantucket Pequots reservation, which had at one point dwindled to only one member, to become one of New England's economic powerhouses.

In the 1970s, new tribal chairman Richard "Skip" Hayward convinced several of his relatives to move onto the 200-acre reservation; had they abandoned it, it would have become property of the state.

Hayward and the other members of the re-established Mashantucket Pequots experimented with a few enterprises, including collecting maple syrup, cutting wood, a gravel business, and owning Mr. Pizza, a restaurant on nearby Route 2.

After securing federal recognition in 1983, the tribe tried several more enterprises before turning to bingo. Most lenders were skeptical of Pequot bingo: strait-laced New England was, allegedly, no place to build a high-stakes bingo parlor. Yet New England had led the nation in reviving lotteries two decades earlier, and bingo had proven popular nearly everywhere in the United States. With a loan from the United Arab-American Bank, Hayward built a $4 million brick bingo parlor on Pequot land near Ledyard.

When the bingo hall opened on July 5, 1986, there were over 100 Indian gaming operations nationwide. The Pequot bingo hall was among the most sophisticated in the country, with electronic boards that displayed the drawn numbers and computers to verify winning tickets. Helped by the Penobscots of Maine, whose own high-stakes bingo game had been curtailed by an unfavorable court ruling in 1984 (a ruling that would be effectively reversed with Cabazon), the Pequots found bingo exceeded all expectations, as players came by car and bus. At times, more than 1,700 of them crowded into the hall, vying for big jackpots and, along the way, helping the Pequots gain financial self-sufficiency.

The next step for the Pequots was opening a true casino. Because Connecticut allowed non-profit charities to run casino games as part of "Las Vegas Nights," the tribe negotiated a compact under which it was able to open a casino. With financing from Malaysian billionaire Lim Goh Tong, who owned Malaysia's Genting Highlands casino resort, and a team of former New Jersey regulators and casino executives, the Pequots opened the Foxwoods casino on February 15, 1992.

Foxwoods was not the first Indian casino to open under the IGRA; the Flandreau Santee Sioux of North Dakota had opened one in 1990. But it quickly became the most profitable. Accessible by car from New York, Boston, and all points in between, it gave Atlantic City its first casino competition on the East Coast. Foxwoods even had a host of games that Atlantic City didn't: Red Dog, pai gow poker, horserace simulcasting, and poker. The tribe's 45-table poker room was the first legal one on the East Coast. Foxwoods never closed, unlike Atlantic City casinos, which had been forced by statute to close at 4 A.M., or 6 A.M. on weekends. (Within five years, New Jersey permitted every game allowed at Foxwoods and had begun twenty-four hour gambling.)

Foxwoods opened with few amenities: it had gift shops, eateries, and a small entertainment venue. Yet it was so profitable that it almost immediately began expanding. Frank Sinatra, the gold standard of casino entertainers since the 1950s, opened the Fox Theater in 1993; he was followed by a string of casino favorites. This gave Foxwoods a new measure of legitimacy, but the casino had already secured something more important: slot machines. Since Connecticut's charity gaming nights were free of slots, the tribe was prohibited from installing them. In hopes that a compromise might be reached, the original casino was ringed with video poker and reel slots set for free play—though no money went in, no money came out.

In 1992, the tribe reached an agreement with Connecticut Governor Lowell Weicker that authorized slot machines in return for a quarter of gross slot revenue or $100 million, whichever was greater. Foxwoods immediately installed new machines and continued to expand; by 1994 it had nearly 4000 machines that grossed at least $800 million a year. It was by then the largest casino in the United States. Further expansions would give it over 7400 slot machines and 388 table games by 2004, making it without question the largest casino in the entire world. With nearly 1500 hotel rooms, restaurants, shopping, and convention facilities, it was a mega-sized Strip-style casino resort, nestled in the backwoods of Connecticut.

Foxwoods' business was so good that not even the 1996 opening of Mohegan Sun 12 miles away in Uncasville slowed its profits. The Mohegan people, once rivals of the Pequots, joined them as casino operators thanks to a three-way 1994 compact between the tribes and the state. Initially managed by South African gaming magnate Sol Kerzer's Sun International, Mohegan Sun grew to be nearly as large as Foxwoods and just as successful.

Other states had similar experiences with the "new buffalo" of Indian casinos. California had, since Gold Rush days, been a state of gamblers, and a good portion of the visitors to Las Vegas and Reno drove up from the Golden State. California Indian tribes argued that since the state's lottery used electronic devices, they were permitted to install electronic gambling devices in their card rooms and bingo halls, which were unambiguously legal under the Cabazon decision. By 1995 twenty tribes across the state operated 8,000 slot machines; one of the largest, the Barona Big Top Casino in San Diego County, had over 1000 of the machines.

These machines were not quite legal, and though they were un-doubtedly lucrative for tribes, most wanted to place their casinos on a more solid regulatory footing: compacts with the state that would permit them to operate Class III casinos with table games and slots. Governor Pete Wilson negotiated such a pact with the Pala Band of Mission Indians of San Diego County, but most tribes felt it was too restrictive and in 1998 pushed for a statewide referendum, Proposi-tion 5, that would force the governor to accept tribal casinos. Termed the "Tribal Government Gaming and Economic Self-Sufficiency Act," the referendum passed handily despite the opposition of Ne-vada commercial casino interests (all told, over $200 million was spent on both sides of the fight). Though it had passed convincingly, Governor Wilson challenged Proposition 5's legality and the Cali-fornia Supreme Court struck the measure down in 1999. A repack-aged measure, Proposition 1A, was approved by voters in 2000. This time, commercial casino companies, sensing that California Indian gaming was inevitable and that there was money to be made by sign-ing management contracts with tribal casinos, backed the proposi-tion.

A new, friendlier governor, Gray Davis, had already begun ne-gotiating compacts with California tribes. Agreements with over 60 tribes brought Nevada-style casino gaming to California, with blackjack and slot machines. Many existing bingo halls added slots and began planning new casinos. Within the next few years, dozens of reservations boasted glittering new casinos. The typical California Indian casino had between 30 and 50 table games, a poker room, and 2000 slot machines, the state maximum. As the state entered a financial and political crisis in 2003 culminating in the election of Arnold Schwarzenegger as governor, the restraints and financial obligations placed on tribal government casinos became a political football which, it seemed, would be in play for years.

Whatever the ultimate fiscal and political settlement reached between the governments of California and its Indian tribes, casinos soon changed the face of California gambling. Card rooms and race tracks, which had long enjoyed monopolies on live-action gambling, felt the pinch almost immediately. California citizens, suddenly presented with casino gambling closer to home, turned out in record numbers; though none of the casinos were as large as the Pequot's Foxwoods, they may have been, machine for machine, just as lucrative. Dotting the California countryside, they were further proof that Californians still loved to gamble.

Riverboats Return

With the proliferation of lotteries, the sudden reality of Indian casinos, and the success of Atlantic City, many states began to reconsider their traditional prohibitions against casinos. With visitation to Las Vegas and Atlantic City breaking new records each year and no major scandals related to the operation of their casinos, allowing legal gambling seemed like anything but a gamble. Yet the inhabitants of many states still felt some compunctions about legalizing casinos: while they might be fine for vacation destinations like Las Vegas or Atlantic City or isolated Indian reservations, they were hardly appropriate for the hard-working, God-fearing communities of the heartland. Still, the potential revenue from gambling halls remained a tantalizing lure, particularly as many states suffered economically in the late 1980s. If only there were some way to legalize casino gambling without the casinos, some thought, all of their problems could be solved.

Iowa did just that when, in 1989, the state approved gambling on board riverboats. By the late 1980s, a recession had gripped the Quad Cities area of the state, as manufacturing and food processing plants closed. Searching for a way to spark local development, Art Ollie, a Democratic state legislator from Clinton, Iowa, hit upon the idea of riverboat excursions featuring gambling. Vaguely citing the heritage of Mark Twain and the legendary exploits of Mississippi riverboat gamblers, Ollie and others began seriously pushing the idea of riverboat casinos, which, they hoped, would draw tourists to the otherwise moribund region.

Bob Arnould, the Speaker of the Iowa House, picked up Ollie's idea and ran with it. In the fall of 1988, Bernard Goldstein, the former owner of the Alter Company, a Quad Cities-based concern that started as a scrap metal yard and diversified into the grain business, barge fleets, and real estate. He articulated plans to build a hotel/entertainment complex with a dock that would provide access to an excursion boat outfitted with slot machines and gambling tables. Goldstein's lobbying and public speaking efforts contributed to the August 1989 passage of a riverboat gaming act by the Iowa Legislature. According to the new law, gambling was legal in licensed boats on the Mississippi, Missouri, and other rivers, if approved by the adjacent county. Riverboat gambling was about to become a reality.

The bill that the legislature passed mandated that gambling could take place only during scheduled cruises, and players were limited to bets of $5 and losses of $200 per trip. The gaming area could only take up one-third of the vessel's floor space. Even with these restrictions, boosters projected that the gambling boats would draw 8 million tourists to Iowa a year. Goldstein commissioned the construction of the Emerald Lady and Diamond Lady, specially designed gambling ships, and eagerly anticipated April 1, 1991, the first day that the boats could legally operate.

In the meantime, residents of Illinois, particularly Moline and Rock Island, began clamoring for a piece of the coming gambling bonanza. The state accordingly legalized riverboat gambling without the onerous bet and loss restrictions of Iowa. Even before the first boat had sailed, Iowans knew this was bad news. Goldstein scaled back plans for his gambling boats, and most of the ancillary hospitality developments never happened, as developers feared that gamblers, primarily drawn from Illinois and Missouri, would simply play at the more convenient and less restrictive Illinois boats.

Marred by competition or not, riverboat gambling still promised to transform the towns that permitted it. On April 1, 1991, a Mark Twain look-alike and hoop-skirted southern belle welcomed visitors on board the Diamond Lady; owner Bernard Goldstein smashed a champagne bottle across its bow and, live on Good Morning America, officially launched the boat. Howard Kiel, a Quad Cities native, placed the ceremonial first bet at a craps table (he rolled a seven and won), while Vanna White gave the boat's wheel of fortune its first spin. Outfitted in mahogany, marble, and chrome, the Diamond Lady evoked Victorian elegance on the Mississippi.

Illinois, which passed a riverboat gaming act in January 1990, also launched its first gambling boats in 1991. Casinos in Alton and East St. Louis siphoned off gamblers from St. Louis, while boats in Elgin, Aurora, and Joliet captured most of the Chicago gamblers. Several of the earliest Iowa riverboats sailed out of state, heading for more lenient jurisdictions. In 1994, the state eased many of its restrictions, but much of the damage had already been done. Since the 1980s, Iowa has legalized bingo, lotteries, horseracing, and riverboat gaming. Yet the failure to stave off competition from Illinois has prevented Iowa from establishing itself as a true gambling destination.

Mississippi did not make the same mistake. In 1990, it had promulgated the nation's most liberal riverboat gambling law, approving an unlimited number of floating casinos on local option on the Mississippi, Gulf Coast, and virtually every other body of water in the state. The casinos did not need to cruise or even be able to sail. Although several working boats relocated from Iowa when gambling started, eventually Mississippi "riverboat casinos" became barges connected to hotel/entertainment complexes.

By a quirk of fate, the same boat that opened Iowa gaming also commenced gambling in Mississippi. Bernard Goldstein, frustrated with mounting losses on his Iowa boats, moved his flagship Diamond Lady and Emerald Lady to Cadet Point, Biloxi. While conducting his due diligence in Biloxi, he learned of the long-gone Isle of Caprice offshore gambling resort. Wanting to make a fresh start, Goldstein redecorated his boats with palm trees and luminous colors and named his new casino, which comprised the boats and a barge to which they docked, the Isle of Capri: both boats opened on August 1, 1993. Other boats soon followed, and Mississippi casinos were an immediate success.

Although some states, like Illinois, initially required riverboat casinos to cruise, others permitted nonsailing barges that were "boats" in name only. Harrah's first riverboat opened in 1993 in Joliet, Illinois, where the Southern Star and Northern Star sailed six three-hour tours daily. Harrah's Vicksburg (which later became the Horizon Vicksburg) was, from the start, an integrated casino-hotel complex whose gaming floor just happened to float on water.

Though legal throughout the state, only two areas became casino clusters: Tunica, close to Memphis in the north of the state, and the Gulf Coast (Biloxi, Gulfport, and Bay St. Louis) in the south.

Tunica County, previously most famous for its Sugar Ditch, a slum replete with shacks, outhouses, and open sewers, became renowned as a boom town. The opening of the Splash Casino in October 1992 cut the county's unemployment rate in half. Casinos worked a similar miracle on the Gulf Coast, reviving the hopelessly stagnant tourist industry.

These casinos catered primarily to drive-in players, and were not much different from completely land-locked casinos in downtown Las Vegas or Atlantic City. Casino barges were large and frequently multi-story. In some, it was difficult to tell exactly when a patron had left the terra firma of the grounded hotel portion for the barge. Steve Wynn's $675 million Beau Rivage, which opened in 1999, featured a barge so spacious and a stabilization system so sophisticated that one might as well be on land. In the aftermath of Hurricane Katrina in late 2005, the Mississippi legislature approved land-based casinos near former riverboat sites on the Gulf Coast, and casinos were lauded as a major tool for the rebirth of the region's economy.

Other states followed Iowa, Mississippi, and Illinois. Louisiana became the fourth riverboat casino state in 1991 when it authorized 15 riverboats; a year later, a land-based casino was approved for New Orleans. Despite the history of legal gaming in New Orleans, which hosted the nation's first legal casinos, casinos in Louisiana have not been the unmitigated success that they were in Mississippi. Like Iowa, Louisiana quickly became a one-stop gambling shop, with racinos, riverboat casinos, Harrah's New Orleans casino on land, and video gambling devices at bars and truckstops.

In 1998, scandal rocked the state when former governor Edwin Edwards was indicted along with six others for racketeering and extortion. Edwards was notoriously corrupt—he had already been the subject of 22 grand jury investigations—but seemed bulletproof, once boasting that the only way he could lose an election was to get caught "with a live boy or a dead girl." He was charged with blackmailing prospective casino licensees to the tune of $3 million. Former San Francisco 49ers chairman Eddie DeBartolo was also enmeshed in the scandal: he later testified that he had given Edwards $400,000 after Edwards had threatened to use his influence to block DeBartolo's license application. Edwards was convicted, and casinos continued to operate in Louisiana without interruption.

Missouri followed in 1992 and Indiana in 1993, bringing the number of riverboat casino states to six. Missouri attempted to limit losses, something that had been tried—and would soon be rejected—in Iowa. Boats were initially required to cruise for two hours, and patrons were limited to a $500 loss limit on each tour. Using player cards, the casino tracked purchases of gaming chips or slot machine credits. When the $500 limit was reached, the player was barred from playing any further. Though the state eventually dropped the cruise requirement and permitted patrons to come and go as they pleased, the $500 loss limit remained in force.

As riverboat gaming became a fixture of the Midwest and central South United States, a score of casino chains soon appeared, some lasting longer than others. Grand Casinos opened three Mississippi properties and invested in Bob Stupak's Stratosphere in Las Vegas before being acquired by Park Place Entertainment and ultimately folded into casino giant Harrah's (today Caesars Entertainment). Argosy grew to become the nation's fifth-largest casino operator before being bought by racetrack and racino operator Penn National. Isle of Capri opened or bought casinos in five states and a Florida racetrack and even expanded internationally with a Bahamas location. Ameristar, a company that began as Cactus Pete's casino in Jackpot, Nevada, grew to own seven casinos. Countless other groups owned one or two casinos, making regional markets a proving ground for smaller casino companies.

Moving Ashore

Even before the first riverboat casino had been launched, South Dakota experimented with a different model of limited gambling. A 1988 referendum permitted legal gambling in Deadwood, South Dakota, the notorious Wild West town. This was not a sweeping enactment of wide-open gambling: only blackjack, poker, and slot machines were permitted, and bets were limited to a five dollar maximum. South Dakotans were more interested in historic preservation than re-creating the Las Vegas Strip, so they limited each establishment to a maximum of thirty slot machines. To prevent monopolization of the market, all licensees had to be state residents, and none could own more than three gambling halls.

Gambling started on November 1, 1989. Operators proved ingenious in combating the restrictions on casino size, combining their properties within a single building to present the appearance of a single large gambling hall. Cadillac Jack's, for example, boasted over 170 slots and nine table games. This was no MGM Grand, but it was certainly a departure from the spirit of the law. The state raised the betting limit to $100 in 2000, which led to a dramatic increase in blackjack play. With the popularity of the HBO series *Deadwood*, record numbers of visitors flocked to the town to soak up the period replica atmosphere and recapture the spirit of the Old West by gambling a bit.

Limited gaming began in Colorado in 1991, when the first gambling halls opened in the historic mining towns of Cripple Creek, Blackhawk, and Central City. Gambling was limited to slot machines, poker, and blackjack and bets capped at $5. Since the state hoped to advance historic preservation and tourism though casino development, it required that all gambling halls conformed to pre-World War I architectural design standards. Still, some of the larger casinos of Blackhawk, in particular, seem to be merely scaled-down versions of Las Vegas casino resorts.

But Colorado limited gaming has also created a unique gambling center. Bennett Avenue, Cripple Creek's main thoroughfare, was soon dotted with dozens of storefront gambling halls whose facades are reasonably faithful reproductions of turn-of-the-century designs. Colorful names like Creeker's, Midnight Rose, Brass Ass, and Virgin Mule adorn a row of unpretentious gambling halls that cling to the spirit of old Colorado. In some, players receive complimentary popcorn and hot dogs, a far cry from the gourmet offerings of the Vegas Strip's celebrity chef eateries, but the right fit for Bennett Avenue. Cripple Creek casinos offered something strikingly different from the Strip and Strip imitators: small, informal gambling halls set within a genuinely historic milieu.

Where Colorado and South Dakota embraced gambling, at least in part, to preserve the past, the city of Detroit courted casinos to help build its future. The city had suffered grievously since the 1970s, its industrial base decimated, many of its businesses closed, and much of its population in flight. When the neighboring province of Ontario opened the government-owned Casino Windsor on the opposite side of the Detroit River in 1994, the Motor City had a new problem: state residents spending their discretionary income in Canada. The state's legislators concluded that three casinos within the city of Detroit would recapture these gamblers and anchor future tourist development.

But the road to casino nirvana was easy. Originally, planners envisioned a waterfront strip of casino hotels that would become a tourist destination. While the city attempted—unsuccessfully— to buy the land, the state allowed the three winning bidders: the Greektown Casino, owned by a local group of investors, the MGM Grand, the Detroit branch of the Las Vegas gaming giant, and the MotorCity Casino, partly owned by the Mandalay Resort Group, to operate "temporary" casinos. By 2001 these casinos were grossing over $1 billion a year, and it was becoming increasingly clear that the original development plan was not feasible. The next year, the state allowed its casinos to open permanent locations away from the waterfront.

The Greektown opened with only one restaurant, but, as the only casino owned completely by Michigan residents, pointedly advertised that it wished its guests to patronize a range of local eateries. This was the exact antithesis of the Las Vegas Strip/Atlantic City model of the self-contained casino resort. The MGM Grand Detroit opened in a former Internal Revenue Service building, perhaps the most creative repurposing of a government office in a long while. The MotorCity, not to be one-upped, was housed in an extensively-remodeled Wonder Bread factory, newly decorated with automobile-inspired murals. Within a few years, each of the three casinos opened its permanent location, and the Detroit gaming industry would earn more than $1 billion a year in casino revenues.

Detroit casinos offered the usual array of games—blackjack, craps, baccarat, roulette, and slot machines—and showcased the new prominence of gambling in American life. Once, elected officials professed to consider gambling halls a disgrace. Now, they celebrated the conversion of government buildings and shuttered factories into lucrative casinos, hungry for both jobs and tax revenues. No oration about the changed place of gambling in American society could be more eloquent.

With land-based casinos a proven winner in major cities like Detroit and New Orleans, the taboo against them crumbled. Pennsylvania legalized casinos at racetracks, slot parlors, and resorts, and casinos in Pittsburgh and Phildelphia added to the roster of urban gambling halls. New York City in 2011 saw the opening of Resorts World at the Aqueduct Racetrack, bringing video lottery terminal gambling to the nation's largest metropolis. Casinos in a quarter of Ohio cities (Cleveland, Toledo, Columbus, and Cincinatti) began opening in 2012, and East Coast states from Maine to Maryland were in various stages of approving new or expanded gambling.

The wave of expansion that seemed to crest in 2012 had started a generation earlier, and it profoundly remade the American gambling landscape. But Las Vegas, the city that didn't invent American gambling but nonetheless came to define it, wasn't standing still. Even before the first dice had been tossed on the first legal riverboat casino, that city's power brokers were plotting their counterattack.

15

A Clockwork Volcano

<><><><><><><>

Las Vegas strikes back

In the 1990s, canny owners and their designers reinvented the Las Vegas Strip as an adult playland that borrowed elements from around the world. Recreations of Venice, Paris, and New York shared the skyline with oversized medieval castles, exploding volcanoes, and dueling pirates. The three-mile stretch of erstwhile highway promised to whisk visitors to worlds of adventure, little more than a cab ride away. But the exotic atmosphere belied the serious business that gambling had become. High-tech cameras followed every throw of the dice, and random number generators determined slot jackpots. Meanwhile, gamblers around the world, logged on to the Internet to bet. Gambling may have seemed edgy and spontaneous, but it was increasingly by the numbers. Just as they tamed the fire that had destroyed Pompeii, making it punctually erupt for the delight of their guests, casino operators channeled the primal force of gambling.

Gambling Goes Electronic

By the end of the 20th century, casino floors had changed remarkably from the days of sawdust and spittoons. Closed-circuit television cameras had replaced direct observation via catwalks, making casino surveillance much more sophisticated. Slot machines, which were once a toy-like diversion on the casino's perimeter, emerged to become the casino's primary money-maker. Slots first out-earned table games in 1981, and twenty years later, they accounted for two-thirds of gaming revenue throughout Nevada, and even higher portions in other states.

The mechanical reel machines of the 1890s, in which customer pulled a handle to set reels into motion, had become electro-mechanical hybrids by the 1960s. Even though they incorporated electronics to illuminate display panels and eventually to make gameplay smoother (and less susceptible to cheating), old-style slot machines were simply not that exciting: play was slow and payouts excruciatingly low. But with advances in electronics came a new generation of slot machines. In 1963, Bally Manufacturing, a longtime slot and amusement builder, introduced a machine called Money Honey, regarded as the first modern slot. With a 2,500-coin hopper it could offer large payouts, and its electronic innards paved the way for future refinements. By the end of the decade, Bally had created five-coin multipliers—machines that let patrons play extra coins in return for higher payouts—and multi-line machines, on which players had several chances to win.

As computer and television technology evolved, video slots appeared. In 1963, Nevada Electronics produced the first game that combined electronics with a video display, a blackjack game called Automatic Blackjack. It was refined by electronic engineer Richard Raven, who renamed it Dealer 21. His Raven Electronics also produced a keno-based game and video versions of reel slot machines. Video slots were initially a tough sell: players, conditioned to the reassuring sound of spinning wheels and buzzing bells, were leery of the newfangled machines. But slot players eventually overcame their skittishness and embraced video gambling, and by the turn of the century, video slots accounted for nearly half of American gaming machines.

Video poker became one of the most popular slot games. In 1978, a former Bally distributor named William "Si" Redd purchased a fledgling video slot manufacturer named Fortune Coin. Redd, who in 1981 renamed his company International Game Technology, introduced Draw Poker the next year. It was not the first attempt at a video poker machine, but it was the most successful. Under Redd, IGT capitalized on its poker machines and a stream of new games made possible by more sophisticated microprocessors, soon supplanting Bally as the world's leading slot maker. In 1986, IGT's Megabucks, a progressive slot machine system that pooled bets from machines throughout the state of Nevada debuted. Several spin-offs followed, and Megabucks became enshrined as one of the casino floor's most exciting slots. The largest single slot jackpot to date, $39,710,826.36, was won in 2003 on a dollar Megabucks machine at Las Vegas's Excalibur by a twenty-five year-old Los Angeles software engineer. IGT's wide-area progressives combine the instant-gratification of slots with the life-changing jackpots of lotteries—a heady combination unimaginable when the first slots were crafted. By 2012, IGT wide-area progressives could be found in virtually every state and reservation land from California to New Jersey.

Technology also allowed casinos to more accurately track play and better evaluate complimentaries or "comps." Traditionally, players got comps based on what casino bosses surmised about their betting: if they seemed to be playing big (or had the potential to do so) casinos gave them up to one-half of their expected losses in free food, drink, entertainment, and even transportation. Seeking to standardize this process, casinos started harnessing technology to better award comps. Beginning in the 1980s and intensifying in the next decade,

Mirage CEO Steve Wynn smiles as lucky winner Elmer Sherwin holds aloft a check signifying his multimillion-dollar winning spin on The Mirage's opening night, November 22, 1989. Megabucks is typical of the wide-area progressive slots pioneered by International Game Technology that combine slots' instant gratification with the lottery's life-changing jackpot.

casinos began to issue player loyalty cards that allowed them to track exactly how much slot players put into the machines. This would take comping decisions out of the hands of casino managers, instead relying on computer software. By 2005, casinos would begin experimenting with radio frequency identification (RFID) chips that would let them track table play with similar sophistication. Though traditionalists decried computer comp systems as yet another sign of the growing impersonalization of casinos, they were simply another adjustment casinos made to their exploding popularity.

No Mirage

As casino gambling became increasingly common, Las Vegas casino operators were forced to offer more than just gambling, lest they fade away like the Monte Carlo casino in the 1930s. This had been the clarion call of casino promoters since the 1940s, but the travelers of the 1990s were more sophisticated than their earlier counterparts, demanding luxury and scoffing at the "cheap eats" and inexpensive entertainment that had long been the defining feature of the Las Vegas Strip. To survive, the Strip would have to change.

Steve Wynn, owner of downtown's Golden Nugget, initiated that change. Wynn had announced plans to build a major casino resort on the Las Vegas Strip as early as 1981. Though that original project never saw fruition, Wynn did not give up. In January 1987, when he announced the sale of the Atlantic City Golden Nugget to Bally's, he revealed that he had bought a parcel of land next to Caesars Palace on which he would build a luxury resort called the Bombay.

This project ultimately evolved into The Mirage, a resort that pulled the Strip into a new realm. The Mirage fused the titanic integrated resort pioneered by Kirk Kerkorian's International with the dreamy, dramatic opulence of Caesars Palace. Yet Wynn built The Mirage to be more than a glitzier version of its predecessors. Earlier Strip resorts were casinos first and entertainment resorts second. The Mirage, by contrast, was planned to be a general vacation attraction that incidentally had a casino.

Other casinos had lustrous neon signs or sweeping porte cocheres to greet visitors; The Mirage had a 4.5 acre South Seas-styled lagoon and an artificial volcano that erupted on cue every fifteen minutes.

Inside, a white tiger habitat showcased the animals of Siegfried and Roy, the illusionists who would define Las Vegas entertainment for over a decade as The Mirage's resident headliners. Guests could walk though a rainforest nestled between the entrance and the casino and check into their rooms while watching the luxuriant lobby's 20,000 gallon aquarium, whose calmly gliding fish provided a counterpoint to the frenetic excitement of the casino floor

As work progressed on The Mirage, pessimists predicted that the resort, which needed to gross $1 million per day to break even, would surely fail, a victim of its sizeable debt load. When the casino opened its doors on November 22, 1989, 100,000 guests had been optimistically projected. But twice that number turned out, a portent of the resort's success. Caesars Palace, long the reigning money king of the Las Vegas Strip, earned $300 million in 1990, The Mirage's first year. The Mirage pulled in $420 million, vivid proof that it had taken the Palace's crown. Wynn's belief that the casino with the highest overhead would enjoy the highest profits was vindicated.

It was a timely victory. Wynn offered an ingenious adaptation to the inevitable expansion of casino gambling throughout the United States. With the success of casinos in Atlantic City and mounting calls for casino legalization in other states, it became clear that Nevada's monopoly on casinos was gone forever. Anyone with foresight could see that, in the future, most Americans would have to fly over thousands of slot machines on their way to Las Vegas.

Which raises the question: why would anyone fly that far to play the same games that they could at home? All things being equal, the answer is that, barring an unusual fetish for air travel, they would not. But, Steve Wynn and others correctly deduced, they would fly twice as far to visit a unique resort destination— to gamble, certainly, but also to be entertained in ways that they couldn't back home.

Wynn's overachieving Mirage had a sequel, the adventure-themed Treasure Island, which opened in 1993 as a lower-budget version of the original—it was distinguished by the pirate battle staged hourly on its Strip frontage. Five years later, Wynn debuted the Bellagio, an even-more-upscale rendition of The Mirage. When it opened, the Bellagio's $1.6 billion price tag made it the most expensive hotel,

With its lavish use of seemingly non-revenue generating space and features like a rain forest, white tiger habitat, and volcano, The Mirage inspired the next generation of Strip resorts after its 1989 opening.

casino or otherwise, yet constructed. The volcano was replaced by an eight acre artificial lake that, every fifteen minutes, erupted into a terpsichorean tangle of lights and towering jets of water.

Inside the Bellagio, guests were wowed by the lobby ceiling, where artist Dale Chihuly created an unmatched aerial garden of 2,000 hand-blown glass flowers. From there, visitors could walk into the casino's botanical gardens, which were regularly updated to keep pace with the seasons. The Bellagio eschewed the over-the-top theming that had come to dominate the Strip: there would be no recreation of Venice's gondolas or Paris's street sweepers. Instead, the casino's more understated décor implied the luxury of its name-sake resort on Lake Como. The Bellagio gave Wynn three Strip show-stoppers along with his original downtown Golden Nugget, a Laughlin Golden Nugget, and Biloxi's Beau Rivage, a Gulf Coast version of The Mirage. Each of these was, in its own way, a casino design triumph, yet there was more to Wynn's empire than attention to architectural detail. A uniquely charismatic leader in an industry that was becoming increasingly impersonal, he inspired rare loyalty in his employees.

The influence of Wynn's model, a high-end property that combined the various functions of a casino resort with a dramatic theme, can be termed the Mirage Effect, and it became the blueprint for the 1990s expansion of the Strip. In a few years, smart operators reversed the existing paradigm; rather than giving away these amenities to get people in the door, they increased their quality—and cost—and created attractions that customers would gladly pay for, and made gambling an increasingly small (though still significant) part of the overall resort.

The growing importance of rooms was a logical, though not necessarily inevitable part of the Mirage Effect. Since the 1950s, many casinos in Las Vegas had had pretensions towards luxury. But, in the 1990s, operators made sincere moves towards elegance. They enlarged and upgraded their rooms; once little more than dormitories, these became spacious and tastefully designed. Originally merely places for gamblers to sleep, rooms became attractions in and of themselves, at least partially because convention travelers were willing to pay higher premiums for better rooms.

The rooms aren't the only part of the Strip that's become a money generator. In addition to paying more for higher thread-count sheets and designer finishes, Strip visitors have eagerly opened their wallets for gourmet cuisine, delivered to them in celebrity chef eateries.

In the Strip's earliest years, casino restaurants had generic menus and service. That began to change in the late 1950s. The Stardust broadened the Strip's palate with Aku Aku, a Polynesian restaurant that played on the then-current rage for all things tiki. The casino also hosted Moby Dick, a seafood restaurant, a venture that would have been unthinkable in the desert city a generation earlier. Other casinos followed, opening their own seafood restaurants (the Dunes' Dome of the Sea) or making stabs at ethnic cuisine.

Then, in 1961, Chester Simms at the Flamingo decided that the Strip was ready for true gourmet dining. Managing the casino at the time, he supervised the creation of the Candlelight Room, the first true gourmet restaurant on the Strip. It offered what was at the time a novelty, fresh Maine lobsters that were flown in daily from Boston. The Candlelight Room closed in the late 1960s, a victim of the management shake-up after Kirk Kerkorian's purchase of the Flamingo, but it was influential: soon other casinos were dipping their toes in gourmet waters.

Casino dining underwent a sea change in the 1990s, and as the Mirage Effect remade restaurants. Casinos went two routes: creating their own in-house upscale dining "brands," and linking with well-known chefs whose culinary stature made them mainstream celebrities.

The celebrity chef invasion began in 1992, when fabled Los Angeles restaurateur Wolfgang Puck opened a branch of his famous California eatery Spago at the Forum Shops in Caesars. Puck would go on to become a Las Vegas fixture, putting his name to Chinois, also in the Forum Shops; Postrio, at the Venetian; Trattoria del Lupo, at Mandalay Bay; Wolfgang Puck Bar and Grill, at MGM Grand, and CUT at the Palazzo.

Spago's was an immediate hit, and within ten years a flood of famous culinary eminences had descended on Las Vegas. Emeril Lagasse, Bobby Flay, Alain Ducasse, Bradley Ogden, Nobu Matsuhisa, Michael Mina, Thomas Keller, and Daniel Boulud, each of them famous far beyond the restaurant world, opened Strip restaurants.

In 2005, MGM Grand scored a coup when the casino lured "chef of the century" Joel Robuchon out of retirement to open his only fine-dining restaurant in the United States. His namesake restaurant features 6- and 16-course tasting menus, and has been hailed as one of the finest in the United States. That's a bold claim, particularly in a town that, not too long ago, was renowned for shrimp cocktail and chuck wagon buffets. But it's not an outlandish assertion. It would be hard to find a higher concentration of haute cuisine anywhere in the world.

Other casinos have also entered the ultra-gourmet sweepstakes. In 2006, Restaurant Guy Savoy, the famed chef's first eatery outside of France, opened in Caesars Palace, and new casino plans give as much importance to their choice of signature celebrity gourmet as they do the resort's architecture or its casino games.

The cost of entertainment has gone up, too, as headliner concerts and installed shows (Cirque du Soleil alone has five today) raised their production values and their prices.

Casino showrooms have evolved considerably over the 25 years, though there are many similarities. Then as now, casinos split their stages between installed production shows and big-name headliners, with smaller and lower-end resorts concentrating on the productions. In January 1981, for example, the Stardust and Tropicana offered their evergreen shows (Lido de Paris and Folies Bergere, respectively), while the Maxim ran "Old Tyme Burlesque," the Hacienda staged "Ice Fantasy," and the Silver Slipper had "Boylesque." Each of these was a production show, with the emphasis on the general entertainment value rather than a name headliner. It's doubtful that anyone traveled to Las Vegas specifically to see Razzle Dazzle at the Flamingo Hilton or Horsin' Around at the Treasury (today's Hooters), but such shows gave patrons a brief break from gambling, at the very least.

Headliners ran the gamut, from a country double-bill of Roy Clark and Tammy Wynette at the Frontier to Shecky Greene and Suzanne Somers at the Sands. Many casinos offered two different shows a night: at the Sahara, guests could see Jerry Lewis and Jack Jones for the dinner show, or Flip Wilson and Vic Damone over cocktails. Generally, these headliners were established acts. Some, like Liberace (then at the Hilton) had been playing Las Vegas for decades, while others, like Willie Nelson (headlining at Caesars Palace) were relative newcomers.

By 1989, the entertainment lineup was, all things considered, weaker. Caesars Palace still had headliners with greater mainstream popularity than other casinos (Ann Margaret, in March of that year). The Hilton had Frankie Valli and the Four Seasons, and the Desert Inn, Ray Stevens and Louise Mandrell, while virtually every other casino showcased revue shows, many of them with considerably fewer frills than the old standbys, Folies and Lido.

Casino entertainment was clearly feeding from itself: lesser revues shuttled up and down the Strip, from casino to casino, and were both formulaic and derivative. Tellingly, impersonators began to be considered headline entertainment: Legends in Concert had begun its run at the Imperial Palace, and Vegas World featured two imitation spectaculars, back to back: "Reflections of Sinatra" at 4 P.M. and "Memories of Elvis" at two hours later. None of these shows cost more than $30 a ticket, and most cost considerably less: Vegas World's ersatz shows charged $5 each.

When Siegfried and Roy began appearing at Steve Wynn's Mirage in 1990, they performed true magic: they permanently raised entertainment prices on the Strip. At more than $70, their show was by far the most expensive in town. And it was also successful, grossing over $1 billion in sales and countless more in incremental gaming revenue during its nearly 14-year run.

By 1996, other operators realized that their customers, too, would pay more for a better entertainment experience. In that year, two shows—Treasure Island's Mystere (the first permanent Cirque show on the Strip) and the MGM Grand's EFX—joined the Bavarian magicians on the north side of the $50 per ticket mark, and many other shows were flirting with the $40 barrier.

There was a generational change underway, as well. Genuine rock acts, from Pat Benatar to Bad Religion, headlined the Hard Rock's venue, The Joint, signaling the new "coolness" of Las Vegas. Once, playing a casino was considered a sign of hopeless has-been-hood for entertainers—now, it was a mark of hipness. The House of Blues at Mandalay Bay would contribute to the trend towards younger acts, and the Grand Garden Arena at MGM would host Vegas stops for a variety of current top-selling acts.

All of these changes would put gambling in the center of increasingly upscale resorts. In 2007, it seemed like the marriage between high-stakes gambling and deep-pockets vacationing would continue forever. The next three years, however, would prove that to be a dream as illusory as anyone's had at the craps table. In 1990, when the world was welcoming The Mirage, however, all of that was in the future.

Send out the Clowns

The Mirage restored the shine to the Strip's luxury aspiration. The next casino to open, The Excalibur, was quite a contrast: behind the timbered chandeliers and paper mache dragons it was a plainly mass-market casino hotel. This 4,000-room casino resort styled as a medieval castle was the last major Strip resort designed before the opening of The Mirage, and is in many ways the anti-Mirage. Called the "granddaddy of all miniature golf castles" by architect Alan Hess, the Excalibur's construction cost less than half than that of The Mirage. Its "Shopping Courtyard" had a string of carnival-like attractions and chintzy stores. While expansions of existing casinos, like the Stardust, Tropicana, Sahara, and Riviera guaranteed a continuing home for the "cheap room/cheap eats" visitor, all subsequent developments on the Strip hewed more closely to Wynn's vision.

Circus Circus Enterprises, the company that built Excalibur, embraced luxe as enthusiastically as anyone. Circus's next project, Luxor, was a dividing point for the company, which had changed significantly since Bennett and Pennington had mastered the low-roller family market in the 1970s. The property was designed as a "class resort," and despite some errors in execution, marked a new direction under the growing leadership of Glenn Schaeffer. In 1984, soon after Circus Circus went public, Schaeffer, whose background included both public relations and finance, joined the company as senior vice president for casino development; he was chiefly responsible for selling Circus Circus and casino gambling to Wall Street. After the successful launch of Excalibur, Schaeffer became Circus Circus's president and heir apparent, but left the company in early 1993 after a split with company chairman Bill Bennett. But Schaefer would return when, in 1995, following Bennett's ouster, Circus Circus acquired Gold Strike Resorts, a company that he had joined. With Schaeffer as president once again, the company began planning a new flagship property, Mandalay Bay. Built along the lines of Mirage rather than Excalibur, it opened in 1999 and was so successful that Circus Circus Enterprises changed its name to Mandalay Resort Group. The company that once championed budget accommodations and coffee shop fare now had as its flagship a luxurious casino resort with a Four Seasons hotel-within-a-hotel, a fitting commentary on the transformation of the Las Vegas Strip.

It had been a remarkable change, as gambling casinos, once considered dangerously seedy or, at best, comfortably tacky, turned into hip vacation spots. Schaeffer and his Circus Circus team were not the only ones to evolve the casino environment. The openings of Mirage and Excalibur signaled the start of an incredible decade of growth along the Strip. The international economy picked up in the early 1990s and, later in the decade, the dot-com boom produced scores of newly-rich young vacationers who thought nothing of playing thousands of dollars over a weekend. As it became clear that, if presented with alluring attractions, visitors would continue to fly to Las Vegas even after casinos had been legalized closer to home, the boom began in earnest.

Grander than Ever

By the early 1990s, Kirk Kerkorian had built the world's largest hotel twice and bought Metro-Goldwyn-Mayer film studios as many times. In 1969, he had opened the International, which he sold to Hilton, and in 1973 he had debuted the MGM Grand, which he sold in 1985 to Bally Manufacturing to satisfy the lawsuits stemming from the tragic 1980 fire. Since then, he had bought and sold the Sands and Desert Inn before purchasing the Marina, a small casino hotel across from the Tropicana, in 1989. In 1991, work began on a second, grander MGM, with more than 5000 guest rooms, a vast casino, and an attached theme park.

This new MGM Grand not only recaptured the title of the world's largest hotel, but was also the first $1 billion Strip resort. When it opened in December 1993, it was roughly twice the size of the average Strip casino. The MGM's green glass exterior, originally intended to evoke the Emerald City of *The Wizard of Oz*, was a clever piece of cross promotion (Kerkorian also owned the MGM movie library, which included that 1939 film classic). But the Oz theme proved uncongenial to gamblers, who wanted less of the Yellow Brick Road and more of sophisticated gambling; in retrospect, a James Bond theme (another MGM franchise) might have been more appropriate. Still, the resort was a success: repositioned as "The City of Entertainment," it formed the genesis for what would become one of the gaming industry's leaders.

MGM Grand, in partnership with Primmadonna Resorts, a company that owned three casinos at Primm on the California state line, built a neighboring casino, the Gotham-themed New York-New York, which famously brought a reproduction of the Manhattan skyline to the Strip in 1997. MGM subsequently acquired Primmadonna and then set its sights on a larger prize: Mirage Resorts. The

Board of Directors of Mirage Resorts, led by Steve Wynn, agreed in March 2000 to a $6.4 billion buyout offer from MGM Grand, Inc. The deal created MGM Mirage, a company that owned 14 casino resorts in Nevada, Detroit, Mississippi, and Australia. At the time, some speculated that Wynn might be content to channel the $400 million in after-tax profit he made from the sale of Mirage Resorts into his art collection, while others noted that the aging Desert Inn was on the market and might present a challenge for the industry's top developer.

Wynn actually already had his eye on the Desert Inn site. He later claimed that, having built at every price point on the Las Vegas Strip, he was bored, and he accepted the buyout offer as a way for his friendly rival, Kerkorian, to help bankroll his next project, which would debut in 2005 as Wynn Las Vegas and again set the bar for casino design on the Strip. (Kerkorian and Wynn present an interesting contrast: the former opened the world's largest hotel three times, while the latter built its most expensive one three times.)

The merger highlighted the consolidation that had come to define the American casino industry. At the turn of the 21st century, American gaming was dominated by five large Las Vegas based firms and a host of smaller competitors. MGM Mirage led the way with five Strip properties, half-ownership of the Monte Carlo, a Strip resort that fittingly had more hotel rooms than the actual Monte Carlo, and assorted other properties across the world. The Mandalay Resort Group owned the other half of the Monte Carlo and its four Strip properties, with interests elsewhere. MGM Mirage in 2010 renamed itself MGM Resorts International.

Park Place Entertainment, the spinoff of Hilton Hotel's gaming division and Bally's Entertainment, had an even larger national presence; after its 1999 acquisition of the Caesars empire from ITT, it owned three of the "Four Corners," (the Flamingo, Bally's, and Caesars Palace), a brand new French themed resort, Paris, the storied Las Vegas Hilton, and casinos in Reno, Mississippi, Atlantic City, and elsewhere. It would soon rename itself Caesars Entertainment. Boyd Gaming, founded by Sam Boyd, had continued to prosper under his son, Bill Boyd, and had a similarly far-flung portfolio, with several casinos in and around Las Vegas (including the legendary Stardust) and other states. In 2003, the company opened the Borgata, the billion-dollar Atlantic City resort that rivaled anything recently built on the Strip. And Harrah's Entertainment, though it had only a single casino on the Strip itself, had become a national powerhouse, with franchises in most major markets and an innovative commitment to customer service and information technology that made it consistently profitable.

Casino ownership would become even further concentrated in 2005 with another merger wave. First, MGM Mirage acquired the Mandalay Resort Group for $7.9 billion, making it the world's largest casino company. By the age of 87, Kirk Kerkorian controlled a company that owned much of the Strip and, thanks to its talented management team, was well poised for future growth. But MGM Mirage was soon dethroned by Harrah's Entertainment. Bill Harrah's name graced a company that, under Phil Satre, had grown into a byword for consistent gambling entertainment. Harrah's capped six years of acquisitions by buying Caesars Entertainment for close to $9 billion: the resulting company had over 100,000 employees worldwide and expected annual revenues of nearly $9 billion. Less than sixty years after Bill Harrah had struggled to establish a bingo parlor in Depression-era Reno, his company was the world's casino king, though in 2010 it changed its name to Caesars Entertainment Corporation.

The growing concentration of ownership on the Strip followed an unprecedented building boom. Twelve new resorts opened along Las Vegas Boulevard from 1989 to 1999, from the Stratosphere, with its namesake observation tower several blocks past the traditional boundary of the Strip at the Sahara, to Mandalay Bay, which brought a slice of the South Seas to the neighborhood of McCarran International Airport. The average new resort was suited for the age of mass market tourism: with 3000 hotel rooms, 80 table games, and 2500 slot machines, convention space, and numerous restaurants, shops, and entertainment venues, it could serve equally well as the backdrop for a bachelorette party, regional sales meeting, second honeymoon, or gambling jaunt.

During the early years of the boom, "family friendly" resorts received a great deal of media attention. With the MGM Grand Adventures theme park, Circus Circus's indoor Adventure Dome, and the pirate-themed Treasure Island, some were predicting that Las Vegas would soon upstage Orlando as a family vacation destination. But after the dot-com bust, Las Vegas was more successful in promoting itself as an "adult Disneyland" (a phrase uttered so often it has become cliché), and a wave of more sophisticated attractions, particularly nightclubs and "ultra lounges" became de rigeur after 2002. New resorts like the Palms and Hard Rock actively catered to twenty-somethings, a real innovation in an industry where Tom Jones had long been considered an edgy entertainer that attracted a youthful crowd.

Despite lines of clubbers winding through its casinos after midnight, the Strip was still about more than nightlife: conventioneers represented an increasing percentage of visitors to Las Vegas, and people continued to bring their families for the weekend in Las Vegas. As the city's annual visitation climbed towards 40 million, Las Vegas casino operators relished their success in transcending the stigma formerly attached to gambling, and had successfully established Las Vegas as a destination for all seasons and temperaments. The surest sign of the new legitimacy of gambling can be found, ironically enough, in a casino named after the first European casino destination: Venice.

Gondoliers in the Desert

The Sands was one of the landmark casinos of Las Vegas from its 1952 opening. It was world-famous in the 1960s as the haunt of the Rat Pack. But by the time Sheldon Adelson bought it in 1989, it's best days were behind it.

Adelson had a different career arc than other casino magnates. Steve Wynn had been in the business virtually all of his adult life; MGM Resorts chief Jim Murren was a Wall Streeter; Caesars Entertainment's Gary Loveman was a former business school professor. Adelson at one point worked as a Boston cabdriver but, in the 1970s, became involved with the expositions industry. In 1979 he founded the COMDEX computer trade show, which became the premier convention in that rapidly-expanding industry. Ten years later, seeing that the real money in conventions was in hosting, not running them, he bought the Sands and added the Sands Expo Center, a massive convention facility.

At the time, he was planning to expand the Sands, adding more hotel towers to the existing property. Most of the classic Strip casinos—the Dunes, Tropicana, Stardust, Flamingo, Riviera, and Sahara—had done that over the years, and it seemed a sensible strategy.

But then Steve Wynn built The Mirage, and suddenly Strip casinos needed more than new room towers to compete. They needed a theme. Adelson hit upon a Venice theme for the property that he now planned to replace the Sands, which he closed in 1996. The Venetian began rising out of the Sands' rubble the following year, and it opened in 1999. With 3,000 suites and direct access to the Sands Expo Center (which was not imploded along with its namesake hotel), Adelson designed the Venetian to appeal to a mix of luxury-seeking vacationers and business travelers.

Hitching the Venetian's wagon to the convention trade was a wise decision. Adelson knew the exposition industry intimately; he sold his expo company, the Interface Group, in 1995 to focus on the Venetian's construction. Las Vegas had been catering to business travelers since the late 1950s, primarily because they helped to fill the casino during the middle of the week, when both diehard gamblers and sun-seeking tourists are rare. Meetings had become an even more integral part of Vegas casinos as they got bigger. Adelson's Venetian was built to capitalize on the tendency of business travelers to spend more than their leisure counterparts on their rooms, entertainment, and meals.

The Venetian added the Venezia tower in 2003, and next door the Palazzo—a taller, more luxurious version of the original—opened in 2008. Together, the properties boast 7,000 suites between them and, along the success of his Asian casinos (see chapter 16) they have made Adelson an extremely wealthy man. In 2012, he was the fourteenth richest man in the world according to *Forbes* magazine, proving that the easiest way to strike it rich in a casino still was to own one.

But beneath all of the business expositions and family-friendly attractions, Las Vegas remained a gamblers' paradise. Casinos staged pitched battles to attract high rollers, known in the local parlance as whales. Casinos built lavish private suites, promised copious comps, and generally catered to all of their wishes. In the late 1990s, about 250 top echelon whales, players with credit lines of $20 million or more, were the prized bounty for casino hosts. While package-tour patrons with fanny packs fretted about blowing $20 while waiting in line for the buffet, managers warily anticipated the next move of the highest of the high rollers, knowing that a lucky weekend for them could mean the difference between the casino's showing a profit or a loss.

In the seven decades since the birth of the casino resort on the Las Vegas Strip, operators have had ample time to create a science of casino design. The science—which is sometimes held to be an arcane art—starts at the floor and ends at the ceiling. The carpet, is carefully selected: loud colors convey a sense of excitement, while not distracting players (who don't stare at their feet while playing), and tight, multi-colored patterns neatly hide stains. Cushioned chairs at slot machines allow a player to comfortably sit while gambling. Above the player, low ceilings and dimmed lights can create a sense of intimacy, which leads to more gambling. The sounds of fun—clanking coins, shouts of triumph, and excited conversation—also stimulate play. Some casinos, hip to aromatherapy, circulate scented air to make their patrons' stay more pleasant.

Las Vegas grew to become something of a paradox. Though it's world-renowned as a center of gambling, it's no longer the leading gaming destination in the world (Macau is; see chapter 16). More interestingly, its casinos no longer make the majority of their money from gambling. High-end hotel accommodations, dining, and entertainment proved ample competition for visitors' dollars. It's certainly the place Americans—and many others—go when they want to gamble, but, increasingly, they're doing much more than just gambling in Las Vegas. And, seeing the massive spread of casinos throughout the United States in the years after the opening of The Mirage, that's likely a good thing.

16

All In

◇◇◇◇◇◇◇◇◇◇

Casino Gambling's Global Spread

Legal gambling, on the decline worldwide at the beginning of the 20th century, was flourishing with unprecedented vigor by its end. It is too early to judge the bigger sweep of history, but it seems that the world is entering a sustained period of gambling's growth not seen since the European gambling boom of 1650-1850.

The Japanese Conundrum

Japan is as enthusiastic a nation of gamblers as can be found. A lottery game named *hobiki* was popular as early as the 14th century. This common form of gambling that, like American lotteries and bingo, was considered "not really gambling," paved the way for a unique form of machine gambling known as pachinko that, in sheer volume, may be the most popular form of gambling in the world.

Pachinko has its roots in the 1920s with the "Corinthian game," an imported American pinball game styled "Korinto Gemu" by the Japanese. As an adaptation to the space-conscious island, an enterprising game maker in Osaka or Kanazawa flipped the machine upright. With a flipper shooting a small steel ball into a vertical maze of pins and holes, the player hoped that his ball landed in a special hole that would entitle him to bonus balls. Known as pachi-pachi and gachanko after the sound of the careening steel ball, the game became popular at street fairs throughout Japan in the 1930s.

During World War II the Japanese government prohibited pachi-pachi, but after hostilities ended it grew in popularity. Improvements to the game, which soon became known as pachinko (a combination of its previous names), made it more appealing to a wider range of players. The introduction of the "machine gun" model made playing far easier: instead of manually inserting balls, players simply had to pull a lever to shoot them onto the board in rapid succession. Even novices could fire as many as 100 balls per minute. Because balls could be redeemed for prizes and, indirectly, cash, the game was for many a way of gambling though, officially, it was not a gambling game. Whatever its legal status, the game was sweepingly popular: by 1953, there were nearly 45,000 pachinko parlors in Japan.

After the government outlawed the continuous-shooting machine-gun version, the pachinko industry went into a decline that was revered only by a relaxation of the ban. The 1980 introduction of the "Fever Model," which combined elements of pachinko with slot machines, sparked another pachinko renaissance. In the 1990s pachisuro machines, thinly-disguised Western slot machines, began appearing in many parlors, and many operators renovated their halls in an effort to attract a more diverse clientele.

Today, an estimated 20 million Japanese men and women (the game is forbidden to minors) regularly play pachinko. The elite players, professional pachipuro, actually earn their living from pachinko. This is possible because the game is a mixture of chance and skill. Parlor owners periodically adjust the pins on non-electronic pachinko machines to vary the payouts, and habitual players work to identify high-paying machines and mercilessly exploit this advantage. Even electronic machines were periodically altered to boost the odds, so professionals continued to work the system in the digital age.

Though millions of Japanese play pachinko for money every day, the game is not officially considered gambling because it is technically not played for money. Players pay a fee to "lease balls" and winners accrue buckets of the glittering globes which they redeem at a parlor booth for prizes, ranging from pickled plums and sausages to home electronics and gold nuggets. To receive cash, players take their prizes to nearby keihin kokanjo (prize-exchange facilities) which are not owned by the pachinko parlor but work closely with them. Literally exchanging the prize for cash through a hole in the wall, players walk away with a return on their pachinko investment, while the exchange agent will sell the prizes back to the parlor, retaining a commission.

Simply considering money wagered, pachinko is the world's biggest gambling industry. Throughout Japan, 17,000 parlors with 5 million machines take in ball rental fees of $300 billion a year, far outstripping total American casino totals: the United States has roughly 600 casinos with 500,000 slot machines. Together, all American casinos make approximately $60 billion per year; total American gaming revenues are about $100 billion.

Because of the huge pachinko haul, Japan is frequently mentioned as a possible site for gambling legalization. As the Asian casino business boomed in the early 2010s calls for legalization have gotten more persistent. To understand why some believe such a major change would be a profitable one, a look at Macau will suffice.

Macau Goes Mega-Gaming

The mainland Communist regime has an official anti-gambling stance, though it permits a thriving lottery. Yet the real story of Chinese gambling, over the past ten years, has unfolded in Macau.

Forty miles west of Hong Kong, Macau stepped onto the world stage in the middle of the 16th century. Under the aegis of Prince Henry the Navigator, the Portuguese had become the outstanding mariners of the world. Seeking to confound the Mediterranean monopoly on Asian trade goods such as gold, sandalwood, silks, and spice, the intrepid Portuguese pushed southward along the coast of Africa until they had rounded the Cape of Good Hope and, ultimately, discovered an ocean route to India. From India, their trade routes continued eastward to China and Japan: Portuguese merchants first settled Macau, a slender isthmus near the mouth of the Pearl River estuary in Guangdong province, in the 1550s, chiefly as a way station between the Indian city of Goa (then the center of Portugal's Asian trade network) and China and Japan.

Chinese fishing settlements had marked the isthmus since at least the 13th century. Despite the initial reluctance of the Ming authorities, the Portuguese established a trading outpost there, initially paying an annual ground rent to the imperial rulers and further gaining their trust by assisting in the suppression of piracy in the surrounding waters. Macau enjoyed a golden age in 16th and 17th centuries as the preeminent commercial and evangelical European gateway to

Asia. But with the Japan's closure to foreign trade in the early 17th century and the emergence of Great Britain as the dominant mercantile power, Macau slowly declined, a slide that could not be offset by its use as a center for trade in opium and semi-slave "coolie" labor. Beginning in the 1840s, British-settled Hong Kong replaced Macau as the area's primary trading center.

Faced with decline, Macau's authorities took a bold step: they legalized gambling. This happened as Macau's political status was changing. Emboldened by China's declining strength, Portugal stopped paying ground rent in 1849 and destroyed the Chinese customs post, in essence declaring its possession of the city; the Treaty of 1887 officially recognized Portugal's sovereignty over Macau. Captain Isidoro Francisco Guimaraes, serving as governor of Macau from 1851 to 1863, took steps to bolster the city-state's economy by regulating and taxing vice, including both prostitution and gambling. Since at least the 1830s, the owners of illegal gambling houses had bribed officials. Guimaraes, by officially licensing gambling houses, diverted this graft to the public coffers. He was immediately successful: gambling never failed to yield revenues for the city's Portuguese masters.

Macau's gambling houses offered Chinese games, including fantan, pai gow, and, after the early 20th century, a game called cussec or "big and small," also known as sic bo. Licensed operators also ran lotteries, with thrice-daily drawings, that inevitably attracted poor and working class citizens.

Fantan was an elaboration of the ancient odd-and-even games in which a dealer covered an unknown number of white buttons with a bowl and then accepted bets on how many buttons would remain after the buttons had been divided into groups of four. Players could bet on one, two, three, or four (zero) and on combinations. Pai gow is played with a set of 32 tiles. Players receive four tiles and divide them into a high (strong) and low (weak) hand. If the player beats the dealer's high and low hands, he wins; if the dealer wins both hands, the house triumphs; a split decision is declared a push, with the player keeping his stakes.

Cussec is something of an anomaly among Chinese casino games: it is played with dice. Three dice placed in a cup, bowl, or cage are shaken, and players bet on the results; they can lay stakes on the total number of points as reckoned by the number of dots on the upturned faces of the dice, big (11 to 17) or small (4 to 10), or triples. Another variation popular in Macau casinos, fish-prawn-crab cussec, replaces the dice's pips with images of a fish, prawn, crab, coin, gourd, and rooster, each of which have an accepted numerical value. These three games were the sole offerings of licensed fantan houses, as no Western games were played in Macau.

Legal gambling took place either in exclusive private clubs that catered to the wealthiest and provided them a venue for player-to-player social gambling or public fantan houses patronized by the poorest. In the 1860s, sixteen of these houses generated respectable revenues for the government, but they did not draw wealthy travelers to Macau. These houses offered "singing girls"—often a euphemism for prostitutes—and doubled as cheap flophouses; though this satisfied some rough-and-tumble visitors, it hardly augured any future as an international destination. Thanks in part to these gambling hells, Macau retained a reputation as a center for prostitution, slavery, gold and opium smuggling, and the domain of what one contemporary called "the flotsam of the sea, the derelicts, and more shameless, beautiful, savage women" than any other port. While this might seem a quite attractive nuisance to some, it could hardly be expected to draw the aristocratic, if not reputable, patrons of Monte Carlo.

Early in the 20th century, the city's gambling was stagnating. Lottery tickets sold in Hong Kong and surrounding areas allowed Macau to extract a few million dollars a year from its neighbors (much to the chagrin of British and Chinese authorities), but the scheme of licensed gambling as practiced through the early 1930s produced few economic gains for Macau, which had no real agricultural, commercial, or industrial development. If gambling were to serve as the linchpin of a tourist-economy—seemingly the only option remaining—Macau's rulers would have to clean it up.

At about the same time that the Nevada legislature rolled the dice on "wide-open" gambling, the Macau government undertook a complete overhaul of its legal gambling. It swept away the rabble of the fantan houses, replacing the proletarian gambling havens with more refined casinos in upscale hotels. Thus, the Portuguese governor argued, Macau would attract wealthy inhabitants of surrounding Chinese cities and perhaps even the sporting gentlemen of Europe. Instead of licensing any operators who applied, the governor granted a monopoly franchise to a single syndicate, the Tai Xing company, run by Kening Gao and Laorong Fu. Starting in 1937 this company opened casinos along the Rua de Felicidade and Rua 5 de Outubro. Despite the governor's original plan that the casinos appeal to Europeans, these houses offered only the traditional Chinese games of chance, something that precluded their appeal to all but the most receptive of occidental visitors.

In the decades after the first casino opened in the Central Hotel, the Tai Xing company successfully maintained its monopoly, working diligently to exclude potential rivals from the bidding process. Because Laorong Fu believed (as do many Chinese), that red is a lucky, and that white and green unlucky, he insisted that all Tai Xing employees never wear red, and that all its casinos, and even his own house, be adorned in white and green. His customers were willing to buck the superstition, and continued to gamble on traditional Chinese games in Tai Xing casinos.

The Tai Xing monopoly survived World War II and the turmoil of the Chinese Revolution, both of which left Macau relatively unscathed. In the postwar period, Tak Iam Fu ran the company. He controlled all gambling and lotteries in Macau and had diversified into real estate (with four apartment blocks) and transportation (he owned several trade vessels). He also owned a Macau-Hong Kong ferry, which shuttled his casino customers back and forth. An absolute prohibition on gambling enacted by the People's Republic of China in 1949 gave Macau, and hence the Tai Xing company, a regional monopoly on casinos, but China's restrictive border controls cut off the flow of visitors from the mainland, although British prohibitions on casino gaming kept Hong Kong a captive market.

As Macau adjusted to the postwar world, its government decided that gambling-related tourism was the colony's best hope for economic development. Law 18267, promulgated by the Portuguese colonial authority, designated Macau a "tourism and gaming region," signaling the increased emphasis to be placed on gambling as an economic driver. The government opened the gaming monopoly to bidding in 1961 and awarded it to the Sociedade de Turismo e Diversoes de Macau (STDM, "the Society for Tourism and Entertainment of Macau"). Founded by Stanley Ho with Yin-dong Huo, De-li Ye, and Han Ye, STDM would extend its control of Macau's gambling monopoly to a near-domination of the enclave, and make its managing director, Dr. Stanley Ho, wealthy and powerful.

According to his official biography, Ho started life with the proverbial silver spoon in his mouth; born November 25, 1921, into a wealthy Hong Kong family (his granduncle Sir Robert Hotung was knighted by King George V and his grandfather was a well-connected businessman), Ho lived the typical life of a rich scion, until, in 1934, his father suffered devastating financial reverses and fled to Vietnam, leaving his wife to raise her children alone. Young Stanley suddenly felt the press of poverty, and from here, his life becomes a true Horatio Alger story, as only his hard work and dedication stood between him and poverty. Ho applied himself anew to his studies, earning a scholarship to Queen's College (Hong Kong), from which he graduated with top grades, and then a place at the University of Hong Kong, where his studies were interrupted by the vicissitudes of the Second World War.

Ho fled to neutral Macau before Japanese forces occupied Hong Kong, arriving with ten Hong Kong dollars in his pocket and an unquenchable ambition. He took a job as a secretary at the Companhia Leun Chong, a trading concern that acted as a middleman between Chinese, Japanese, and Portuguese interests. Ho later said he had acted as a "semi-government official," obtaining much-needed rice, sugar, and beans from the Japanese for the Macau government. He learned Japanese and Portuguese (he was already fluent in English and Chinese) and parlayed his knowledge and skill into a partnership in the firm. After the war, he pursued shipping, finance, and trade, and returned to Hong Kong in 1953 as a young millionaire.

When the Macau administration opened the gambling monopoly, Ho jumped at the chance to extend his fortune, despite his personal distaste for gambling. One of his oft-repeated aphorisms, that "success is not by luck," refutes the gambler's trust in fortune, and though called the "king of casinos" and even the "god of gambling," he has never been known to gamble himself. Nevertheless, Ho applied himself to the administration of STDM with the same fire he showed in school and with Leun Chong.

STDM started with a single casino in the Estoril Hotel and a floating casino moored in the Inner Harbor, the immodestly-named Macau Palace. By 1975, STDM operated three other casinos: the Casino Kam Pek, the Jai Alai casino, and the STDM flagship, the Casino Lisboa. STDM continued to expand its selection of betting vehicles, offering greyhound racing, jai alai (from 1972 to 1990), horseracing, instant lotteries, and eventually soccer betting.

Betting on horses in Macau is centuries old. As early as the 17th century, Portuguese colonists imported Iberian tests of equestrian skill, snatching rings with lances and conducting mock battles. By the early 19th century, a racecourse built near the barrier gate crossing into China hosted regular races. Portuguese and Chinese crowds representing a cross-section of Macau's society boisterously cheered their favorites, betting heavily on the outcome.

In 1963, STDM absorbed greyhound racing at the Macau Canidrome sponsored by the Yat Yuen Canidrome Club. The only greyhound racing track in Asia, the Canidrome still hosts 16 races four night a week, and the public (as of early 2005) could watch and bet on the races online. The syndicate built a large modern track on Taipa Island for trotting in 1980, but it struggled and in 1989 STDM acquired the Macau Jockey Club and reconfigured the track for thoroughbred racing.

Following a new franchise contract in 1983, casinos become more than a major source of revenue for Macau's government: they became its majority revenue producer. Rising from around 30 percent of the public revenue to nearly two-thirds of it, STDM's gaming taxes kept Macau's administration afloat throughout the 1980s and 1990, when Stanley Ho's enterprises contributed around 80 percent of Macau's tax revenue.

Still, with Macau's 1999 reversion to China came the possibility that the communist Chinese authorities might suppress Macau's casinos. But with an eye on both prosperous Hong Kong (which returned to Chinese control in 1997) and Taiwan (which Chinese authorities still wanted to reunite with the mainland), the People's Republic guaranteed no interference in Macau's economy for the next fifty years.

Stanley Ho's casinos represent a unique mélange of eastern and western gambling. Casino Lisboa, his flagship, has expanded over the decades to include 1000 rooms. Though STDM introduced western games in 1962, many Asian favorites remain, including sic bo, fish-prawn-crab sic bo, pai gow, mahjong pai gow, pacapio (the original keno), and the venerable fantan. Though these games, particularly sic bo, have their devotees, they all bow to baccarat, now the most popular game in Macau. Other western games, like blackjack, roulette, and boule, can be found in Macau, along with newer imports like three-card baccarat, three-card poker, though the American signature game of craps is rare.

The Lisboa hosts weekend bingo games, and scattered around the main casino's perimeter are slot machines, another American gaming innovation that has yet to truly catch on with Macau gamblers. Slots are called tigers, with the intimation that they will inevitably prey upon their players. Still Macau's operators—Chinese and Western alike—have attempted to widen the appeal of slots. New casinos

Stanley Ho's Casino Lisboa became the hub of his Macau gambling, transportation, and real estate empire.

have modern slot machines, and several slots-only halls owned by Melco, a company chaired by one of Stanley Ho's sons, have opened throughout the city. One machine plays on the reputation of slot as "hungry tigers" by incorporating a traditional legend about a hero who defeated a ravenous tiger. When a player hits a jackpot, he is treated to a video re-enactment of the hero's triumph.

Chinese gamblers subscribe to a set of superstitions that seem bizarre and perhaps even silly to Westerners, who often forget that their own superstitions are no less arbitrary or foolish. Crossing under ladders, black cats, the number thirteen, broken mirrors, and spilled salt shakers elicit little response in China, reminding Westerners that there is nothing universal about luck. Instead, the visitor to a Macau casino would do well to avoid the unlucky number of four and exult in the supremely lucky eight. She should not carry a book into the casino, because, owing to the sound of the Cantonese word for "book," it is considered unlucky.

To those familiar with American casinos, with their uniformly spaced slot machines and orderly assortments of table games, the Lisboa, and other STDM casinos might seem downright unruly. Gamblers crowd the tables, staking wagers while stacked two or three deep, shrouded by thick clouds of cigarette smoke. Away from the hullabaloo of the main floor at the Lisboa, American visitors might be perplexed at another Macau institution—private gaming clubs. Subleased by the gaming operator to a string of junket operators and concessionaries, these rooms host high-stakes gambling in relative privacy. Regularly allowing maximum bets of up to a half-million patacas ($65,000 US), these rooms attract the cream of China's gamblers, who chiefly play baccarat. With their play, STDM revenues soared, and the city administration, collecting over one-third of all casino earnings as taxes, enjoyed one bumper budget surplus after another.

By the time of the reversion, Stanley Ho had become a Macau colossus: not the most powerful man in the city, but simply *the* powerful man in the city. Under his leadership, STDM became a tourism giant and the biggest employer in Macau. In addition to its gaming enterprises, STDM owned or invested in several hotels, Macau's largest department store, the Macau Tower Convention and

Entertainment Center (opened in 2001 and featuring the world's 10th tallest tower), the Turbojet Macau-Hong Kong ferry service, Macau International Airport, and a host of other projects. Ho was also the group executive chairman of Shun Tak Holdings, chairman of Seng Heng Bank, and a member of numerous community and philanthropic groups. Ho, the non-gambler, has parlayed his Macau casino franchise into riches, influence, and (despite whispers of connections to organized crime triads), respect. For years, when Chinese gamblers planned a trip to Macau, they said that they were "going to visit Uncle Stanley."

Yet Ho's domination of Macau's casino market did not long outlast the enclave's return to Chinese rule. His monopoly franchise expired in 2001, and the new government of the Macau Special Administration Region (SAR) reopened the bidding and awarded the right to operate casinos to three entities: a subsidiary of Dr. Ho's STDM called Sociedade de Jogos de Macau (SJM); a joint venture of Las Vegas Sands, Inc. (owners of the Las Vegas Strip's Venetian) and Galaxy, a Chinese company; and Steve Wynn's Wynn Resorts. Macao's extension of casino privileges to these three groups struck a balance between preserving its history and identity and allowing new entrepreneurs to bring fresh ideas and a wave of new construction to the city.

Though they combined to bid for a casino license, Las Vegas Sands and Galaxy soon went their separate ways, with the SAR government splitting the license in two. To compensate the other successful bidders, the government permitted them to sell subconcessions. Wynn sold his to a partnership between PBL (today Crown Limited) and Lawrence Ho's Melco International Development for $900 million in March 2006. Stanley Ho sold his subconcession to MGM Grand Paradise, a partnership between his daughter, Pansy Ho, and MGM Mirage, for approximately $200 million.

At the same time, as the Chinese government liberalized border restrictions, a flood of new visitors descended upon Macau. Chinese authorities gradually expanded the number of cities allowed to issue tourist visas to Macau, thus virtually guaranteeing a steady rise in that city's guests. Macau's annual visitation nearly doubled to 15 million, and with the prospect of continued liberalization, its boosters nervously anticipated infrastructure improvements that would let the city cope with a doubling of that number.

The new entrants into Macau promised to transform the city into a true international tourist attraction. Las Vegas Sands opened its Sands Macau first, in May 2004, a stone's throw from the Macau ferry terminal, the point of debarkation for most arrivals from Hong Kong. The opening was not without drama; when someone spread a rumor that the casino would give away free chips on its first day, a near-riot enveloped the casinos and eager crowds literally broke down the doors to get inside and begin playing. Since then, the action has settled into more consistent frenzy, and the success of the Sands Macau has demonstrated that Western operators can profitably run casinos in Macau.

Steve Wynn opened Wynn Macau in September 2006, replicating the look—and success—of his Las Vegas flagship. In 2010, an expansion to the resort, called Encore, opened. The MGM/Pansy Ho partnership opened MGM Grand Macau in 2009. Melco Crown and Galaxy also opened new casinos, leading to a boom in Macau casino supply that was more than matched by an increase in revenues. In 2002, before U.S.-based companies entered the industry, Macau posted revenues of $2.7 billion. By 2006, with the Sands and Wynn projects open, the city's casinos pulled in $7 billion—more than the Las Vegas Strip. By 2011, Macau casinos were making $33.5 billion a year, three times the combined revenues of all of Nevada's casinos.

The biggest growth in Macau gaming is slated for the Cotai Strip, an area of reclaimed land between Coloanne and Taipa islands that was projected to rival the famous Las Vegas Strip. In 2007, Las Vegas Sands opened the massive Venetian Macao on a Cotai parcel, with 800 table games and 3,400 slots. By contrast, most Strip casino resorts, themselves no slouches, have about 100 tables and 2,000 slots. Las Vegas Sands also partnered with worldwide hotel brands like Conrad, Holiday Inn, Sheraton, and Four Seasons to develop hotels and a full retinue of luxury shopping, entertainment, and convention facilities. Not to be outdone, Melco Crown opened the City of Dreams, a massive casino resort featuring unique architecture. A Grand Hyatt and Hard Rock Hotel complement the Crown Towers hotel, giving the property several well-known brands under one roof (albeit in four towers).

As of early 2013, both MGM Resorts and Wynn Resorts were in the early states of developing their own Cotai projects. Macau is currently the world's top casino gambling destination, and it's going to continue to be one of the most interesting stories in gambling for years to come.

Around the World

Even before Macau made clear the success of Asian casinos, a few other Asian countries permitted casinos, often with the caveat that their own citizens were forbidden from entering them. South Korea's casinos date from 1967. Located in hotels, they cater primarily to Japanese and Taiwanese visitors. Cheju Island, billed as "Korea's Hawaii," developed as South Korea's honeymoon resort of choice, though for foreign visitors, the island's eight casinos became a major attraction. As foreign casino visitation dropped in the late 1990s, the South Korean government allowed Koreans to visit a single casino, Kangwon Land, opened in 2000 in a depressed area. Though isolated, the casino proved successful, as more than two thousand Koreans passed through its doors each day, sometimes sleeping on the floor while waiting for a spot at a table.

By the 1990s, Nepal, Cambodia, and Myanmar had casinos and there was a thriving casino industry in the Philippines, whose Philippine Amusement and Gaming Corporation (PAGCOR) opened nearly twenty casinos throughout the country and became a chief source of government revenue. Even North Korea, one of the world's most isolated nations, opened foreigner-only casinos in Pyongyang in the late 1990s. Supplementing its usual income streams (chiefly the sale of arms and counterfeit currency), the government in 1999 opened the Emperor Casino in isolated Raijin. It struck gold catering to Communist Chinese, at least until the Chinese government, discovering that officials were carting embezzled funds to the casino, forbade its citizens from traveling there.

Malaysia's casino monopoly has been parlayed into an empire by Tan Sri Lim Goh Tong. Lim, born in Fukien province, China, moved to Singapore in his teens and found work in construction. He gradually established himself as one of Malaysia's most influential developers. Lim was seized in 1964 by a vision for a Malaysian resort "above the clouds" that would offer a cool respite from its tropical climate. He personally oversaw the construction of a hotel, utility services, and an access road for his Genting Highlands, perched 6,000 feet above sea level about 45 miles from Kuala Lumpur. The project received a boost when, in 1969, Malaysian Prime Minister Tunku Abdul Rahman awarded Genting the nation's only casino license, with the caveat that Malaysian Muslims were barred from gambling at the casino, though Muslims from other nations were free to play without interference and non-Muslim Malaysians also were welcome. Despite Muslims making up about half the nation's population, the enthusiasm of ethnic Chinese in Malaysia and Singapore represented a tremendous gambling market, and Lim enjoyed a monopoly.

Over the next quarter century, Lim developed Genting Highlands into one of the world's major resorts. Six hotels, including three five-star operations, offered guests over 8,000 rooms. With its convention center, entertainment venues, and restaurants, it was a supersized Las Vegas Strip casino set "on top of the clouds" (the Chinese translation of "Genting") in a predominantly Muslim nation. The Casino de Genting offered a range of Western games from blackjack to Caribbean Stud Poker, and Asian favorites like sic bo (called tai sai) and pai gow. The casino had five separate themed gaming areas, and in 2004 a neighboring Starworld casino, geared towards the "young at heart," offering patrons the chance to watch MTV and sip coffee while playing.

Under Lim's leadership the Genting Group became Malaysia's leading corporation, developing casinos worldwide and diversifying into non-casino hotel resorts and cruise lines, as well as seemingly unrelated areas: power generation, paper and box manufacturing, palm oil plantations, and information technology. Lim's investment in the Foxwoods casino enabled the Pequots to start a casino giant of their own in the 1990s. Genting also began acquiring British casinos in 1976, slowly building up a portfolio that would grow to 46 casinos by 2012, including the Maxims and Mint brands as well as one of the oldest names in London's gambling scene, the venerable Crockford's. Though Lim had already established himself as an important Malaysian developer before he gained the nation's casino franchise, it is unlikely that he would have become so fabulously wealthy without it (with a personal net worth of over $2 billion, he regularly made Forbes Magazine's list of the world's richest people). Worth more than even Stanley Ho, he was the world's wealthiest casino operator. In 2003, at the age of 85, Tan Sri Lim Goh Tong, stepped down as Chairman of the Genting Group and was succeeded by his son, Tan Sri Lim Kok Thay, who had been with the company since 1976. The elder Lim's career is a testament to the powerful attraction of a casino, particularly where it is marginally forbidden.

After Lim's 2007 death, the Genting empire continued to evolve. Under the Resorts World banner (Genting Highlands itself became Resorts World Genting in 2010), Genting ramped up its international investments, opening a video lottery terminal operation at New York's Aqueduct racetrack in 2011 that, as of 2012, is the only casino gambling in the Big Apple. Combined with Resorts World Singapore, Genting remains a casino powerhouse, an outcome few could have imagined when Lim first dreamed of a heavenly resort in 1964.

In contrast to Malaysia's partial ban, the prohibition of gambling was almost absolute in the predominantly Muslim countries of the Middle East and northern Africa. But as oil-rich sheikhs became legendary high rollers in Monte Carlo, Las Vegas, and Atlantic City, several Islamic nations experimented with casinos open to foreigners. In cosmopolitan Lebanon, Beirut's Casino du Liban opened in 1959. Routinely profitable until it was forced to close in 1975 due to the ongoing civil war, it reopened in 1996, admitting all foreigners and even those Lebanese who were not government or military employees, cashiers, or earners of less than $20,000 a year.

Egypt has for decades encouraged a small casino industry, chiefly to generate revenues and acquire foreign currency: Egyptian nationals are barred from entering, though anyone else with a passport is welcome. In the small casinos, games include blackjack, baccarat, and even poker, and bets are often made with American dollars. Saudis are the most common visitors to Egypt's casinos, though they are joined by a healthy sprinkling of American and European tourists. Morocco and Tunisia have similar casinos, and Turkey has, since 1969, alternated between permitting and prohibiting casinos—as of 2013, they are forbidden.

Israel, laboring under no significant doctrinal objections to gambling, failed to develop land-based casinos, though casino cruise ships operated out of the Red Sea port of Eilat. In 1998, the Oasis Casino opened in Jericho under the Palestinian Authority; it was the single largest private investment in the Authority's territory. By permitting a casino that would cater to Israelis, who are esteemed as serious gamblers, the Palestinian Authority was emulating American Indian nations who used their sovereignty to offer gambling in hopes of economic development. Amid political turmoil, the casino closed in 2000, a victim of the crossfire between Hamas terrorists and the Israeli army. It has not reopened since then, "due to the ongoing situation," though Casinos Austria, the casino's one-time operator, insists that, should the political situation change, its 120 table games and 300 slot machines will be ready to welcome gamblers.

Singapore Joins In

As explosive as Macau's growth was in the 2000s, another Asian gambling destination emerged to be the star of the 2010s. Singapore is a city-state adjacent to Malaysia which, since its 1965 independence, has pursued its own path to economic success, focusing on shipping, manufacturing, and technology. Tourism also contributes significantly to Singapore's economy, belying the "all work/no play" image the city, which has strict laws covering everything from the import of narcotics to gum-chewing, has earned. In order to expand the city's tourist appeal (and to replicate, in some fashion, the success of Macau and Resorts World Genting), Singapore opened up bidding for casinos in 2004. Combining gambling with Singapore's other attractions, it was thought, would boost the city's tourism even further.

There is little better commentary on the status of gambling in the new millennium than the fact that, despite the enviable economic success of Singapore, many felt it was still lacking a key element of a world city. Prime Minister Lee Hsien Loong, in announcing the opening of Singapore to casinos, spoke of wanting to capture the

"X-factor" of cities like London, Paris, and New York. And casino gambling was the way to do it.

But this would be a much different kind of casino than had been seen in Las Vegas or Macau, at least according to the bidding rules. Gambling was to be consciously de-emphasized: the projects weren't even called "casinos" or "casino resorts" but "integrated resorts," featuring convention facilities, entertainment, shopping, dining, and even museums. This was the Las Vegas casino resort, only more so, with gambling—at least initially—appearing to be an almost-incidental part of the whole.

Nineteen companies, including such U.S. stalwarts as Wynn Resorts, Las Vegas Sands, MGM Mirage, and Harrah's Entertainment, submitted bids to build integrated resorts on two parcels: Marina Bay, a waterfront parcel near the entertainment district, and Sentosa Island, a resort connected to Singapore proper by a causeway. On May 26, 2006, the government announced the first winning bidder: Las Vegas Sands, which was selected to build an integrated resort on Marina Bay. Sands carried the day because of its history of building and operating diversified resorts—the Venetian in Las Vegas, for example, was an all-suite hotel that boasted capacious convention facilities and, at one point, two Guggenheim museums. This was the kind of beyond-baccarat bid the government was looking for. All told, the bid specified a $3.6 billion project that, when fully built, would feature 2,500 hotel rooms, 1 million square feet of shopping, a 1.2 million square-foot convention center, and a 200,000 square-foot arts and sciences museum. This wouldn't be a themed resort, a la the Venetian Las Vegas or the under construction Venetian Macau. Instead, the complex, designed by Moshe Safdie (an architect known for structures like Jerusalem's Yad Vashem Holocaust memorial, the Skirball Cultural Center in Los Angeles, and Salem, Massachusetts's Peabody Essex Museum), was bold and iconic: above the large structure holding the resort's many amenities, three towers, looking something like decks of playing cards splayed open at the bottom, support a SkyPark, itself hosting gardens, restaurants, nightclubs, and an infinity edge pool.

The Sentosa development was awarded to Genting, which built Resorts World Sentosa, a tourist development featuring several hotels, including a Hard Rock Hotel and a Michael Graves-designed "art lovers hotel," and a Universal Studios theme park.

Sentosa opened first, with its first hotel debuting in January 2010 and its casino launch coinciding with Chinese New Year. The Marina Bay Sands began welcoming guests in April en route to a grand opening in June. Both properties won kudos for their design but, more importantly, their casinos generated a great deal of income. In 2011, its first full year of operation, Marina Bay Sands earned $2.4 billion in total casino revenues—more than five times the amount won by the company's two Las Vegas casinos. Within a year, Singapore stood poised to become the world's second-largest gaming destination by revenue, knocking Las Vegas down another notch in the global gaming hierarchy.

More importantly to the Singaporean government, casinos boosted tourism arrivals by 15 percent in their first full year of operation, and led to an increase in spending in several other areas. Singapore had hoped to tame the tiger of gambling, using it as a way to create development and lure more tourists to its shores. In the initial years of its casino gambit, at least, it appears to have succeeded.

Casinos Down Under

Singapore showed that there was a tremendous pent-up demand for gambling in Asia, but the region has long been a hotbed of gambling. Australians have a reputation for being some of the world's least inhibited gamblers. They've had plenty of practice. Pokies, or poker machines, have been widely played in Australia since the early 20th century. These are not American-style video poker machines; early on Australians began calling American slot machines "poker machines," because many of them retained the original card-based symbols on their reels. (The British, on the other hand, adopted "fruit machine" for the same device, focusing on the symbols that appeared on most machines.) Through the 1920s and 1930s, pokies appeared intermittently in clubs and hotels, sometimes supported by the law but illegal at other times. In 1956, New South Wales sanctioned pokie gambling in clubs, provided that they adhere to state licensing requirements. It was an auspicious decision; by 1980 the state had more than twice as many pokies as the gambling mecca of Las Vegas. By the 1990s, every state, save Tasmania, had legalized pokies in clubs, and Australia had nearly 185,000 gambling machines. These clubs were not the gilded aristocratic hells of London's West End, or even the gentleman's retreats of 19th century Australia. They were open to anyone interested in spending time with those who share common interests, including sports like bowling and golf. Revenue from the slot machines enables club members to enjoy discounted meals, drinks, and entertainment. In addition, clubs sponsor a variety of community activities and charitable projects. Sports betting, particularly on soccer and rugby, became another popular democratic gamble in the late 20th century. But pokies continued to account for almost two-thirds of all Australian gambling in 2004.

The Wrest Point Hotel Casino in Hobart, Tasmania, opened in 1973 as Australia's first legal casino, becoming Australia's largest hotel and a popular convention destination. The MGM Grand Darwin, opened in 1979 in a temporary facility, was Australia's second casino; it was sold in 2004 to New Zealand-based Sky City and became the Sky City Darwin. A host of other casinos opened in the 1980s. Lasseter's, in Alice Springs, was a relatively small resort, deep within in Northern Territory. Casinos in Adelaide, Gold Coast, Perth, and Townsville, followed in the 1990s, trailed by Canberra, Brisbane, Melbourne, and Sydney. Australian casinos are, in general, slightly scaled down versions of their Las Vegas Strip counterparts, with lounges, restaurants, showrooms, swimming pools, and all the accoutrements expected of vacation resorts.

Given their reputations as fierce gamblers, Australians are well-represented in the ranks of gambling celebrities. The winner of the 2005 World Series of Poker, for example, was Australian pro Joseph Hachem. While winning a WSOP bracelet is no mean feat, no Australian could match media baron Kerry Packer as the nation's biggest gambler. Majority shareholder in Publishing and Broadcast Limited, an Australian multimedia combine, Packer also owned an interest in Melbourne's Crown Casino and Perth's Burswood Casino, making him a rarity: the casino owner who is also a dedicated gambler. One of the world's most notorious high rollers, Packer was known to win or lose millions of dollars in a single weekend. It was said that Packer beat several Las Vegas casinos so consistently, winning tens of millions of dollars over two years, that they refused to allow him to play anymore. At the time of his death, whether because of lucky gambling or not, his net worth was estimated at $4.7 billion.

Gambling in nearby New Zealand often overlapped Australia's, with legal casinos (in Christchurch, Auckland, Dunedin, Hamilton, and Queenstown) appearing in the 1990s. While casinos in Australia have been somewhat overshadowed by the tremendous boom in Asian gambling over the past decade, their continued success is a testment to the Australian gambling urge.

North of the Border

Canadians had a similarly restrictive relationship with gambling until relatively recently. Canada's 1892 Criminal Code had made all gambling illegal, with three exceptions: raffles for charitable or religious organizations, which eventually included bingo, carnival games of chance at agricultural fairs, and betting at racetracks. Though charitable and carnival games were widely varied, none of them were permitted to use dice, as a 1922 amendment to the 1893 law had specified that dice games were indisputably illegal.

In 1969, the Canadian legislature amended the Criminal Code to permit provinces to operate lotteries and slot machines, and to license charities, fairs, and social clubs to do the same, though slots were only permitted if the provincial governments themselves owned them.

Canadian casinos, therefore, are either owned by provincial governments or dedicated to charitable organizations. This system took shape slowly. First, in 1975 an Alberta children's summer camp received permission to operate a casinos for four days to raise funds. The casino was such a success that hundreds of groups followed suit, and British Columbia, Saskatchewan, and Manitoba joined Alberta in promoting a system of permanent casinos that allowed different charity groups to participate.

From the outside, these charity casinos looked much like privately-owned gambling halls. Indeed, private companies own the casinos themselves and rent out their facilities to charities, who operate the table games and keep the lion's share of profits—minus government taxes and fees. Charity casinos often turn up in unlikely places. The West Edmonton Mall, billed as the world's biggest entertainment and shopping center, has a charity casino of its own, the Palace Casino. Games offered include all of the Las Vegas favorites. Even dice were legalized in 1999 and are used to play craps and sic bo.

Eastern Canadian provinces took a different tack, figuring that, if casinos were to be run for the public benefit, there were no more deserving charities than the provinces themselves. In 1993, Quebec's Casino de Montreal, one of the largest casinos in the world, opened to immediate success. The following year, the Province of Ontario opened the Casino Windsor, a gambling hall a mere mile from downtown Detroit. Government-owned casinos opened in Nova Scotia in 1995, making it the sole Atlantic province with casinos. Even though these casinos are owned by the provinces, private management companies, sometimes American, often managed them, taking a share of the profits. The lucrative Casino Windsor was managed by an affiliate of Park Place Entertainment, and, after 2005, Harrah's (later Caesars) Entertainment. This has caused some consternation in Canada, as economic nationalists chafe at the flow of "public money" south of the border.

There is also controversy over government ownership of video lottery terminals (VLTs), which are essentially slot machines run by provincial lottery commissions. These machines first appeared in Atlantic provinces in 1990 and spread rapidly throughout the nation. Because they are easy to play and accessible in the course of everyday life (Nova Scotia initially permitted VLTs in convenience stores and gas stations), VLTs have drawn fire from those concerned about problem gambling. Critics wonder how a provincial government can balance its desire for higher revenues with a need to "protect" its citizens from the ravages of gambling. Though this quandary is more obvious because the provinces actually own the machines, governments around the world increasingly face these difficult questions, as their interest in gambling has shifted from control to regulation to, in many cases, active promotion.

South of the Border

Latin American nations from Costa Rica to Chile have encouraged the growth of casino industries of various sizes, usually to encourage tourism and the importation of foreign currency. In general, they have alternated between state and private ownership. Panama, Uruguay, Chile, and Argentina (with the biggest industry) have all had legal casinos for decades. Until 1944, all Argentine casinos were privately owned. In that year, a presidential decree closed all private casinos; some were nationalized, while others were simply forced to close. The government placed responsibility for running the casinos in the hands of the National Lottery Administration, which had been running draw games since 1893.

In the 1940s and 1950s, the national government opened new casinos and reopened old ones. National casinos had dress codes, high betting limits, and no slot machines. This was supposed to encourage a ritzy atmosphere but, from a practical point of view, it limited revenues. In the 1960s, the national government began transferring control of casinos to provinces and authorized provinces to build their own casinos. These gambling halls usually scrapped the dress code, permitted smaller-scale betting, and installed slot machines. Predictably, they became popular with locals, and several national casinos were forced to close. In the 1980s, support for the privatization of the casino industry grew, and in the following decades many of the casinos were sold. By 2004, there were more than 70 casinos throughout the country, and casino advocates were hopeful to finally opening one in Buenos Aires itself.

In the Caribbean, a diversity of casinos sprouted near the glittering beaches, all intent on enticing the lucrative tourist trade. They had varying degrees of success. Puerto Rico, a United States commonwealth, had small casinos in several hotels by the 1960s. The Caribe Hilton, Sheraton, and San Juan casinos were the largest and most popular. The remote El Conquistador, located in Fajardo, was one of the best known, but though it was filled to capacity with gamblers during the four-month winter season, players were scarce in the off-season. Other Puerto Rico resorts faced this problem, to a lesser extent, complicated by the government's mandating lower betting limits and barring locals. Elsewhere the casino business proved more lucrative. The Bahamas, which first allowed casinos in the 1960s, hosted first Resorts International, then the Atlantis on Paradise Island; by 2005 four casinos had opened. Other island nations, particularly Aruba, Curacao, and the Dutch Antilles, have small casinos catering to foreign tourists that, tacitly or explicitly, discourage locals from playing.

South Africa's Sun rises

Although gambling was common among the indigenous peoples of Southern Africa and the first waves of European sailors, soldiers, and settlers to inhabit the area in the 17th and 18th centuries, gambling was outlawed in 1889 in areas under British control, as it already was in the Boer Republics. The gambling ban (which excepted horse bookmaking) continued after the consolidation of British and Boer governments into the Union of South Africa in 1910. A 1933 law stiffened anti-gambling penalties, and six years later the ban was extended to pin-table machines and other mechanical gambling contrivances, though totalisators were specifically excluded, as they were an integral part of the conduct of legal pari-mutuel gambling. As many other nations looked to legalize gambling in the 1960s, South Africa turned in the other direction, passing a comprehensive Gambling Act in 1965 that forbade all lotteries, sports betting, and games of chance.

Despite the ironclad prohibition against gambling, many South Africans still wanted to play. In 1976, the creation of "independent" black homelands within South Africa (though they were ostensibly separate nations, only the South African government recognized them as so) allowed for the legalization of casino gambling in the four nominally independent states of Bophuthatswana, the Ciskei, the Transkei and Venda; Bophuthatswana and the Transkei became famous for their casino resorts built on the Las Vegas model, offering guests gambling and entertainment.

Southern Sun, the biggest casino owner, started in 1977 with a single casino in Mmabatho, the capital of Bophuthatswana, in the north of South Africa. Its chief executive, Sol Kerzner, had, in 1964, built his first hotel in Durban with borrowed money, using pictures of Miami hotels he'd clipped from travel brochures for inspiration. Kerzner followed the Mmbatho casino with a resort that was to become South Africa's most famous, Sun City. Located in a section of Bophuthatswana only about 100 miles from Johannesburg, the Sun City resort opened in 1979 with many of the amenities usually associated with the Las Vegas Strip (and lacking in South Africa): roulette, slot machines, an 18-hole golf course, discos, restaurants, softcore pornographic movies, and a buffet of sequined, multiracial showgirls. Half of the profits went to the government of Bophuthatswana, and though few blacks had the money to register at the hotel, many patronized the discos, restaurants, and slot machines, taking their places along a multicultural mix of South Africans of Indian, Chinese, Afrikaner, and English descent. In a 1981 *New York Times* interview, Kerzner tactfully expressed a hope that, having learned to live together while on vacation, South Africans might be able to co-exist someday at home.

Sun City triggered controversy. Kerzner, eager to establish it as an international destination, opened his checkbook to entertainers and athletes: Frank Sinatra inaugurated the 7000-seat Sun City Superbowl with a nine-night stand in 1981 for a reported $1.6 million, and Sun City hosted several boxing matches. Opponents of apartheid charged that Sun City legitimated the system of apartheid and called on travelers and entertainers to boycott Sun City.

Yet Sun International continued to expand, owning over a dozen homeland casinos and a string of resort hotels. In 1992 Kerzner opened the Lost City, a $300 million casino resort complex at Sun City, complete with a three-story water slide, massive wave pool, artificial volcano, and a giant casino. The audacious resort opened when homeland casinos were already in transition. The process of creating majority rule in South Africa had already begun and it was clear that the days of the homelands were numbered. Perhaps the new government might outlaw all casinos; perhaps it might allow casinos closer to Johannesburg. Neither possibility boded well for homeland casinos. In addition, a recession and the international stigma of its associations with apartheid rule had dimmed the luster of Sun City.

Kerzner, dogged by charges that he had bribed several homeland government officials, divested himself of his South African interests and moved to London. Sun International South Africa continued to operate casinos and hotels in that country, while Kerzner, with his Sun International Hotels (later renamed Kerzner International), relocated to the Bahamas. In 1994, Kerzner bought the former Resorts International from Merv Griffin, who had owned it since 1988. He opened Atlantis on Paradise Island, an aquatic casino-hotel that he billed as the world's first amphibious resort, and bankrolled Connecticut's Mohegun Sun casino. In 1996 Sun International acquired Merv Griffin's Resorts, once Resorts International, Atlantic City's first casino. Sun International's originally-announced plan to embark on a $500 million transformation of the resort into an Atlantic City Atlantis were later scaled back, and in 2001, after more than $300 million in losses, the company sold Resorts.

By the time Sol Kerzner had passed the reins of Kerzner International to his son Butch in 2004, the company had emerged as an international casino and hotel powerhouse. Meanwhile, South Africa's casino industry had seen a decade of turmoil. Even before the dissolution of the homelands, their casinos faced competition from scores of unlicensed casinos that sprang up throughout South Africa. Before they were suppressed, as many as 3000 of them were in operation; some had as many as 800 slot machines.

In 1996, South Africa's new government passed the National Gaming Act, which provided for the inauguration of a national lottery and set out the rules for the opening of as many as 40 casinos. Sun International was forced to divest itself of half of its homeland casinos but remained the country's dominant casino operator. Foreign companies invested in the new South African casino industry; in 2001, Park Place Entertainment opened Caesars Gauteng on the former site of the World Trade Centre, where the multi-party negotiations that led to South Africa's first multi-party elections were held in 1992, a sure commentary on the place of gambling in the new South Africa.

Casinos in the rest of sub-Saharan Africa were small and scattered, usually found in hotels catering to foreigners. The first African casino of note, Ghana's Casino Africa, opened in Accra in 1960. Before the development of homeland casinos, gambling resorts in Swaziland and Lesotho catered to South Africans. Kenya developed a relatively large casino industry, with nine casinos catering to tourists (though winnings could not be converted into foreign currency) as well as horseracing. Oil-rich Nigeria likewise supported many casinos. Elsewhere, casinos were less common. Nations like Uganda, Benin, and Congo sported a single casino. Throughout the continent, lotteries and horseracing proved to be the most popular forms of gambling. Here, as elsewhere, 20th century governments invariably turned to gambling for help when facing problems of underdevelopment and revenue shortfalls.

A European Renaissance

European casinos grew dramatically during the 20th century, as nations that had previously banned gambling discovered that maybe it wasn't so bad after all. The casino revival had started in 1907, when France legalized baccarat. Casinos at Cannes, Antibes, Juan-les-Pins, Deauville, and Nice really prospered after 1933, when the government permitted them to try roulette and *trente-et-quarante.* Slot machines were permitted only after 1987. Though this provision was modified in 1988, when casinos were permitted in larger cities, France retained many of its smaller casinos; there were over 180 throughout the country by 2004. French casinos have sponsored many cultural events; the International Film Festival at Cannes is underwritten by the Groupe Lucien Barriere, a group that owns casinos in every corner of France.

This was an arrangement followed elsewhere; the famous Montreux Jazz Festival, for example, began in the Montreux casino (also owned by the Group Lucien Barriere) in 1967 and became an internationally-celebrated music event. French casinos adhered to stricter rules than their come-as-you-are American cousins, with formal dress codes and entrance fees. Many casinos around the world adopted these policies, while others favored more lax "Las Vegas-style" rules. A dozen or so large casinos account for much of the country's casino business. Baccarat, blackjack, and roulette remain the most popular games, though American poker and craps have made inroads, particularly in the larger casinos. Boule and *trente-et-quarante* are still found, and some smaller casinos have only boule and slot machines. Despite their sophistication, with the coming of slots, they have become considerably more open than in years past, and often appeal to the mass market: by the late 1900s, slots accounted for 90 percent of French casino profits. Still, the image of tuxedoed chemin de fer players remains a powerful draw.

In the 20th century, no single political system had a monopoly on gambling: fascist, socialist and even communist governments chartered lotteries, and Germany's National Socialist party, in 1933, re-opened the casino at Baden-Baden. Though German Chancellor Adolf Hitler himself approved the opening of the casino, some Nazis were distressed to learn that the French lessee designated to actually run the casino (the Brownshirts knew nothing about roulette), Paul Salles, was actually a front for other financiers, the most influential of whom were Jewish. Gambling continued at Baden-Baden until August 1944. Until the collapse of the Third Reich was imminent, a single casino operated in German-occupied Austria and another in Poland.

In the immediate postwar period, when Baden-Baden was the headquarters for French military forces in Germany, locals planned to reopen the casino as soon as possible—no matter what the political system (monarchy, dictatorship, or democracy) they were sure that a casino was the best bet for their prosperity. Elsewhere, German casinos were returning. In 1948, Bad Durkheim and Bad Neuenahr, two municipalities in the state of Rhineland-Palatinate, opened legal gambling houses, the first outside of Baden in the 20th century. On April 1, 1950, Badeners rejoiced as the gambling rooms originally built by Benazet nearly a century earlier re-opened. Other German states licensed casinos, despite the disapproval of the federal government, and, though taxes on revenue are sometimes higher than 80 percent (Nevada casinos, by contrast, pay taxes of 6.75 percent on gaming revenue), the industry expanded; by the time that East and West Germany reunified in 1990, West Germany had 35 casinos; by 1992, six casinos had already opened in the formerly-Communist east.

In Austria, private gambling rooms had been the norm since the 1920s, and in 1933 the national government got in on the action by licensing casinos at several resorts. The company chosen to operate the monopoly concession, Austrian Casinos AG/Laxenburg, was, curiously, dominated by Canadians. When Hitler's Germany annexed Austria in 1938, all casinos, save the one at Baden bei Vien, were closed. In 1944, that casino closed as well. Almost immediately after the war, Austrian casinos reopened in the western, Allied-controlled, regions of the country. After Soviet withdrawal from the east in 1955, casinos reappeared there as well. Following a turbulent decade, the Austrian government stripped Austrian Casinos AG/Laxenburg of its casino concession and formed a new group, Casinos Austria, owned by a combination of government bodies, and travel, banking, and utility companies.

Under the leadership of Leo Wallner, Casinos Austria came to operate 12 casinos in Austria. Prevented from opening more casinos in its native land by the terms of its government concession, Casinos Austria grew internationally. By 2005, the company operated—and often held ownership stakes in—51 casinos in 35 different countries, including Egypt, South Africa, Argentina, Greece, Australia, and Switzerland. It also operated over a dozen casino cruise ships—a bit of an irony for a casino monopoly in a landlocked European nation with no known nautical heritage.

Elsewhere in Europe, restrictive casinos licenses became the norm in the years after World War II. Casinos from Ireland to Greece catered to both tourists and visitors; some were state-owned, others privately-held. But none had the bizarre history of Belgian gambling halls. Casinos had been legal in that small nation (it was home of the original Spa) until 1902, when, reportedly, the Prime Minister (disturbed by his son's gambling problem) prompted Parliament to ban all gambling, and the nation's casinos were closed.

But there was a complication: nearly a decade later, King Albert I, seeking to amuse a few visiting royal guests, was told by his councilors that gambling was now illegal. It was good to be the king; he used his influence to convince the nation's procurators, or prosecuting attorneys, to tolerate a few casinos that catered to "the right people." These opened in 1911 and, though the law clearly said that gambling was illegal, continued to operate without any further supervision until 1952. In that year, procurators, still acting beyond the law, placed several restrictions on the casinos: they were to be private clubs owned by their host cities and had to verify the identities and collect membership fees from all gamblers. Over one-third of Belgium's population, including those under twenty-one, lawyers, public officials, soldiers, and public employees, were excluded from gambling. Any sort of external advertising or promotion was banned, and the number of casinos limited to eight. The benign under-enforcement of Belgium's gaming laws ended in 1999, when its Parliament finally declared casinos legal and permitted them to install slot machines, which had been forbidden under the old regime. The number of casinos was still restricted, and they remained relatively small, with a few table games and slots each.

Great Britain had, in 1853, suppressed legal gambling almost entirely. Still, illegal betting, particularly on horses, continued. In 1960, Parliament re-legalized bookmaking, with great success. The legislation led to an unintended explosion in unregulated "social clubs" that were actually gambling casinos. Over 1,200 of them were in operation when, in 1968, Parliament changed the law and drastically curtailed the growth of casinos. Gambling could now take place only in private clubs; a prospective visitor had to wait at least 48 hours after applying for admission to enter the premises, something that put a damper on catering to spontaneous tourist drop-ins. The law also limited the number of slots—increasingly the most lucrative game—to two per casino.

There were further limitations. Advertising and even overly-elaborate signage was banned, and hours of operation were limited. Clubs strictly enforced their own codes of conduct, permanently barring players who flouted them. One London casino tore up the membership cards of 167 patrons who committed the offense of parking within three blocks of the casino in violation of the club's agreement with surrounding residents. This was clearly not the free-wheeling "Last Frontier" of Las Vegas or Reno.

While their casino gambling took place under straitened circumstances, Britons enjoyed betting on horses and sports with unparalleled freedom. The United Kingdom is the last major holdout against pari-mutuel betting, as fixed-odds wagering with bookmakers continued to dominate that country's betting. British betting was dominated by a few major betting chains: Ladbrokes, William Hill, Coral Eurobet, and Stanley Leisure. In the late 1990s, casinos began to catch up to bookmakers: in 1997, Parliament loosened restrictions a bit, and slot machines were allowed in more locations

Further changes came in 2005, when Parliament passed a comprehensive Gambling Act. Putting regulation of all commercial gambling—arcades, race and sports betting, bingo, and casinos—under the authority of a new Gambling Commission, the act eased some existing restrictions on casino advertising and allowed for the creation of a limited number of larger casinos. The first of these, Aspers Westfield Stratford City, opened in a shopping center in east London in late 2011. With 40 roulette and blackjack tables, 92 electronic game terminals, and a 150-seat poker room, Aspers would have been dwarfed by the giants of the Las Vegas Strip or Macau, but for Britain, this was a true "super casino." The biggest impact of the 2005 legislation, however, might be the advent of online and mobile gambling in the United Kingdom (see chapter 17).

To the east, casinos have been proxies for the transitions to capitalism in many nations. In the postwar period, Josip Broz Tito's Yugoslavia boasted the largest casino industry of any Communist nation, and after the dissolution of that country, casinos in many of its former provinces, particularly Croatia and Slovenia, became reasonably successful. Throughout Eastern Europe, the fall of the Iron Curtain brought an explosion in casino development. Bulgaria, Hungary, and the former Yugoslav republics saw many new casinos, but the former Soviet Union was perhaps the region where the mushrooming of gambling halls was the most astounding. By 2005, there were 60 casinos in Moscow alone, though many of them were small and operating on the margins. Still, Russian casinos brought in $5 billion in the previous year, more than Atlantic City, New Jersey.

But Russian casinos' luck ran out in 2009, when Prime Minister Vladimir Putin supported a decree that shut down every gambling casino in Russia, putting 400,000 employees out of work overnight. The law permitted casinos only in four areas: the Baltic exclave of Kaliningrad, south Siberia's Altai Territory, Primorye on the Pacific Coast, and in Azov City in southern Russia. By the following year, casinos had begun to open in those disparate locations, but it was clear that, barring major legislative changes, Russian casinos would not regain their former dominace.

As casinos spread throughout Europe, any semblance of exclusivity that Monte Carlo may have retained vanished. Its casinos were now distinguished only by their history, never a quality held in high esteem by those eager to get the best odds and the highest action. Now outfitted with slot machines and featuring punto banco (American baccarat), craps, and even double-zero roulette, the four casinos of Monte Carlo still sought to cater to elite customers in the age of mass marketing. Though the name continued to inspire visions of elegance, the resort had clearly been surpassed: the four hotels of venerable Societe des Bains de Mer, for example, had about one-sixth as many rooms between them as Las Vegas's Monte Carlo casino resort—the Nevada theme park version was bigger than the original.

The international spread of the Las Vegas-style casino resort was one of the most significant developments of the late 20th and early 21st centuries. It speaks to both the growing economic clout of Nevada-based gaming companies and the increasing homogenization of global gambling cultures. Where once regional and national games had dominated, now gambling took place in casinos that looked more and more alike. And the globalization of gambling would only intensify as cards and dice took to their next, and for now final, frontier: cyberspace.

17

Reinventing the Wheel

Las Vegas hangs on as gambling goes digital

When the 20ᵗʰ century closed, gambling was on the upswing world-wide. An unprecedented string of legalizations brought legal casinos to more places than ever before. The continent of Asia was about to experience a remarkable explosion of casino gambling. The future seemed to be boundless. But the casino world's center, Las Vegas, was on the brink of a decade that would see it reach highs—and lows—it couldn't have imagined. At the same time, gambling world-wide continued to evolve, moving from "bricks" to "clicks," as gam-blers increasingly moved online.

Retooling the Las Vegas Strip

As gambling proliferated across the United States in the 1990s, it was hailed as a thing that could defy gravity. Casinos, it was said time and again, were recession-proof. Even in down years, they would continue to thrive, balancing budgets and providing jobs. That was, strictly speaking, never the case. But casinos enjoyed enough of a good run to create the impression that they would continue to prosper indefinitely.

The 2000s, however, gave the United States gaming industry a one-two punch from which it is only just recovering. First, early in the decade, the combination of a cooling economy and the post-9/11 economic disruption depressed winnings in destination (and quasi-destination) markets Las Vegas and Atlantic City. Regional markets, as had grown up throughout much of the country in the 1990s, gener-ally fared well. People might not be taking the time or money to travel long distances to gamble as much, but they still wanted to play.

Both Nevada and Atlantic City casinos confronted increased competition as well. The chief threat to Nevada casinos came from Indian casinos that now dotted much of the Pacific Northwest, California, and Arizona—key feeder markets for Nevada destinations as disparate as Lake Tahoe, Reno, Mesquite, Laughlin, and Downtown Las Vegas. All of these areas suffered declines during the 2000s—in the case of Lake Tahoe's South Shore, a 40 percent drop from 2000 to 2011. That's why, even before the Great Recession, the Nevada gambling industry began to contract. The total number of slot machines in the state fell by 14 percent from 2001 to 2011—this despite the opening of several large casinos on the Las Vegas Strip.

The Strip itself responded to the crisis by doubling down on the Mirage Effect, a strategy made most clear by the profound shift in the revenue structure of large Strip casino resorts during the 1990s. Unable to compete with new casinos in California and elsewhere on the gambling floor, Strip casinos added a new customer to its mix of business travelers, international tourists, fun-seeking bargain hunters, and serious gamblers: young men and women in search of nightlife filled the nightclubs, ultralounges, beach clubs, and plain honest bars that proliferated during the 2000s, effectively bringing a new generation of customers to the Strip.

The nightclub trade, which skews to a 20s and 30s demographic, represented a departure for Strip casinos, which traditionally considered 45-year olds as youngsters. There might not seem to be as much money in club beats and cocktails compared to high-stakes baccarat, but bottle service makes nightclubs extremely remunerative for casinos, as model, select patrons bypass the line and receive reserved tables along the dance floor in exchange for purchasing several bottles of liquor, at charges of up to $500 per bottle. By opening clubs and lounges along these lines, operators met two objectives: they captured an extremely lucrative business, and they effectively oriented new patrons to the casino. One day, club-goers will tire of pounding music, Red Bull and Grey Goose, and even gyrating bodies. But when they do, they'll be accustomed to vacationing along the Strip, and will then come more for gambling, high-end dining and, perish the thought, Barry Manilow.

This reversed a long-standing trend in Las Vegas. With the post-Mirage gentrification of the Strip, the average customer got older. The mean age of Las Vegas visitors huddled around 47 for much of the early 1990s, steadily trending upwards to top 50 in 2000. Those between 40 and 65 years of age accounted for over half the total visitors to the city in that year. Las Vegas was not unique in this regard—most casinos catered extensively to retirees, since there was a big population of empty-nesters with some discretionary income who wanted to have fun.

Even though Las Vegas casino operators found it was profitable to cater to this age cohort (the Baby Boomers, by no coincidence, aged into this group during the booming 1990s), they were wary of painting themselves into a demographic corner. What if the younger generation associated casinos with stale music, boring games, and stuffy design? Would they reject gambling like their parents had turned their noses up at their parents' Ted Lewis and Glenn Miller records, embracing instead the 21st century vacation equivalent of Jefferson Airplane or the Rolling Stones? Would casinos become, by the 2010s, irredeemably musty?

To attract the next generation of patrons, casinos took a bold step: they got into the nightclub business. Strip resorts had had lounges since the 1940s: places where busted-out gamblers (or the waiting spouses of those not yet busted) could relax, enjoying light comedy and music for the price of a drink. In most of these, a dance floor would have been out of the question. Casino lounges were strictly a place to go before or after the main event, be it gambling or the dinner show.

In the late 1960s, some Strip resorts (and the Mint downtown) advertised late-night dancing. The music was usually soft, the lights low, and the setting intimate. Live bands provided most of the entertainment. By the mid-1970s, a string of discos and night-clubs had opened up, outside of casinos, in and around the Strip. Casinos featured dancing in some of their lounges—as early as 1972, the Tropicana advertised "discotheque dancing" from midnight to 6 A.M. in its Tiffany lounge. There was no cover charge, or line to get in, and the lounges were, still, on the periphery of Vegas nightlife.

The situation remained much the same into the 1990s. Clubs like P.J. Bottoms, the Brewery, the Shark Club, and Palladium, came and went on and around the Strip. In the early part of the decade, about a half-dozen "disco clubs" could be found around Las Vegas. For those who wanted to venture outside of casinos, it was something to do.

The 1996 opening of the Club Utopia brought techno and house music to the Strip, and made casino executives consider the salability of full-fledged nightclubs—with celebrity DJs, cover charges, and lines to get in. The year before, the first major casino nightclub, Club Rio, had opened in the Copacabana Lounge of the Rio, a few blocks west of the Strip on Flamingo Road. The Club Rio, which split the Copacabana with headliners like Danny Gans, was squarely in the tradition of lounges converting to dance halls after hours, but it brought the idea of casino nightclubbing to a new level.

In the late 1990s, the Strip's biggest casino, MGM Grand, was fervently seeking to distance itself from its opening Dorothy in Oz theme and reposition itself as the "City of Entertainment." The opening of Studio 54 there in 1997 was an epochal moment: it was a full-fledged, single purpose nightclub, with an enviable pedigree as the successor to New York's most famous spot for disco dissolution. With the openings of Ra at Luxor (1998) and Baby's at the Hard Rock (1999), casino nightclubs had become a fixture. This first generation was followed by a string of other clubs, and, with an average lifespan of five to eight years, some clubs are into their third incarnation now.

The explosion of ultra-hip nightspots was a godsend for those who keep the hotel rooms of the Strip full and the blackjack tables humming. Because while the older attractions of the New Strip were doing a great job of luring conventioneers, retirees, international travelers, and older Americans to Las Vegas, they weren't setting twenty-somethings on fire. When Vince Vaughn and Jon Favreau drove up to "Vegas, baby" in 1996's *Swingers*, they were consciously going against the grain—in fact, they joked about just how "old school" the "Stardust" (actually downtown's Fremont) was. In those salad days of the mid-to-late 1990s, Vegas was big, but it wasn't yet cool. Part of the appeal of Vegas in those days was its retro chic: *Swingers* was an up-to-date story about relationships, but it was also an homage to the Rat Pack.

Swingers might have put Las Vegas back on the hipster retro radar, but as swing dancing's star faded, Las Vegas's shone brighter. It took a television show aimed at an even younger demographic to really re-launch the Vegas brand. The 2002 season of MTV's everlasting reality series *The Real World* was shot in the newly-opened Palms. The show turned a welcome light on the youthful indiscretions to be had in Las Vegas, and was remarkably prescient in portraying the city not as the fabled haunt of yesterday's legends, but as today's hot party spot.

The Palms might have been in the right place at the right time, but it was uniquely poised to capitalize on the attention brought by *The Real World*. Palms owner George Maloof and others—the Hard Rock casino in particular—have helped spark a profound demographic shift in Las Vegas tourists. Since 2000, visitors to Las Vegas have gotten younger, better educated, and wealthier: in 2000, the mean age of sampled visitors was well over fifty; today it is just over 49. Thirty-eight percent had only graduated high school or less; by 2011 that number dropped to 20 percent; over three-quarters of visitors had been to college. And whereas in 2000 only 25 percent of visitors made over $80,000 a year, in 2011 49 percent fell into that category.

These younger visitors were drawn to nightclubs because they offer the perfect milieu for the twenty- and thirty-something crowd, not averse to gambling but not obsessed by it, drawn to Las Vegas by "reality" TV and celebrity magazines. Once, the casino was the place to be seen; now, with the casino floor more resembling a slot machine warehouse than a swank hideaway, the nightclub became the exclusive place to be seen.

And exclusive is the right word. The conventional wisdom has been that Las Vegas casinos have prospered because they are profoundly democratic—anyone can get in and rub elbows with the rich and famous. Reality was far more complex, as patrons with wealth and power always enjoyed a finer cut than those pitching nickels into the slots—comps at the steakhouse instead of the coffee shop, for starters. But despite the sometimes-rigid segmentation of patrons by dollars gambled, casinos always had at least the appearance of egalitarianism. One could walk freely into the baccarat pit, and, if he didn't mind the insinuating stares, perhaps even watch a hand or two.

The club life of 21st century Vegas is profoundly different. It is built on the principle of exclusion. A night at XS is made that much sweeter knowing that others might wait in vain for three hours and not get in. Thus, the line outside becomes a big part of the night for those not on the VIP list. Even those who get in aren't going to enjoy everything inside: after waiting in line for hours and paying the cover charge, one gets the privilege of access to the dance floor and the bar, and the chance to watch the true cognoscenti, those with bottle service, rest between gyrations at tables (in some clubs, luxury boxes) with a view of the action.

Previously, casinos used free cocktails to get patrons in: now, nightclubs are giving away tables to customers who buy outrageously-priced alcohol. This is another reversal, and should prompt casino managers, even those who don't have nightclubs, to reconsider some basic tenets of the business. If people in a casino are willing to pay hundreds of dollars for something that's being given away free to gamblers, it's possible that many other aspects of the gambling biz might be due for a rethink.

Even if club-goers only represent a small percentage of casino patrons, they are significant. They are younger and often wealthier than the average casino visitor, so their preferences might dictate how casinos evolve over the next decade. Those who go to nightclubs are willing to pay dearly for the privilege of exclusiveness, and they want to be the stars of the show. It's the Mirage Effect for the Facebook generation.

And the Las Vegas Strip, which in early 2002 seemed to be stuck in neutral (revenues and visitation down, many operators delayed or abandoned plans for new projects) found itself booming again by 2004. As in the late 1980s, Steve Wynn provided the spark. He had already sold his Mirage Resorts empire to Kirk Kerkorian's MGM Grand and bought the Desert Inn. While other developers waited to see whether the economy would rebound, Wynn went full bore into a project built on the Desert Inn site. First called Le Reve, after the Picasso masterpiece in Wynn's personal collection, then Wynn Las Vegas, the project out-Bellagioed the Bellagio, becoming the high-

est-end property in town. Opening just as the wave began to crest on
the Strip, Wynn Las Vegas seemed to betoken a future where bigger and better casinos would pull in wealthier and higher-spending
customers.

So, up and down the Strip, operators imploded old casinos and
started building anew. Some simply added hotel towers: Mandalay
Bay, the Venetian, Bellagio, and Caesars Palace all added to their
supply of hotel rooms without adding a single slot machine to their
casinos. Next door to the Venetian, the Palazzo opened, while Wynn
got its own companion casino, Encore. Others thought even more
boldly. Developers new to the Strip began building the Cosmopolitan and Fontainebleau, large-scale casinos that also included substantial condominium components. MGM Mirage imploded the
small Boardwalk casino hotel, whose grinning clown façade terror-
ized many a young (or old) visitor to the Strip to make way for
CityCenter. Originally planned as a mixed-use leisure/residential
concept, CityCenter was to utilize the acreage between the Monte Carlo and Bellagio, now owned by a single company following
MGM Mirage's acquisition of the Mandalay Resort Group.

The dream of reinventing the Strip, wiping away the last ves-
tiges of the pre-Mirage era, proved a contagious one. Boyd Gaming
imploded the storied Stardust to make way for a hotel/retail/con-
vention center casino project named Echelon, while the venerable
Frontier was purchased and imploded, with a resort bringing New
York's Plaza brand to the Strip planned for the site. MGM even began planning another "CityCenter North" project adjacent to Circus
Circus.

Then, in late 2007, the bubble burst. The onset of the national
recession, combined with a slowdown in business travel, chilled the
growth prospects of Las Vegas and its casinos. The Nevada gaming
industry's gross gaming revenue stopped growing and actually de-
creased in the fourth quarter of 2007, a slump from which it would
not emerge until early 2010, and even then only hesitantly. Both
visitation and overall revenue fell on the Strip in 2008 and 2009.
Suddenly, projections that had seemed sensible, perhaps even con-
servative, in 2005 were hopelessly pollyannish. Boyd delayed construction on Echelon indefinitely in the summer of 2008; the owners

Steve Wynn's namesake Las Vegas resort, which opened on April 28, 2005, epitomized the luxury and aspirations of the post-9/11, pre-recession Las Vegas Strip.

of the Frontier site delayed and then canceled the Plaza Las Vegas; the Fontainebleau ultimately ran out of money, was acquired by Carl Icahn, and sat incomplete on the North Strip for years.

Others soldiered on. MGM plunged ahead with CityCenter, opening the centerpiece Aria casino resort in late 2009. Although initial results were underwhelming, the casino has since found its footing as a standard Strip resort, without any pretensions to greater pseudo-urban glory. Deutsche Bank acquired the Cosmopolitan in foreclosure and opened the property in late 2010.

As of early 2013, Las Vegas appeared to be on the mend. Both visitation and revenues had risen for two consecutive years, and, buoyed by smaller-scale renovations and improvements on the Strip and a Downtown renaissance, a guarded optimism was in the air. Just like gamblers who never forget an early lucky streak, those who own the casinos of Las Vegas were sure that good times were just ahead.

Moving Online

As spectacular as the highs and lows of the casino industry in Las Vegas might have been, the real story of the new millennium was the shift of gambling from terrestrial casinos to online ones. This happened in stages, and it matched the increasing growth and sophistication of digital commerce and communications.

In the mid-1990s, millions discovered the Internet, a communications medium that promised to accelerate scientific study, speed business, and allow instantaneous communication. Many users, though, logged on chiefly to download pornography, chat online, and gamble. The first "gambling" websites appeared in 1995, but these were primarily "free" sites that offered only simulated games. Playing with valueless credits, players might as well have been mindlessly clicking on Freecell. Though this wasn't really gambling, some predicted at the time that, should live wagering be introduced, online gambling revenues could surpass $10 billion a year.

These projections bore out what many gambling operators knew: that, given the convenience of gambling over the computer, an online gaming site could be phenomenally lucrative. Later in 1995 and 1996, sites that let players deposit money via credit cards or wire transfers appeared. Many governments, not wishing to jeopardize the millions they annually took in by licensing other gambling schemes, declared Internet gambling illegal (the United States relied on an interpretation of a 1961 anti-bookmaking statute), but others legalized the new betting medium, frankly to create revenues and business development.

The small Caribbean nation of Antigua was one of the first to take the iniative. Antigua already had casinos catering to foreigners and, in the mid-1990s, created a free trade zone that let American bookmakers (using toll-free numbers to accept bets from the mainland) operate. Immune from American gambling prohibitions, they paid licensing fees and agreed to submit to Antiguan regulation. In a sense, Antigua treated online gaming like any other business: the island was already a minor haven for other offshore shelter businesses like ship registries and banking. With their advertisements airing on American radio stations and appearing in popular sports magazines, these Antiguan-regulated betting businesses claimed to be completely legitimate.

In 1995, these offshore sportsbooks began to take advantage of the Internet: several posted odds and other information as well as a toll-free number that visitors could call to place bets. In the United States, some licensed gambling operators did the same. New York's Capital OTB horseracing monopoly began posting its odds on a "virtual tote board" in 1996. Within a few years, Capital OTB used the Internet to transmit betting information and even broadcast races, though bettors still needed to use their phone to wager from home. In 1997, Idaho's Coeur d'Alene Indian tribe posted digital lottery games that it argued were Class II games permitted under the National Indian Regulatory Act. Wisconsin's attorney general begged to differ, and as a result of a court action the site was closed.

As online commerce became more sophisticated and consumers became more comfortable with transmitting financial data over the Internet, Antiguan sportsbooks made the natural transition to complete online wagering. The World Sports Exchange pioneered when it went online in early 1997 as a full-service Internet sportsbook that let players actually "bet with the click of a mouse." Based in Antigua, the World Sports Exchange was the creation of Jay Cohen and Steve Schillinger, two former traders on the Pacific Stock Exchange. For years, Schillinger had run office pools, letting fellow traders swap sports "futures" and bet on the outcome of the O.J. Simpson trial and other public events. Cohen persuaded Schillinger to move the operation online. Researching the field, they concluded that a sportsbook based in Antigua using the Capital OTB model was legal and, potentially, very lucrative.

Soon, others followed, and by early 1998 there were more than two dozen fully-operational online sportsbooks accepting bets from Antigua. Most looked quite similar, with pages featuring the latest odds, site rules, information about payment, and links to both sports news and problem gambling sites. Some let players bet illusory credits for fun, while most ran aggressive promotions, offering bonus cash to new sign-ups and those who referred them. Sports betting had come a long way from the street-corner bookie, though the operators of pool rooms at the turn of the previous century would not have been surprised by the marriage of high technology and gambling.

Sportsbooks were best suited to the Internet because they were really just another medium for an age-old pastime. Whether one places his bet in person, or by telegraph, telephone, or wireless connection doesn't influence the outcome of the game or the odds offered. Provided one knows that the bookmaker will promptly pay off winners, the method of placing the bet is immaterial. (The speed with which sportsbooks paid their winners, though, was another story.) Online casinos were different. Players anted up real money on virtual games. No real roulette dealer spun the wheel, dropped the ball, and announced the winner—a digital random number generator simply spat out data for software to translate into a player win or loss. Slot machines had been using random number generators for years, but playing online was still a big leap of faith. Slot machines in Atlantic City were certified by the state of New Jersey to be fair., and if one felt otherwise, he could easily prompt regulators to investigate. Should a disgruntled bettor suspect an online gaming site of cheating, he had no recourse save an appeal to a distant government. When several fly-by-night operators bilked players before disappearing, unproven online casinos faced a credibility problem.

Millions of players quickly found sites they trusted. In 1996, about 15 sites accepted real money. A year, later, over 200 sites existed. In 1999, that number more than tripled to 650, and by 2002 it had leveled off at about 1800 gaming sites. These sites included sportsbooks, casinos, lotteries, and horseracing sites. The reaction of land-based gaming operators was, originally, dismissal, followed by opposition. But many soon reasoned that, with their established names and reputations for both gaming action and probity, they could become leaders in the field. Governments, too, watched the steadily rising revenue of online gambling sites and saw a potential cash cow. In many nations, though, technological and moral conservatives prevented the quick jump of governments and private gaming concerns into cyberspace.

Several European lotteries experimented with online games, and in 1999 Alice Springs, Northern Territory (Australia) made gambling history when its sole casino, Lassetters, became the first terrestrial casino to go online. The Australian federal government had permitted state and territorial legislators set parameters for the extension of land-based operations online. Several TABs went online, but in the next year the Australian government placed a moratorium on all new online gaming sites, and in 2001 the Interactive Gaming Act, though it maintained horse and sports wagering sites, criminalized the act of offering virtual card, dice, or slot-based games to Australians. Australians wagered money with legal betting sites in ever-growing numbers but they could not enjoy the protection of betting with an Australian-regulated online casino—though foreigners did.

Larger brick-and-mortar casinos in the United Kingdom and United States cautiously explored going online. They were leery of jeopardizing their land-based licenses, and thus could not accept bets with the same impunity as Caribbean-based sites that only existed in cyberspace. Britain's Aspinalls, a casino operator since 1962, launched an online casino in 2002, as did Kerzner International, which attracted a half-ownership investment from Las Vegas's Station Casinos. Las Vegas giant MGM Mirage operated a site based in the Isle of Man. Because of the unresolved legal status of online gaming, MGM Mirage Online accepted bets from citizens of only six countries. It was unprofitable and soon closed, as did the Kerzner venture, though both held out the promise that, in a less tenuous regulatory environment, well-known casinos would successfully make the transition to cyberspace.

Other nations followed Antigua, Australia, and the Isle of Man and quickly tried to maximize revenues from online betting. In March 2005, for example, the Philippine casino monopoly PAGCOR announced plans to implement Telesabong, the world's first Internet-based cockfighting system. Telesabong would allow online bettors to wager on a series of fights from the nation's 1700 cockpits. Even before creating this system, PAGCOR had 312 betting stations that, linked by the Internet, let Filipinos bet online from designated locations. One of the world's oldest sports had made the transition to the 21st century.

Despite federal intransigence in the United States—the Justice Department under both the Clinton and Bush Administrations insisted that, according to the Wire Act, any kind of Internet gaming was illegal—several foreign governments and even American states began exploring regulation rather than prohibition. In April 2001, the Nevada legislature passed Assembly Bill 578, which created a theoretical framework for the eventual licensing and regulation of online gaming operations within the state—contingent, of course, on federal approval. But legalization seemed far off. In March 1998, the Justice Department charged fourteen online sportsbook operators from Costa Rica and Antigua with violating the Wire Act. Three of the fourteen were in the United States at the time and surrendered to authorities; most pled guilty to lesser crimes. Those still abroad, though, were in the Caribbean. The United States could not extradite them. Should they wish to return to the United States, though, they might be arrested and put on trial.

Some returned, pled guilty, and put the charges behind them, while others elected to remain abroad, technically fugitives from American justice. Though his associates in the World Sports Exchange took this option, company president Jay Cohen chose to clear his name by returning to New York to face trial. But Cohen was found guilty in 2000 and, after exhausting his appeals, served nearly two years at Federal Prison Camp Nellis, about twenty miles from the Las Vegas Strip. The "March Madness" prosecutions (named for the month in which prosecutors unsealed the indictments) were a reminder that, in the United States at least, betting on the Internet remained illegal.

Antigua soon challenged American enforcement of the Wire Act. Along with U.S. government threats to disallow the use of credit cards for online payment, the specter of prosecution for running legal businesses hurt the Antiguan Internet betting industry. In 1999 the country boasted 119 operators that employed 3,000 Antiguans; four years later, the number had fallen to nearly one-sixth of that. Antigua blamed American "aggression" for the loss, and pursued a settlement under the General Agreement on Trade in Services. The GATS, which dates from 1995, bound all member bodies (which included both Antigua and the United States) to give each other equal access. Antigua argued that the United States was compelled to accept its "cross border gaming services," an assertion that the United States denied, claiming the matter was one of criminal enforcement rather than trade in services. A World Trade Organization dispute resolution panel ruled in favor of Antigua in 2004. The United States appealed, and though the panel affirmed its original decision, the powers of the World Trade Organization to prevent the federal government from enforcing its laws against gambling were spurious at best, and the case was far from over.

Besides sports betting, which was a natural for the Internet, the biggest expansion in online gaming has been the American classic: poker. Despite trust issues similar to that of online casino games—one doesn't know for sure whether virtual cards are randomly chosen, if other players at a virtual table are in collusion or, indeed, are a single user logged in under multiple accounts—online poker swiftly became one of the most popular games of the new millennium.

Online poker combined with an older medium, television, to spur the old game to unforeseeable levels of popularity, both in the United States and worldwide. Televised poker, in particular, expanded dramatically after 2002. The use of innovative camera techniques which allowed viewers to see players' hole cards (dealt facedown) made watching games online almost hypnotic. Soon, the World Series of Poker (which aired on ESPN), the World Poker Tour, and a host of celebrity poker shows were common.

The new visibility of poker sent many players online, where they found a place to learn the game in an anonymous, non-threatening place. Instead of having to venture into a casino poker room and play against professionals, or compete against one's own friends at home, a player could gradually gain confidence (and skill) playing against people she never met, winning or losing money without embarrassment. Online poker burst into prominence when, in 2003, Chris Moneymaker, an online player who had never sat in a live tournament before, won the World Series of Poker in Las Vegas. He had earned his spot by winning an online satellite tournament held by PokerStars.com, parlaying a $40 investment into a $2.5 million payday. Suddenly, online poker had a face, and many who watched him go all-in against seasoned pro Sam Farha had the dream of parlaying skill and luck into careers as professional poker players. Attendance—and jackpots—at the World Series of Poker soared, and after casino giant Harrah's purchased the tournament from Binion's in 2004, became the center of a year-long series of satellite tournaments and sponsored poker events.

Harrah's maintained a "don't ask, don't tell" policy, refusing to acknowledge that many of the tournament's players were primarily online players. Wary of crossing Nevada regulators or Justice Department prosecutors, they and other American casino companies left the online poker field to a variety of international sites. Visitors to these sites played poker against each other, while the site, in return for providing an online betting forum, charged a rake. This was exactly what casino poker rooms did and, in fact, what ten percent houses had done as far back as the 1830s.

One company, thanks to skillful promotion, soon came to dominate the field. Founded in 2001, Party Gaming was a model for the international Internet economy. With offices in London, the company was headquartered in Gibraltar (taking advantage of liberal tax and Internet gaming laws), while most of its employees lived and worked in India. The company's chief venture, Party Poker, grabbed over half of the world's online poker market by 2004. Taking no direct risk in the games, the site's owners earned an estimated $100,000 an hour. Poker had come a long way from cigar store backrooms and dingy basements. It was part of a global Internet gaming market that was estimated to have pulled in revenues of over $7 billion in 2004. Little had changed since the earliest humans wagered over coin flips and the roll of bones: the gambling lure was just as potent.

Yet not everyone welcomed the reality that gambling could only be a mouse-click away. The March Madness prosecutions ultimately did little to curb American online gambling; companies offering games to U.S. gamblers simply made sure that they had no financial exposure to in the United States. With no one prosecuting gamblers for placing bets and no employee of the operators in the United States to be charged with a crime, there didn't seem to be much for the federal government to do.

As it turned out, the Wire Act was merely one tool in the Justice Department's arsenal. In July 2006, federal prosecutors arrested BetOnSports CEO David Carruthers while he was changing planes in Texas, en route to Costa Rica from the United Kingdom.

He and ten others were charged with racketeering and an array of other charges related to their accepting bets from U.S. bettors. The prosecution of BetOnSports was noteworthy because the company was publicly traded in the United Kingdom and Carruthers had long been arguing for the American legalization and regulation of online gambling. Yet Carruthers and several others associated with the company, including founder Gary Kaplan, ended up serving prison sentences, even as online casinos were close to becoming legal in Carruthers' native United Kingdom.

Those arrests were just the beginning. Congress has been mulling legislation that would specifically and unambiguously criminalize online betting for years, but proponents of a ban couldn't marshal support for their cause. In September 2006, however, that changed, as an amendment tacked on to the SAFE (Security and Accountability for Every) Port bill sought to throttle online gambling by cutting off its funding. That amendment, known as the Unlawful Internet Gaming Enforcement Act, criminalized facilitating the transfer of or accepting funds from U.S. gamblers online. U.S.-based financial providers quickly stopped processing payments to gambling sites, and several online poker sites stopped accepting bets from the United States.

Even this legislation proved to be less than completely effective, however, as players and online gambling operators found ways around the law. With prohibition seemingly faltering, many assumed that it was merely a matter of time before the United States legalized online play and provided for its taxation and regulation—a particularly strident call as the national economic situation deteriorated in the late 2000s. Even as the terrestrial United States casino business—including major players like Caesars Entertainment, MGM Resorts International, and Wynn Resorts—came out on the side of legalization, however, the online poker world was rocked by a wave of arrests on April 15, 2011. Known as "Black Friday," the date went down in infamy for online poker players, particularly those who had accounts with PokerStars, Full Tilt Poker, and Absolute Poker, the three sites targeted in the prosecutions. The Justice Department charged owners and employees of the sites with bank fraud, money laundering, and illegal gambling offenses and issued restraining orders against

more than 75 bank accounts used by the companies and their payment processors.

Those who ran the sites did themselves no favors. Looking at
the books, the Justice Department charged Full Tilt with running
a "global Ponzi scheme," a not unreasonable charge seeing how the
site owed its players $390 million, money that they had on deposit
and should have been free to withdraw at any time, but had only $60
million in the bank. It seemed that online poker operators were following in the footsteps of the cheating blacklegs who had plied their
trade on the Mississippi River in the antebellum South.

Still, by the end 2011 American legalization seemed more a matter of when than if. The state of Nevada codified its "interactive
gambling" regulations and began processing applications for online
poker providers. Though these online poker rooms would only be
permitted to accept bets from within the state, should the federal
government legalize online play, Nevada-licensed companies would
be in the cat-bird seat. Several casino operators and equipment man-
ufactures quickly filed for licenses. And, in late December, a Justice
Department ruling effectively opened the door to the proliferation
of online gambling throughout the country, as it announced that the
Wire Act only applied to sports betting, and that states wishing to
authorize online lotteries or other forms of gambling within their
borders were well within their rights.

As a result, states began considering a move online; in March
2012, Illinois became the first U.S. state to sell lottery tickets online,
and others scrambled to follow. With cash-hungry states looking to
profit from online gambling as they had previously benefited from
lotteries and casinos, it seemed that legalization was finally in the
cards.

Epilogue
Still Betting

A hard seven

When I sat down to write the final chapter of the first edition of *Roll the Bones* back in May of 2005, I had no problem picking a framing device: the opening of Wynn Las Vegas which, a few weeks earlier, had given me occasion to reflect on the history of gambling. I was doing a lot of that in those days, as I hurried to finish my first draft of *Roll the Bones*, but the setting of Wynn—brand new, but nonetheless steeped in millennia of gambling tradition—proved a powerful tonic. I'll reproduce a few paragraphs here:

> April 28, 2005, 12:02 A.M. The doors open at the $2.7 billion Wynn Las Vegas, the most expensive casino yet built and the self-proclaimed masterwork of visionary Steve Wynn. As the seconds tick down before the opening, he has little time to reflect on the significance of the hour: this is the third time he has opened the world's most expensive resort, and, after having sold his Mirage Resorts to MGM in 2000, represents a leap back into the casino world. When the doors open and the first guests hurry through, his mind is on the million technical problems that can be revealed under the strain of the opening. There is not much of a chance to enjoy the sight of patrons finally inside his casino, and, though confident that his masterpiece will speak for itself, at the moment his best hope is to not be embarrassed by an errant glitch.

> Thousands pour through the entrances, excited to be part of the most eagerly anticipated casino opening in years. Drawn by an urban legend (unfortunately false) which says that slots on opening night are set to pay back over 100 percent, locals crowd the floor, as tuxedoed VIPs fresh from an earlier charity dinner enjoy the ambience, and guests from around the world snap pictures and hurry to

the tables. A perceptive visitor walking through the property, could see the resort as the culmination of seven thousand years of gambling history.

Wynn's latest manipulation of the environment, an artificial mountain whose Lake of Dreams faces inwards to the casino, ensuring that its wonders are seen only by resort guests. Under the chandeliered valet porte cochere, a pair of cast-bronze guardian lions imported from China welcome visitors. They exactly match the pair sitting in front of the Bank of China and are said to prevent bad luck and negative energy from entering the building. In the casino atmosphere, they symbolize both the past of gambling (the playing cards and numerous games invented in Asia, and that regions intrepid gamblers) and this resort's present: many of its international high rollers will hail from the Far East.

Inside the doors, a bas relief inspired by 18th century French design but calling to mind the classical era suggests the ancient Greeks and Romans casting lots and rolling bones. A visitor might linger in the glass-ceilinged Atrium, with its balls of color fashioned from flowers. This indoor garden recalls the famous gardens of the German spa resorts, and its flower patterns appear in the ceiling all the way into the adjacent retail promenade. Stepping into the casino, the visitor moves along a marble pathway with exquisite mosaics that pick up patterns from the casino's carpet—even this typically garish feature of the gambling hall has been elevated to high art, and "carpet joint" operators from William Crockford to Jay Sarno would have approved.

From there, I took the reader on a tour of Wynn Las Vegas and, drawing on talks with Steve Wynn, his chief designer Roger Thomas, and my own historical interpolations, saw in the surroundings the culmination of a history of gambling that began so long ago.

At the time, it made sense. After all, Las Vegas was the world's capital of gambling, and Wynn Las Vegas was the epitome of Las Vegas. I could make an honest claim to be standing at the crux of the gambling world when I watched the doors to Wynn open on that warm April night.

Gambling history, too, seemed to follow a natural progression, with things seamlessly clicking into place. Simpler games begat more complex ones, and, in the big picture, gambling itself became more accepted across the world. There might be a few hold-outs here and there, but gambling was undoubtedly on a winning streak.

The 20th century seemingly marked a turning point, from which the scales would continue to slide from prohibition to legalization.

Seven years later, I'm not entirely sure that's the case. I no longer live in the world's gambling capital. Since 2008, Macau's less-than-three dozen casinos have brought in more money than all of Nevada's. In 2011, Macau casinos pulled in $33.5 billion, more than three times the Nevada total. Singapore, with only two casinos, is on the fast-track to knock Las Vegas out of its runner-up spot.

Since that night in 2005, Las Vegas has taken a few on the chin. The recession, combined with the ascendancy of Asian gambling, has prompted an identity crisis for the city, one that it has not yet come to grips with. There have been speed bumps before—the recessions of the early 1980s and 2001-2 were particularly acute—but never before had the specter of decline hung over Las Vegas as it has the past few years. The unfinished Fontainebleau gives the city's new anxiety physical form; an immense failure, it gives the lie to the idea that Las Vegas's luck will never run out.

And my hometown, Atlantic City, has been knocked to the canvas. Its casinos, facing new competition as never before, have seen their annual gaming revenues fall by more than one-third since 2006. On some level, the Atlantic City I grew up in, where stately old hotels were demolished to make way for casinos that, whatever their aesthetic demerits, represented jobs, opportunity, and the future, shaped how I conceptualized and wrote about gambling. But now, casino gambling does not appear to have given Atlantic City much of a future—only to have borrowed a generation's prosperity.

Still, people are gambling more than ever, and they don't look like they are going to stop anytime soon. Despite all the doubts, I still believe that my original closing line stands, and I'll paraphrase it here: Wherever humanity ventures, they will surely bring a fascination with gambling along for the ride, and they will continue to dream about their next tangle with fortune.

Notes

Credit where credit's due

Prologue: Rainmaker Reborn

xii   Information on the Mystic Massacre and its consequences: Herbert Milton Sylvester. *Indian Wars of New England. Volume 1.* Cleveland: The Arthur H. Clark Company, 1910. Chapter 3, "The Pequod War;" William Hubbard. *A Narrative of the Troubles with the Indians from the first planting thereof in the year 1607 to this present year 1677...to which is added a Discourse about the warre with the Pequod.* Boston: John Foster, 1677. 127; John Mason. A Brief History of the Pequod War. Boston. S. Kneeland and T. Green, 1736. 8-9; Steven T. Katz. "The Pequot War Reconsidered." In Alden T. Vaughan. *New England Encounters: Indians and EuroAmericans ca. 1600-1850.* Boston: Northeastern University Press, 1999. 121-2.

xiii   On the Pequot resurgence: Kim Issac Eisler. *Revenge of the Pequots: How a Small Native American Tribe Created the World's Most Profitable Casino.* New York: Simon and Schuster, 2001. 52, 87.

xiy   Statistics from American Gaming Association. "Gaming Revenue: Current Year Data." Accessed online at: http://www.americangaming.org/industry-resources/research/fact-sheets/gaming-revenue-10-year-trends

Chapter One: The Ridotto Revolution

1   Macaque gambling: Allison N. McCoy and Michael L. Platt. "Risk-sensitive neurons in macaque posterior cingulate cortex." *Nature Neuroscience* 8, 1220 - 1227 (2005).

2   Divination: Florence N. David. *Games, Gods, and Gambling: The Origins and History of Probability and Statistical Ideas from the Earliest Times to the Newtonian Era.* New York: Hafner Publishing Company, 1962. 15; Clifford A Pickover. *Dreaming the Future: The Fantastic Story of Prediction.* Amherst, New York: Prometheus Books, 2001, particularly 133-7.

3   Early astragalus finds: Laszlo Bartosiewicz. "A Systematic Review of Astragalus Finds From Archaeological Sites." *Anteus.* 24. 1997/1998. 37-44, 594.

4   Mesopotamian dice games: R. C. Bell. *Board and Table Games from Many Civilizations.* London: Oxford University Press, 1960. 23; James Christie. *An Inquiry into the Antient Greek Game Supposed to Have Been Invented by*

Palamedes, Antecedent to the Siege of Troy. London: W. Bulmer and Co., 1801.

4   Asian gambling propensity: John A. Price. "Gambling in Traditional Asia." *Anthropoloica.* N.S. Vol 14, N. 2, 1972. 123-5.

4   Chinese gambling: J. M. Roberts, *A Short History of the World.* New York: Oxford University Press, 1997. 69, 74.

5   Ancient cricket fighting: Price, 171.

5   Modern cricket fighting: "HK Police Smash Illegal Insect-Fighting Ring." *Channel News Asia.* September 21, 2004.

5   Hua-Hoey lottery: Stephen M. Stigler. "Casanova, "Bonaparte," and the Loterie de France." 7 (unpublished paper).

5   *Han Shu*: Price, 174.

6   Chinese dominoes: Stewart Culin. Korean games with notes on the corresponding games of China and Japan. Philadelphia: University of Pennsylvania, 1895. 102-3, 114.

6   Additional Chinese games: Price, 176.

6   Other Asian gambling: Price, 169-170.

8   Lansquenet: David Parlett. *The Oxford Guide to Card Games.* Oxford: Oxford University Press, 1990, 76-77.

9   Venetian gambling: Russell T. Barnhart. "Gambling with Giacomo Casanova and Lorenzo Da Ponte in Eighteenth Century Venice—The Ridotto: 1638-1774." In Russell T. Barnhart Papers, University of Nevada Reno Special Collections. Box 14. 2. Cited as Barnhart (Casanova); Jonathan Walker. "Gambling and Venetian Noblemen." *Past and Present.* No. 162. February 1999. 32-33, 77.

10   Basset: Parlett, 77.

10-11   The Ridotto: Barnhart (Casanova),4-5, 13, 16; Maurice Rowdon. *The Fall of Venice.* London: 1970. 45.

12   The genesis of faro: Parlett, 78.

12-3   Lorenzo Da Ponte at the Ridotto: Barnhart (Casanova), 9, 19-20.

13   Casanova at the Ridotto: Barnhart (Casanova), 10, 12.

13   Closure of the Ridotto: Andrieux, 131, Barnhart (Casanova), 20.

14   Spread of casini: Barnhart (Casanova), 4; Andrew Steinmetz. *The Gaming Table: Its Votaries and Victims, in All Times and Countries, Especially in England and in France.* Originally published 1870. Reprint published in Montclair, New Jersey: Patterson Smith, 1969. 70-72.

15   French gambling through Louis XIII: Steinmetz, 75, 84-5.

16   Louis XIV, Mazarin, and gambling: Steinmetz, 87-88; Nancy Mitford. *The Sun King.* New York: Penguin Books, 1994. 64-65.

16   Spread of French gambling: Thomas Kavanagh. *Enlightenment and the Shadows of Chance: The Novel and the Culture of Gambling in Eighteenth-Century France.* Baltimore: the Johns Hopkins University Press, 1993. 32; Steinmetz, 88, 99.

16   French rationales for gambling: Kavanagh, 42, 46.

17   French games: Russell T. Barnhart. "The Invention of Roulette." New

York: Russell T. Barnhart, 1987. 11. Cited as Barnhart 1987; Thomas M. Kavanagh. "The Libertine's Bluff: Cards and Culture in Eighteenth-Century France." *Eighteenth-Century Studies.* V. 33, N. 4. 509. Cited afterwards as Kavanagh, 2000.

17   French gaming hells and spas: Steinmetz, 103-105.
18   French attempts to legalize gambling: Steinmetz, 105-107.
18   The Palais Royale: Russell T. Barnhart. "Gambling in Revolutionary Paris- The Palais Royale: 1789-1838." New York: Russell T. Barnhart, 1990. 2-11. Cited as Barnhart 1990.
19   The origin of roulette: Barnhart 1987, 5-8, 14-20.
20   Napoleon legalizes gambling: Barnhart 1990 12-16.
20   Blackjack: Parlett, 78-81.
21   Continuation of French legal gaming: Steinmetz, 108.

Chapter 2: Seeking the Cure

23   Spa's 16ᵗʰ century emergence: Russell T. Barnhart. *Gamblers of Yesteryear.* Las Vegas: GBC Press, 1983. 53-4.
23   Early attractions at Spa: Barnhart, 58-61.
24   Early gambling at Spa: Barnhart, 79.
24   Opening of the Redoute: Barnhart, 79-80.
24   Horseracing at Spa: Barnhart, 71.
24   Velbruck's resolution of inter-casino tensions: Barnhart, 80-1.
25   The English Club: Barnhart, 81.
25   Fire at the Redoute: Barnhart, 79-80.
25   Scandal at the Redoute: Barnhart, 83.
27   Trente et quarante: Barnhart, 80; Parlett, 78.
27   The French Revolution's impact at Spa: Barnhart, 88-90.
28   The decline of Spa: Barnhart, 90-3.
28   "the ball spins more slowly..." Andrew Steinmetz. *The Gaming Table: Its Votaries and Victims, in All Times and Countries, Especially in England and in France.* Originally published 1870. Reprint published in Montclair, New Jersey: Patterson Smith, 1969. Vol. 1.171-2.
28   Railroads bypass Spa: Barnhart, 90-3.
29   Early years of Baden-Baden: Klaus Fischer. *Faites Votre Jeu: History of the Casino Baden-Baden.* Baden-Baden: Hans Werner Kelch, 1975. 7, 22.
29   The Promenade House opens: Barnhart, 100.
29   Other gambling operations: Fischer, 25.
30   Johann Peter Hebel's praise of Baden-Baden: Fischer, 16.
30   Growing popularity of Baden-Baden: Fischer, 17.
30   Chabert: Barnhart, 100.
30-1 Jacques Benazet: Barnhart, 100-1.
31   End of Parisian gambling (1837): Barnhart, 101-2.
32   Benazet moves to Baden-Baden: Barnhart, 114.
32   Benazet's success at Baden-Baden: Fischer, 44.
32   Old Father Martin: Barnhart, 111-3.

33   Edward Benazet's continued success: Barnhart, 115-6.

33   "all bearing the semblance of gentility…", description of Baden-Baden: Steinmetz, 159-60.

34   Leonie Lablanc: Steinmetz, 168-9.

34-5   If the public were not such simpletons…" Barnhart, 108.

38   Brahms at Baden-Baden: Barnhart, 106-8; Leon Botstein, ed. *The Compleat Brahms: A Guide to the Musical Works of Johannes Brahms.* New York: W. W. Norton and Company, 1999.144; Malcolm McDonald. Brahms. New York: Schirmer Books, 1990. 132.

38   Offenbach and Strauss at Baden-Baden: Barnhart, 106-8.

38-9   Last years of Baden-Baden as a gambling resort: Fischer, 60-1.

39   Countess Kissileff: Barnhart, 145-8.

39   Gogol at Baden-Baden: Barnhart, 104-5.

39   Tolstoy at Baden-Baden: Barnhart, 110.

39-40 Turgenev and Tolstoy: Ivan Turgenev. "Dying Plea to Tolstoy." In John Cournos, ed. *A Treasury of Classic Russian Literature.* New York: Capricorn Books, 1961. 75.

40   Dostoyevski writes The Gambler: Count Corti. *The Wizard of Homburg and Monte Carlo.* London: Thornton Butterworth, Ltd. 1934. 210-11.

41   Dostoyevsky's July 1867 trip to Baden-Baden: Barnhart, 121.

41   "Apart from my own gains…" Fyodor Dostoyevsky, "Meeting with Turgenev." In John Cournos, ed. *A Treasury of Classic Russian Literature.* New York: Capricorn Books, 1961. 48.

41   Dostoyevksy's growing desperation: Cournos, 48.

41   Existing tensions between Dostoyevski and Turgenev: Barnhart, 121-2.

42   Dostoyevsky/Turgenev confrontation: Cournos, 49-50.

42   Dostoyevsky stops gambling: Barnhart, 124.

42   Closing of Rhine spa gambling resorts: Fischer, 22.

43   Development of Weisbaden: "One of Europe's Most Attractive Casinos." Informational brochure in Promotional and Publicity Material: Spielbank Casino, Wiesbaden, Germany. UNLV Special Collections.

44   Weisbaden in 1868: Steinmetz, 207-13.

44   "ghastly creatures…" Steinmetz, 213-5.

44   An edifying sight is this venerable dame…"Steinmetz, 215-7.

45   The Blanc brothers' early years: Corti, 17-26, 30-3.

47   Landgrave Ludwig negotiates with the Blancs: Corti, 38-41.

47   Blanc strikes a deal with Landgrave Phillip: Corti, 42-4.

47   Casino dedication ceremony: Corti, 45-6.

48   Blanc efforts to lure visitors to Homburg: Corti, 45, 47-9.

48   Opening of the permanent casino at Bad Homburg: Corti, 50.

49   Description of Bad Homburg casino: Barnhart, 139; Steinmetz, 180-1.

49   Suicide at Bad Homburg and dealers' nonchalant response: Steinmetz, 188-9.

49   Non-gaming amenities at Bad Homburg: Barnhart, 140.

50   George Augustus Sala's description of Bad Homburg: Barnhart, 153-4.

50 "We are throwing sprats..." Corti, 104-5.

51 Cheating at Bad Homburg and Blanc's countermeasures: Corti, 90-2.

51-2 The Prince of Canino comes to Bad Homburg: Barnhart, 141-2; Corti, 93-9.

52 "Red sometimes wins..." Charles Kingston. *The Romance of Monte Carlo.* London: John Lane, 1925. 36.

52 Blanc's marriage and prosperity: Corti, 100-2.

52-3 Thomas Garcia's wins and Blanc's countermeasures: Corti, 113-4, 118-26.

53-4 The German National Assembly's anti-gambling edict and Blanc's maneuvering: Corti, 63-74.

54 Dostoyevsky on the press's favorable coverage of gambling resorts: Dostoyevsky, 27.

54-5 Prussian consolidation of Rhine states and the end of gambling: Corti, 200-1, 203-4.

56 The end of German gambling: Corti, 204, 248-9; Barnhart, 168.

56 Blanc transitions to Monaco: Corti, 249.

Chapter Three: A Sunny Place for Shady People

57-8 Early history of Monaco: Count Corti. *The Wizard of Homburg and Monte Carlo.* London: Thornton Butterworth, Ltd. 1934. 130-2, 137-8.

58 Eynaud's investigation: Corti, 139.

59 Blanc's doubts about Monaco: Corti, 85, 141.

59-60 Langlois and Aubert's attempts to run a "bathing establishment:" Corti, 142-9.

60 Daval tries his hand at Monaco: Corti, 155-159.

61 Duc de Valmy's company strikes out: Corti, 159-168, 179.

61 Francois Blanc signs a contract with Charles III: Corti, 177-180.

62 Blanc's successes at Monaco: Corti, 182-7, 193-9, 218-9, 225-6; Charles Kingston. *The Romance of Monte Carlo.* London: John Lane, 1925. 16.

63 Blanc's entrance card system's genesis: Corti, 252-3.

63 *London Times* article on Monaco: "Monaco." *New York Times.* April 23, 1873. 4.

64 Blanc's largesse towards the French government: Corti, 259.

64 Blanc's death: "Gambling at Monte Carlo." *New York Times.* September 17, 1877. 2; Corti, 266.

64 Monaco at Blanc's death: Stanley Jackson. *Inside Monte Carlo.* New York: Stein and Day, 1975. 45.

64 Monte Carlo and casino chips: Barnhart. 181; Dale Seymour. *Antique Gambling Chips.* Revised Edition. Palo Alto, California: Past Pleasures, 1998. 7-14, 66-72, 109-120.

66 Marie Blanc's death: Jackson, 48-9.

66 Camille Blanc's improvements at Monte Carlo: Jackson, 49; Graves 1951, 112.

66-7 Monte Carlo's dealer school: Graves, 1951, 113.

67 Expansion of the casino: Barnhart, 183-4.

67-8   *New York Times* criticism of Monte Carlo: "An Italian Gambling Hell." *New York Times*. April 7, 1878. 2.

68-9   Misadventures of a railroad scion, 1882: "An American at Monte Carlo. *New York Times*. December 18, 1882. 3.

69   Queen Victoria and Prince Edward at Monte Carlo: Barnhart, 185-6; Jackson, 53.

69   The lucky churchman's hymns: Adolphe Smith. *Monaco and Monte Carlo*. London: Grant Rirchards, LTD, 1912. 449-455.

70   Monte Carlo superstitions: Smith, 456-662.

70-1   Monte Carlo during and after World War One: Smith, 345, 440-4; Graves 1951, 95, 145.

72   Martingale and Grand Martingale: Darwin Ortiz. *Darwin Ortiz on Casino Gambling: The Complete Guide to Playing and Winning*. New York: Lyle Stuart, 1992. 73, 175-6.

72-3   Labouchere system: Ortiz, 177-8.

73   The d'Alembert system: Ortiz, 179-80.

73   Patience system: Ortiz, 181.

74   Gagnante Marche system: Ortiz, 182.

74-5   Francois Blanc on systems: Graves 151, 61.

75   "Breaking the bank" ritual: Graves 1951, 90.

75-6   Pair of Parisian swindlers: "Their System Didn't Work." *New York Times*, June 26, 1887. 11.

76-7   Jaggers' "system:" Graves 1951, 76-7; Mordaunt Hall. "'Breaking the Bank' Costly to Tourists." *New York Times*. September 2, 1923. XX4.

77-8   Charles Deville Wells: Jackson, 72; Graves 1951, 90-1.

78--9 Lord Rosslyn vs. Sir Maxim: Russell T. Barnhart. Gamblers of Yesteryear. Las Vegas: GBC Press, 1983. 191-4; "Rosslyn Ahead in Gambling Test." *New York Times*. September 28, 1908. C1; "Rosslyn's Defeat Easy." *New York Times*. October 8, 1908. C1; For Maxim's book-length exposition of the falsity of systems, see Hiram S. Maxim. *Monte Carlo: Facts and Fallacies*. London: Grant Richards, 1904.

81   Chemin de fer's spread: Charles Graves. *None But the Rich: The Life and Times of the Greek Syndicate*. London: Cassell, 1963. 1-2.

81-2   French gambling clubs: Eugene Villiod. Russell Barnhart, trans. *The Stealing Machine*. Las Vegas: Gambler's Book Club, 1906. 24, 27, 31, 35, 46.

83   Taxes on French casinos: Charles Graves. The Price of Pleasure. London: Ivor, Nicholson, and Watson, Ltd., 1935. 1-2.

83-4   The Greek Syndicate: Graves 1963, 11-21,. 29, 40; Graves 1951, 27-8.

85   "Never bet on a race horse..." "Famed Gambler Dies in Switzerland at 68." *New York Times*. April 23, 1953. 6.

85   The Deauville casino: Graves 1963, 56-7.

85   Zographos's death and the survival of the Greek Syndicate: Graves 1963, 61-4, 101, 165.

86   Camille Blanc's ouster and death: Jackson, 12, 123-4, 130-1; "Blanc, Who Grew Rich in Monaco, Dies at 81." *New York Times*. December 23, 1927. 19.

86-7 Rene Leon's career at Monte Carlo: Jackson, 132, 140.; Clair Price. "A Roulette Battle Resounds in Europe." *New York Times.* March 4, 1934. SM5.

87 San Remo: Price, 5.

87 France legalizes roulette: Price, 19.

88 Leon leaves Monte Carlo: Jackson, 163.

88 Monte Carlo in the late 1930s and early 1940s: Graves 1935, 4-6.

89 Postwar Monte Carlo: Jackson, 183-4.

89 Aristotle Onassis buys, sells, controlling interest in SBM: Jackson, 228, 244-6.

89 Monte Carlo in the 1970s: Jackson, 252.

89 Monaco gaming revenues: Rachel Billington. "A Promenade in Monte Carlo." *New York Times.* March 13, 1988. SMA24.

Chapter Four: Baiting John Bull

90-1 Early years of Bath: Russell T. Barnhart. *Gamblers of Yesteryear.* Las Vegas: GBC Press, 1983. 10-11; Willard Connely. *Beau Nash: Monarch of Bath and Tunbridge Wells.* London: Werner Laurie, 1955. 22-23.

91-2 Beau Nash's early years: Barnhart, 7-8; Connely, 24.

92 Captain Webster: Connely, 22-23, 27.

93 Nash's redevelopment of Bath: Connely, 28-34; Barnhart, 13-15; Trevor Fawcett. *Bath Entertain'd: Amusements, Recreations, & Gambling at the 18ᵗʰ Century Spa.* Bath: Ruton, 1998. 45-49, 69.

94 Parliamentary acts against gambling: Barnhart, 31.

96 Decline of Beau Nash: Barnhart, 43-47.

96 Decline of Bath: Barnhart, 49-50.

97 Early 18ᵗʰ century London gaming houses: Ashton, 22-24, 58-9.

98 Coffee houses: Nevill. 2-3; A.L. Humphreys. *Crockford's: or The Goddess of Chance in St. James's Street 1828-1844.* 13, 20.

98 Growth of gambling clubs: Nevill, 182-184. Ashton, 90.

99 The Earl of Sandwich: Waddy, 137.

99 Montagu biographer N. A. M. Rodger has cast doubt on the famous story of the sandwich's origin. He believed the legend originated with a passage in a 1765 travel book that relates the story as it is known today, but claims that during that year the earl was serving as a cabinet minister and routinely worked at his desk without pause. It was here, Rodger says, that the sandwich made its debut. But two other sources insist that the sandwich has its origins at the gaming table. Edward Gibbon wrote in 1762 that a number of gentlemen supped on "a bit of cold meat, or a Sandwich" at the Cocoa Tree, and the Beef Steak Club, a gambling fraternity that met at the Shakespeare Tavern, also claimed to have invented the sandwich. Linda Stradley. "What's Cooking America: The History of Sandwiches." Accessed at: http://whatscookingamerica.net/History/SandwichHistory. htm; N. A. M. Rodger. *The Insatiable Earl: A Life of John Montagu, Fourth Earl of Sandwich, 1718-1792.* New York: W.W. Norton and Company,

1994. 76-79.

99   The rules of Almack's: Ashton, 90-91.

99   Public outcry against clubs: Ashton, 83.

100   Low hells: Ashton, 133-36.

100   Sharpers: Andrew Steinmetz. *The Gaming Table: Its Votaries and Victims, in All Times and Countries, Especially in England and in France.* Volume Two. Montclair, New Jersey: Patterson Smith, 1969, 193-194.

100   Lord Chesterfield's playing with sharpers: Barnhart, 27-28.

100   Sharpers as vegetarians: Steinmetz, 32.

100-1   "For this end they studied ..." Steinmetz, 32.

101   Lady Archer and Lady Buckinghamshire: Ashton, 76-82.

101   Increased police harassment of gambling houses: Steinmetz, 200-202.

101   Continued prevalence of social gambling: Ashton, 83.

102   The game of Macao: Steinmetz, 185-186.

102   William Crockford: Humphreys, 39-48; Nevill 190-191.

102-3   Description of Crockford's club: H.T. Waddy. *The Devonshire Club—And Crockford's.* London: Eveleigh, Nash, and Company. 1919. 120-136, 147; Nevill, 191; E. Beresford Chancellor. *Memorials of St. James's Street, Together with the Annals of Almack's.* New York: Brentano's 1922. 164-6.

104   Crockford's retirement and death: Waddy, 137, 143-4; Ashton, 148.

105   "Come and once more let us greet..." Humphreys, 13.

105-6   Whist's evolution: William Pole. *The Evolution of Whist: A Study of the Progressive Changes which the Game Has Passed Through from Its Origin to the Present Time.* London: Longmans, Green, and Company, 1897. 10-19, 26, 35-6; An Amateur. *Whist: Its History of Practice.* London: Bell and Wood, 1843. 18, 27, 29.

106   Early British gaming guides: David Parlett. *The Oxford Guide to Card Games.* Oxford: Oxford University Press, 1990. 55-58.

106-7   Hoyle and his rules: Pole, 41-42, 46, 48-49; Amateur 41; Parlett, 59-60.

107   Whist becomes intellectual: Pole, 73-83.

Chapter Five: Star-Spangled Gamblers

110   Native American games: Stewart Culin. *Games of the North American Indians.* New York: Dover Publications, 1975. 346-9.

111   Noquilpi and his temple: Kathryn Gabriel. *Gambler Way: Indian Gaming in Mythology, History, and Archeology in North America.* Boulder: Johnson Books, 1996. 88-9, 100-1.

112   Chungke: Gabriel, 51.

112   Persistence of Native American gambling: Gabriel, 8-9.

112-3   Montezuma, Cortez, and gambling: Gabriel, 129-31.

113   Gambling and the Ghost Dance: Gabriel, 72-3.

113-4   Colonial Virginia: Walter A. McDougall. *Freedom Just Around the Corner: A New American History 1585-1828.* New York: HarperCollins, 2004. 42-3, 149.

114   Early Virginia gambling: T.H. Breen. "Horses and Gentlemen: The Cul-

tural Significance of Gambling Among the Gentry of Virginia." *The William and Mary Quarterly*, 3rd Series, V. 34, N. 2. (April, 1977). 239, 248; Louis B. Wright and Marion Tinling, eds. The Secret Diary of William Byrd of Westover, 1709-1712. Richmond, Virginia: The Dietz Press, 1941.442.

114-5   Puritan/New England gambling: Emil Oberholzer, Jr. *Delinquent Saints: Disciplinary Action in the Early Congregational Churches of Massachusetts.* New York: Columbia University Press, 1956. 230; Larry Gragg. "Gambling." In James Ciment, ed. *Colonial America: An Encyclopedia of Social, Political, Cultural, and Economic History*. New York: M.E. Sharp, 2006; Bruce C. Daniels. Puritans at Play: Leisure and Recreation in Colonial New England. New York: St. Martin's Press, 1995. 144, 152, 158, 176-81.

116   Penn's charter and the elder Penn's gambling: McDougall, 83-4.

117   Colonial gambling prevalence:"Gambling (1600-1754)." *American Eras*. 8 vols. Gale Research, 1997-1998. Reproduced in History Resource Center. Farmington Hills, Michigan: Gale Group; Chafetz, 16.

118   Howe's anti-gambling edict: General Sir William Howe's Orderly Book. Port Washington, New York: Kennikat Press, 1970. 37.

118   Gambling in the British armies: Chafetz, 30.

119   Washington's gambling: Marvin Kitman. *The Making of the Prefident 1789*. New York: Harper and Row, 1989. 39-42.

119   Washington's anti-gambling edict: Chafetz, 29.

120   Betting on Yellow Fever: Chafetz, 37.

120   Frontier gambling: Chafetz, 44-6.

121   Henry Clay and Daniel Webster's gambling: Chafetz, 48.

121   Andrew Jackson's gambling: Chafetz, 45.

121-2   American Faro: Asbury, 7-9, 15.

123   Elijah Skaggs and the spread of professional faro dealers: Chafetz, 51-4.

124   Gambling in Washington, DC: Asbury, 134; Chafetz, 180.

124-5   Scandal over John Adams' White House billiards table: Edwin A. Miles "President Adams' Billiard Table." *The New England Quarterly*, V. 45, N 1 (March 1972). 31, 36-42.

125   All presidents from Van Buren to Cleveland (minus Hayes) as poker players: Lillard, 17-8.

126   Hall of the Bleeding Heart: Asbury, 141-2, 144-6.

Chapter Six: Wild Cards

128   "Those who live in the midst of democratic fluctuations..." Alexis de Tocqueville. *Democracy in America*. Book 2, Chapter 19. Accessed at: http://www.marxists.org/reference/archive/de-tocqueville/democracy-america/ch31.htm.

128-9   Louisiana's legal gambling: Asbury, 110-2.

129-30 John Davis's gambling house: Asbury, 114-5.

130-1   The genesis of poker: David Parlett. "The History of Poker." Accessed at: http://www.pagat.com/vying/pokerhistory.html.

131-2 The evolution of craps: Barnhart, 23-4, 27-8; Asbury, 46-7; John Scarne. *Scarne on Dice. Eighth Revised Edition.* New York: Crown Publishers, 1980. 19-21.

132 The shell game and bunco: Asbury, 52-6.

133 Gambling in Southern river towns:Chafetz, 55.

133-5 The Vicksburg vigilante hangings: Asbury, 219-24; Chafetz, 56-7.

135 New Orleans continuing gambling: Asbury, 122.

135 Riverboat regulation: Kermit L. Hall. *The Magic Mirror: Law in American History.* New York: Oxford University Press, 1989. 93.

136 Riverboat gamblers: Asbury, 201-2; Chafetz, 74.

136-7 Blacklegs: Asbury, 204-5.

137-8 George Devol's career and recollections: Geroge Devol. *Forty Years a Gambler on the Mississippi.* Cincinatti: Devol and Haines, 1887. 129-30, 148.

139 General Benjamin Butler in New Orleans: Devol, 119-120.

139 Gambling among Union troops: Bell Irvin Wiley. *The Life of Billy Yank: The Common Soldier of the Union.* Baton Rouge: Louisiana State University Press, 2001. 149-50, 250-1.

140 Gambling among Confederate troops: Bell Irvin Wiley. *The Life of Johnny Reb: The Common Soldier of the Confederacy.* Baton Rouge: Louisiana State University Press, 1996. 36-40.

141 Gambling across the lines: Wiley, Johnny Reb, 318-9.

141-2 "The first orders we would receive...": Devol, 117-8.

143 Gambling en route to the goldfields: J. S. Holliday. *The World Rushed In: The California Gold Rush Experience.* New York: Touchstone, 1981. 76, 94, 96, 412.

144 Gambling at the goldfields: Holliday, 355, 364.

144 "Where men are congregated..." Roger D. McGrath. *Gunfighters, Highwaymen, and Vigilantes: Violence on the Frontier.* Berkeley: University of California Press, 1984. 11-2.

144 Typical Western saloon: McGrath, 111.

144 Animal sports and betting: Rodman Wilson Paul and Elliott West. *Mining Frontiers of the Far West, 1848-1880.* Albuquerque: University of New Mexico Press, 2001. 214-5.

145 San Francisco gambling halls: Asbury, 53, 312-5.

146 Chinese gambling in San Francisco: John Phillip Quinn. *Fools of Fortune, or, Gambling and Gamblers.* Chicago: G. L. Howe & Co., 1890 449-50.

146 Revenue of San Francisco gambling houses: Asbury, 317.

146 California gambling prohibitions: Roger Dunstan. History of Gambling in California. Sacramento: California State Library, 1997. Accessed at: http://www.library.ca.gov/CRB/97/03/crb97003.html#toc.

147 Gambling in Western cities: Asbury, 328-33, 335, 341.

147 Gambling in Santa Fe and Kansas City: Asbury, 340.

147-8 Gambling in cowtowns: Chafetz, 146.

148 "He was too much of a gambler..." Bret Harte. "The Outcasts of Poker

Flat." In *9 Sketches.* West Virginia: West Virginia Pulp and Paper Company, 1967. 36.

148-9 Wild Bill Hickok: Robert K. DeArment. *Knights of the Green Cloth: The Saga of the Frontier Gamblers.* Norman: University of Oklahoma Press, 1982. 333-6; Chafetz, 156; Bill Kelly. *Gamblers of the Old West: Gambling Men and Women of the 1800s, How They Lived—How They Died.* Las Vegas: B & F Enterprises, 1995. 18-20.

149-50 Doc Holliday: Kelly, 80-1, 84-5.

150 Bat Masterson: Kelly, 113-8.

151 Dona Maria Gertrudis Barcelo (La Tules): DeArment, 229-237.

151 Belle Siddons (Lurline Monte Verde): Kelly, 31-6.

152 Eleanor DuMont: DeArment, 240-1, Chafetz, 172-5.

152-3 Poker Alice: DeArment, 269-76.

Chapter Seven: Fools of Fortune

154-5 Early New York gambling: Herbert Asbury. *Sucker's Progress: An Informal History of Gambling in America from the Colonies to Canfield.* Montclair, NJ: Patterson Smith, 1969. 156-7.

155-6 Wolf-traps: Asbury, 185-7, 272-4.

156 Second-class houses: Asbury, 176-7.

157 Brace rooms: Asbury, 181-4.

158: At these dens..." Asbury, 175-6.

158 Horace Greeley's estimates of New York gambling losses: Asbury, 162.

158 New York's first class houses: Asbury, 160-1.

159 New York Association for the Suppression of Gambling statistics on gambling: Asbury, 163.

159-60 Reuben Parsons: Asbury, 167-8.

161 Henry Colton: Henry Chafetz. *Play the Devil: A History of Gambling in the United States from 1492 to 1955.* New York: Bonanza Books, 1960. 236.

161 Patrick Herne: Chafetz, 231-4.

161-2 Other noted New York gambling operators: Chafetz, 233-9.

162 John Morrissey's early years: Asbury, 360-2.

164-5 Morrissey's later career: Asbury, 367-88.

165-6 Rondo: Edmund Hoyle. *Hoyle's Games: Autograph Edition. Revised, Enlarged, and Brought up to Date.* New York: A. L. Burt Company, 1907. 334.

166 Keno: Hoyle, 247-8

166 Cincinatti gambling: Chafetz, 209-10.

166-7 Midwestern gambling: Chafetz, 205.

167 Professional gamblers in the Midwest: Chafetz, 206.

167-8 Milwaukee gambling: Asbury, 264-6.

168 Early Chicago gambling: Asbury, 286-91.

170 Wat Cameron: Asbury, 291.

170-1 George Trussell: Asbury, 293-5.

171-2 Louis Cohn and the Chicago fire: Chafetz, 417.

172 Mike MacDonald: Asbury, 295-7.

172   "The town was literally handed over…" John Philip Quinn. *Fools of For-tune*. Chicago: G. I. Howe and Company, 1890. 402.

172   The Store: Asbury, 298-9.

173   MacDonald's decline: Asbury, 300-5.

174   "They wore every variety of dress…" Edgar Allen Poe. "The Man of the Crowd." in *The Annotated Tales of Edgar Allen Poe*. New York: Doubleday and Company, 1981. 189.

174-5   Fakirs and their games:Quinn, 284-891.

175   Wheel of fortune odds: Robert C. Hannum and Anthony N. Cabot. *Practical Casino Math. Second Edition*. Reno: Institute for the Study of Gambling and Commercial Gaming, 2005. 117.

175-8   Honest John Kelly's life: Julien J. Prosauker. *Suckers All! The Life of Honest John Kelly as Told from His Diaries*. New York: The Macaulay Company, 1934. 23-53; 93-179; 182-199, 200-91; 317-8.

178   John Phillip Quinn: John Philip Quinn. *Gambling and Gambling Devices*. Las Vegas: GBC Press (originally copyright John Philip Quinn, 1913). 27-8.

178-9   Gambling devices: Quinn 1913, 136, 145-6.

179-80 Punchboards: Quinn 1913, 226-30.

Chapter Eight: Wise Guys and One-Armed Bandits

181   Early Saratoga: Jon Sterngass. *First Resorts: Pursuing Pleasure at Saratoga Springs, Newport, and Coney Island*. Baltimore: Johns Hopkins Press, 2001. 150.

182   Saratoga racetrack and the Travers Stakes: Sterngass, 148.

182   Morrissey's role in Saratoga race betting: Sterngass, 149.

182   Morrisey's clubhouse: Asbury, 383-4.

183   Morrisey successful at Saratoga: Asbury, 387.

183   Johnny Chamberlain, Long Branch, and Monmouth Park: Asbury, 393-6.

183-4   Canfield's early years: Asbury, 419-27.

184   Canfield's style: Asbury, 420-01.

185   Canfield at Saratoga: Asbury, 439-40.

185   Canfield's administration of his gambling clubs: Asbury, 444-5.

185-6   "Bet a Million" Gates: Asbury, 448-50.

186   Canfield's death and legacy: Asbury, 466-8.

187   Gambling machines: Quinn 1913, 188-197, 219.

187   Early slot machines: Marshall Fey. *Slot Machines: A Pictorial History of the First 100 Years. Fourth Edition*. Reno: Liberty Belle Books, 1994. 13-21.

188   Charles Fey and the Liberty Bell: Fey, 40-2, 53-4.

189   Slot machines dispensing gum: Fey, 106.

189   Frank Costello's slot empire: Fey, 104-5.

190   Mark H. Haller. "The Changing Structure of American Gambling in the Twentieth Century." In Eric H. Monkkonen, ed. *Crime and Justice in American History. Volume 8: Prostitution, Drugs, and Organized Crime*. Part I. Munich: K.G. Saur, 1992. 318.

190-1   New York Gambling Commission: "This City's Crying Shame." *New York Times.* March 9, 1900. 1.

191   Chicago gambling syndicate: John Phillip Quinn. *Fools of Fortune, or, Gambling and Gamblers.* Chicago: G. L. Howe & Co., 1890. 405.

191   Minneapolis gambling syndicate: Asbury, 270.

191   San Bernardino: Noah Sarlat, ed. *America's Cities of Sin.* New York: Lion Books, 1950. 63-4.

192   Bergen County resorts: Noah Sarlat, ed. *Sintown USA.* New York: Lion Books, 1952. 123-7.

193   Palm Beach: Henry Chafetz. *Play the Devil: A History of Gambling in the United States from 1492 to 1955.* New York: Bonanza Books, 1960. 409-414.

193   Biloxi: Deanne Nuwer and Greg O'Brien. "Gambling: Mississippi's Oldest Pastime." In Denise Von Hermann, ed. *Resorting to Casinos: How the Mississippi Casino Resort Industry Was Made.* Jackson: University of Mississippi Press, 2005. 14-32.

194   Hot Springs, Arkansas: Hank Messick and Burt Goldblatt. *The Only Game in Town: An Illustrated History of Gambling.* New York: Thomas Y. Crowell Company, 1976. 68, 70.

194   Newport, Kentucky: David Wecker. "Before there was Vegas, there was Newport." *Cincinnati Post.* September 9, 2004.

194:    "A never to-be-forgotten chapter..."Advertisement, *New York Times,* April 15, 1951. P 4XX.

195   Cuban revolution and the closure of casinos: "Batista and Regime Flee Cuba; Castro Moving to Take Power; Mobs Riot and Loot in Havana." *New York Times,* January 1, 1959; "Havana's Last Casino Closed." *New York Times,* September 30, 1961.

196   Agua Caliente (Mexico) casino: Messick, 115-6.

196   Montreal gambling: Sarlat 1950, 107.

Chapter Nine: Hard to Resist

197   "Of all the seductive vices extant..." John B. Reid and Ronald M. James, eds. *Uncovering Nevada's Past: A Primary Source History of the Silver State.* Reno: University of Nevada Press, 2004. 66.

197   Early Nevada tolerance, prohibition of gambling: Barbara and Myrick Land. *A Short History of Reno.* Reno: University of Nevada Press, 1995. 33; Eric Moody. *The Early Years of Gambling in Nevada, 1931-1945.* Reno: University of Nevada. Doctoral dissertation. 1997. 10-11.

198   1869 legalization of gambling: Moody, 11-2.

198   1871, 1875 amendments to gaming law: Moody, 14-5.

198-9   1877, 1903, and 1905 amendments to gaming law: Moody, 16-9.

199   1909 prohibition of gambling: Moody, 20-1.

199   Permitted gambling after 1909: Moody, 22-31.

200   Boxing in early 20th century Nevada: Phillip J. Earl. *This is Nevada.* Reno: Nevada Historical Society, 1986. 178-9.

200 McKay and Graham: Moody, 180-1.
201 Failure of gambling decriminalization in the 1920s: Moody, 32-34, Moody, 51-2.
202 Graham and McKay take advantage of legal gaming: Moody, 174.
203 The game of pan: Murray M. Sheldon. *Pan (Panginguie): Rules of Play and How to Win*. Miami Beach: Pan Book Publishers, 1969. 15-6.
203 Graham and McKay's legal struggles and imprisonment: Moody, 184.
204 The Palace Club: Moody, 186-88.
204 African-American and Asian casino entrepreneurs in 1930s Reno: Moody, 234-7.
204-5 Bingo (tango): Moody, 188.
205 Keno: Moody, 189-90.
205-6 Harold's Club: Land and Land, 87-91; Moody, 191, 193, 195.
206-8 Harrah's Land and Land, 94-6; Moody, 215-217; Mando Rueda Oral History Interview.
208-9 Other Reno casinos: Moody, 197-9, 204-6.
209 Slot routes: Moody, 113-5.
210 Reno redline: Land and Land, 100-2.
210 The Cal-Neva: Moody, 272-4.
210-1 The Commercial Hotel: Moody, 280, 420.
212 Las Vegas gambling hall licenses: Las Vegas City Commission Minutes. 156-7, 162-3, 183.
213 J. Kell Houssells: Moody, 258.
213 Women in early Las Vegas gambling: Moody, 105, 126-7, 140-1; Thomas "Taj" Ainlay and Judy Dixon Gabaldon. *Las Vegas: The Fabulous First Century*. Charleston: Arcadia Publishing, 2003. 49-51; Moody, 105, 126-7.
214 Las Vegas keno: Moody, 129-31.
214 African-Americans and early Las Vegas gambling: Moody, 269.
215 Nevada legalizes pool rooms: Moody, 293.
216-7 Former illegal gambling operators in Las Vegas: Moody, 263-5, 296-9.

Chapter Ten: A Place in the Sun

218-9 Early evolution of casino resorts: David G. Schwartz. *Suburban Xanadu: The Casino Resort on the Las Vegas Strip and Beyond*. New York: Routledge, 2003, particularly chapter 2.
220 Nevada Biltmore: Moody, 389-90.
220-1 The Last Frontier: William Moore. Oral History. Elizabeth Nelson Patrick, interviewer. Reno: University of Nevada Oral History Project, 1981. 5, 13..
222-4 Billy Wilkerson and the Flamingo: W. R. Wilkerson III. *The Man Who Invented Las Vegas*. Los Angeles: Ciro's Books, 2000. 98, 104, 110-1, 166-7, 225-6.
224-5 The Mayfield Road Gang: Wallace Turner. *Gamblers' Money: The New Force in American Life*. Boston: Houghton Mifflin Company, 1965. 288.
226-7 Evolution of gambling syndicates: Mark H. Haller. "The Changing Struc-

ture of American Gambling in the Twentieth Century." In Eric H. Monk-konen, ed. *Crime and Justice in American History. Volume 8: Prostitution, Drugs, and Organized Crime. Part I.* Munich: K.G. Saur, 1992. 315-316.

232   Commercial gaming overtaking mining as Nevada's leading revenue source: Moody, 459.

233   Tax Commission role in collecting gaming taxes: Moody, 446-8.

233   Nevada's gaming regulatory system: A. L. Higgenbotham. *Legalized Gambling in Nevada: Its History, Economics, and Control.* Carson City: Nevada Gaming Commission, 1971. 11.

235-6 "Money moves the world..." Robert Thomas King. *Fighting Back: A Life in the Struggle for Civil Rights.* From oral history interviews with Dr. James B. McMillan; conducted by Gary E. Elliott; a narrative interpretation by R.T. King. Reno: University of Nevada Oral History Program, 1977. 98.

236-7 John Scarne's early years: John Scarne. *The Odds Against Me.* New York: Simon and Schuster, 1966. 9.

237   Scarne during World War II: John Desmond. "Help for G.I. Suckers." *New York Times.* October 10, 1943. SM14.

237   Scarne's later years: Joan Cook. "John Scarne, Gambling Expert." *New York Times.* July 9, 1985. B6.

237-9 Nick Dandalos: "Nick the Greek Arrested." *New York Times.* June 2, 1929. 22; Gladwin Hill. "Why They Gamble: A Las Vegas Survey." *New York Times.* August 25, 1957. 60; "Nick the Greek is Dead on Coast.' *New York Times.* December 27, 1966. 35.

240-1 Edward Thorp and card-counting: Edward O. Thorp. *Beat the Dealer: A Winning Strategy for the Game of Twenty-One.* New York: Blaisdell Publishing, 1962. 5-6, 15-7, 78.

241-2 Ken Uston and team play: Ken Uston with Roger Rapoport. *The Big Player: How a Team of Blackjack Players Made a Million Dollars.* New York: Holt, Rhinehart, and Watson, 1977. 76-10.

242   The MIT team: Ben Mezrich. *Bringing Down the House: The Inside Story of Six M.I.T. Students Who Took Vegas for Millions.* New York: Free Press, 2002.

Chapter Eleven: The Sky's the Limit

243-4 Jay Sarno and Caesars Palace: Jack Sheehan. *Players: The Men Who Made Las Vegas.* Reno: University of Nevada Press, 1997. 92-5; George Stamos, Jr. "Caesars Palace." *Las Vegas Sun Magazine.* October 14, 1979. 92-6.

244   Tanya the Elephant and Circus Circus employees: Interview with Joyce Marshall.

245   Sarno's personal habits: Sheehan, 97-8.

245-6 Circus Circus after Sarno, his plans for the Grandissimo: Sheehan, 99-100.

246-8 Howard Hughes in Las Vegas: Omar V. Garrison. *Howard Hughes in Las Vegas.* New York: Lyle Stuart, 1970. 47-50; "Mark on Nevada by Hughes Staggering." *Las Vegas Review-Journal,* April 6, 1976; Robert Maheu and

Richard Hack. Ne*xt to Hughes: Behind the Power and Tragic Downfall of Howard Hughes by his Closest Advisor*. New York: HarperCollins, 1992. 198-9; "Mark on Nevada by Hughes Staggering." *Las Vegas Review-Journal*, April 6, 1976.

248   "A freak, or amusement-park category..." Michael Drosnin. *Citizen Hughes*. New York: Holt, Rinehart, and Winston, 1985. 107.

248-9   Benny Binion: A.D. Hopkins. "Benny Binion: He Who Has the Gold Makes the Rules." in Sheehan, *Players*, 55-6.

249   William Lee Bergstrom: *Weekly Variety*, February 20, 1985.

249   Binion's legal troubles: Hopkins, 54-60.

250   Though in his memoirs Moss claimed the contest took place at the Horseshoe, Binion did not open that casino until 1951. Either the game was at the Westerner, which Binion owned at the time, or Moss misremembered the year.

250   "Mr. Moss, I have to let you go..." A. Alvarez. *The Biggest Game in Town*. Boston: Houghton Mifflin, 1983. 17-24.

250-1   Origins of the World Series of Poker: Crandell Addington, "The History of No-Limit Texas Hold'em," in Doyle Brunson, ed. *Super System 2: A Course in Power Poker*. New York: Cardoza Publishing, 2005. 78-80.

252   Origins of Texas Hold'em: Personal communication, Crandell Addington.

252   Texas Hold'em: Oswald Jacoby. *Oswald Jacoby on Poker*. Garden City, New York: Dolphin Books, 73-77; Hopkins, 61-2.

253-4   Steve Wynn and the Golden Nugget: Mark Seal. "Steve Wynn: King of Wow!" In Sheehan, *Players*, 174-7.

254   Jackie Gaughan: Bill Moody with A.D. Hopkins. "Jackie Gaughan: Keeping the Faith on Fremont Street." In Sheehan, *Players*, 123-6, 129-31.

254-5   Sam Boyd and Boyd Gaming: Jack Sheehan. "Sam Boyd's Quiet Legacy." In Sheehan, *Players*, 104-18.

256   Ernest Primm: Land and Land, 113.

258   Del E. Webb and corporate ownership of Nevada casinos: David G. Schwartz. *Suburban Xanadu: The Casino Resort on the Las Vegas Strip and Beyond*. New York: Routledge, 2003. 105-6.

259   Corporate Gaming Acts: Lionel Sawyer & Collins. Nevada Gaming Law. Las Vegas: Lionel Sawyer & Collins, 1991. 81-3.

259-60 Alex Shoofey and the Flamingo. Alex Shoofey. Oral History Interview. Las Vegas: University of Nevada Las Vegas Oral History Program, 2003. 35-8.

260   The International: Full-page advertisement. *Las Vegas Now*, July 1970; Schwartz, 152.

Chapter Twelve: America's Playground...Again

262-3   Nucky Johnson's vice empire: Jonathan Van Meter. T*he Last Good Time: Skinny D'Amato, the Notorious 500 Club, and the Rise and Fall of Atlantic City*. New York: Crown Publishers, 2003. 40, 50, 60-1.

264   Atlantic City post-Nucky: Van Meter, 109-110.

263-4　Early casino lobbying efforts in Atlantic City: Ed Davis. *Atlantic City Diary: A Century of Memories, 1880-1985*. McKee City, New Jersey: Atlantic Sunrise Publishing Company, 1980. 113.; Van Meter, 230-1.

264　Failure of 1974 New Jersey casino referendum: John Alcamo. *Atlantic City: Behind the Tables*. Grand Rapids, Michigan: Gollehon, 1991. 12-3.

265　Success of 1976 casino referendum: Alcamo, 17-9.

265:　Reaction to referendum: Donald Janson. "Election's Spin of a Wheel Elates the Faded Resort of Atlantic City," *New York Times*, November 4, 1976. 43.

265　"Keep your filthy hands off Atlantic City …"Alcamo, 35.

266　Resorts International History: http://www.fundinguniverse.com/company-histories/Resorts-International-Inc-Company-History.html

266　Nevada's regulatory reaction to New Jersey legalization: Robert D. Faiss and Gregory R. Gemignani. "Nevada Gaming Statutes: Their Evolution and History," Occasional Paper Series 10. Las Vegas: Center for Gaming Research, University Libraries, University of Nevada, Las Vegas, 2011. 5.

266　Resorts application fee: Donald Janson. "Jersey Expects to Charge $550,000 to Investigate a Casino Applicant." *New York Times*. January 11, 1978. B21.

266　Resorts $16 million in loans: Donald Janson. "A Casino Operator Obtains Financing." *New York Times*. January 12, 1978. B21.

267　Temporary licenses: Martin Waldron. "Byrne Working on Temporary Plan To Open First Casino By Summer." *New York Times*, March 3, 1978. B16.

267　Rooms booked: "First Atlantic City Casino Hotel Booked Solid Through Labor Day." *New York Times*, May 4, 1978. B23.

267　Resorts International's licensure: Donald Janson. "Gambling Board Gives a Go-Ahead To Open first Atlantic City Casino." *New York Times*, May 16, 1978. 73.

267-8　Atlantic City's opening bet: Alcamo, 40.

269　Holdings of Caesars World: Caesars World, Inc. Annual Report, 1973.

269　Traymore Hotel site: Caesars World, Inc. Annual Report, 1974.

269　Caesars financing plans: David G. Schwartz. "Hail Caesars." *Casino Connection*, V.6 N. 8. August 2009.

269-70　Planned Boardwalk Regency opening: Caesars World, Inc. Annual Report, 1979.

270　Malnik/Cohen connection: Donald Janson. "2nd Casino in Jersey Accepts Strictures." *New York Times*, June 3, 1979. 45.

270　Caesars opens: David G. Schwartz. "Hail Caesars." *Casino Connection*, V.6 N. 8. August 2009.

270　Perlmans' departure: Schwartz, "Hail Caesars." ; David G. Schwartz. "Mothballing the Mob." *Vegas Seven*, July 27, 2011.

270　Caesars Atlantic City growth: Schwartz. "Hail Caesars."

271　Resorts International's daily profits: "2 Casinos Report Winnings for July," *New York Times*, August 7, 1979. D3.

271-2 The Marlborough Blenheim/Bally's Park Place: David G. Schwartz. "Castle in the Sand: The Marlborough-Blenheim and its place in Atlantic City history." *Casino Connection*. V. 2 n. 2, February 2005.

272: Bally's opening and growth: Schwartz, "Castle in the Sand."

272 New Jersey casino regulations: New Jersey Casino Control Commission.1979Annual Report. Trenton: Casino Control Commission,1979. 8.

273 Ramada Inns: David G. Schwartz. "Empire Builders." *Casino Connection*, V 6 N 12. December 2009.

274 Development and opening of the Tropicana: Schwartz, "Empire Builders."

275 1984 Atlantic City statistics: New Jersey Casino Control Commission.1984Annual Report. Trenton: Casino Control Commission,1984. 17.

275 Harrah's Marina revenues: Keith H. Hammonds. "Holiday Inns Scramble." *New York Times*, April 22, 1984. F6.

276 Prime rate: http://www.infoplease.com/ipa/A0908373.html

276-7 Development of Harrah's Trump Plaza: David G. Schwartz. "Plaza Suite: History of Trump Plaza." Casino Connection. V. 7 N. 2. February 2010.

278 Hilton denied license: Donald Janson. "Hilton Rejected for License To Operate a Jersey Casino." *New York Times*, March 1, 1985. B2.

278 Trump empire grows: David G. Schwartz. "Plaza Suite: History of Trump Plaza." *Casino Connection*. V. 7 N. 2. February 2010.

280 Plans for Atlantic City: "Atlantic City to be transformed by 2012." Associated Press via MSNBC.com, November 20, 2007.

Chapter Thirteen: The Burger King Revolution

282 "has eliminated organized crime…" National Gambling Impact Study Commission. Final Report. Washington, DC: Government Printing Office, 1999, 3-1.

282-3 Creation of Gaming Control Board, Black Book: David G. Schwartz. *Suburban Xanadu: The Casino Resort on the Las Vegas Strip and Beyond*. New York: Routledge, 2003. 137.

283 Generational changes in organized crime: Daniel Bell. "Crime as an American Way of Life." In Nikos Passas, ed. *Organized Crime*. Brookfield, VT: Dartmouth Publishing Company, 1995. 131-154.

284 Table of state gaming revenues at: http://gaming.unlv.edu/abstract/1967-71 percent20P91.jpg

284 Rising cost of casino construction: Schwartz. *Suburban Xanadu*, 152-4.

287 Cohen, Lansburgh convictions:"Vegas Hotelman Pleads Guilty in Skimming." *Los Angeles Times*, February 1, 1973. P. 26.

288 Caesars Palace raid: Gene Blake. "U.S. Seized $1.5 Million in Las Vegas Raid," *Los Angeles Times*, December 15, 1970. 3.

289 Resorts International revenues: 1978 New Jersey Casino Control Commission Annual Report.

290   Surging Atlantic City: "Casinos in NJ Will Surpass LV," *Las Vegas Sun*, May 22, 1978. 1; 1979, 1980, 1982, 1985 New Jersey Casino Control Commission Annual Reports.

290   1985 Las Vegas Strip revenues: 1985 Nevada Gaming Abstract.

290   Las Vegas fears about Atlantic City: Kim Foltz with David T. Friendly. "The Bad Luck in Las Vegas." *Newsweek*, November 14, 1983. 94.; http:// gaming.unlv.edu/abstract/ac_annual.html.

290   *Las Vegas Sun* coverage of Atlantic City: "Jersey Voters Okay Casino Gambling," *Las Vegas Sun*, November 3, 1976. 1.

291   Las Vegas anxieties: Penny Levin. "LV's Unruffled by NJ Casinos," *Las Vegas Sun*, November 4, 1976. 1.

291   Hank Greenspun's reaction to Atlantic City: Wade Cavanaugh. "Mob Will Fleece Jersey: Publisher," *Las Vegas Sun*, May 27, 1978. 1.

291   Blackjack comparisons: "Las Vegas' Blackjack Rules Easier on Bettor than NJ's," *Las Vegas Sun*, May 31, 1978. 1.

291   "God love 'em…" A.D. Hopkins. "Vegans Don't Fear New Jersey," *Valley Times*, November 4, 1978. A 2.

292   "Not an island unto itself," Thomas F. Cargill. "Is the Nevada Economy Recession Proof?" Paper No. 79-4. Reno: Bureau of Business and Economic Research, 1979. 2.

292   Declining visitation: "Historical Las Vegas Visitor Statistics." Las Vegas Visitors and Convention Authority. LVCVA.com.

293   Rising bad debts: Iver Peterson. "While Atlantic City Rolls On, Las Vegas Comes Up Losing," *New York Times*, October 21, 1984. E2.

293   Las Vegas pessimism: "Vegas revival wears a blue collar," *Chicago Tribune*, December 5, 1985.

293   MGM Grand fire: Jane Anne Morrison. "In Depth: MGM Grand Hotel Fire: 25 Years Later: Disaster Didn't Have to Be," *Las Vegas Review-Journal*, November 20, 2005.

294   *Boston Globe Magazine* article: Connie Paige. "Can Las Vegas Beat the Odds?" *The Boston Globe Magazine*, July 25, 1982. 8.

294   Recession impact survey: "Nevada Hotel/Casino Industry Recession Impact Survey." Summer 1980. Laventhol and Horwath. 3.

294   "Now we are into mass marketing…" Al Martinez. "The New Las Vegas: A Bet on Burgers," *Los Angeles Times*, March 31, 1984.

295-6 Riviera's Burger King saga: Al Martinez. "The New Las Vegas: A Bet on Burgers," *Los Angeles Times*, March 31, 1984.

296   Silver's rationale for Burger King: Personal communication, Jeffery Silver, March 10, 2009.

296   "We're targeting Middle America:" Nicholas D. Kristof. "Strategy Part of Comeback," *New York Times*, November 28, 195. D1.

296   Development of funbooks: Bill Moody with A.D. Hopkins. "Jackie Gaughan: Keeping the Faith on Fremont Street." In Jack Sheehan, *The Players*, 130.

297   "Vegas has changed:" Iver Peterson. "While Atlantic City Rolls On, Las

Vegas Comes Up Losing," *New York Times,* October 21, 1984. E2.

297   Marv Leavitt quote: Nicholas D. Kristof. "Strategy Part of Comeback," *New York Times,* November 28, 195. D1.

297   Nevada Gaming Revenue Reports, 1983-7.

298   Changes at Circus Circus: Circus Circus Enterprises Annual Report for the Year Ended January 31, 1984.

298   Shift from tables to slots: Nevada State Gaming Control Board Gaming Revenue Analysis, 1983-1989.

299   Dan Lee quote: Kathy Rebello. "City of Glitter Rolls Dice for Middle Class," *USA Today,* January 15, 1986. 1.

299   Slots-A-Fun, Silver City purchases: Circus Circus Enterprises Annual Report for the Year Ended January 31, 1989.

299   Circus Circus eschews high rollers: Kathy Rebello. "City of Glitter Rolls Dice for Middle Class," *USA Today,* January 15, 1986. 1.

299   Circus Circus growth: Circus Circus Enterprises Annual Report for the Year Ended January 31, 1984; Circus Circus Enterprises Annual Report for the Year Ended January 31, 1989.

299   "Basically, we are mass merchandisers:" Nicholas D. Kristof. "Strategy Part of Comeback," *New York Times,* November 28, 195. D1.

300   "For the first time…" and subsequent quotes: Kathy Rebello. "City of Glitter Rolls Dice for Middle Class," *USA Today,* January 15, 1986. 1.

301   Glenn Schaeffer quote: "Atlantic City in a stall as Las Vegas Expands," *USA Today,* April 5, 1985. 6B.

301   Paul Rubeli quote: Kathy Rebello. "City of Glitter Rolls Dice for Middle Class," *USA Today,* January 15, 1986. 1.

301   Growing room inventory: "Historical Las Vegas Visitor Statisics." Las Vegas Visitors and Convention Authority. LVCVA.com.

301   Circus Circus RV park: Circus Circus Enterprises Annual Report for the Year Ended January 31, 1984.

Chapter Fourteen: Runaway American Dream

304   1924 Bureau of Indian Affairs recognition of tribal gaming: S. Rep No. 99-493. 3.

304   "It's more than beads…" Jennings Parrott. "Bingo Name of the Game in Indian War." *Los Angeles Times.* July 14, 1981. OC2.

305   Yaqui high-stakes bingo: William E. Schmidt. "Bingo Boom Brings Tribes Profit and Conflict." *New York Times.* March 29, 1983. A1.

305   Indian high-stakes bingo: "Cherokee Bingo Session Attracts Thousands." *New York Times.* July 3, 1983. 14; "Big-Stakes Bingo Brings the Into Oklahoma by the Busload." *New York Times.* December 27, 1984. A1.

305-6   Cabazon decision: U.S. Supreme Court. California v. Cabazon Band of Mission Indians, 480 U.S. 202 (1987). Accessed online at http://caselaw.lp.findlaw.com.

306   Reagan Administration encouragement of Indian gaming: S. Rep No. 99-493, 5.

306-7 Congressional legislation on Indian gaming: Senate Report 100-446. "Indian Gaming Regulatory Act." Cited in *The Indian Gaming Regulatory Act, Annotated.* Washington, DC: Hobbs Straus, Dean, and Wilder, 1989. A-3. Hereafter cited as IGRA Annotated.

307 The first Indian casino: Howard Blum. "In Garage Casino, Sky Is a $5 Limit." *New York Times.* February 26, 1984. 24.

307-8 Mashantucket Pequot struggle for recognition and gaming enterprises: Kim Issac Eisler. *Revenge of the Pequots: How a Small Native American Tribe Created the World's Most Profitable Casino.* New York: Simon and Schuster, 2001. 51-60, 106-7; Richard D. Lyons. "Pequots Adding New Venture to Enterprises." *New York Times.* January 26, 1986. CN1; Dirk Johnson. "Tribe's Latest Enterprise: Bingo." *New York Times.* July 12, 1986. 29.

308 The opening of Foxwoods: Mark H. Spevack. "A User's Guide to Foxwoods Casino." *New York Times.* June 21, 1992. CN10.

309 Foxwoods statistics: Peter Passells. "Foxwoods, a Casino Success Story." *New York Times.* August 8, 1994. D1.

310 Spread of Indian gaming: Nina Munk. "Two-Armed Bandits." *Forbes.* May 22, 1995. 151-4.

310 Proposition 5 and California tribal gaming: David J. Valley with Diana Lindsay. *Jackpot Trail: Indian Gaming in Southern California.* San Diego: Sunbelt Publications, 2003. 26-7.

312 Efforts to legalize Iowa riverboats: Bernard Goldstein with William Petre. *Navigating the Century: A Personal Account of Alter Company's First Hundred Years.* Chantilly, Virginia: The History Factory, 1998. 131-5.

312 Riverboat gambling begins in Iowa: Goldstein, 140.

313 Iowa riverboats move to Mississippi: Goldstein, 153-4.

315 Success of riverboat casinos: Ronald Smothers. "With Casino, the Poor See a Change in Luck." *New York Times.* December 22, 1992. A18.

315 "With a live boy or a dead girl." http://www.cnn.com/2000/ALLPOLITICS/stories/05/10/edwards5_10.a.tm/; for a book-length treatment of the Louisiana scandals see Tyler Bridges. *Bad Bet on the Bayou: The Rise of Gaming in Louisiana and the Fall of Governor Edwin Edwards.* New York: Farrar, Straus, and Giroux, 2001.

315 Edwin Edwards convicted of casino corruption: George Loper. "Louisiana Politics: Is Edwin Edwards Running out of Luck?" January 2000. Accessed online at: http://www.loper.org/~george/archives/2000/Jan/60.html

316-7 Deadwood, South Dakota casinos: Geoffrey Perret. "The Town That Took a Chance." *American Heritage.* V. 56 N. 2 (May 2005). 54.

318 Detroit casinos: Evans, 62.

Chapter Fifteen: A Clockwork Volcano

321 Bally Manufacturing: Robert N. Geddes. *Slot Machines on Parade.* Long Beach: The Mead Company, 1980. 167, 190-1; Basil Nestor. "The 10 Most

Influential People in the History of Slots."

321   Raven Electronics: Richard M. Bueschel. *Lemons, Cherries, and Bell-Fruit-Gum.* Denver: Royal Bell Books, 1995. 280-2.

323   Steve Wynn's first plans on the Strip: Robert Metz. "Marketplace." *New York Times.* February 3, 1981. D8.

323   1987 plans for Mirage: "Golden Nugget's Leader Hailed for Sale Move." *New York Times.* January 20, 1987. D2.

324   Success of The Mirage: Mark Seal. "Steve Wynn: King of Wow!" In Sheehan, *Players,* 1 170; Anne Raver. "Fooling with Nature." *New York Times.* July 11, 1993. V5.

329   "Granddaddy of all miniature golf castles" Alan Hess. *Viva Las Vegas: After Hours Architecture.* San Francisco: Chronicle Books, 1993. 105-7.

330   Glenn Schaefer and Mandalay Resort Group: Dave Berns, "The Ringmaster." *Las Vegas Review-Journal.* February 28, 1999.

331-2   Steve Wynn's sale of Mirage Resorts: David Strow. "Casino Observers Speculate on Wynn's Future." *Las Vegas Sun.* March 7, 2000.

335   Sheldon Adelson's wealth: http://www.forbes.com/profile/sheldon-adelson/

335-6   High rollers in Vegas: Brett Pulley. "Casinos Paying Top Dollar to Coddle Elite Players. *New York Time*s. January 12, 1998. A1.

336   Casino design: Bill Friedman. *Designing Casinos to Dominate the Competition: The Friedman International Standards of Casino Design.* Reno: Institute for the Study of Gambling and Commercial Gaming, 2000. 89, 136, 139-40.

Chapter Sixteen: All in

337   Hobiki: Tsutomu Hayama. "Pachinko: The Lonely Casino." In Atsushi Ueda, ed. *The Electric Geisha: Exploring Japan's Popular Cultur*e. Tokyo: Kodansha International, 1994, 41-2.

33   Corinthian game: Hayama, 37.; Elizabeth Kiritani. "Pachinko, Japan's National Pastime." In John A Lent, Ed. *Asian Popular Culture.* Boulder: Westview Press, 1995. 203.

338   Postwar and current popularity of pachinko: Hayama, 38-9.

338   Professional pachinko players: Kiritani,206-8.

338   Pachinko balls exchanged for cash: Eric Prideaux. "The Trickle-down effect: Pachinko is a national obsession—but who's winning?" *Japan Times.* April 7, 2002.

339   American gaming revenues: http://www.americangaming.org/Industry/factsheets/statistics_detail.cfv?id=7

339-40   The Portuguese settlement of Macau: Geoffrey C. Gunn. *Encountering Macau: A Portuguese City-State on the Periphery of China, 1557-1999.* Boulder, Colorado: Westview Press, 1996. 8-9.

340   Macau legalizes gambling: Gunn, 6-7, 88-9; A. Pinho, "Gambling in Macau." In R.D. Cremer, ed. *Macau: City of Commerce and Culture.* Hong Kong: UEA Press LTD, 1987. 157.

340-1 Games of Macau: Pinho, 155-156; *Macau's Journey*. Macau: Sociedade de Jogos de Macau, S.A., 2004. unpaginated.

341 "The flotsam of the sea…" Jonathan Porter. *Macau: The Imaginary City: Culture and Society, 1557 to the Present.* Boulder, Colorado: Westview Press, 1996. 94.

342 Macau creates casinos in the 1930s: Gunn., 88-89.

342 Laorong Fu: A. Pinho, 157.

342 Tak Iam Fu. Gunn, 135; Pinho, 135.

343-4 Career of Stanley Ho: Jason Zhicheng Gao. An Overview of Macau Gaming Industry. Lecture presentation. University of Macau, 2004; Stanley Ho. Beijing: Xinhua News Agency, 1999. 62, 156-158; Gunn, 124.

344 STDM: Pinho, 158.

344 Macau racing: Porter, 147; *Macau's Journey*.

344 Prosperity of STDM: Pinho, 162.

347 Widespread business operations of STDM and Stanley Ho: *Macau's Journey*; Stanley Ho, 198-199.

347 "Uncle Stanley:" Stanley Ho, 198-199.

348 Cotai Strip: Gilberto Lopes. "Gaming Rouses Macao." September 2004.

349 South Korean Casinos: Anthony N. Cabot, William N. Thompson, Andrew Totteham, and Carl Braunlich, eds. *International Casino Law. Second Edition.* Reno: Institute for the Study of Gambling and Commercial Gaming, 1993. 435.

349 South Korean casino opened to Koreans: "Booming Locals Casino in Korea Selling Stock." *Las Vegas Sun.* October 25, 2001.

349 PAGCOR: Cabot, 529-531.

349 North Korean casino: "Odds Against North Korean Casino as China Stops Flow of "Dirty Cash."" *Casino City Times.* http://www.casinocity-times.com/news/article.cfm?contentId=148872

350-1 Lim Goh Tong and Genting Highlands: Lim Goh Tong. "My Dream." http://www.genting.com.my/en/mydream/mydream12.htm

351 Beirut's casino: Anthony N. Cabot, William N. Thompson, Andrew Totteham, and Carl Braunlich, eds. *International Casino Law. Third Edition.* Reno: Institute for the Study of Gambling and Commercial Gaming, 1999. 493-4.

351-2 Egypt's casinos: Cabot, 493.

352 The Jericho casino: Edward B. Miller. "An Oasis or Just a Mirage: The Jericho Casino and the Israeli-Palestinian Peace Process." *Richmond Journal of Global Law and Business.* 2. 33-60.

353 Singapore's attraction to casinos: Le-Min Lim. "Singapore Casinos Won't Cut Macau's Gaming Revenue, Analysts Say." Bloomberg. April 19, 2005. http://www.bloomberg.com/apps/news?pid=newsarchive&sid=aykIrK0 ax.u4&refer=asia

353 Las Vegas Sands winning Marina Bay bid: Linus Chua. "Las Vegas Sands Wins $3.2 Bln Singapore Casino Bid." Bloomberg. May 26, 2006. http://www.bloomberg.com/apps/news?pid=newsarchive&sid=aUJq83MND4u

c&refer=asia

354 Marina Bay Sands revenues: Las Vegas Sands. Form 10-K. http://investor.lasvegassands.com/secfiling.cfm?filingID=950123-12-4305

354 Gambling impacts on Singapore tourism: Your Singapore. "Quarterly Tourism Focus 2011: July to September." Singapore Tourism Board, 2012.

354-5 Early gambling in Australia: Peter Charlton. *Two Flies Up a Wall: The Australian Passion for Gambling.* North Ryde, Australia: Methuen Haynes, 1987. 9-15, 38; John O'Hara. A Mug's Game: A History of Gaming and Betting in Australia. New South Wales University Press, 1988. 10-11.

354-5 Pokie machines: John O'Hara. *A Mug's Game: A History of Gaming and Betting in Australia.* New South Wales University Press, 1988. 198-200; Terri C. Walker. *The 2005 Casino and Gaming Market Research Handbook.* Atlanta: Terri C. Walker Consulting, 2005. 354-5.

355 Australian casinos: Walker, 352-4.

356 Kerry Packer barred from Las Vegas casinos (allegedly): "For Las Vegas Gamblers, Getting the Heave-Ho." *New York Times.* November 15, 1998. A1.

356 Canadian gambling: Suzanne Morton. *At Odds: Gambling and Canadians, 1919-1969.* Toronto: University of Toronto Press, 2003. 10-11; Cabot, 170-1.

357 Candian VLTs: National Council of Welfare. 6.

358 Argentine casinos: Cabot, 207; Cabot, 277-280; Walker 337.

358-9 Puerto Rican casinos: Clement McQuade, ed. *Gambler's Digest.* Northfield, Illinois: DBI books, 1971. 267.

359 South African Gambling: Lotteries and Gambling Board. *Main Report on Gambling in the Republic of South Africa.* Pretoria: Lotteries and Gambling Board, 1995. 29-33.

359-60 Sol Kerzner and Sun City: Joseph Lelyveld. "Bringing a Bit of Vegas to South Africa's 'Homelands.'" *New York Times.* July 19, 1981. F7; Bill Keller. "Resort (Not Too African) For Rich Tourists." *New York Times.* December 3, 1992. A1.

360 Sun (Kerzner) International: Larry Rohter, "Waterscape in the Bahamas." *New York Times.* May 28, 1995. A1; Seth Lubove. "Atlantis Rising." Forbes. November 11, 2004; Cabot, 495-8.

361 Post-apartheid South African casinos: Cabot, 495-8; Walker, 348.

362 20th century European casino resurgence: Clair Price. "A Roulette Battle Resounds in Europe." *New York Times.* March 4, 1934. SM5; http://www.lucienbarriere.com/localized/en/portail/casinos/mythes_realites/index.asp?art_id=4121.

363 Baden-Baden reopens under the Nazis: Klaus Fischer. *Faites Votre Jeu: History of the Casino Baden-Baden.* Baden-Baden: Hans Werner Kelch, 1975. 80-3.

363 Postwar German casinos: Cabot 2, 287-8.

363-4 Casinos Austria: Cabot 2, 253-54; Casinos Austria. Essentials. http://www.casinosaustria.com/downloadDocument.aspx?id=131.

364-5   Belgian casinos: Cabot 2, 259-61; Walker, 361-2.

365-6   British casinos: Cabot 2, 302-12.

366   Moscow casinos: Peter Finn. "Gambling Proves a Tough Hand to Beat in Russia." *Houston Chronicle.* July 9, 2005.

367   Monte Carlo in recent years: Richard Bos. "Monte Carlo on the Mend." *International Gaming and Wagering Business.* March 1998. 22-8.

Chapter Seventeen: Reinventing the Wheel

369   Changes in Nevada gaming industry: "Nevada Gaming Footprint, 1963-2011." Las Vegas: Center for Gaming Research, 2012. http://gaming.unlv.edu/reports/nv_gaming_footprint.pdf

370   Changing demographics of Las Vegas: Las Vegas Visitor Profile Study. LVCVA, 1995, 2000.

370   Late 1960s entertainment: *Sonnett's Guide to Las Vegas.* Pub. City unknown, Robert Sonnett, 1969. 27.

371   Opening of Club Utopia: Martin Stein. "Line Pass: Utopia is back." *Las Vegas Weekly,* February 9, 2006. URL: http://www.lasvegasweekly.com/2006/02/09/linepass.html

371   Club Rio: Dave Renzi. "Impressionist Danny Gans jumps to the Rio." *Las Vegas Sun.* January 17, 1997. URL: http://www.lasvegassun.com/sunbin/stories/sun/1997/jan/17/505495165.html?"club percent20rio"

372   Changing demographics of Las Vegas: Las Vegas Visitor Profile Study. LVCVA, 2000, 2005, 2011.

374   Recession's impact on Las Vegas: David G. Schwartz. Nevada Gaming: Charting the Recession, 2007-2010. Las Vegas: Center for Gaming Research, University Libraries, University of Nevada Las Vegas, 2011. http://gaming.unlv.edu/reports/nv_revchanges.pdf

376   Early Internet casinos: Joshua Quittner. "Betting on Virtual Vegas." *Time.* June 12, 1995. 63-4.

376   Antiguan sportsbooks: Brett Pulley. "With Technology, Island Bookies Skirt U.S. Law." *New York Times.* January 31, 1998. A1.

377   Early online sportsbooks: Personal interview with Jay Cohen, December 15, 2003. Federal Prison Camp Nellis, Las Vegas, Nevada.

377   World Sports Exchange: Jack Boulware. "Online Pirates of the Caribbean." *SF Weekly.* December 15, 1999.

377   Capitol OTB: David Rohde. "Upstate OTB Wants to Put Horse Wagering on Internet." *New York Times.* December 26, 1996. B4; David Kushner. "Racing's Brains: Handling the Bets at Tracks and Elsewhere." *New York Times,* January 28, 1999. G5.

378   Statistics on number of gaming sites: Sue Schnieder. "The Market—An Introduction," in Mark Balestra, ed. *Internet Gambling Report, Sixth Edition.* St. Charles, Missouri: The River City Group, 2003. 56.

378-9   Australian Internet gaming: Jamie Nettleton. "Australia." In Mark Balestra, ed. Internet Gambling Report, Fifth Edition. St. Charles, Missouri:

The River City Group, 2002 . 431-443, 449.

379   1998 online gaming: Brett Pulley. "With Technology, Island Bookies Skirt U.S. Law." *New York Times.* January 31, 1998. A1.

379   Terrestrial operators go online: "Aspinalls Online to Outsource Casino Operations to Golden Palace." Rolling Good Times Online. April 3, 2002. Accessed at: http://www.rgtonline.com/Article.cfm?ArticleId=345 58&CategoryName=News&SubCategoryName=Featured ; Liz Bentsen. "Station Casinos Shelves Net Gambling Plans." *Las Vegas Sun.* August 26, 2002; Liz Bentsen. "Kerzner Drops Internet Gambling Operation." *Las Vegas Sun.* January 3, 2003; Liz Bentsen. "Kerzner Drops Internet Gambling Operation." *Las Vegas Sun.* January 3, 2003.

379   Philippine online betting: "PAGCOR Okays Philweb's Online Cockfight Betting System." *The Philippine Star.* March 3, 2005. http://www.philwebinc.com/template.asp?target=news/2005/P_mar03_ism

380   "March Madness" charges: "Online Sports Books Charged." *Las Vegas Review-Journal.* March 5, 1998.

380-1   Antigua vs.. United States, WTO case: World Trade Organization. United States—Measures Affecting the Cross-Border Supply of Gaming and Betting Services: Report of the Panel. WT/DS285/R10. November 2004. Accessed at: http://www.wto.org/english/tratop_e/dispu_e/285r_e.pdf. Cited hereafter as WTO. Page 5; Liz Benston. "WTO 'Net Gambling Details Remain Secret." *Las Vegas Sun,* March 25, 2004; WTO, 272.

382   Party Poker: Michael Friedman. "The Poker Party is Just Beginning." Poker News. July 15, 2005. http://www.pokernews.com/news/2005/07/poker-party-just-beginning.htm.

383   Black Friday prosecutions: David G. Schwartz. "In Poker and Business, Be Careful Who You Trust." *Las Vegas Business Press,* January 23, 2012. http://www.lvbusinesspress.com/articles/2012/01/23/opinion/columnists/schwartz/iq_50346189.txt

384   Global Ponzi scheme:" "Feds call Full Tilt Poker "global Ponzi scheme." CBS News, September 20, 2011. http://www.cbsnews.com/2100-201_162-20108950.html

384   Illinois goes online: Illinois Lottery website, "History," http://www.illinoislottery.com/en-us/About_Illinois_Lottery/Lottery_History/history-2011-2019.html

Illustrations

Cover   Sands Collection, UNLV Special Collections

7   Astragali
Stewart Culin. *Chess and Playing-Cards*. Atlanta, Georgia, 1895. 828.

26   Trente-et-quarante
Ralph Nevill. *Light Come, Light Go*. London: MacMillan and Company, 1909. fr.

34   Baden Baden
Harvey's Collection, UNLV Special Collections

46   Francois Blanc
Monte Carlo: Its Sin and Splendor. New York: Richard K. Fox, 1893. 93.

51   Bad Hamburg roulette
Ralph Nevill. *Light Come, Light Go*. London: MacMillan and Company, 1909. 309.

68   Monte Carlo casino exterior
Harvey's Collection, UNLV Special Collections

70   Monte Carlo casino interior
Harvey's Collection, UNLV Special Collections

93   Beau Nash
Ralph *Nevill. Light Come, Light Go*. London: MacMillan and Company, 1909. 83.
94   Pump Room
Oliver Goldsmith. *Beau Nash*. London: Grolier, c. 1900.

103   Crockford's
Ralph Nevill. *Light Come, Light Go*. London: MacMillan and Company, 1909. 99.

107   Whist
"Cavendish." *The Whist Table*. London, John Hogg, 1895

122   Faro
John Nevil Maskelyne. *Sharps and Flats: A Complete Revelation of Cheating at Games of Chance and Skill.* New York: Longmans, Green, and Co., 1894. 190.

137   Riverboat gamblers
George H. Devol. *Forty Years a Gambler on the Mississippi.* Cincinatti: Devol and Haines, 1887.193.

140   Civil War chuck-a-luck
Harper's Weekly, July 15, 1865. In UNLV Special Collections

145   White Pine faro
Harper's Weekly, April 24, 1869. 288. In UNLV Special Collections

160   New York City faro
Harper's Weekly, February 23, 1867. In UNLV Special Collections

163   John Morrissey
George W. Walling. *Recollections of a New York Chief of Police.* New York: Caxton Book Concern, 1887. 376.

179   Punchboard
Evan D. Rangeloff Collection, UNLV Special Collections

188   Mills Liberty Bell
Harvey's Collection, UNLV Special Collections

207   Harrah's Bingo
Harrah's Entertainment Collection, UNLV Special Collections

209   Harrah's Club
Harrah's Entertainment Collection, UNLV Special Collections

215   Boulder Club
Manis Collection, UNLV Special Collections

219   El Rancho Vegas
Manis Collection, UNLV Special Collections

225   Desert Inn
Union Pacific Railroad Collection, UNLV Special Collections

231   Dunes
Dunes Hotel Collection, UNLV Special Collections

235   Dean Martin
Sands Hotel Collection, UNLV Special Collections

238   Nick the Greek and Benny Binion
Nevada State Museum and Historical Society

245   Caesars Palace
Las Vegas News Bureau Collection, UNLV Special Collections

251   Johnny Moss and Jack Binion
Binion's Horseshoe Collection, UNLV Special Collections

252   Doyle Brunson and Hal Fowler
Binion's Horseshoe Collection, UNLV Special Collections

268   Haddon Hall
Resorts International Annual Report 1976, in UNLV Special Collections

277   Atlantic City, 1986
New Jersey Casino Control Commission Annual Report, 1986, in UNLV Special
Collections

297   Circus Circus, 1986
Jay Sarno Collection, UNLV Special Collections

314   Harrah's riverboats
Harrah's Entertainment Collection, UNLV Special Collections

322   Elmer Sherwin and Steve Wynn
MGM Resorts International Collection, UNLV Special Collections

325   The Mirage
MGM Resorts International Collection, UNLV Special Collections

345   Casino Lisboa
Photograph by author

365   Wynn Las Vegas
Wynn Las Vegas Promotional and Publicity File, UNLV Special Collections

Index

◇◇◇◇◇◇◇◇◇◇◇

Page numbers in *italic font* indicate illustrations

A

Aachen, 43
Adams, John Quincy, 124
Addington, Crandell, 251
Adelson, Sheldon, 334–35
Agua Caliente, Mexico, 195–96
America, early, gambling in
  during California Gold Rush, 143
  by Chinese immigrants, 146
  in colonies, 113–21
  in frontier cowtowns, 147–48
  by Mexicans, 146
  in mining camps, 144
  during Revolutionary War, 118–19
  on Western frontier, 143–53
  by women, 150–53
Ameristar Casinos, 316
animal fighting/racing, betting on. *See also* cockfighting; horseracing
  in China, 5
  in colonial America, 115
  in Kazakhstan, 6
anti-gambling societies, 135
Antigua, online gambling in, 376–77, 380–81
Aoyama, Freddie, 204
Apache, 248
Argent, 288
Argosy, 316
Arnould, Bob, 312
Aspers Westfield Stratford City (Britain), 366
astralagus (astragali), 3
Atlantic City, New Jersey, 387

Boardwalk, casino development on, 268–76
Boardwalk, history of, 262–65
  as casino destination, 275
  earned revenue from gaming, 290
  Indian gambling and, 279–80, 308–9
  Las Vegas and, 290–91
  recent development, 279–81
Australia, gambling in, 354–56
  online gambling, 378–79
Austria, gambling in, 363–64
Automatic Blackjack, 321
Aztar (corporation), 275

B

baccarat
  Greek Syndicate players, 83–86
  history of, 80–83
  in Macau, 345, 346
  in Monte Carlo casino, 87–88
backgammon, 117
Bad Homburg, gambling at, 45–56, *51*
  Kursaal casino, 48–50
Baden-Baden, Germany
  health resort at, 29–30, 32, 33, *34,* 35–42, 363
Bahamas, gambling in, 359
Bally's Park Place (Atlantic City), 271–72
Bank Club (Reno), 203
"bank craps," 132
bank games, 7–8, 9–10, 17
Banque a Deux Tableaux. *See* baccarat

Barcelo, Maria Gertrudis, 151

Bartolf, Jim, 162

basset (bassetto), 9–10, 12

Bath, England, 90–96, *94*

Beach Club (Florida), 192–93

Beat the Dealer (Thorpe), 240–41

Beaux Strategem, The (Farquhar), 105–6

Belgium, gambling in, 364–65

Bellagio (Las Vegas), 324–25

Benazet, Edward, 32–33, 38

Benazet, Jacques, 30–32, 46

Bennet, William (Bill), 245, 298, 299, 330

Bergen County, New Jersey, gambling in, 192. *See also* Atlantic City, New Jersey

Bergstrom, William Lee (Phantom Gambler), 249

BetOnSports, 382–83

billiards, 117, 124–25

Billie, James, 304–5

Biloxi, Mississippi, 193–94

Biltmore (Las Vegas), 220

bingo
Indian gaming, 304–5, 306, 308
in Macau, 345
in Reno, 204

Binion, Benny, *238,* 248–49

Binion, Jack, *251*

Black Book, 283

Black Friday arrests, 383–84

blackjack
Automatic Blackjack, 321
card counting, 291
card tracking, 239–42
in Las Vegas *vs.* Atlantic City, 291
team playing, 241–42

Blanc, Camille, 66, 86

Blanc, Francois, 45–56, *46*
death of, 64
on gambling systems, 74–75
investing in French spas, 58–59
refurbishing Villa Bellevue, 61–62

Blanc, Louis, 45–56

Blanc, Marie, 64, 65

Blasdel, Henry, 197–98

Board of Trade Wheel, 175

Boardwalk (Atlantic City), history of, 262–65

Bonaparte, Charles Lucien, 51–52

Bonaparte, Napoleon, 20

bookmaking, 199, 215–17

bootleggers, 227

Borgata (Atlantic City), 280, 332

Boulder Club (Las Vegas), 212, *215*

Boulder Strip, 256

boule, 87

boxing, 200, 202

Boyd, Sam, 254–56

Boyd Gaming, 332, 374

Bradley, Edward Riley, 192–93

"breaking the bank," at Monte Carlo casino, 75, 77–78, 237–38

bridge, 109

Bringing Down the House (Mezrich), 242

Britain. *See* Great Britain, gambling in

Brunson, Doyle, *252*

"bucking the tiger," 121

Burger King restaurant, Las Vegas Strip, 295–96

Burger King Revolution, 294–302

Burrell, "Shell," 161–62

Byrne, Brendan, 264

C

Cadillac Jack's, 317

Caesars Boardwalk Regency (Atlantic City), 269–70

Caesars Entertainment Corporation, 332, 333

Caesars Palace (Las Vegas), 243–44, *245,* 284, 285, 288, 327, 328

Caesars World (corporation), 269–71

Cal-Neva Lodge (Lake Tahoe), 210

California (Las Vegas), 255

California state, Indian gaming in, 310–11

California *vs.* Cabazon Band of Mission Indians, 305–6

Canada, gambling in, 356–57
Canfield, Richard, 183–85
Capital OTB, 377
cappers (shills), 157, 175
"Card Bell" (Liberty Bell), 188, *188*
card counting, in blackjack, 239–42, 291
card playing, history of. *See also* individual games
  in colonial America, 115–17
  in France, 14–18, 19
  in frontier America, 121
  during Revolutionary War, 118–19
  twenty-one (blackjack), 20
Cargill, Thomas, 292
Caribbean, gambling in, 358–59
carnivals, 174–75, 356. *See also* Kelly, "Honest" John
Carruthers, David, 382–83
Casanova, Giacomo, 13, 72
Casino Africa (Ghana), 361
Casino de Montreal (Canada), 357
Casino Lisboa, 345, *345*
Casino (Scorcese film), 288
Casino Windsor (Canada), 357
casinos. *See also* financing of casinos; marketing of casinos; ownership of casinos; specific casinos by name
  business travelers as players, 234
  casino, definition, 14
  challenges to, in U.S., 368–69
  as Class III IGRA games, 306
  demographics of customers, 369–70
  economic/social benefits from, 281
  effects of recent recession on, 292–93, 387
  European, growth of, 362–67
  Indian operations, 307–11
  innovations at, in Reno, 206–8
  nightclubs in, 370–71
  online casinos, 378
  skimming scandals, 257–58
Casinos Austria, 363–64
Castro, Fidel, 195

Chamberlin, Johnny, 183
charities
  in Canada, 356–57
  in Connecticut, 309
cheating
  by cappers (shills), 157
  by double-dealing, 51
  exposing, on Las Vegas Strip, 237
  by fakirs, 174–76
  at faro, 123
  in gambling houses, 1830s, 156–58
  by grifters, 176–78
  at Monte Carlo, 65–66
  on needle wheels, 174–75
  at punchboards, 180
  by ropers, 157
  at roulette, 75–77
  by sharpers, 100–101
  at shell games, 132
  at slot machines, 189
  at Spa, 25, 28
  at three-card monte, 132, *137*
  using online gambling, 383–84
  using police as enforcers, 158
  in wolf-traps, 155
chemin-de-fer, 80–81
Cherokees of North Carolina, 305
Cheyenne, Wyoming, 147
Chicago, Illinois
  1893 World Columbian Exposition, 173
  crime in, 169–70
  gambling operators in, 168–73
  gambling syndicates in, 191
  Great Chicago Fire, 171–72
  Sands, 169
  The Store, 172–73
Chihuly, Dale, 325
China
  casinos in Macau, xvi
  gambling in, early history of, 4–6
  Haua-Hoey Lottery (lotto), 5
  kwat pai (dominoes), 5–6
Chinatown
  in New York, 165

in Reno, 204
in San Francisco, 146
Chinese lottery, 204–5
chips
    at Monte Carlo, 64–65
    radio frequency identification
        (RFID) chips, 323
    in United States, 65
chocolate houses, gambling at, 98–99
chuck-a-luck, 132, *140*
Cincinnati, Ohio, gambling in, 155–
    56, 165–66
Circus Circus Enterprises, 301, 330
Circus Circus (Las Vegas), 244–45,
    297
    earned revenue from, 299
    loss leaders applied to grind
        business, 299, 300
    marketing to families, 298–300
City of Dreams (Macau), 349
CityCenter (Las Vegas), 374, 375
Civil War, gambling during, 138–43,
    140, 182
Clan of the Mystic Confederation,
    133–34
Clark, Wilbur, 224–25, 283
Clay, Henry, 121
Club Fortune (Reno), 208–9
Club Rio (Las Vegas), 371
Club Utopia (Las Vegas), 371
cockfighting
    in America, 117–18, 120
    online, in Philippines, 379
Coeur d'Alene Indian tribe, 377
coffee houses, 98–99
Cohen, Jay, 377, 380
Cohn, Louis, 171–72
Colorado, 317
Colton, Henry, 160–61
Colvin, Harvey, 172
COMDEX computer trade show, 334
Commercial Hotel (Nevada), 210–11
Compleat Gamester, The (Cotton), 107
Connecticut, gambling in
    at casinos, xiv–xvi

by Indians, 307–9
    revenue from Indian gaming, xv, xvi
Conversation House (Baden-Baden),
    30
Corporate Gaming Acts, 285
corruption and gambling
    in France, 45–46
    in New Orleans, 315
    in New York City, 190
    in San Francisco, 146
Cortes, Hernan, 112–13
Cotai Strip, 348–49
Cotton, Charles *(The Compleat
    Gamester)*, 107
craps
    with African-Americans, 132
    "bank craps," 132
    in Monte Carlo, 88–89
    in New Orleans, 131–32
Crockford, William, 102–4
Crockford's, 104
Crosby, James, 267, 289
croupiers
    at Bad Hamburg, 51
    at French clubs, 81
    at Kursaal, 49
    at Monte Carlo, 65–67, 70–71
    at Spa, 25
Crumley, Newton, Jr., 211
Cuba, 194–95
Curtis, Martin, 167
cussec (sic bo), 340–41

D
Da Ponte, Lorenzo, 12–13
Dakota, Frederick, 307
d'Alembert system of betting, 73
Dalitz, Moe, 224–26, 283
D'Amato, Paul "Skinny," 263–64
Dandolos, Nick "the Greek," 237–39,
    238, 250
Davis, Gray, 310
Davis, John, 129–30
dealers. *See also* bank games
    at Baden-Baden, 32–33

Italian Executors against
  Blasphemy, 9
  at wolf-traps, 155, 156
  as women dealers, 206, 213, 255
Deauville Casino (France), 84–85
Deauville (Reno), 208
DeBartolo, Eddie, 315
Democratic National Convention, 263
Denver, Colorado, 147
Desert Inn (Las Vegas), 224–26, *225*,
  246
Detroit, Michigan, 317–19
Devol, George, 137–38, 139, 141–42
Diamond Lady riverboat (Iowa),
  312–13
dice (casting of lots). *See also* chuck-a-
  luck; craps
  astralagus, 3
  at Crockford's, 104
  cussec (sic bo), 340–41
  klondike, 202
  at Monte Carlo, 88–89
  prehistory of, 2–3, *3*
  "rolling the bones," 2–3
divination, 2–3
dog racing, in Macau, 344
dominoes, in China, 5–6
Dostoyevsky, Fyodor, 40–42
Duc de Valmy, 60–62
Dumont, Eleanore, 152
Dunes (Las Vegas Strip), *231*, 231–32

E
Earp, Wyatt, 149
Eastern Europe, casinos in, 366–67
Echelon (Las Vegas), 374
Edwards, Edwin, 315
Egypt, gambling in, 351–52
El Cortez (Las Vegas), 220, 248
El Dorado (San Francisco), 145–47
El Rancho Vegas, 218–20, *219*, 221
Eldorado (Las Vegas), 249
Elko, Nevada, 210–11
English Club (Spa), 25
entertainment at casinos

in Atlantic City, 263, 267–68
  at Foxwoods, 309
  in Las Vegas, 211, 234–35, 243,
    327–29
  in South Africa, 361
  World Series of Poker, 250–53
Entratter, Jack, 234–35
Epsom health resort, 90
euchre, 117
Excalibur (Las Vegas), 322, 329–30
exposition industry, 334–36

F
fairgrounds, 174–75, 356
fantan, 340
faro, *122*
  basset and, 12
  in Britain, 97, 101–2
  in frontier America, 121
  at mining camp, *145*
  in New Orleans, 130
  in New York City, *160*
  rules of, 122–23
  at Saratoga Club House, 185
  in Washington, D.C., 126–27
Fey, Charles, 187–88
financing of casinos
  by corporate developers, 258–61
  by debt collecting, 228, 229–30, 286
  by mainstream capital, 285
  by organized crime, 228–29, 256–58
fires at casinos
  at Las Vegas Hilton, 293–94
  at MGM Grand (Las Vegas), 261,
    293, 331
fish ponds, 178
Fisher, Kate, 149
500 Club (Atlantic City), 263
Flamingo (Las Vegas), 222–26, 259–
  60, 287, 326–27
Flandreau Santee Sioux of North
  Dakota, 308
Forty Years a Gambler on the Mississippi
  (Devol), 137
Fowler, Hal, *252*

Fox, Mildred, 263–64
Foxwoods Resort Casino, xiv–xv, 307,
  308–9, 350
France
  baccarat playing in, 81–82
  before/after French Revolution,
    18–21, 27–28
  casinos in, 18–20, 21, 24–25,
    362–63
  history of gambling in, 14–18
  poque playing in, 130–31
  royals' investment in gambling, 58
  Spa, 22–29
  whist playing in, 108
Fremont Street (Las Vegas), 212–17,
  220, 249, 254–56
Fremont (Las Vegas Casino), 248
French Revolution, 18–21, 27–28
Friedrich II, 35
Frisch, Roy, 203
Fu, Laorong, 342
Fu, Tak Lam, 342
Full Tilt, prosecution of, 383–84
funbooks, 254, 296–97

G
Gagnante Marche (streak or hot and
  cold), 74
Gambler, The, 40–41
gamblers, professional
  blacklegs, 121, 135–38, *137*
  during California Gold Rush, 147
  description of, by Poe, 173–74
  Dumont, Eleanore, 152
  "fakirs," 174–76
  gamblers' brigade, during Civil War,
    141–42
  Gates, John "Bet-a-Million,"
    185–86
  grifters, 175–78, 180
  Hachem, Joseph, 355
  Hickok, James Buttler "Wild Bill,"
    148–49
  Holliday, John Henry (Doc),
    149–50

Ivers, Alice (Poker Alice), 152–53
  in Louisiana and Mississippi,
    133–35
  Masterson, William Barclay "Bat,"
    150
  Morrissey, Jim, 162, *163*, 163–65
  Packer, Kerry, 355–56
  reformed gamblers, 178
  Scarne, John, 236–37
  Skaggs, Elijah, 123–24
  in smaller Midwestern towns,
    166–67
gambling. *See also* global gambling;
  mercantile gambling; online
  gambling
  prehistory of, 3–4
gambling clubs, 81–82, 355
gambling houses, *160. See also*
  cheating; individual city names
  during California Gold Rush,
    144–45
  in Chicago, 169, 170–71
  during Civil War, 139
  in early America, 124
  as illegal gambling resorts, 191–92
  in London, 96–109
  in Midwest, 165–67
  in New Orleans, 129–30
  roped games at, 156–58
  in San Francisco, 145–47
  syndicate ownership of, 159
  in Washington, D.C., 125–26
  on Western frontier, 142–43
  wolf-traps (snap houses), 155–56
gambling syndicates. *See also* organized
  crime
  in Chicago, 173, 191
  evolution of, 189–90, 226–27
  in Minneapolis, 191
  in New York City, 190–91
game cards, 179–80
Gaming Control Board, Nevada,
  282–83, 289
Gaming Fraternity Convention. *See*
  World Series of Poker

Gao, Kening, 342
Garcia, Bobby, 191–92
Garcia, Thomas, 52–53, 61
Gates, John "Bet-a-Million," 185–86
Gaughan, John D. "Jackie," 254
Gaughan, Michael, 291
gender and gambling
  in colonial America, 117
  female dealers, 204, 206
  female owners/managers, 213–14
  female players, 33–34, 39, 44, 101,
    182
  women of the West, 150–53
General Agreement on Trade in
    Services (GATS), 380–81
Genting Group, 350–51
Genting Highlands (Malaysia),
    350–51
George III, 35
Germany. *See also* Baden-Baden
  Aachen, gambling at, 43
  Bad Homburg, gambling at, 45–56
  bank games in, 8
  gambling spas in, 29–30
  gambling towns, 42–45
  Wiesbaden, gambling at, 43–45
  during WWII, 363
global gambling
  in Australia, 354–56
  in Austria, 363–64
  in Belgium, 364–65
  in Canada, 356–57
  in Caribbean, 358–59
  in China, 4–6
  in Egypt, 351–52
  in France, 14–18, 80–81, 362
  in Germany, 29–30, 35–38, 42–56,
    363
  in Great Britain, 90–109, 365–66
  in Israel, 352
  in Japan, 337–39
  in Korea, 6
  in Latin American countries, 358
  in Lebanon, 351
  in Macau, China, 339–49

  in Malaysia, 350–51
  in New Zealand, 356
  in North Korea, 349
  in Russia, 366–67
  in Singapore, 352–54
  in South Africa, 359–61
  in South Korea, 349
  in sub-Saharan Africa, 361–62
Gluck, Henry, 270
Gogol, Nicholai, 39
Gold Strike Resorts, 330
Golden Nugget (Atlantic City), 273,
    281
Golden Nugget (Las Vegas), 216,
    253–54
Goldstein, Bernard, 312, 313
golf courses
  at Agua Caliente (Mexico), 195
  at Desert Inn (Las Vegas), 226
  at Foxwoods Resort Casino, xv
  at Tunbridge Wells, 90
gourmet restaurants, in Las Vegas
    casinos, 326–27
Graham, William, 200–201, 202, 203,
    215
Grand Martingale system of betting,
    72
Great Britain, gambling in, 90–109,
    365–66
  baccarat playing in, 81
  Bath health resort, 90–96
  Epsom health resort, 90
  London gambling houses, 96–109
  online gambling, 379
  Tunbridge Wells, 90
Great Depression, 201
Greektown Casino (Detroit), 318
Greenspun, Hank, 291
Grimaldi family, in Monaco, 57–58
Guys and Dolls, 150

H
Hachem, Joseph, 355
Hall, Joe, 161
Hall of the Bleeding Heart, 125–26

Haller, Mark, 227
Han Shu, 5
Hannifin, Phillip, 290–91, 291–92
Hard Rock (Las Vegas), 334
Harolds Club (Reno), 205–6, *207*
Harrah, William Fisk, 206–8, 256, 286–87
Harrah's Atlantic City, 280–81
Harrah's Entertainment, 333, 381–82
Harrah's Heart Tango (Reno), 207–8, 208, *209*
Harrah's Las Vegas, 261
Harrah's Las Vegas (Holiday Casino), 285
Harrah's (Marina) Atlantic City, 276, 277
Harrison, Carter, 172–73
Harte, Bret, 148
Haua-Hoey Lottery (lotto), 5
Hayward, Richard "Skip," xv, 307–8
health resorts, gambling at, 22–56
    Aachen, 43
    Baden-Baden, 29, 30–32, *34*, 38–42
    English Club, 25
    German spas, 29–30
    Homberg, 37–38
    Kursaal, 48–50, *51*, 51–54
    Redoute, 24–25
    Spa, 22–29, 25–29
    Wiesbaden, 43–44
Heath, Monroe, 172
Hebel, Johann Peter, 29–30
Henry III, 15
Henry IV, 15
Herne, Patrick, 161
Hickok, James Buttler "Wild Bill," 148–49
high rollers (whales), 335–36
Highway 91 (Las Vegas Boulevard), 219
Hilton Hotels
    in Atlantic City, 278
    on Las Vegas Strip, 260–61
Ho, Stanley, 343–44, 346–47
Holiday Casino (Las Vegas), 261

Holiday Inns, 261
Holliday, John Henry (Doc), 149–50
Holtz, Theodore, gaming inventor, 187–88
Hoover Dam, 211
horseracing
    in Chicago, 171
    during Civil War, 140
    in colonial America, 115
    in frontier America, 120
    in Great Britain, 365
    in Macau, 344
    at Monmouth Park, 183
    in New Jersey, 264
    online gambling on, 377
    at Reno, 199
    at Saratoga Springs, 182
    at Spa, 24
Horseshoe (Las Vegas), 249, 251
Hot Springs, Arkansas, 194
Hotel Last Frontier, 220–21
Houssels, J. Kell, 213, 249
Hoyle, Edmund *(Whist According to Hoyle)*, 106, 107–8
Hughes, Howard Robard, 246–48
Hull, Thomas, 219

I
Illinois, gambling in, 312–13, 317–18
Indian gaming
    bingo, 304–5
    as challengers to Nevada casinos, 369
    history of, 303–11
    online gambling, 377
Indian Gaming Regulatory Act (IGRA) of 1988, 306–7
Indiana, gambling in, 316
innovations at casinos
    funbooks and giveaways, 254
    popular entertainers, 211
    slot machine technologies, 321
International Film Festival (Cannes, France), 362
International Game Technology

(IGT), 321–22
International (Las Vegas), 285
  cost of, 284
International (Las Vegas Hilton),
  259–60
Iowa, gambling in, 311–12
Isle of Capri, 313, 316
Isle of Caprice (Biloxi), 193
Israel, gambling in, 352
Italy
  Ridotto, 8–12
  Venice, 8–10
Ivers, Alice (Poker Alice), 152–53

J
Jaggers, Joseph, 76–77
Japan, 337–39
Jefferson, Thomas, 119
jenny wheel, 175
Johnson, Enoch "Nucky," 262–63
Johnson, Jack, 200
junket trade, 229, 285–86

K
Kefauver, Estes, 196
Kefauver Committee hearings, 192,
  196, 263
Kelly, "Honest" John, 175–78, 180
Kennedy, Robert F., 194, 196, 287
keno parlors
  in Cincinnati, 165–66
  in Las Vegas, 214
  in Reno, 205
  rules for keno, 166
Kentucky, gambling in, 194
Kerkorian, Kirk, 259–61, 331, 333
Kerzner, Sol, 359, 360, 361
Kiel, Howard, 313
Kissileff, Sophie, 39
klondike, 202
Kursaal, 48–50, *51*, 51–52

L
Labouchere (cancellation system of
  betting), 73

Lake Tahoe, Nevada, 210
Landmark, 247
Lanni, Terry, 270
Lansky, Meyer, 224, 228, 287
Las Vegas. *See also* Las Vegas Strip; *see
  also* specific clubs
  Atlantic City and, 266, 290–91
  casino fires in, 293–94
  club ownership in, 212–13
  customer demographics, 372
  development of, 248, 333–34
  downtown gambling halls in, 214
  early history of, 211
  effects of recessions on, 292–93, 387
  exclusivity of casinos, 372–73
  as family-friendly destination,
    333–34
  female owners/managers in, 213–14
  licensing authority in, 212
  mass marketing of (Burger King
    Revolution), 294–302
  revenue from grind players, 300
  segregation of clubs in, 214
  weakening national economy and,
    291–92
  zoning casino district in, 211–12
Las Vegas Club, 212–13
Las Vegas Hilton fire, 293–94
Las Vegas Sands, 334–36, 353
Las Vegas Sands, Inc., 347–48
Las Vegas Strip. *See also* specific clubs
  building boom on, 333–34
  celebrity chefs on, 327
  as convention center, 233–34
  desegregation of, 235–36
  earned revenue, Atlantic City *vs.*,
    290
  earned revenue, slot machines, 298
  effects of recessions on, 294–95, 369
  gourmet restaurants on, 326–27
  marketing casinos on, 220–21,
    229–30
  Mirage Effect, 325–26
  organized crime on, 222–25,
    227–30

origin of highway name, 230–31
redevelopment of, 323–29, 331–33,
    373–74
segregation on, 232
slot machine players, 300–301
Last Frontier Village, 221
Latin American countries, gambling
    in, 358
Leavitt, Marv, 297
Lebanon, gambling in, 351
Leblanc, Leonie, 34
Lee, Dan, 298–99
Lee, Robert E., 140
legalized gambling
    in Atlantic City, 263–65
    in Baden-Baden, 29–30
    in France, 17–21, 31
    in Germany, 363
    in Macau, China, 340–43
    in Nevada, 199–200, 201–2
    in New Orleans, Louisiana, 128–29
    in Reno, 200–201
    at Ridotto, 10–13
Leon, Rene, 86–87
Levoz, Noel, 27
Lewis, Kevin, 242
Lim Goh Tong, 350–51
Lim Kok Thay, 351
London gambling houses, 96–109
    Crockford's, 102–5, *103*
Long Branch, New Jersey, 183
Loong, Lee Hsien, 353
lotteries
    in Canada, 356
    early scratch-offs, 178–80, *179*
    Indian, 306
    lotto, 166
    in South Africa, 361
    state lotteries, 264
Louisiana, riverboat gambling in, 315
Loveman, Gary, 334
low rollers (grind players), 297–98,
    299, 300
Luxor (Las Vegas), 330

M
Macau, China, 339–49
    casinos in, xvi, 387
    conversion to communist authority,
        344–45, 347
    cussec (sic bo), 340–41
    fantan playing in, 340, 341
    history of, 339–40
    legalized gambling in, 341–43
    new entrepreneurs in, 347–48
    pai gow playing in, 340
    popular games in, 345–46
    private gaming clubs in, 346
    as tourism destination, 342–43
Maheu, Robert, 246
Maine, Indian gaming in, 304
Malaysia, gambling in, 350–51
Mandalay Resort Group, 330, 333
March Madness prosecutions, 380,
    382
Marina Bay Sands (Singapore), 353,
    354
marketing of casinos
    annual visitors, Atlantic City, 275
    annual visitors, Las Vegas, 275
    to convention (exposition) industry,
        233–34, 244, 284, 334–36
    design science of, 336
    exclusivity of, 372–73
    to families, 245–46, 298–300,
        333–34
    to grind business, 299
    to junket trade, 229, 285–86
    mass marketing strategy, 254, 294–
        302, 329–30
    Mirage Effect, 325–26
    nightclub trade, 369, 370–72
    to slot-players, in Las Vegas,
        297–98
    tracking complimentaries (comps),
        322–23
    using entertainment, 327–29
    using themes, 220–21, 272
    as vacation attractions, 323–29
Martin, Dean, *235*

Martingale progression system of betting, 72

Mashantucket Pequot Indians, 307–8
Foxwoods Resort Casino, xiii–xiv, xiv–xv
Hayward, Richard "Skip," xv
tribal history of, xiii–xiv

Mason, John, xiii–xiv

mass market tourism, 333–34. *See also* Burger King Revolution

Masterson, William Barclay "Bat," 150

Matthews, Thomas, 108

Maugham, Somerset, 63

Maxim, Hiram, 78–79

Mazarin, Jules, 15–16

McAfee, Guy, 216, 230

McDonald, Mike, 172–73

McDonald's restaurant, Las Vegas Strip, 296

McKay, James, 200–201, 202, 203, 215

McMillan, James, 235, 236

Meadows (Las Vegas), 216–17

Megabucks, 321–22

mercantile gambling
bank games, origins of, 7–8
as Class III IGRA game, 306
origins of, 6–7
Ridotto, first casino, 8–12
social shift against, in Britain, 101–2

Mesopotamia, astragali (dice) in, 3–4

MGM Grand (Detroit), 318

MGM Grand (Las Vegas), 260, 261, 268, 285
chef Joel Robuchon, 327
CityCenter, 374
earned revenue, 290
fire at, 293, 294
redevelopment of, 331–32
Studio 54, 371

MGM Mirage/MGM Resorts International, 280, 331–32, 333, 383

MGM Mirage Online, 379

MGM Resorts (Macau), 349

Milwaukee, Wisconsin, gambling in, 167–68

mining camps, gambling at, 144, *145*, 150–53

Minneapolis, Minnesota, gambling syndicates in, 191

Mint 400, 248

Mint (Las Vegas), 255

Mirage, 323–25, *325*, 329

Mirage Effect, 325–26, 369

Mississippi, riverboat gambling in, 313–15, 316

Missouri, riverboat gambling in, 315–16

Mohegan Sun casino, 309

Molly (Trussell's mistress), 171

Monaco, 55–56, 57–60, 62–63

Money Honey slot machine, 321

Moneymaker, Chris, 381

Montagu, John, 98–99, 395n99

monte, 146

Monte Carlo casino, *68, 70*
amusements at, 71
baccarat at, 87–88
"breaking the bank" at, 75, 77–78, 237–38
craps at, 88–89
description of, 67
gambling currency at, 64–65
gambling in, 367
reputation of, 62–63, 67–69

Monte Verde, Lurline, 151–52

Montezuma, 112–13

Montreal, Canada, 195–96

Montreux Jazz Festival (France), 362

Moore, Bill, 221

Morgan, Helen, 213

Morrissey, John, 162, *163*, 163–65, 181–83

Moss, Johnny, 250, *251*

MotorCity (Detroit), 318

Moulin Rouge (Las Vegas), 232

Mound Builders, gambling by, 112

Murren, Jim, 334

Muslims, gambling by, 350, 351

myths, 112–13

N
Nash, Richard "Beau," 91–96, *93*
National Gambling Impact Study
    Commission, 282
National Indian Gaming Commission,
    306
Native Americans, 110–13. *See also*
    Indian gaming; specific tribes
Navajos, 111–13
needle wheel, 174–75
Nevada
    casino developments in, 256
    changes in gaming law in, 285
    debt collection from casinos in,
        286–87
    Gaming Control Board in, 282–83
    gangsters as gamblers, 210
    legalized gambling as tourist
        strategy, 201–2
    legislating bookmaking in, 199
    online state gambling regulations,
        384
    regulations against gambling,
        197–99
    regulations taxing gaming revenue,
        232–33
New Orleans, Louisiana, 128–33
    chuck-a-luck, 132
    craps in, 131–32
    gambling houses in, 129–30
    legal gambling in, 128–29
    poker playing in, 130–31
    riverboat gambling in, 315
New York City
    Chinatown, 165
    epidemic and gambling in, 120
    first-class gambling houses in,
        158–59, 159–60
    gambling houses in, 154–55,
        156–59
    gambling syndicates in, 190–91
    penny poker dens in, 157–58
    video lottery terminal gambling,

319
New York-New York (Las Vegas),
    331–32
New Zealand, gambling in, 356
Newport, Kentucky, 194
nightclubs, 369–71
91 Club (Las Vegas), 216, 218, 221
North Korea, gambling in, 349
Northern Club (Las Vegas), 213
Nye, James, 197

O
Ohio, gambling in cities of, 319
Ollie, Art, 311–12
Onassis, Aristotle, 89
online casinos, 378, 379
online gambling, 376–84
    in Antigua, 376–77
    online poker, 381–84
    sportsbooks, 377–78
    in United States, 376, 378
"Optimum Strategy in Blackjack"
    (Thorp), 240
organized crime
    in Atlantic City, 262–63, 270, 278
    changes in, 284
    financing of casinos, 228–29,
        256–58
    income from illegal racewires, 216
    in Las Vegas, 214–15, 216–17
    on Las Vegas Strip, 222–25, 227–30
    out of gambling, 285
    out of Las Vegas, 282–84
    public outrage against, 196
    relationship with law enforcement,
        226
    skimming scandals by, 287–89
    use of slot machines by, 189
origins of gambling, 2–3
    Indian gaming, xiii–xiv, xv–xvi
Otoe Missouria Indians of Oklahoma,
    305
ownership of casinos
    by corporate consolidations and
        mergers, 331–33

by corporate developers, 259–61, 265–68, 269–71 (*see also* Wynn, Stephen A.)

by criminal gangs, 162–63

by gambling syndicates, 189–96

by Howard Hughes, 246–48

by Indian tribes, xiv–xvi

by John D. "Jackie" Gaughan, 254–55

by limited partnerships, 212–13

by organized crime, 194, 210, 222–24, 227

by partnerships, 245–46

by Sam Boyd, 254–56

by SBM partnership, 66–67, 83, 87–88, 89

ownership of gambling houses

by gambling partnerships, 164–65, 170–71

by promoter Richard Canfield, 183–86

by syndicate partnerships, 159–65

P

pachinko, 337–39

pachisuro machines, 338

Packer, Kerry, 355–56

PAGCOR (Philippine Amusement and Gaming Corporation), 349, 379

Page, Connie, 294

pai gow, 340

pakapoo (White Pigeon Ticket lottery), 204–5

Pala Band of Mission Indians of San Diego County, 310

Palace Club (Reno), 204–5

Palais Royale (Paris), 18–20

Palley, Reese, 271–72

Palm Beach, Florida, 192–93

Palms (Las Vegas), 334, 372

panguingue, 202–3

pari-mutuel betting, in Great Britain, 365–66

Paris, France, 81–82

Park Place (Caesars) Entertainment, 332

Parlett, David, 130

paroli (parlay), 72

Parsons, Reuben, 159–61, 161

Party Gaming, 382

patience system of betting, 73–74

Peavine (Reno), 204

Pendleton, Edward, 125–26

Penn, William, 116

Pennington, William, 245, 298

Pennsylvania, gambling in, 319

penny poker dens, 157–58

Penobscot Indians of Maine, 304, 308

Perlman, Clifford, 269–70

Philadelphia, Pennsylvania, 120

Philippines, gambling in, 349, 379

Pilgrims, xiii–xiv

pinball machines. *See* pachinko

piquet, 117

Playboy (Atlantic City), 275

Poe, Edgar Allen, 173–74

poker

in Australia, 354–55

as Class II IGRA Indian game, 306

early poker-playing machines, 187–88

historic roots of, 130–31

online poker, 381–84

Texas Hold'em, 251–52

video poker, 321–22

World Poker Tour, 381

World Series of Poker, 248, 250–53, *252*

pool rooms (race books), 215–16

Poole, Butcher Bill, 164

Prell, Milton, 258

Primm, Ernest, 256

Principles of Whist, The (Cavendish), 108–9

prizefighting, 200, 202

Prohibition, 189

prohibitions against gambling

at Baden-Baden, 38

in Bath, England, 95–96

in Belgium, 364–65
in Canada, 356–57
in colonial America, 114–15
in early Italy, 9
in Great Britain, 366
in Homburg, 55
in London, England, 96–97, 104–5
in Milwaukee, 168
online, 379
online, in US, 379–80, 383, 384
by Senate anti-gambling
    investigations, 196
Puck, Wolfgang, 327
Puerto Rico, gambling in, 358
punchboards, 178–90, *179,* 205

Q
Quakers, gambling by, 116
Quinn, John Philip, 178, 191

R
racehorse keno, 205
Ralenkotter, Rossi, 295
Ramada Inns (Atlantic City), 273–75
Rat Pack, 234–35
Reagan, Ronald, 306
Real World, The, 372
recessions, 292–93, 369, 374–75, 387
Red Rock Bingo Palace, 305
Red Rooster, 218
Redd, William "Si," 322
Redoute, 24, 28
Reed, Charles, 184
regulations against gambling
in Atlantic City, 263–65, 274, 275,
    276, 278, 286–87
in Canada, 356
in City of Saratoga Springs, 186
during Civil War, 139
in colonial America, 117–18
in frontier America, 121
in Illinois, 313
by immigrants, 202
of Indian operations, 306–7, 308,
    310

in Iowa, 312
in Las Vegas, 211–12
licensing allowed to corporations,
    259
licensing of casinos, in Atlantic
    City, 267, 270–71
licensing of casinos, in Nevada,
    256–57
in Mississippi, 313
in Nevada, 197–99, 201–2, 232–33,
    266, 282–83
in New York, 159
in San Francisco, 146–47, 188
in South Africa, 359, 361
in South Dakota, 316–17
Reno, Nevada, 202–10. *See also*
    individual casinos
anti-gambling legislation in, 199
gambling halls in, 203
legal card rooms in, 200–201
popular games in, 202–3
segregated clubs in, 204
zoning casino district in, 210
Resorts International (Atlantic City),
    265–68, *268, 277*
earned revenue, 289
new owners, 278–79
Resorts World Genting, 351
Resorts World Sentosa (Singapore),
    353–54
Restaurant Guy Savoy, 327
revenue from casinos
in Atlantic City, 263, 268, 269, 271,
    275, 280–81, 289–90
in Detroit, Michigan, 318
at Flamingo, 259
at Foxwoods Resort Casino, xv, 309
from Hughes' portfolio, 247
at Indian bingo halls, 304–5
in Las Vegas, 275, 284, 290, 298,
    299
in Macau, 348, 387
from mass marketing strategy,
    301–2
at Mirage (Las Vegas), 324

at Mohegan complex in
Connecticut, xv
in Singapore, 354
revenue from gambling
at Baden-Baden, 32
in Bergen County, 192
by grind players, 300
from online poker, 382
during recessions, 292–93, 374
in San Francisco, 146
in Sarasota Springs, 182
from slot machines, 320
Revolutionary War, gambling during,
118–19
Rickard, Tex, 200
Ridotto, 8–14
ridotto, definition, 9
riverboat gambling, 135–38, *137*,
311–16
casino barges, 315
Harrah's Vicksburg (Horizon
Vicksburg), *314*
loss and cruise limits, 316
riverboats, *314*
Riviera (Las Vegas), 231, 295
Rochefort, Henri, 34–35, *35*
Rock, Chris, xiv
Rodger, N.A.M., 395n99
ropers, 157
Rosenthal, Frank "Lefty," 288–89
Roslyn, James Francis Harry, 78–79
Rothstein, Arnold, 238
roulette
at Bad Homburg, 48, *51*
as battlefield, 74
boule and, 87
in early France, 17
at Kursaal, 50
at Palais Royale, 19–20
at Saratoga Club House, 185
at Spa, France, 25, 27
systems of betting on, 72–75, 76–77
Rousseau, Jean-Jacques, 12
Royal Nevada (Las Vegas Strip), 231
Rubeli, Paul, 301

Russia, gambling in, 366
RV parks, 295, 301

S
Safdie, Moshe, 353
Sala, George Augustus, 50
Salles, Paul, 363
Sam's Town (Las Vegas), 255–56
San Bernardino, California, 191
San Francisco, California, 145–47,
187–88, 192
Sands (Atlantic City), 272
Sands (Las Vegas), 234–35, 334
Sands (Macau), 348
Sandwich, Earl of, 98–99, 395n99
SAR (Macau Special Administration
Region), 347
Saratoga Club House, 183, 185–86
Saratoga Springs, New York, 181–86
Sarno, Jay, 243–46, 298
Satre, Phil, 333
Scarne, John, 236–37
Schaeffer, Glenn, 300, 301, 330
Schillinger, Steve, 377
Scribner, Ben, 181
Sears, John, 168
Seminoles of Florida, 304
shell games, 132
Sherwin, Elmer, *322*
Shoofey, Alex, 259–60
Showboat (Atlantic City), *277*
Siddons, Belle, 151–52
Siegel, Benjamin "Bugsy," 216, 222–24
Siegfried and Roy, 329
Silver, Jeffrey, 295
Silver Club (Las Vegas), 213
Simms, Chester, 326–27
Sinatra, Frank, 210, 234–35, 283, 309,
360
Singapore, gambling in, 352–54
Skaggs, Elijah, 123–24
skimming scandals, 257–58, 287–89
skinning houses, 169, 170–71
slot machines
in Australia, 354–55

in California Indian casinos,
310–11
in Canada, 356
early machines, 187–89, *188*
in Foxwoods Casino, 309
in Las Vegas, 297–98
in Las Vegas Strip, 298
in Macau, 345–46
in Monte Carlo, 87
new technologies, 321
pachisuro machines, 338
during Prohibition, 189
as regulated Indian operations, 306
in Reno, *209,* 209–10
video slots, 321
winners, *322*
Smith, Harold, 205–6
Smith, Raymond I. (Pappy), 205–6
Societe des Bains de Mer (SBM),
66–67, 83, 87–88, 89
South Africa, gambling in, 359–62
South Dakota, gambling in, 316–17
South Korea, gambling in, 349
Spa, 22–29, 24–29
Spago's, 327
Spencer, Albert, 184
sportsbooks, 248, 377–78, 380
S.S. Rex (Las Vegas), 217
Stamp Act of 1765, 118
Stardust (Las Vegas), 256, 284, 326,
328
STDM (Sociedade de Turismo e
Diversoes de Macau), 343,
344–45, 345, 346–47
steamboats, 135. *See also* riverboat
gambling
Stern, Martin, Jr., 259
Stocker, Mayme, 213
Stralla, Antonio Cornero (Tony
Cornero), 216–17
Strawman investigation, 288–89
Studio 54 (Las Vegas), 371
sub-Saharan Africa, gambling in,
361–62
Sudyam, Sam, 161

Summerlin, 247
Sun City Resort (South Africa), 360
Sun International South Africa,
359–61
superstitions
of African-Americans, 188
of Chinese, 342, 346
of Civil War soldiers, 141
at Monte Carlo, 69–70
surveys
of gaming houses (1731), 97
of Paris legal gaming tables, 21
recession impact survey (1980),
294–95
swindles. *See* cheating
Swingers (1996), 371–72
systems of betting, 71–79
"breaking the bank" at Monte
Carlo, 75, 77–78
calculating probabilities, in whist,
108–9
card counting, in blackjack, 239–42
by Charles Deville Wells, 77–78
d'Alembert system, 73
fraudulent systems, 75–76
Gagnante Marche (streak/hot and
cold), 74
Grand Martingale, 72
by James Francis Harry Roslyn,
78–79
Labouchere (cancellation system),
73
Martingale progression, 72
mechanics of roulette, 76–77
Monte Carlo Fallacy (Gambler's
Fallacy), 79
Paroli (parlay), 72
patience, 73–74

T
Tai Xing company, 342
Tampa, Florida, 193
tango, 204
Teamsters Central States Pension
Fund, 285

Telesabong (internet cockfighting), 379
Texas Hold'em, 251–52
Thomas, E. Parry, 253
Thorp, Edward O., 240–41
three-card monte, 132
Tolstoy, Leo, 39–40
Tong, Lim Goh, 308
trade stimulators, 178–80
Treasure Island, 324
trente-et-quarante (thirty and forty), 25–27, *26*
Tropicana (Las Vegas), 301, 328
Tropicana/TropWorld (Atlantic City), 274–75
Trump, Donald, 276–79
Trump Plaza (Atlantic City), 277–78
Trump Taj Mahal (Atlantic City), *277*, 279
Trump's Castle/Trump Marina, 278, 281
Trussell, George, 170–71
Tunbridge Wells health resort, 90, 95
Turgenev, Ivan, 39–40, 41–42
Tweed, William "Boss," 164–65
twenty-one (blackjack), 20

U
Union Plaza (Las Vegas), 248, 255
United Kingdom. *See* Great Britain, gambling in
Unlawful Internet Gaming Enforcement Act of 2006, 383
Uston, Ken, 241–42

V
Van Buren, Martin, 124
Vaux Hall (France), 24–25
Velbruck, Francois de, 24–25
Venetian (Las Vegas), 335–36
Venetian (Macao), 348
Venice, 8–10
Vicksburg, Louisiana, 133–35
Victoria, Queen of England, 69
video lottery terminals (VLTs), 357

video poker, 321–22
video slots, 321
Villa Bellevue (Monaco), 59, 61

W
Wallner, Leo, 364
Waltzman, Arthur, 296
ward heelers, 163
Washington, D.C., gambling in, 124–27
Washington, George, 118–19
Webb, Del E. (corporation), 258–59
Weicker, Lowell, 309
Weiner, Sanford, 265
Wells, Charles Deville, 77–78
Wentworth, "Long" John, 169–70
wheel of fortune, 175, 178–79
whist, 105–9, *107*
    in colonial America, 115, 117
    how-to-play books, 106–8
    Principles of Whist, The (Cavendish), 108–9
Whist According to Hoyle, 106, 107–8
White, Vanna, 313
Wicks, Tom, 167–68
Wiesbaden, gambling at, 43–45
Wilhelm IX, 35–37
Wilkerson, Billy, 222, 223
Wilson, Pete, 310
Wilson Rangers, 141–42
Wire Act, 379–80, 382, 384
World Poker Tour, 381
World Series of Poker, 248, 250–53
    winners, *251, 252,* 355, 381
World Sports Exchange, 377, 380
Wrest Point Hotel Casino (Australia), 355
Wynn, Stephen A., *322*
    Beau Rivage and, 315
    Golden Nugget and, 253–54, 273
    in Macau, 348
    Mirage and, 323–25, *325*
    Mirage Resorts sale, 331–32
    Wynn Las Vegas and, 373–74, *375*
Wynn Las Vegas, 332, *375*

opening of, 373–74, 385–86
Wynn Macau, 348
Wynn Resorts (Macau), 347, 349

Y
Yaqui (Arizona tribe), 305
Yugoslavia, gambling in, 366

Z
Zarahoff, Basil, 86
Zarowitz, Jerry, 288
Zographos, Nicolas, 83–86

CPSIA information can be obtained
at www.ICGtesting.com
Printed in the USA
LVHW040107301118
598739LV00007B/166/P